MUSIC PRODUCTION

For Producers, Composers, Arrangers, and Students

Second Edition

Michael Zager

Published by Scarecrow Press, Inc.
A wholly owned subsidiary of The Rowman & Littlefield Publishing Group, Inc.
4501 Forbes Boulevard, Suite 200, Lanham, Maryland 20706
http://www.scarecrowpress.com

Estover Road, Plymouth PL6 7PY, United Kingdom

British Library Cataloguing in Publication Information Available

Library of Congress Cataloging-in-Publication Data

Zager, Michael.
Music production : for producers, composers, arrangers, and students / Michael Zager. — 2nd ed.
p. cm.
Includes bibliographical references and index.
ISBN 978-0-8108-8201-0 (pbk. : alk. paper) — ISBN 978-0-8108-8202-7 (ebook)
1. Music trade—Vocational guidance. 2. Sound recordings—Production and direction—Vocational guidance. I. Title.
ML3795.Z14 2012
781.4—dc23 2011027564

∞™ The paper used in this publication meets the minimum requirements of American National Standard for Information Sciences—Permanence of Paper for Printed Library Materials, ANSI/NISO Z39.48-1992.

Printed in the United States of America

This book is dedicated to
my wife, Jane.
Thank you for all of your love,
encouragement, and support.

Contents

Preface

> For the first time in the history of the Internet, traffic in paid contact has passed piracy. (Spring Traffic Report from Sandivine 2011)

The global music industry continues to experience a major reconstruction. Illegal music downloading, brick and mortar (retail) stores and chains closing, combined with counterfeiting and legitimate competition for leisure income, has caused the record companies to investigate and also modify corporate business models. (iTunes has become the largest retail store and most physical facilities are departments rather than stand-alone brick and mortar stores. Some boutique, independent retail stores are still in existence.)

Legal digital downloading continues to increase and the sale of physical CDs continues to decline, in most genres. Unfortunately, the increase in legitimate downloads has not replaced the loss of revenue incurred by the decrease of physical sales. It is most difficult, if not impossible, to control the Internet and its impact on the music industry. The negative effects are primarily a result of illegal peer2peer file sharing and Web sites that sell music and do not pay royalties to the copyright owners and/or content providers. (These websites are primarily housed out of the U.S.) Yet, many new opportunities for producers and artists are available. There are myriad new independent record labels, which sell their content solely on the Internet, artists—both established and unestablished—who sell their music and merchandise directly to consumers, and Web marketing and promotions (social networking), which is relatively inexpensive (e.g., YouTube videos and streaming services).

360 record contracts have become the norm rather than the exception. 360 deals allow record labels to become partners with artists by sharing income derived from performances, music publishing, merchandising, and

additional income generating ventures. To entice superstar artists to sign 360 agreements, companies offer them very large advances (e.g., Madonna and Jay-Z); new artists will be fortunate if they ever receive a generous income stream from the sale of recordings. In return for signing these agreements, artists receive an increased share of record royalties. Record sales have become a marketing tool rather than a primary source of income for most artists. It is problematical for labels to generate a profit strictly from the sale of albums. Artists rely primarily on the income derived from live performances to produce the bulk of their revenue stream. Labels want to share in this income because, from their viewpoint, the label's marketing, advertising, and promotional efforts provide the artists with exposure, which translates into concert and merchandise revenue and income from other sources.

Artists, managers, and agents must work jointly with labels to achieve success. Many artists have chosen not to sign with labels or with managers or agents. The Internet has allowed them to receive exposure with virtually no cost or very little cost. Social networking has become the norm (e.g., Facebook and similar sites).

The public loves music. The guidance of a skilled music producer will always be essential to music production. A music producer's job is analogous to that of a film director. The director brings a script to "life" on the screen. The music producer's mission is to bring an artist's music to "life" on a recording, in the most creative manner. Quentin Tarantino has a unique style of directing films, and Phil Spector had a unique style of producing music. Spector's imprint is referred to as a "Wall of Sound" and is discussed later in this book. In most creative areas, this is referred to as, "Having your own voice." Most successful artists have their own "voice," as do creative producers.

Music production is a craft, and to achieve a high-level of expertise requires many years of experience. The Revised Edition of this book updates information included in the First Edition and discusses the morphing music industry. Licensing, marketing, and producing music for film, television, games, Internet programs, Internet advertising, and more are discussed in this Edition. The expanded role of music supervisors, new production techniques, additional interviews with eminent industry professions, and new terms included in music industry contracts are also discussed.

Extensive study of the subjects discussed in this book, in addition to experience and innate talent, form a "cocktail" of knowledge that is necessary to achieve success as a music producer. Unfortunately, experience and talent cannot be taught. So why write a book about music production? Subjects associated with music and music production *can* be taught and learned. Dissecting compositions, understanding studio technology, coaching musicians and vocalists, arranging and orchestration, musicianship, editing, marketing, advertising, and promotion *can* be learned. Knowledge of these subjects is essential to learning music production.

Many music producers specialize in one or two musical areas, which may include record production, film music production, advertising music production, television music production or supervision (not only music underscoring for programs but also generic music used on news programs and station promotions), music for documentaries, corporate video music production, industrial show music production, and additional multimedia genres.

Synthesizers and samplers, computer music-sequencing programs, and home studios, also referred to as a project studios, have greatly influenced the craft of music production. All aspects of music production can be self-contained in today's extensive electronic music world. The project studio has become commonplace with new artists, producers, and professionals alike. Many artists and producers produce basic tracks at home and record overdubs and mix in a professional studio. Others complete entire projects in home studios. Software programs and hardware equipment is affordable; therefore, most producers and artists own home studios.

Artists, producers, and/or arrangers may have very little artistic contact with other creatives, since they tend to live in a creative cocoon. This can be both beneficial and detrimental to one's artistic development. Affordable technology has allowed average artists and producers a chance to be creative without incurring considerable studio costs. What may be detrimental is the probable lack of creative interaction with other engineers and musicians. Collaboration encourages a creative flow of ideas. To counter that theory, not knowing "the right way to do things" can become the "mother of invention." In my opinion, a delicate balance between the two working methods is the best solution.

The subjects covered in the book, in conjunction with extensive practice, will help to develop a nascent producer's natural ability. Experimentation also contributes greatly to innovative production techniques.

Acknowledgments

Teaching is the best way to learn!

I would like to thank the following individuals for sharing their knowledge and their friendship: Ira Abrams, Esq.; Michael Abbott; Dick Asher, Esq; Bob Fernandez; Trevor Fletcher; Doug Frank; Kevin Gershan; Dr. Stuart Glazer; Darren Higman; Robert Rainier; Alejandro Sanchez-Samper Aram Schefrin, Esq.; Dr. Edward Turgeon; Dan Warner; and Scott Wynne.

Thank you to David Tcimpidis (of the Mannes College of Music, a division of New School University) for his continued support and friendship.

I would also like to thank colleagues in the Department of Music at Florida Atlantic University, for their support and friendship.

A special thank-you to Henry and Ellie Stern for their generous support of the Commercial Music Program at Florida Atlantic University.

Thank you to Fookloy Ford, administrator and the coordinator of the Commercial Music Program at Florida Atlantic University. Cover photograph by Fookloy Ford.

Introduction

> Let us describe the education of our men. What then is the education to be? Perhaps we could hardly find a better than that which the experience of the past has already discovered, which consists, I believe, in gymnastic, for the body, and music for the mind.
>
> —Plato

The book is divided into three parts: I, Music Production; II, Recording Technology; and III, The Music Business. When reading part I, there will be references to recording technology. Refer to part II of the book for explanations.

Although music production is intertwined with recording technology, I did not want to begin the book by having the students read about technology. Instead I have opted to begin by covering the creative aspects of music production.

I advocate *the creative use of technology*. Producers should relate to technology in the same manner as they relate to the music. Understanding the recording console, music computer technology, and audio engineering requires the same study and dedication as is required to learn how to play an instrument or to compose, arrange, and orchestrate music. Students interested solely in the technological aspect of the music business should study audio engineering as a separate discipline.

This book is not intended to be a technological guide but rather an overview of the numerous areas of study that apply to music production. Studying music production, as well as current audio production technology, will prepare students to enter the exciting world of music production.

The Meaning of Music

> The whole problem can be stated quite simply by asking, "Is there a meaning to music?" My answer would be, "Yes." And "Can you state in so many words what the meaning is?" My answer to that would be, "No."
>
> —Aaron Copland

Music (which stems from the Greek word meaning *dance*) is generally considered to consist of pleasant sounds that are either played on instruments and/or sung. Music consists of pitch, melody, harmony, rhythm, meter, timbre, tempo, form, and dynamics. Music producers must be familiar with these elements in addition to having the ability to arrange, orchestrate, analyze songs and instrumentals, coach recording artists, and understand recording technology. Review the following definitions:

Pitch: The pitch of a note refers to its frequency range. If the general intonation of a piece is poor, the average person will notice that the music is "out of tune." Poor intonation, in any musical style, can be a persistent problem. Many popular musicians and singers are not properly trained and therefore may have faulty intonation. A producer has to be acutely aware of this problem and has to correct it either by recording multiple takes of a performance and editing the best parts together or by electronically fixing the problem.

Antares Auto-tune is a software plug-in (a digital signal processor) that can be used with most computer music-sequencing programs. When the program processes a vocal or instrumental performance, the program either manually or automatically corrects poor intonation (pitch). Most popular recorded vocal performances are processed through this device. (Other companies manufacture pitch-correction software and hardware.)

Melody: Melody is created by a succession of notes in a musical form. Random notes do not create melodies. Melody is important in popular music because it is, generally, the prime musical element that emotionally connects the audience to a song or composition. Popular songs are usually easy for the listener to sing and remember. Standards are songs that have survived for many years and are considered a part of the popular musical lexicon. In popular music, strong melodies are usually notated within a singable range and constructed using conjunct motion rather than disjunct motion.

Harmony: Harmony generally refers to the simultaneous sounding of different pitches called chords. Harmony can be perceived as being pleasant (consonant) and/or unpleasant (dissonant). It is a matter of personal artistic perception. Harmony often provides the background support for the melodic structure of a composition. Frequently, melody and harmony are perceived as being inseparable.

Constructing chords is not the only way to create harmony. Contrapuntal musical lines also outline harmony. Two or more musical lines moving, weaving, and interacting with each other can achieve the same musical results as listening to pitches played simultaneously (chords).

Rhythm: Rhythm refers to rhythmic patterns, which are also called "beats" or "the beat" when producing popular music. Rhythmic repeated patterns are called "grooves" (in the vernacular of commercial musicians). The term *rhythm section* refers to musicians who play keyboards, guitar, drums, percussion, and bass. The rhythm section is responsible for giving the music a "feel" (mood) and a groove. Skilled rhythm section players have "good time," meaning they do not waver from the tempo (assuming the composition is at one tempo).

A drummer might play "behind the beat," which gives the music more of a laid-back or funky feeling. Sometimes, drummers anticipate a beat—called "pushing"—and it might appear as though the drummer (or other musicians) is "rushing" (playing in front of the tempo), but the tempo remains steady. Pushing can create a feeling of anticipation.

Meter: Meter divides the music into strong and weak beats. The rhythmic patterns aid musicians in reading the rhythmic values assigned to the notes. Meter is one of the most important compositional tools available to a composer. The flow of the music is an integral part of how meter is used by a composer. It helps a musician interpret the rhythmic intention of the composer; the misuse of meter can cause musical chaos. Understanding meter is challenging for the novice musician and requires the study of music theory, including exercises in dictation and sight singing.

An example of meter: 4/4 time means that there are four beats per measure and the quarter note receives one beat. 6/8 time means there are 6 beats per measure and the eighth note receives one beat.

Timbre: Timbre means tone color. The timbre of a musical instrument is the actual sound that is produced. All instruments vary in tone color. Tone color emanates from the harmonics (overtones) that construct the tone. An oboe does not sound the same as a bassoon, although both are played by blowing into a double reed. They have different overtones, different tessitura, different physical shapes, and different timbres. For instance, all B♭ clarinets generally sound the same although each instrument has individual and unique characteristics, which slightly alters the timbre. Stradivarius violins—considered by some to be the greatest violins ever made—may cost millions of dollars, primarily due to the instrument's timbre. The tone color is that of incomparable beauty. When instruments of various timbres play in a section, as in an orchestral setting, the result is a beautiful sonic texture. The mix of colors used by a painter is analogous to a mixture of orchestral timbres. Timbres also vary with voices. No two humans are genetically the same; consequently, their timbres differ.

Tempo: Tempo is the speed at which a composition is played. Tempo is measured in beats per minute (bpm). Thus a quarter note =120 bpm means that 120 quarter notes are played in one minute. The tempo has a direct effect on the mood of the composition. A composition played quickly evokes a different emotion than the same piece played slowly. Choice of tempo is important to a music producer because if a song is performed slightly too fast or too slow, the musical mood is affected.

In traditional classical music, using general Italian terms indicates tempo markings, which communicates to the musicians and the conductor the musical intent of the composer. The terms are merely guidelines and offer the interpreter flexibility rather than exact tempo indications. Following are some of the most common tempo markings:

- *Largo* indicates a slow tempo. *Largo* is also used to create a feeling of importance. (Terms such as *largamente* (stately) or *larghetto* (slower than *largo*) are attempts to be more precise in communicating the feeling of the piece. Once the interpreter knows the music, the exact tempo becomes an artistic choice.)
- *Adagio* indicates a slow feeling.
- *Andante* means slow but faster than *adagio.*
- *Moderato* indicates a moderate tempo. *Moderato* is often used as an adjective (e.g., *andante moderato*—moderately slow).
- *Allegro* indicates a fast tempo.
- *Vivace* means that the tempo and musical feeling should be lively.
- *Presto* means that the music should be played quickly.

The above terms are merely broad tempo indications, and more precise markings are usually indicated. In modern popular music, tempos are typically determined by current trends in some forms of music. For example, in the late 1970s the average tempo of dance (club) music was 120 beats per minute; average tempos became faster with the creation of various styles of dance music.

When hip-hop (rap) music became popular, the average tempo was 95 bpm, primarily due to the time it takes for a rapper to recite the lyrics. Most popular composers and arrangers (in English-speaking territories) use the English language to determine the tempo.

Form: Form brings order to music; Without musical form the notes or musical phrases are not "threaded together." For example, sonata form consists of an exposition, development, and recapitulation. Sonata form is used in symphonies, chamber music, and other musical genres.

When composing film music composers often have to create form. The sequence of pictures restricts composers from writing in traditional musical forms. For example, a scene might change on the upbeat of a note located in the middle of a measure. That is an unnatural place to change the flow of the music. Film composers have various musical solutions to deal with these problems (e.g., changing the meter in the previous measure). Scenes are not generally edited to accommodate completed pieces of music (called *cues*). Some directors edit scenes to accommodate prerecorded music (cues). For instance, if a composition is exceptionally rhythmic, the director might edit pictures that "hit" each beat, creating musical and visual syncopation.

Dynamics: Dynamic markings within a musical composition alter the overall musical mood. Without dynamics, the composition would have basically one mood and the music would most likely become monotonous. Following is a list of some of the most common dynamic markings:

- *Pianissimo*—to play very quietly; indicated in the score with a *pp*.
- *Piano*—soft; indicated in the score with a *p*.
- *Mezzo forte*—not too loud; indicated in the score with *mf*.
- *Forte*—loud; indicated in the score with *f*.
- *Fortissimo*—very loud; indicated in the score with *fff*.

These dynamic markings have numerous variations.

Conclusion

Music producers, including those who are not musicians, should become familiar with the above-mentioned subjects. Melody, harmony, rhythm, meter, timbre, tempo, form, and dynamics are applied in music production. For example, music producers suggest changes in melodic and lyrical content, adjust tempos, alter rhythm patterns, and so forth.

Chronology of Recorded Music and Music Production

Alexander Graham Bell and Elisha Gray worked on developing recorded sound, but it was Thomas Alva Edison who invented the process. He was trying to create a telephone answering machine that could also be used for dictation. In 1877, Bell patented a machine that crudely reproduced the human voice. In the same year, he invented the first phonograph, which he operated by turning a tin-foil-covered cylinder with a hand screw. He could record audio, store it, and play it back. That was the beginning of the recorded-music industry.

The following is a timeline of events leading up to the current DVD technology.

1877: Thomas Edison records "Mary Had a Little Lamb," the first recording of the human voice. Edison invents a phonograph having a tin-foil cylinder that can play for two to three minutes. Emile Berliner invents the microphone.

1887: The flat record player, invented by Emile Berliner, is called a gramophone. That format is expected to be more appealing to the public than the cylinder phonograph. The gramophone uses zinc discs.

1888: Cylinder recordings are sold for entertainment purposes.

1889: The coin-operated cylinder phonograph precedes the jukebox. The average recorded time per cylinder is two minutes.

1890: John Philip Sousa's Marine Band records the first recordings for the Columbia Records catalogue. The first duplication process is used in North America.

1891: International copyright agreements are initiated, but sound recordings are not included in the agreements.

1892: Cylinders for the home and coin-operated markets are made available in the United States.

1894: *Billboard*, the music industry trade magazine, begins publishing.

1895: Edison begins mass-producing the phonograph, consisting of a horn to amplify the sound and cylinders to store it. The cylinders, however, are impossible to mass-produce. The Berliner Gramophone Company begins storing music on shellac, which is easier to reproduce and lasts longer. Wax, instead of zinc, is used to create the master recording, a process that greatly improves the quality of recorded sound. In addition, Eldridge Reeves Johnson, a New Jersey machinist, invents a clockwork motor, which enables people to play the phonograph without having to manually turn the motor. By the turn of the century, thousands of recordings are being sold. Three companies are in the forefront of the industry; The Columbia Graphophone Company and Edison's National Phonograph Company produce cylinders, and the Victor Talking Machine Company, a Berliner and Johnson–owned company, produces discs. The Victor Talking Machine Company records the great tenor Enrico Caruso on a 10-inch disc instead of a 7-inch disc. A 10-inch disc stores more audio and can play for four minutes. Caruso's legendary 1903 recordings are released on the Victor Red Seal Label. Other famous opera singers are recorded on 10-inch discs, which advance the popularity of the disc over the cylinder. A cylinder provides better audio quality than a disc, but a disc can be played back at a louder volume, which makes the format more appealing to the audience.

♫ This was analogous to the format competition between Beta and VHS videotapes, vinyl and CD audio recordings, VHS and video DVDs, and CDs and audio DVDs. The audience supports a format based on price and features. DVDs have replaced VHS tapes as the preferred video format. Downloading digital audio will most likely replace CDs as the preferred audio format. The newest format (as of this publication) is the DualDisc, a combination CD (audio) and DVD (video) on one disc.

1896: Columbia manufactures a basic cylinder player called The Eagle, which sells for $5.00.

1900: Eldridge Johnson produces the first discs with recordings on both sides. The recordings are children's music.

1903: Pirated records appear, but sales are small and do not have a significant effect on the industry.

1904: Double-sided discs become available to the public, which adds more value to the format.

1906: The Victor Talking Machine Company releases the Victrola. Designed as a piece of furniture, the Victrola not only establishes the disc as the preferred recording format but also becomes the state-of-the-art record player for the next two decades. For years, the word *Victrola* is used as the generic term for any record player. Victor adapts the 78 rpm (revolutions per minute) speed as the standard. When purchasing records the consumer asks for "78s." Many companies do not adopt the standard until the 1920s.

1909: The term *album*, which refers to the format used to store pictures, is first used in connection with the release of Tchaikovsky's *The Nutcracker Suite*, recorded on four double-sided discs.

1910: There are multiple disc sizes: 7-inch, 10-inch, 12-inch, 14-inch, 16-inch, and 21-inch, which all play at 78 rpm. Some discs can hold up to eight minutes of information. Music halls and movie theaters close during World War I, making records a popular form of entertainment (many patriotic songs are recorded). The first portable record player, the Decca, is released, which also adds to the popularity of recorded music.

1917: The first jazz recording is made. The song is "Livery Stable Blues," by The Original Dixieland Jass Band, from New Orleans (*jass* is the original spelling of *jazz*.) Jazz, America's original art form, becomes a national craze and furthers the popularity of recorded music.

1920: In the early 1920s, radio becomes a popular form of free entertainment, negatively affecting record sales. The Radio Corporation of America (RCA) mass-produces radios. The public can not only listen to music for free but also hear news and dramatic programming. The record companies refuse to allow signed artists to perform on the radio for fear that the public will not purchase music that can be heard without paying. **October 20, 1920:** KDKA in Pittsburgh—the first commercial radio station to receive call letters—begins broadcasting. **November 2, 1920:** KDKA initiates regularly scheduled programming by broadcasting the results of the presidential election. Record sales increase when recorded sound quality improves. The introduction of high-fidelity (hi-fi) sound and the invention of the condenser microphone are contributing factors. Rivalry between record companies and radio stations stops with the realization that radio airplay helps record sales.

1926: The Vitaphone Company (owned by Warner Bros. and Western Electric) produces a product that can record sound on a 16-inch disc. The audio can be played back in synchronization with film, creating the first "talking pictures." The disc plays at 33 1/3 rpm and stores the same number of minutes of sound as the accompanying film. The first talking picture is *The Jazz Singer*, starring Al Jolson.

1929: After the stock-market crash, record sales decrease from 100 million units a year to six million; people purchase only necessities.

1930s: The jukebox is credited with saving the music industry. During the 1930s, jukebox distribution increases from 25,000 to more than 300,000. That gives tremendous public exposure to records, thereby increasing sales.

1930: Guitarist Les Paul develops the first recording process that enables additional music (information) to be added to an existing recorded track; the process is now referred to as *overdubbing*. It is the beginning of multitrack recording. Paul accomplishes multitrack recording with the use of two acetate-disc machines; each time he records to the second machine, he adds a part.

1931: Famous opera singer Lawrence Tibbett and the great jazz musician Sidney Bechet use the multitrack recording technique. Tibbett overdubs a baritone part on his recording of "The Cuban Love

♫ Les Paul's recordings during the 1940s were recorded in this manner. (Acetate is a soft substance that begins to scratch and lose quality after being played several times.) He presented his concept to record companies, but the labels did not see the practical application for what they considered to be a novelty. That process, however, was the beginning of record production.

Paul invented delays, phasing, echo, and recording at various speeds—effects that are still used (effects processing will be explained later in the book). He also developed the solid-body electric guitar. Guitars were amplified in the 1930s because they could not be heard when other instruments were playing. Open-body guitars were noisy, and Les Paul eliminated the problem with his new invention. The Les Paul guitar is considered one of the finest electric guitars and is still used by some of the best guitar players.

Bing Crosby, the famous singer, bought Les Paul a gift: the first Ampex 300 series tape recorder. After analyzing how the machine operated, Paul felt he could adapt sound-on-sound recording by adding an additional recording head to the three heads on the machine. Multiple "bouncing" of tracks causes a sound-quality loss each time a track is recorded to another track, and after experimenting and altering the recording process, he was able to achieve high-quality sound with minimal quality loss.

Song," and Bechet plays multiple instruments on his recording of "The Sheik of Araby."

1939: Magnetic tape is invented. It completely transforms the manner in which music is recorded.

1940: When the Japanese invade Southeast Asia in 1940, there is a depletion of shellac, the material used to manufacture records; the lac beetle of southern Asia is the source of shellac. That event curtails the ability to manufacture records. Shellac is replaced by vinyl—a derivative of petroleum—which has superior sound quality and is more durable.

1948: Shellac records can hold only up to ten minutes of information while vinyl records can store thirty minutes of information per side. The vinyl disc is called the LP, or long-playing record.

1949: RCA releases the first 7-inch recordings called *singles*. They hold two songs, one song per side, and the record has a doughnutlike hole in the middle. The format of singles, also called "45s" because they play at 45 rpm, is used in jukeboxes.

1950: Les Paul and his wife Mary Ford record "How High the Moon," the first hit using the multitrack recording process. The record remains at number one on the charts for nine weeks. Record production is forever changed. Prior to recording "How High the Moon," Les Paul invents a way to achieve tape delay and uses the technique on "How High the Moon." Paul's other signal-processor inventions are still used in both analog and digital formats.

1954: Bill Haley and His Comets record "Rock around the Clock," the first rock 'n' roll hit (1955) to be documented on the *Billboard* magazine chart. (*Billboard* is still the most significant and respected music industry publication.) This recording begins a new genre of popular music.

1958: Stereo recordings are released to the public.

1960s: James T. Russell invents the digital compact disc in the late 1960s. He wants to improve the quality of reproduced music. Because vinyl scratches, it causes an unpleasant array of pops and repeating sections when the disc is damaged. His mission is to invent a storage system that can read back the recorded information without any physical contact. Russell is familiar with digital data recording and knows that it is based on a binary system

♫ Some consider the first rock 'n' roll record to be "Good Rockin' Tonight," recorded in 1947 by Roy Brown on the DeLuxe label. The recording was not a major hit and therefore did not have much influence on the popularity of the rock 'n' roll genre.

comprising ones and zeros, If he can mimic the system with dark and light, he can store huge amounts of data, not just music. The technology is accomplished by recording the dark and light bits of information onto a photosensitive platter; the data are read by a laser light and then converted into an electrical signal by a computer. Russell spends years developing the system. He patents the process in 1970, while working as a senior scientist for the Battelle Memorial Institute in Richland, Washington. Russell continues to work on the process by developing the CD-ROM, which can be used for storing and/or reading back almost any kind of computer data.

1982: Philips and Sony corporations bring the compact disc (digital audio) to the marketplace. The compact disc holds approximately seventy minutes of audio, is recorded at a sampling rate of 44.1, and is 16-bit. **Fall:** The compact disc is introduced in Europe and Japan.

1983: In the spring of 1983, the compact disc debuts in the United States. **January:** *Musical Instrument Digital Interface* (MIDI) is introduced to the public. Two synthesizers are locked together by using a 5-pin DIN cable. One keyboard is played while the other is triggered to play the same notes simultaneously. The invention revolutionizes the popular-music business. Today, all keyboards (and rack-mounted versions, which have the same electronics minus a keyboard) and effects processors can be controlled via MIDI. MIDI information is routed to devices that play back either analog or digitally sampled sounds.

> ♫ MIDI is an independent platform that can control either analog or digital devices.

1987: CDs (compact discs) are used to store and play back videos. Digital audiotape (DAT) players, a digital-tape-based system, are brought to the public. The Fraunhofer Institute for Integrated Circuits in Germany begins to develop the MP3 format. *MP3* means Moving Picture Experts Group-1 Audio Layer 3.

1988: Recordable Compact Discs (CD-Rs) are launched. CD-Rs enable digital information to be stored on a compact disc. CDs replace vinyl discs as the preferred consumer format.

1990: Digital radio is introduced in Canada. Digital transmission provides improved sound quality (e.g., Internet and satellite radio).

1991: Nielsen SoundScan becomes the most accurate system of tracking legitimate CD (as well as DVD and similar formats) sales. Each purchase is scanned, and the sales information is stored in a database. The recording charts (e.g., *Billboard*) become more accurate as a result of calculating accurate information.

1994: Six major companies—Philips, Sony, Thorn EMI, Time Warner, Bertelsmann (BMG), and Universal—control the music industry, which grosses more than $30 billion annually. Each parent company owns and/or distributes subsidiary labels, which are called imprints.

1996: DVD players were sold in Japan. The Fraunhofer Institute for Integrated Circuits in Germany is granted a U.S. patent for MP3.

1997: DVD players are sold in the United States. Michael Robertson forms MP3.com.

1998: DVD-RAM and DVD-R (recordable DVD) become available to the public. The first 24-bit, 48 track digital recording is produced in Nashville, Tennessee. The DVD becomes the medium of choice for video, storage, and—in the near future—playing back music. Streaming audio and satellite audio are introduced.

2000: IMAX theaters introduce the 6-channel digital sound system. The first film to use the system is *Fantasia/2000.*

2004: In August, DualDisc, a combination CD and DVD on one disc is offered to the public. The record companies believe that this format will help revitalize traditional terrestrial retail sales. The global music industry continues to fight illegal peer-to-peer (P2P) file sharing and physical CD piracy. The RIAA (Recording Industry Association of America) continues to prosecute consumers who illegally download and share music.

2011: The digital distribution of music continues to grow (e.g., Internet [downloading and streaming], Satellite and Cable radio). Cloud Storage, which offers the ability to access and store music (and other files) without having to save it on computers or mobile devices, could possibly become the preferred choice to access music. Since *Cloud Storage* can handle massive amounts of data, if there is a demand for high quality files, such as AIFF or Wave files, compared to MP3s or AAC files, it is possible. As the digital market increases, consumers will have the opportunity to hear the music the way it is intended to be heard.

Conclusion

The laws are beginning to help protect the music and film industries from users who share music files and film titles without paying for the rights to do so.

This timeline is a brief summary of most of the seminal events that have affected the record industry to date. Many additional events could have been reported.

I

MUSIC PRODUCTION

1

An Overview of Record Production

> A record producer is responsible for the sound "shape" of what comes out. In many ways, he's the designer—not in the sense of creating the actual work itself, but he stages the show and presents it to the world. It's his taste that makes it what it is—good or bad.
>
> —George Martin (producer of The Beatles)

Record Production

The skills of record producers vary. Some producers, such as Prince, are able to arrange music, play multiple instruments, sing, *and* engineer. They are referred to as "quadruple threats." Others might not possess any of these attributes, but they have "good ears"—an uncanny ability to choose artists (and projects) who will achieve commercial success. Even with limited musical training they can appropriately communicate with performers and engineers to achieve their creative goals. Speaking in artistic rather than musical terms is a common technique: "The bass line is too dark" or "The keyboard part sounds too happy" can be descriptive enough for artists who need to communicate with producers.

Record producers are essentially music critics and amateur psychologists. The term *music critic* is used to describe people who comment on or review recorded music and concert performances, but music producers, also critics, have the opportunity to improve musical works. The effectiveness of their criticism depends on the relationship producers establish with artists. *A producer's goal should be for the artist (at the least) to experiment with the producer's creative suggestions; some ideas will work and others will not. Generally, there is an amicable compromise.*

Most musicians and singers are highly sensitive. The manner in which producers communicate with artists is the key to achieving positive results. Autocratic producers are usually ineffectual. Accomplished producers are hired because of their creative vision and expertise. Therefore, a producer must appear confident and create an atmosphere of mutual respect and friendship with artists. If a producer does not pose a strong "artistic vision" to an artist, the artist will eventually lose respect for him or her, and the relationship will ultimately deteriorate.

Most successful artists and producers have unique creative imprints—the artist's or producer's "voice" (individuality). A singer has a unique voice; a writer also has a unique voice, as do music recording engineers, arrangers, musicians, and others who are directly involved in the creative process. Talent is an indescribable phenomenon, which cannot be taught but *can* be developed. Producers coordinate the overall recording process, and the manner in which producers communicate with the various personalities has a direct effect on the success of the final recording.

> ♫ Béla Bartók would not teach music composition because he felt that composition was not teachable. John Corigliano, an accomplished contemporary composer, feels that composition is teachable.

The process of creating recorded music is analogous to giving birth. This "product" (an industry term) is the creator's child, and just as mothers protect their young, artists and producers protect their artistic visions.

Conflicts between artists and record-label executives have existed since time immemorial. Most label executives view an artist's work as something that must be commercially viable, although still reaching the highest level of artistic achievement. If an artist's sales do not generate a profit, most labels will eventually terminate his or her contract. In the past, major labels routinely nurtured and developed artists over long periods of time, but today that is a rarity due to the financial commitment necessary to achieving commercial success. Labels are costly to operate, and profits are expected beginning with the first releases of new artists. If the label truly believes that an artist has a bright future, the label may release 2 albums before terminating the contract due to insufficient sales.

Internet piracy (and physical piracy) has had an enormous financial effect on the global music industry, and labels have become ultra-cautious about making financial commitments to artists. That is why the preface compares the state of the music business on a worldwide basis to the settling of America's Wild West. Basically, the Wild West was a lawless society, and so is the Internet.

Author's Opinion: The business of music and the piracy of music directly affect music producers. If consumers refuse to pay for music, there will be no need to hire music producers. Obviously, this is an exaggeration, but not far from the truth. Successful producers can command large advance payments (often recouped against royalties). Labels will not risk paying large advances when it is difficult to forecast the chances of financial recovery. That is a very serious problem for folks interested in pursuing a career in the music business. It has become a worldwide epidemic. There have been attempts to help curtail piracy; iTunes (developed by Apple), Amazon.com, and other legal digital downloading services have lowered prices and afforded consumers an opportunity to download individual songs or instrumentals and to create personalized compilation albums. Some record labels (e.g., Universal Music Group) have lowered CD prices; the price of downloads now varies. For instance, in place of the one-price model, iTunes now offers a three-tiered pricing system. Consumers who illegally download and share recordings are being fined and prosecuted in the courts. To date, this model has not been effective and no new business paradigms have solved this colossal, global epidemic.

Record production is analogous to film directing. A film director is responsible for the overall look and mood of a production; a record producer is responsible for the overall sound and creative quality of a music production.

Most record producers specialize in one style of music (e.g., pop, Rhythm & Blues, classical, country, jazz, rock, and so on). Before specializing, a student should learn the basic music techniques that apply to all musical genres. We will dissect the elements of a successful production and describe the tools used by producers to achieve artistic and commercial success. Physicians complete a basic medical education before training in a specialty; music producers should take the same approach by receiving a solid musical education and then pursue a specialty.

Some successful producers do not have formal music education. Music education

♫ Reported by the RIAA (Recording Industry Association of America)

One credible analysis by the Institute for Policy Innovation concludes that global music piracy causes $12.5 billion of economic losses every year, 71,060 U.S. jobs lost, a loss of $2.7 billion in workers' earnings, a loss of $422 million in tax revenues, a loss of $291 million in personal income tax, and $131 million in lost corporate income and production taxes.

expands a producer's musical scope, and from a technical standpoint, helps him or her verbalize artistic suggestions in musical terminology (e.g., "Go to bar 32, change the B to a G, and play bars 32 and 33 staccato"). The ability to communicate in musical rather than abstract terms can be an advantage, especially when producing film music, jazz, or classical music.

Successful music producers have an innate talent analogous to that of a gifted performer. Musically educated producers understand music theory and recording technology. Successful producers must also feel an emotional attachment to the music. They communicate with artists in artistic terms—as well as in musical terms—and do not necessarily approach music from an intellectual perspective.

Some producers cannot verbalize creative thoughts musically; they express themselves in various ways, such as "Make that synthesizer sound less dense" or "Make the flute sound yellow and sunny." That is not an unusual means of expression. In fact, trained *producer-musicians* who want to express an abstract feeling without sounding overly technical or sterile also speak in abstract terms. This often makes communication with artists more accessible. Listening to music or viewing a piece of art evokes similar emotional reactions. A painting may appear soft and peaceful to a viewer, and a piece of music can project the same feeling to a listener. Complementary relationships between artists and producers are paramount to achieving artistic success.

The goal of a producer should be to enhance an artist's creative vision through inspiration, and also to remain true to an artist's artistic identity. Some producers may make creative choices that could bring instant success but are not necessarily appropriate choices for the long-term development of an artist's career. Developing a career is an arduous task, involving not only creative choices but also business choices. This book addresses various techniques that will help achieve these goals.

If an artist is not an arranger, the label will most likely hire a producer who has a substantial background in arranging. The producer's job is to mold the backing tracks that both complement the creative vision of the artist and sound marketable. Quincy Jones's productions of Michael Jackson's albums showcase a "creative marriage" that became a benchmark for popular-music production (for example, *Thriller*).

> ♫ Backing tracks are the instrumental tracks (and background vocal tracks) accompanying a song or a melody of an instrumental track.

Record producers must have the ability to critique arrangements. After selecting the songs to be recorded, critiquing arrangements is the primary function of a record producer. A producer must guide an artist and/or arranger. Arrangements are crucial to an artist's success. The instrumentation, the rhythmic feel, the harmonic structure, and the background vocal arrangements all contribute to the success, or lack of success, of a recording.

It can be problematic for artists to critique their own work. To remain objective is difficult after repeatedly listening to a music track. That is one reason many artists hire producers. Artists also choose to coproduce with producers.

Most artists enjoy collaborating, if they are able to find synergy with a collaborator. The chemistry that develops between a producer and an artist can be compared to the partnership that evolves between a husband and a wife. After a period of time they begin to trust and respect each other's opinions. If both parties are not respectful to one another, the relationship is most likely doomed. Artistic relationships are sensitive, since dealing with artistic matters is generally subjective.

Some production and musical elements are *not* subjective. For example, if a percussion part is out of time (not playing in the "groove") with the rest of the track or distortion is heard on the bass track, the problems must be repaired. The average music production is collaboration between an artist, a producer, an engineer, and an A&R (Artists & Repertoire) representative from the label. Making unilateral artistic and technical decisions does not work in a collaborative endeavor. Picking that right team is essential to achieving successful recordings.

For collaboration to be successful, a producer must share the same artistic vision as an artist. When an artist signs a recording contract, the label makes both an artistic and a financial commitment to the artist. The most important creative decision—other than choosing the music to be recorded—is the selection of a producer. *The one common element shared by all successful music producers is a great love of music.* It is this love and passion for the music that enables producers to communicate with artists.

Trying to explain the craft of music production is difficult because it is intangible. A music producer applies his or her artistic expression in an unusual manner. A painter takes a brush and strokes a canvas; a music producer is *telling* the artist how to take the brush and stroke the musical canvas. Of course, that is an exaggeration. If it were a literal statement, the producer could maneuver a robot and achieve the same results. *Communication and mutual respect are necessary for success.*

Producers are selected in various ways. Most established artists choose producers in conjunction with an A&R label representative.

- Established artists often coproduce their albums with a producer.
- Many artists co-write with producers and co-produce the song(s).
- If an established artist's career is floundering, a label might insist on choosing one producer or multiple producers. Because labels make substantial financial investments in artists' careers, they are rightfully protective of the risks.

- Artists often fail to notice that record labels are businesses. Internet piracy, physical piracy, and the ever-changing music business paradigms have made label executives even more aware of their financial responsibilities. The financial waste that routinely occurred in the not-so-distant past has virtually stopped. In many ways that has benefited artists. When record labels financially advance money to support artists' careers, it is generally recoupable against artists' royalties. Young artists are not normally aware of this until reviewing their royalty statements. "Why am I not receiving any royalties?" is the age-old artists' response. The problem will be discussed in Part III: The Music Business.
- The label might offer new artists a choice of producers. It is rare for new artists to self-produce or to hire whomever they desire.

In all styles of popular music (pop, R&B, hip-hop, etc.), record labels might hire multiple producers to work on the same album. Many producers are songwriters and arrangers, and they tend to write and arrange the tracks they record. Some producers submit an almost completed master demo, which contains a pilot (demonstration) vocal. Demos, or demonstration records, are minimally produced recordings designed to showcase a song. That enables the label and the artist to hear—basically—the "sound" of the finished product. The singer replaces the pilot vocal, the artist and the producer overdub additional parts, and the producer and engineer mix the final track.

> ♫ With hip-hop music, artists generally hear a rhythm track, and if they are inspired, they write and record the rap, in some instances adding background vocals. The creative process is based upon a visceral reaction to the "music bed." In the heyday of Motown Records, the producers and songwriters worked in a similar manner. They recorded rhythm tracks, and various artists auditioned until they found the ideal fit. Occasionally the lyrics and the melodies were not written until the producer chose an artist. They wrote a portion of a song and listened to several artists sing it. That provided the songwriters with the opportunity to tailor the remainder of the song specifically for the artist.

That is not the procedure normally used with rock bands. Rock bands usually write and arrange the songs they record. Many rock producers are also engineers, which enables them to achieve sonic excellence in addition to providing a "fresh creative ear." That is not to suggest that band producers do not make substantial contributions to the entire production—quite the contrary. Band producers have as much influence on the creative outcome of a production as producers working in other musical genres.

Many music engineers have become accomplished producers. Engineers are critical listeners, analyzing both technical and creative issues. Many have worked with gifted musician-producers and, through osmosis, learned to think like musicians. Talented engineer-producers have a natural musical ability coupled with engineering skills.

The sonic quality of a recording contributes greatly to an artist's success. For example, the "Wall of Sound" (cavernous sound) created by producer Phil Spector became his trademark. His creative concept involved an ambient sonic image, created by the engineer. Microphone leakage (the recording of instruments not directly in front of a specific instrument) and the use of room ambience created the uncommon sonic concept, which has been emulated by many engineers and producers.

Some successful producers have unusual backgrounds. Dance-club DJs are an example. Club DJs have developed a reputation for remixing records. They utilize the original production elements (e.g., vocals and synthesizer parts) in addition to adding new parts, such as replacing the original drum and bass parts with new parts and new sounds. (The purpose of a club mix is to make the original track more danceable.)

In the past 25 years, remixing has become a specialized field and requires a dedication to the music. Club music is trendy and changes rapidly. A remixed version of a song completed 6 months prior to its release could be outdated by the time it is available to the public. Producers specializing in dance music must be aware of the current popular rhythm patterns, tempos, drum, and synthesizer sounds that are in vogue. Remixers' productions must remain contemporary.

Sometimes remixers begin the production process by using only the vocals from the original recording session and develop a completely new arrangement (feel and tempo) for the backing track. Remixers who are not synthesizer programmers or musicians generally hire a programmer and communicate their musical vision. Playing examples, the ability to express musical thoughts to a programmer, can sometimes be sufficient to achieve the desired results.

Most DJs are not musicians. DJs play and mix records (in a club or at a radio station) in a unique and creative manner. Some trend-setting DJs—Junior Vasquez, for example—attract 15,000 patrons when playing in a club. Some of them become excellent producers.

Labels are willing to pay large fees for the services of DJs who are tastemakers. Sales of club records (CDs, downloads, and vinyl) are relatively small compared to the sales of mainstream CDs or downloads, which are designed to attract a commercial-radio, Satellite, cable, or an Internet audience. Some popular club records have crossed over and become top 10 pop singles, resulting in greater sales. Many remixed versions of songs have become the primary versions played on the radio. Club records usually contain four or five different remixes to accommodate the variety of musical styles played in clubs. When the principal radio mix is beginning to lose airplay, some labels release a remixed version of the song, which can generate a new awareness to the record.

Marketing records in dance clubs is appealing to labels for several reasons:

- Dance clubs have traditionally been a relatively inexpensive method to market *and promote recordings.*
- Club hits can garner radio play, and radio performances generate sales.
- A label might think that a track (song or instrumental) has the potential to become a hit recording but the feel, or rhythmic groove, of the original production is not conducive to dance clubs. In this scenario a remixer(s) is generally hired to give the track a new feel that will not only spawn club play but also, the label hopes, expose the artist to a new audience. Many club records have become successful pop hits, in addition to being licensed for use in commercials, television programs, and feature films (*pop*, in this context, is being used as a generic term, encompassing most forms of popular music).

Conclusion

Various production techniques are explored throughout this book. With experience, producers eventually develop a personalized approach to music production. It is advisable to study each technique in depth. To be a successful producer requires a clear artistic vision and the knowledge of how to achieve that "mental picture."

2

The Creative Concepts of Production

> There is two kinds of music, the good and bad. I play the good kind.
>
> —Louis Armstrong

> Producing music is making choices!

Note: Throughout the book, the term *popular music* is being used as a generic term for all genres of commercial music.

The Production Process

The production approach to most styles of popular music is basically the same. Music producers are responsible for:

- Production concepts
- Arrangement concepts
- Song selection
- Coaching singers and musicians
- Audio engineering
- Mixing and mastering
- Music videos (not always a producer's responsibility)
- The business of music production

Overview

Producers should listen to and become familiar with popular recordings in the style of the music they are planning to produce. Listen carefully and analyze production techniques. The most difficult choice producers of popular music encounter is whether to mimic the music heard in the current "market-place" or to venture into new creative territory. Generally, the answer is somewhere in between.

Producing records that emulate current hits creates certain inherent problems. The production values (sound) of the recordings could be out-dated by the time the new production is released. The lack of originality makes artists less attractive to labels even if the recordings sound like hits. "Cookie-cutter" records are sometimes successful and can be profitable, but artists who are not unique generally have brief careers.

Artists and producers want their recordings to sound distinctive, but originality cannot be manufactured. Many artists who may not be considered artistically original still have successful careers.

Barbra Streisand and Celine Dion have recorded immaculately produced records, and their voices are exceptional and distinct. But are the records original? There are many fine singers who are surrounded by well-crafted arrangements, but Barbra's and Celine's extraordinary voices, choice of songs, and impeccably produced recordings have made them superstars. (Also, they are both extraordinary performers and their concerts engender record sales.)

Frank Sinatra, arguably the greatest male pop artist, is unique. The sound of his recordings also established his distinct identity. Sinatra's choice of songs and arrangers (Nelson Riddle, Billy May, and others) created a sound that continued throughout his career. If an audience was able to listen to a Frank Sinatra arrangement minus his vocal, the listeners could easily identify it as a Sinatra arrangement or an arrangement emulating his style. Steely Dan and Sting are also unique artists. They have established musical identities, which should be the goal of any artist.

A distinct artistic identity is also characteristic of successful producers. Most producers find a creative niche. Singers and musicians usually specialize in one musical genre. The same is true of music producers. They produce music in one or two styles. That applies not only to record production but also to other forms of music production such as library music, film music, and so forth.

The primary motive to produce a project should be a love of the music. If a producer is not fond of the music, the creative process will be laborious and the results, most likely, uninspiring.

The ability to "listen" is a prerequisite to producing music. Listening is a skill that requires development. The art of listening refers to the ability to analyze the component parts of compositions, arrangements, and productions, from both a creative and musical perspective. Gain an understanding of why the emotional content and the complexity of a piece evoke emotional reactions from listeners. (Listening in this context refers to any style of music—not just forms of commercial music.)

Music producers enhance artists' musical visions by helping them effectively communicate their emotions to the listener. Music producers are also usually musicians, artists, composers, arrangers, and/or engineers. Diverse backgrounds prepare them to analyze and critique music.

Critiquing one's own work can be difficult. Therefore many artists hire co-producers. A rock band might be more comfortable with an engineer-producer; an R&B artist may want to work with a producer who is also an arranger and a synthesizer programmer. A producer's background should complement the artist's needs.

Attorneys do not learn how to practice law in law school; they learn how to think like lawyers. Attorneys learn law by practicing law! The same is true for music producers. A music producer may not possess the ability to arrange or perform music, but a producer who has studied music production and who understands musical structure can successfully guide artists through the recording process. Competent producers must be able to analyze compositions, performances, and technical issues in addition to guiding songwriters, artists, and arrangers within the confines of an overall creative concept. *A combination of musical and technical skills is required to achieve success.*

Author's Note: Listening to the work of skilled producers is the best tutorial. Although taste cannot be learned, absorbing the techniques used by successful producers unlocks new avenues of creative thought.

Producers who want to achieve successful artistic and personal relationships with artists must become amateur psychologists and understand artists' motivations and artistic temperaments. If they do not believe in the artistic integrity of an artist, it will be difficult to achieve success. Artists and producers must agree on artistic visions and goals. This does not mean there will be no differences of opinion. Relationships should be based on mutual respect and willingness to compromise. *Creative conflicts often produce positive results.*

Listen to the songs, rhythms, and sounds in contemporary hit recordings. Production techniques continually change, and new trends evolve. Cutting-edge producers are aware of changing trends and have the ability to quickly analyze and attempt to predict future trends. The popular-music

> ♫ In some musical genres, such as hip-hop, R&B, and pop, multiple producers are employed, which has proven to be a successful formula. In other forms of music, such as rock and jazz, there is usually one producer.

business is analogous to the fashion-design business. Each year the styles and trends completely change or morph into something new, yet remain based in tradition. *Musical evolution* keeps the public's interest. Popular-music listeners are fickle, and audiences' tastes rapidly change.

Not all genres of popular music are trendy. Contemporary jazz (Kenny G), traditional jazz (Diana Krall), and traditional rock (Aerosmith) remain popular musical styles. Their listeners do not expect their recordings to follow current trends. Those genres rely less on technical wizardry and overly produced contemporary popular music. The latest drum sound and newest reverb or digital delay is not necessarily used when producing classic-sounding albums. Listeners want to feel as though they are in the room with an artist. They expect a well-produced recording and artistic integrity.

Pristine engineering and immaculate production remain a constant in all forms of recorded music.

How Do Trends Affect the Music Business?

Trends are often the catalysts that encourage entrepreneurs or producers to start independent labels. Trends initiate in various locations. For example, many new styles begin in dance clubs. The island of Ibiza (off the coast of Spain) has become a summer haven for college students. A genre of dance music called Chillout began in Ibiza. It is interesting to analyze how a musical genre(s) spreads from such a small territory.

European club DJs were hired to perform in Ibiza dance clubs. The DJs brought new recordings back to their countries, and a new style of music was born. Radio eventually began playing the music because sales resulted from the club play. If the public reacts to radio play and sales continually increase, a domino effect occurs, with other territories following the trend. Imitators oversaturate the market, the trend evaporates, and the labels and the public await the next trend.

Dance clubs are places to uncover inventive music. Artists and producers generally experience creative freedom on small dance labels, and they can afford to take risks. Creative freedom enables new music to surface and develop.

Trend setting is easier to write about than to achieve. Trends are also difficult to predict.

In the competitive atmosphere of the professional music business, success is usually linked to a complete commitment to a project. Producers must address the minutest details of production. The phrase "Dot every *i* and cross every *t*" certainly applies to music production. Attention to details is essential, but the feel of the music is more significant. A production will most likely not be a commercial or artistic success if each song (instrumental) does not have a distinct mood (ambience). Music evokes a visceral response from listeners, and it is a producer's obligation to help artists achieve that objective. *If a production is immaculately produced but lacks emotion (feel), listeners will not react.*

Production Concept

Developing a production concept is the most crucial stage of the production process. A *production concept* is the framework of an album. Many composers write a sketch before completing a composition; most authors write an outline before writing a book; film directors hire storyboard artists to sketch each scene in a cartoonlike drawing prior to shooting a movie. Record producers outline a *creative and sonic image (concept)* before recording an album.

What is the music going to "say" to the listener? The choice of songs (instrumentals) is the first step in developing a production concept; the second step is for the artist and producer to agree on a sonic image. The production concept has to incorporate the artist's physical image, which will most likely be included on the album cover and in the music videos. The music must reflect that image. How does the artist plan to project his or her image within the music? Such concerns have to become one combination of ideas.

An album that sounds romantic and intimate illustrates a production concept. Thus a producer might choose reverberation settings (such as a small-room reverb) that virtually transport the audience from a living room into an intimate nightclub setting; using a small ensemble rather than a large orchestra also helps to achieve intimacy. Psychoacoustics plays a considerable role in the musical relationship between artists and the listeners. *The audience has to connect with the artist's vision.* (Psychoacoustics is the manner in which a listener perceives a musical environment.)

Some artists strive to create recordings that simulate their live performances. Capturing a live performance in the recording studio is the paramount objective of some producers. To accomplish that, artists perform "live" in the studio. Following the recording of the "basic track," they will generally record a series of overdubs to enhance the "live" performance. For instance, the rhythm guitar might be doubled to add power of the original part. This provides the engineer/producer with the ability to pan one guitar to the left and the other to the right thereby creating a stereo image; solos and percussion might be added, and so forth. Artists overdub additional parts and repair mistakes made during the live recording. The objective is to capture the same energy achieved during concert performances.

Producers might choose not to overdub numerous additional parts since artists cannot reproduce all of the parts during live performances. The sound would be inconsistent with the overall ambience of the group.

Many producers record one instrument at a time. A common technique is to program a track on synthesizers (and samplers) and subsequently replace the synthesized tracks with live musicians or combine live musicians with the synthesized tracks.

♫ Most studio effects are able to be reproduced during a concert. The audience is generally disappointed if artists do not basically reproduce their recordings during their live performances. Frequently when an audience member is asked, "How was the concert?" the response is, "They sounded just like their recordings." That is the ultimate compliment from a fan.

Once an artist and a producer agree on a production concept, it is the producer's responsibility to remain focused throughout the recording process. A production concept is analogous to a corporation's mission statement. If the concept of the production is not adhered to, the album will not sound cohesive. It could sound like myriad tracks with a lack of musical focus like a compilation album consisting of songs or instrumentals from various genres, such as a heavy metal track followed by an R&B track. This example is an exaggeration, but close to a listener's perception of the album.

Producers and Artists

If the foundation is not solid, the house will fall! Building an album is analogous to building any structure. When a newly built home is purchased, the builder offers a basic model, and upgrades are available. Upgrades depend on the buyer's taste and budget. The same basic concept applies to designing an album.

The songs are the foundation of the majority of popular-music albums. Creating a well-crafted arrangement and/or a pristine production will not enhance a mediocre song. If the songs are not commercial or artistically interesting, the album will fail. Song selection continually changes until the final material is agreed on. Artists' original songs are replaced, rewritten, and/or edited. The building process emanates from a creative concept. If artists choose to record "covers" (songs that have been previously released), or if a song has already been a hit, the new arrangement must differ substantially from the original version. There is no purpose in releasing "cover band" versions. Although retaining the basic feel of "I Heard It Through the Grapevine," Michael McDonald's recording is slower and differs enough from the original, by Marvin Gaye, to make it an outstanding cover of a classic recording. McDonald's first *Motown* album was extremely successful.

Producers and/or A&R executives search for unique artists. Originality is the main ingredient in the recipe for superstardom. In this context stardom is not defined in the traditional sense of mere fame but refers to the distinctive characteristics of great musical personalities. Mick Jagger, Barbra Streisand, Aretha Franklin, Luciano Pavarotti, and Leonard Bernstein are formidable examples.

> ♫ Mick Jagger, of the Rolling Stones, is a songwriter and a dynamic performer. Streisand, Franklin, and Pavarotti are vocal icons in their respective musical arenas and have all become benchmarks for other performers. Leonard Bernstein was a master conductor, composer, and educator.

Producers should appreciate artists from both a musical and personal perspective. Understanding one's artistic personality helps a producer explore an artist's musical psyche. Most substantial artists have a mission, which is to bring a musical message to the public. Music is the defining factor of an artist's psychological structure. If an artist does not "live the music," it would be unwise for a producer to devote the time and energy required to create a successful production.

Design a production concept after gaining a thorough understanding of the artist. Most important is that an album has a consistency of sound. Each track should sound as if it is part of a collection. Creating an overall mood for a project provides a unified quality. Each song/instrumental should be connected to the others either by a general lyrical concept, sound design, instrumental combination, or alternative method that sews the project together. Artists who achieve longevity have an identity and a producer's job is to *enhance* their musical images. Producers guide artists' recording careers.

> ♫ The great jazz trumpeter Miles Davis continually explored new ways to transport his musical message to the public. He was never creatively stagnant. Sinatra had an image, which emanated from his music. Most great artists *are* the music they perform. Music cannot be separated from an artist's psyche. Many artists have "something to say" and their music provides a forum for expression.

The artistic motivation of an artist is of primary concern to a producer. Commitment and a unique artistic vision are the driving forces behind most successful artists. They have a musical vision and also the ambition to pursue a career. Creating the best music is always their primary motivation; financial rewards follow.

A global hit reaches millions of listeners in a very short period of time. Downloading, terrestrial radio, Internet radio (including streaming), cable, HD, and Satellite radio, videos, mobile music downloads, and broadcast and cable television stations provide instant access to music. Public awareness can be achieved quickly with intensive airplay and touring.

In the 1950s, when folk music was at its peak in popularity, folk artists communicated through music. Many rock 'n' roll bands and hip–hop artists are also passionate about delivering messages to the listeners (sans preaching). Dedication to the music helps artists achieve success. Mature audiences generally react to artists' creative achievements and they remain loyal fans. Billy Joel, Elton John, Steely Dan, Paul McCartney, and James Taylor are superstars partially because of fan loyalty.

Production techniques and recording technology keep evolving, but the basic premise of recording—capturing a performance—will never change. Capturing a performance does not necessarily refer to emulating a live performance (vocal or instrumental) in the studio. It means to *capture* an artist's and producer's creative objectives. For instance, a synthesizer programmer may spend months creating a track; the process involves myriad musical parts that eventually collide to form one musical composition. The final composition is not merely based on the selected sounds (synthesized and sampled) and the compositional form but also includes the creative use of technology. Composers might use reverberation, delays, equalization, compression, and so forth, as essential components of a composition. A flute note might have an eighth-note delay written into the score, or a bass might trigger a 50-millisecond tap echo. Signal processing can also become part of the ambience created during a live performance; it helps generate a sonic image.

The evolution of music production is directly related to music technology. As technology became more sophisticated, so did the creative use of technology. Just the simple ambience that can be created with the proper use of reverberation can transform a recorded piece of music into an emotional experience. Since music is, arguably, the most sensual art form, having the ability to manipulate recorded music into virtually any imaginable sonic atmosphere is possible; purchasing the software to do so is financially affordable for most musicians.

One of the greatest gifts both artists and music producers possess is the ability to create without financial restrictions. The music that can be created and recorded in a bedroom could previously only be accomplished in a technically sophisticated and costly recording studio. When the creative urge strikes an artist, the process of documenting the music must happen immediately. A songwriter can record with a small digital recorder; a symphonic composer can notate on score paper or on a computer notation program such as Finale or Sibelius. Now, any artist can immediately document his or her work in a computer-sequencing program. When the creative spirit appears, a programmer can use a laptop computer and not only experiment with the sonic quality of a production but actually hear what it will sound like by listening to instrumental samples of real instruments or by creating synthesized sounds. The incredible development of real orchestral samples has afforded composers and orchestrators an opportunity to hear their compositions prior to hiring musicians, if that is the ultimate goal. They simply play the notes on a keyboard (or another instrument that can trigger MIDI), which triggers the sound of the real sampled instrument. (The notes can also be typed into the program.) Synthesizers and samplers are also manufactured as virtual instruments (analogous to a physical instrument), which are stored on a computer's hard drive. With a computer-sequencing program, an electronic keyboard, and virtual synthesizers and samplers, almost any recording can be accomplished on demand.

Contemporary popular-music productions customarily follow trends. Listen to the musical elements used in hit recordings, and analyze the marketing approaches used to market successful recordings. In the music business, music and marketing are inseparable. If an artist produces a musically viable album and the public is not aware that it has been released, there will be relatively few sales. Success in the music industry is based upon 50% artistic achievement and 50% business acumen.

Study the overall production concepts of successful albums. Listen carefully to the compositions and the production qualities. Try to analyze analogous elements that are found in various styles of music such as rhythm patterns, bass sounds, and the use of signal processing.

- *Why does the song (instrumental) selection build an organized artistic concept?* Most successful albums are designed as a project and song selection is the *key* to success. The songs (instrumentals) are chosen to fit together like the pieces of a puzzle, although "fitting together" is not meant to imply that all albums are designed as concept albums.
- *Concept albums* are intended to work as a story. The Who's *Tommy* is a concept; there is an explicit relationship between the lyrics of the songs, even if there is no definitive storyline. The lyrics may contain an emotional thread that ties them together.
- *Is there a synergy between the lyrics on the album?* Society changes, and mores change, and the lyrics of popular songs usually mirror those changes. Contemporary popular music reflects popular culture. Some lyrics have substance while others are designed as unadulterated entertainment. For instance, hip-hop music reflects a lifestyle—a subculture, such as Southern, East Coast, or West Coast hip-hop.
- Listeners relate to lyrical content. At the beginning of rock 'n' roll, the lyrics were trite, but the music and culture helped promote civil

rights by obliterating musical racism on U.S. radio stations. During the Vietnam War, many lyrics reflected an antiwar sentiment. The perils of love have consistently been the most popular subject of lyrics.

- Singer-songwriters have a definite point of view. Lyrics that reflect popular culture in an entertaining manner have to echo current popular thought, or attracting a youthful audience, the primary consumers of popular culture, will be difficult. For instance, Britney Spears or Justin Bieber must record records with cutting-edge production values, but the lyrical content of the songs should also appeal, primarily, to a young demographic. (Britney Spears had to morph from a young artist to a mature artist without losing her core fan base.) Usher sang about being unfaithful, and Eminem rapped about family problems and growing up poor. The fans can relate to the lyrics.
- Producers have to address these issues when designing albums. Artists without a point of view are probably not worth producing.
- *Does the sonic quality remain constant throughout the album?* An overall sound is vital to achieving sonic cohesiveness. Some artists develop a sonic identity (e.g., The Beatles, Coldplay, and Linkin Park). The audience expects to hear an identifiable ambience. Artists, producers, and engineers all contribute to creating a sonic identity.
- *How is the album going to be marketed and advertised?* The music dictates the most suitable approach. If an album has a theme, the record label will design the advertising, marketing, and promotions around the concept. (This subject is addressed in the business section of this book.)
- An artist's music and stage performance are the most significant ingredients of the image-building process. Music videos reflect an artist's image, and advertising (photos and graphics) and public relations (interviews) project his or her image.
- Usher is an example of an artist who wants the public to perceive him as being "cool" and entertaining. Alicia Keys sings, plays the piano, writes songs, and projects a contemporary image. Her style of music will most likely afford her a long career that will continue after her record sales decline.

To arrive at a viable album concept, producers and artists must agree on artistic goals. The following questions should be taken into consideration:

- *What message does the artist want to deliver?* The choice of songs should be an affirmation of an overall concept. If the concept is to record *The Greatest Love Songs*, the lyrics should suggest a variety of emotions so the listener remains stimulated throughout the album;

the lyrical *messages can vary but remain related to one another.* A concept album *A Tribute to Frank Sinatra* could include songs recorded by Sinatra (a compilation) or recorded by new artists recording Sinatra classics. A title can instigate a diversity of conceptual ideas and can be the primary tool for building a production concept.

- Achieving an overall musical design for an album is a producer's most crucial consideration before recording begins.
- *Should the emotional-technical ambience of a recording be intimate or spacious?* Is the listener going to be mentally transported into a small nightclub, to Carnegie Hall, or to a large stadium?
- The choice of a studio and an engineer affects the sonic atmosphere of the album. Large studios, such as studios designed to record orchestral music, produce a spacious ambience created by natural reverberation that is carefully calculated during the design of the studio. Studios designed to record rhythm sections, or smaller instrumental ensembles generally have a less ambient studio room and the natural sound of the recording has less reverberation. (This is not to imply that a small studio cannot have natural reverberation.) Ambient effects are added during the mixing process with the use of signal processing (e.g., reverberation, delay, and equalization).

Successful producers are detail oriented. This can sometimes be misconstrued as being too compulsive or too restrictive like areas of a production that some may feel are not significant. *All areas of production are essential.* Calculating delay and feedback, compression ratios, the selection of echo and/or reverberation, the model of a guitar used on a particular song (e.g., Fender Stratocaster or Fender Telecaster), the programmed sounds of synthesizers and samplers, the microphone selection, the choice of an engineer and the selection of musicians, and many other facets of the production process are substantial concerns of producers. *Producing is a musical and technical potpourri.*

> ♫ Many rock bands prefer to record in large studios to attain a sound similar to the sonic atmosphere of a large concert venue.

Arranging

The sound of the arrangement. The arrangements are crucial to the success of a project. A hit song will not be a hit record if the arrangement does not complement the music and lyrics. Producers guide arrangers and help shape and select the most inventive creative path. Arrangers *are* composers. They "set" and enhance a basic composition. An arrangement may be referred to as a "surrounding composition" since the arrangement surrounds the basic song (instrumental) structure.

- *A band has a sound; their arrangements are the sound of the band. If an arranger(s) is hired, the producer has to be concerned that the arrangements throughout the album have a consistent sound.* The artist and the producer must agree on the ambience of the arrangements. The grooves and basic instrumentation should be similar throughout an album. Naturally, there are exceptions, e.g., The Beatles enhanced instrumentation used on the *Sgt. Pepper's Lonely Hearts Club Band* album.
- *To achieve a coherent sonic image, use essentially the same instrumentation, musicians, engineer(s), and studio(s) throughout the recording of an album.* That is not always possible and most likely not probable. The executive producer is responsible for overseeing the overall sound of the project and has to coordinate all the musicians and singers to achieve a sonic image.
- *Does the arrangement complement the lyric?* Does the mood of the arrangement surround the lyric? Some lyrics can be musically accented, which will enhance the impact of a song. Experienced arrangers instinctively address these concerns; it is a basic skill of professional arrangers.
- *Does the arrangement complement the lead vocal?* Consider the sonic quality of the lead vocalist before writing an arrangement and before choosing the instrumentation. An arrangement for a powerful voice will differ from an arrangement designed to complement a softer voice (e.g., Sade as compared to Aretha Franklin). These subjects are discussed in detail in chapter 5.

Producers must monitor each section of a production to make certain that it does not stray too far from the desired sonic concept. Since most albums are recorded over an extended time period, producers should continually listen to rough mixes, analyzing the abovementioned concerns.

♫ A rough mix is a mix used for review.

Song Selection

Producers and artists usually begin an album by selecting songs. If the budget permits, it is best to record more songs than will actually be used on the final album. Song demos (basic productions of songs) that sound appropriate for a project or also sound suitable during rehearsals will not necessarily be included on the album. It is wise to have replacements. For example, a song might not fit the final creative concept of the album. That might become a dilemma for a producer, an artist, and the label because a song that sounds like a radio hit could be out of character with the remainder of the song selection. Therefore, it is wise to keep the song for a future project rather than risk ruining the album's overall sonic image. The final song selection has to work as a unified collection rather than a grouping of individual tracks that do not musically relate to each other.

> ♫ The terms *song* and *instrumental* are used interchangeably.

The source of future compositions is a primary concern of label executives and producers. Artists who are also songwriters are appealing to labels. Labels prefer not having to rely on independent songwriters or music publishers as a source of material. Artists who can write radio-friendly songs are sought after.

Artist-songwriters are not necessarily "hit" songwriters. Many artists insist on writing their own material, although the songs are not commercial. Some artists have ruined their careers by refusing to record songs written by other songwriters. Most successful popular artists record any appropriate song that has a chance to top the charts. (It is foolish not to record songs from outside sources, since hits attract concert promoters who hire artists. Besides, one hit song generates album sales. Most record labels are willing to sell one song from an album via Internet stores, such as iTunes and Amazon. This has become a paradigm for Internet sales.)

> ♫ When a producer discovers an artist, he or she usually signs the artist to the producer's production company or the producer's record label. A production company usually "shops" the album or single tracks to various labels for distribution, or it has an exclusive deal with a label to distribute all of the company's productions. A label has a distribution deal (physical and digital) through either a major label or an independent distributor(s).

Many producers are also songwriters. They sign artists who will record their songs. Successful relationships have been built between producer-songwriters and artists; *the songwriter and the interpreter.* A stellar example is Dionne Warwick, who recorded multiple hits by singing the songs of Burt Bacharach and Hal David. It is analogous to a comedian's relationship with a joke writer. Some comedians write their own jokes, but many rely on independent writers to supply them with jokes and routines. The comedian becomes the interpreter.

Producers are responsible for editing songs (instrumentals) and arrangements prior to recording. That is done in collaboration with artists. Most new artists

♫ Producers have to be concerned with all aspects of the business of music when conceiving an album. In addition to a cohesive sonic image, the cover design and graphics should mirror the musical content. In retail stores, albums are displayed (racked) in categories—rock, R&B, world music, and so on. For marketing purposes, the record company targets the proper audience; therefore, the overall sound of the album should be within a musical genre. That is one of the keys to strategic popular-music marketing. An artist must focus on his or her image, which, hopefully, will appeal to a targeted demographic.

need help with song formats and arrangements. For example, an introduction may become 4 instead of 8 measures; the second chorus could be sung 2 times instead of once. The editing process is crucial to the artistic and commercial success of the final product. Skilled producers have an innate ability to detect creative flaws and experiment with various ways to repair them. It is a form of coaching, consistent with the importance to success of mutual artistic respect between producers and artists.

Coaching Singers

Producers coach singers. A producer must "get a performance" from an artist. That is a complex subject, and there are no concrete methods for guiding artists.

Producers develop their own system of working with singers; the modus operandi differs from artist to artist. Personal relationships affect the interaction between producers and artists. *Trust is the crucial element.* If an artist does not have confidence in the producer, the project is doomed to failure. This subject will be discussed, in detail, later in the book.

Coaching Musicians

Coaching musicians, whether band members or studio musicians, requires the same skills as coaching a lead vocalist or solo instrumentalist. The psychological approach producers take with the musicians (and background singers) is vital to drawing out the best possible performances from artists. Creating a comfortable ambience in the studio relaxes performers, and in such an environment they will most certainly deliver better performances. A musician must have confidence in and respect for the producer or it will be difficult for the producer to coach an artist into achieving a stellar performance.

Certain styles of music sound best when programmed on synthesizers (e.g., trance music) while other styles sound best performed by live musicians (e.g., rock or traditional jazz). A producer may choose to combine live musicians with synthesizers or select the most appropriate instrumental combination to complement a song. When possible, it is advisable to experiment. Experimentation can produce new sounds and combinations. If a producer coaches and encourages a programmer to be inventive, a fresh crop of ideas may take a music track in new directions.

Engineering

Recording engineers who specialize in music are responsible for the sonic qualities of albums. Recording engineers are artists. Some have studied music, whereas others developed musical skills through the process of osmosis. They listen carefully and work with skillful producers and musicians. Experienced engineers operate recording consoles, both hardware and software. SSL and Neve consoles interact with computer audio programs, such as Pro Tools.

Effects, such as reverbs, delays, and compression, enhance the recorded music tracks and become an intrinsic part of the final sonic image. Psychoacoustics plays an important role in a listener's emotional response to recorded music. For instance, a delay behind a lead vocal adds depth to the sound of the vocal; a long reverb on a snare drum creates a shooting effect through the track and adds power; a tap echo can add a rhythmic delay to a sound. When creating a recording, which is a permanent representation of a composition, the effects become—in some cases—equal in importance to the other components of the arrangement. Using effects properly is an example of *the creative use of technology.* Effects are discussed in a later chapter.

Mixing

Creating the final sonic image is called mixing. A musical sketch has been completed, the colors have been added (orchestration), and the individual components are ready for assembly into one complete unit.

Mixing is an art form that is both a technical and creative process. At this phase in the production process, producers and artists ought to agree that the basic tracks and vocals (or instrumentals) are acceptable, and the necessary overdubs (additional parts) have been recorded. Signal processing, such as equalization, compression/limiting, panning, volume levels, and the balancing of these elements, all contribute to the final sonic image. *Mixing is the artistic blending of these elements.* Each of these components is discussed in the technology section of this book.

> ♫ Some engineers only mix and do not record. Some producers do not mix but rely on mixing engineers. The record label may choose the mixer in consultation with the artist and the producer. It is not unusual for several producers and engineers to mix one song. Multiple mixes might be included on one album; most often the additional mixes are dance mixes, e.g., Katy Perry.

Many albums are recorded in multiple studios. Because of the differences in sound, some producers and engineers choose to mix in one studio, which helps to create sonic continuity. Since it is commonplace for multiple producers and engineers to work on one album, mixing in one location can sonically "glue" a project together. An executive producer oversees the process of the production. (This concept might not be practical.)

In the chapter devoted to the mixing and mastering process, in addition to the information previously mentioned, the following elements are discussed:

- The importance of a sonic concept
- Signal processing
- Monitor selection
- The control room
- Console selection
- Attention to detail during the original recording sessions
- Live tracks that can be fixed only by rerecording, for which the cost might be prohibitive
- The placement of the lead and background vocals in the mix
- The sonic relationship between the lead and background vocals
- The artistic reasons for this relationship

> ♫ Standards vary according to the musical genre. For example, rock 'n' roll vocals are usually placed at a lower level in the mix than R&B vocals. The placement of pop vocals is usually similar to the placement of R&B vocals.

Arrangements are affected by the vocals. If the vocals will be loud in a mix, an arranger has to design the rhythm track so that it can also be prominent in the mix without masking the vocals. One technique is to write the arrangement so that the frequency ranges of the instrumental parts do not conflict with the frequency ranges of the vocals. The same is true of strings, horns, or additional instrumental parts. Carefully placed fills (e.g., snare-drum fills) can be prominent in the mix if they surround the vocals and do not cover them. More will be said about this in the chapters devoted to arranging, mixing, and mastering.

Mastering

Mastering is the final creative and technical process before manufacturing. The mix (stereo or surround sound) receives its final sonic manipulation in the mastering lab (producers usually oversee mastering sessions). Mastering is a synthesis of art and technology, and mastering engineers are artists. Although the final sound of a recording is created during the mixing process, the mastering engineer is responsible for technical excellence (e.g., no distortion or digital error, and the track levels match throughout the album), and the final equalization process, which should not drastically change the overall sound of the mixes, adds a final *sonic gloss*.

Mastering can be either advantageous or detrimental to the final sonic quality of a production. For instance, an excess of compression can eliminate the dynamics in a music track; overemphasizing the higher frequencies can create a piercing sound. Many factors can either detract from or greatly enhance the final sound. A producer usually attends the mastering session or approves the mastering before the album is manufactured.

The choice of a mastering engineer and a mastering studio is as essential to the recording process as the other creative and technical choices typically made by a producer.

Music Videos

A music video is a visual representation of a song or instrumental composition. Not only must a story be told but the director also has to capture the artist's image. The director should be thoroughly familiar with the artist's persona since the video must capture the essence of the artist. An ill-conceived video could damage an artist's image with fans.

The choice of a director is a primary consideration. Some directors specialize in directing music videos and are also genre-specific in the assignments they accept. Viewing directors' demonstration reels narrows the selection process.

Record labels are involved in choosing a director, and they have relationships with directors and video production companies. Since cost is a factor, it is wise for the artist (and sometimes the producer) to consult with the record label when choosing a director. Hire a director who will work within the budget and deliver a quality video.

The artist and director must develop a synergy similar to that an artist develops

> ♫ Most major labels spend between $500,000 to $1,000,000 per video for high-profile artists. Prior to the rampant illegal downloading and physical pirating that reduced profits, major labels were spending (infrequently) as much as $2,000,000 to produce a superstar's video. Small labels spend a fraction of that cost. Many independent artists produce their own videos and post them on websites such as YouTube. Videos seen on the Internet have been instrumental in launching careers for artists such as Justin Bieber.

with a music producer. Trust and mutual respect are primary considerations.

A creative and contemporary choreographer should be hired. If an artist wants to project a contemporary image and the dancing is outdated, the artist's image will appear dated. Choreographers are also hired to help an artist with movement. Not all artists are competent dancers, and choreographed movements help keep an artist from appearing static.

Music producers are not always consulted before a music video is shot. If the producer feels that the artist is being misguided and the music is not being visualized properly, the producer should voice his or her opinion to the artist and the label. Videos are a significant sales tool, and if a video does not properly represent a song, the production may be compromised. (Some labels are charging for the use of videos in venues such as the Internet.)

The Business of Music

The business of music is the subject of numerous books. Students wishing to become music executives or informed creatives should study, in depth, each of the subjects noted in this chapter and the additional chapters dedicated to the business of music.

The contemporary music industry has made it necessary for industry people to think entrepreneurially. The continuing growth of digital distribution has made it essential to understand all aspects of the business. New independent labels, managed by two or three executives, make it necessary for each person to have a working knowledge of all aspects of the industry.

Producers and executives must comprehend the following subjects:

- Negotiating master recording contracts
- Negotiating artists' contracts
- Negotiating production contracts
- Music distribution contracts
- Personal artist management contracts
- Talent agent contracts
- Production budgets
- Securing record deals
- Record sales
- Music promotions
- Music marketing

- Music advertising
- Studio selection
- Engineering
- Copyrights and music publishing
- Musicians' union agreement (AFM)
- Singers' union agreements (SAG, AFTRA)
- Performance-rights organizations (BMI, ASCAP, and SESAC in the U.S., and similar organizations throughout the world)
- Foreign music licensing

♫ These topics, and more, are discussed in the chapters concerning the business of music.

Conclusion

Music production is a complex topic. Successful producers are knowledgeable in both music and business. (Iconic producer Quincy Jones is a schooled musician, arranger, and music executive. The late Arif Mardin had the same background.) They manage production businesses and not being thoroughly conversant with the subjects discussed in this chapter will make it difficult for them to sell or negotiate master sound recording licenses. (Production companies, copyright owners, or record labels that finance and own recordings, often license the use of those recordings for a time period (term), which is negotiable. The recordings are referred to as masters or master recordings.)

Familiarity with these topics will help producers develop a modus operandi. It cannot be stated often enough: *The only way to learn music production is by producing music.*

Assignment

You are planning to produce an album. Answer the following questions. (Choose a fictitious artist.)

- Describe the artist (solo artist, band, image, performance traits, etc.).
- Why do you choose to produce the artist?
- What is your production concept? Justify the concept.
- What is the title of the album?
- Why did you (and the artist) choose the title?
- Does the title relate to the songs (instrumentals)?
- Describe the graphic design of the cover.
- Why is the cover design important?
- What style of songs (instrumentals) do you plan to record and why?

- You may record in several recording studios. Why did you select those studios?
- What are the attributes of your engineer and how will his or her experience directly enhance your project?
- How do you plan to promote and market the album?

3

The Artist

> You have to be singular, instead of saying, "These are the hit records of the moment; how do I make my music sound like that?"
>
> —Sting, *USA Today*

Being Good Is Not Good Enough!

Record labels take a considerable financial risk when signing artists. They try to minimize financial risk by carefully selecting artists and producers. The process is discussed in this chapter.

A producer's mission should be to enhance an artist's musical vision; any attempt to reinvent a musical image rarely results in success. It is a mistake to try to transform an artist into a producer's artistic visualization. If a producer has to perform a "makeover," the artist is not ready to begin or sustain a recording career. Artists must have a strong self-image and a true musical sense about themselves. Most successful performers have a creative vision and an air of self-confidence. *An artist's "mission" is usually the foundation of a successful career.*

♫ Some producers view themselves as artists and the singers or instrumentalists as interpreters. That formula can be successful if the artistic mission is stated at the outset of the relationship. For instance, producers of dance music (club music or disco) usually establish this type of relationship.

Artist development is a lengthy and involved process. Talent is only half of the formula needed to "break" (popularize) a contemporary artist. Producers must carefully consider many factors before signing an artist to a production contract or agreeing to produce an artist for a label. Artistry, songwriting ability, quality of live performance, physical appearance, and charisma are all primary considerations. Because of the competitive nature of the music business and the financial commitment required to achieve success, close attention to the overall artistic picture is crucial.

The success of most artists is dependent upon 50% talent and 50% business sense. As a producer scouting to sign new artists, you must carefully investigate the business executives who are counseling the artist. If the artist has a manager and/or an agent, do those advisors have the clout to enhance the artist's career? For instance, a talent agent might book a new artist as an opening act on a major tour with a popular artist who is also represented by the same agent. Such exposure is invaluable when trying to enhance an artist's career.

Some labels will not sign artists who are represented by powerless business people. Labels rely on managers and agents to parlay artists' careers, particularly when the label's promotion department has provided radio and television airplay followed by album sales.

In the early stages of most artists' careers, it is unwise to make long-term business commitments. Some producers and label executives help artists develop business relationships, but usually at a time when proper representation will be beneficial.

Artists are discovered in numerous ways. Producers and A&R executives, who sign artists to recording contracts and labels, develop business relationships with managers, agents, music publishers, concert promoters, music-business attorneys, and club owners for whom it is advantageous to expose A&R executives to unsigned artists or signed artists whose contracts will shortly terminate. Basically, artists are found from various sources. Artists who have been dropped from labels are often signed to new labels and become stars (e.g., Alicia Keys and Aretha Franklin).

Established A&R executives, managers, and agents receive an inordinate number of artist demo (a demonstration CD of songs or instrumentals) submissions. Rarely does an unsolicited demo fuel a professional relationship. Without a "story," labels are normally not interested in artists unless there are unusual circumstances surrounding their careers (e.g., John Lennon's son, Julian Lennon) or an artist is extraordinarily gifted. If a manager or agent promotes an artist to a label and promises that the artist will be touring, be supported by public relations and additional support services, the label will seriously consider signing the artist—assuming that the label executives are excited about the artist's music and performance skills.

♫ Major label executives are instructed not to open unsolicited packages (e.g., containing demos). They fear lawsuits claiming plagiarism. In most circumstances, reputable personal managers, agents, music publishers, and music business attorneys submit demos.

The process usually begins by listening to countless demos. A demo (demonstration CD) consisting of three or four original songs is the most suitable presentation. If a label or producer becomes interested in the artist he or she will request a submission of additional material. An experienced A&R executive or producer can judge from the first listening whether an artist is gifted and fits the label's creative standards.

It is rare for a demo to sound as polished as a master sound recording (a completed production), although many inexperienced artists believe their demos *are* master quality. Unless an artist is confident that his or her submission is master quality, it is wiser to represent the recordings as demos.

Affordable technology has made home recording available to artists. Most artists record demos in a home studio (also called a project studio). Prior to the popularity of project studios, a studio-rental budget was necessary. Not only was that costly, but creative experimentation was also limited because of the expense.

Digital audio offers unlimited, affordable editing capabilities without loss of audio quality and at a reasonable cost. On analog audio tape, bouncing (combining tracks) causes a generational loss of audio quality. Digital technology affords the artist unlimited, nondestructive editing capabilities (all original recorded information can be recalled) without the loss of audio quality. (Analog audio tape is rarely used with the exception of transferring final mixes to 2 track audio tape for mastering. Some producers and engineers prefer the sound of audio tape to the sound of digital audio.)

The professional audio quality of home studio technology has also afforded artists the opportunity to record either all or part of the master recordings at a considerably reduced cost. Sizable studios are normally used to record live rhythm sections (e.g., rock bands) or large ensembles such as orchestras or horn and string sections; sophisticated recording consoles are sometimes used for mixing, if the budget allows. Most home studio owners can now afford to purchase outboard gear (reverbs, compressors, etc.) and are able to mix home-studio project with stellar results. (Music sequencing programs come with most outside gear so it is not necessary to purchase hardware versions unless the producer/engineer prefers the sound quality.)

♫ The Foo Fighters album *Wasting Light*, released April 11, 2011, was recorded on analog tape. They inserted pieces of the master tape in copies of the album so the fans could own a part of the master. Dave Grohl of the Foo Fighters said, "We recorded the record in my garage to analog tape, and probably wound up with 20-30 reels of tapes."

Choosing a suitable record label is crucial to artists' careers. An artist and a label are committing to a "marriage," of sorts, when agreeing to sign a recording contract. Most artists would prefer to sign with a major label. There are several reasons:

- Financial stability is usually the primary concern. Many independent labels have cash-flow problems, which may affect financial accountability to artists.
- Major labels have the financial resources and the business relationships to market and promote albums to a greater degree than most independent labels.
- Many major labels sign artists to worldwide contracts, which offers artists international exposure. That is not always desirable from an artist's perspective. It does not necessarily follow that branch territories (e.g., Spain, France, UK) are as productive as the flagship territory (e.g., U.S.). Some artists prefer to choose multiple distributors, but most major U.S. labels will sign artists to a worldwide deal only. (Most digital distribution is global although the clients have the ability to choose in which territories they want distribution.)

An independent label may not have the same financial resources as a major label, but for some artists signing with an independent might be wiser than signing with a major.

- Major labels have the ability to outsell independents but may not excel in promoting certain styles of music. A&R executives at boutique labels are usually experts in a specialized genre of music (e.g., jazz or new age) and become involved in the creative shaping of an album. They hope to guide artists in a focused direction.
- Often an artistic synergy exists between an artist and an independent label, since there is a mutual passion for a musical style. Similar relationships also exist at major labels but usually do not develop to the same extent unless there is financial success.

♫ Independent labels usually have sublicensing deals with labels in either territories or individual countries. Some large independent labels have offices in various territories. Therefore, they might have the same influence as a major label.

Many successful independent labels specialize in musical genres that are not necessarily of interest to major labels (e.g., dance music). Small and successful independent labels are able to operate with 3 or 4 employees, the owner being the CEO. Low overhead enables the labels to make a profit with relatively inconsequential sales, as compared to major or mini-major label sales. (Many small labels only sell their music on the Internet. Some labels, such as beatport.com, are highly successful. As compared to Amazon, which offers only MP3s, Beatport offers consumers high quality audio files. They sell MP3, MP4, and WAV file formats.)

Independent labels often start, rather than follow, musical trends. They can afford to experiment and take risks. The major labels, hoping to piggyback on the success of smaller labels, emulate most trends started by independents. The independent labels are viewed as focus groups. If sales do not produce enough income to warrant the financial commitment needed for a major label to staff and fund the promotion of a specific musical genre, the offshoots are usually disbanded within several years.

Some major labels purchase or partner with independent labels rather than start a new division; BMG bought the new age label, Windham Hill Records. That does not assure the survival of the former independent. If the smaller label is not generating a profit, the major often keeps the lucrative artists and returns the remaining ones to the original owners or drops them from the label.

Before signing an artist, consider the following:

- *Most successful artists have unique musical personalities.* They possess "musical fingerprints," which often is a reflection of their lifestyles. They "live" the music (e.g., Eminem). Like any artistic endeavor, popular music offers artists opportunities to achieve international exposure.
- Musical trends traditionally dominate the popular-music market. A style develops, and clones follow. Britney Spears, for example, has been cloned by a series of young female singers. In the music industry these artists are referred to as "cookie-cutter artists"—all out of the same mold. Labels tend to flood the marketplace with clones—up to a point. After a trend has been exhausted and sales decline, labels are no longer interested in signing clones.
- Radio stations always search for something new to program, and trends often begin when a unique record hits the charts. Popular-music audiences are fickle and are continually seeking new musical experiences. YouTube has become the outlet where most of the younger audience discover new artists and listen and watch videos of established artists. On YouTube, Usher discovered Justin Bieber and the 13 year-old singer Rebecca Black, also not signed to label, has received 153,653,217 hits on YouTube, as of the writing of this book. She signed a recording contract after receiving notoriety on YouTube.
- Trends translate not only into the cloning of music but also into the "look" (image) and performance style of popular artists. The

> ♫ Cloned artists can generate substantial incomes before the public's interest begins to wane. Generally, one of the group members initiates a solo career, and the group eventually disbands (e.g., Diana Ross from Diana Ross and the Supremes and Justin Timberlake from 'N Sync).

cookie-cutter acts usually have a style of dress and choreography similar to that of their predecessors. Sometimes two or three clones achieve popularity simultaneously, such as 'N Sync, O-Town, and the Backstreet Boys. The artists may not be unique, but their recordings are well produced and contain memorable songs with contemporary rhythmic grooves. Their live performances create excitement, spectacle, and, of course, sales.

Record labels search for unique artists. Major labels are primarily interested in artists who have the potential of generating significant sales. It generally takes a minimum investment of one million U.S. dollars to even *attempt* to break an act, without any guarantee of sales. The recordings must be promoted, marketed, and advertised on radio and television stations, in stores, and on tours; the videos must be shown on television. These endeavors are costly, and require sizable financial commitments from labels. (Social networking, described later in the book, is an inexpensive method to gain visibility.)

Charisma is one of the most essential attributes of an artist. Charisma cannot be learned and can mean the difference between success and failure. The Beatles had it; Mick Jagger and Lady Gaga have it; Marlon Brando and Cary Grant had it; Mozart and Beethoven had it. The genre is irrelevant—the gift is the same.

It has been my experience that the artists I have known who achieved success and fame had unique personas prior to achieving success.

Someone asked Louis Armstrong, "What is jazz?" and Louis replied, "Man, if you got to ask, you'll never find out!" Charisma is indefinable.

An artist's image is crucial to his or her success. The backgrounds of superstars in all artistic endeavors contribute to the artists' public images. The audience does not usually relate to a contrived image. The relationships artists build with their fans help them achieve artistic integrity. In hip-hop music an artist's image is referred to as his or her "street credibility"; audiences want to empathize with artists. Frank Sinatra had an image as a great entertainer who lived a lavish lifestyle. Many rock bands project an image of being unconventional and rebellious or political, such as Bono of the band U2.

The Grateful Dead is a band that has maintained longevity despite relatively minor record sales compared to their stature. The group has a loyal and truly fanatical audience. Some fans literally follow the band while they tour. Jerry Garcia, the deceased lead singer, became a rock icon. The audience identifies with the band's overall musical message, which depicts a life of freedom.

Note: Many of the most successful touring artists in the U.S. are established artists (e.g., Cher, Paul McCartney, Barry Manilow). The more mature audience's financial ability to purchase pricey tickets partially contributes to this unusual scenario—unusual because the touring artists may not achieve the same album sales figures as many younger popular artists who do not necessarily attract sizable concert audiences.

Artist-songwriters are more appealing to labels than artists who do not write. They do not rely on either producers or independent songwriters to supply songs. (The country-music market is an exception because most country artists do not generally write the songs they record.) Producing a hit is the goal of most pop-music producers. Therefore, the songs are the main ingredient for success.

The songs (instrumentals) should reflect the musical persona of an artist. Artists must remain true to their artistic sensibilities. It is inherent in the work of artist-songwriters, but artists who rely on outside sources for songs must assemble a repertoire that defines their musical personality—as in the case of Frank Sinatra, whose entire public persona emanated from his music.

Most artists perform new material prior to recording. The reaction of the audience can be helpful in determining if a composition is "commercial." This is not to imply that every song has to be a commercial success, but most artists want audiences to empathize with their music. A song may require a new arrangement, or the basic rhythmic feel might have to change. The producer should have the ability to step back and listen to the music not only as a creative artist but from the audience's perspective as well. If the song and the production are not well crafted, the attention span of the audience will wane, and the final production will not be successful.

Some artists are strictly entertainers and not necessarily trying to "preach" to the audience. Elvis Presley was an entertainer, while Bruce Springsteen makes a statement in most of his songs *and* he entertains.

Generally, artists who achieve career longevity record songs that have a lasting effect on the public. They are also charismatic and entertaining performers. Trendy artists might have a contemporary performance style and a modern image, but the songs are poorly constructed. They may be memorable, but they might also sound like the "flavor of the month."

♫ Producers must be concerned with the attributes of a solo artist or band member. There are usually two categories of popular-music artists: exceptional singer-performers, (e.g., Barbra Streisand, Celine Dion, Michael Bublé), or singers who are also exceptional writers, such as James Taylor, Elton John, and Billy Joel. Most band members write the band's songs. It is unusual for bands to record songs composed by other writers. (The Beatles, The Rolling Stones, and Aerosmith are examples of superstars who have recorded outside material.)

Exceptionally talented artists normally achieve longevity with the public. Artists such as James Taylor, Barry Manilow, Steely Dan, Aretha Franklin, The Eagles, Neil Diamond, and Willie Nelson will always attract an audience. It is not necessary for them to have a hit single in order to attract a concert audience. An artist's career is molded by careful image planning and intelligent management decisions, combined with a strategic-minded booking agent concerned with protecting the artist's image.

It is unusual for a new artist to receive an offer to sign with a label without a live showcase (audition). For example, labels are usually attracted to artists who sell out clubs in a regional market since that is often a forecast of the artist's national or global market potential. Most music executives are familiar with the nightclubs that showcase new talent, and they are constantly scouting them for new artists. It is analogous to scouting for athletes; in fact, bidding wars occur between labels as well as athletic teams. Some executives have strong relationships with nightclub owners who tout them when a "hot act" is booked to perform.

Pollstar Magazine, a trade publication, tracks most clubs and arenas throughout the United States. The magazine provides information on the seating capacity of a club or arena and the percentage of seats sold by the artists. A&R executives and producers use the information in the magazine to follow an artist's progress. If the artist has a personal manager and/or agent, a demo is requested; if not, the artist is contacted directly. This can initiate the process that leads to a recording contract.

Record labels reward artists who are cooperative and appreciative of the label's support. That is an important consideration for a producer because artists have a better opportunity of achieving success if they cooperate with the label.

When an artist generates income for a label, the company's personnel are obligated to support that artist. When an uncooperative artist's popularity diminishes, it is human nature to do the minimum. The label might appear to be assertive, but it is relatively easy for promotion and marketing executives to concentrate on artists who welcome and acknowledge the label's efforts.

Certain musical genres do not routinely generate sizable sales, such as jazz or classical music. The A&R executives of jazz and classical labels seek out artists who they feel will eventually develop a solid fan base and establish a career. That can evolve into almost guaranteed sales for each new project, consequently lowering the label's financial risk. Jazz and classical labels are primarily interested in the artistic attributes of artists, although some artists have unique personas, such as Louis Armstrong, Leonard Bernstein, and Wynton Marsalis, who have achieved great popularity. These artists have spawned substantial sales partially due to their engaging personalities and showmanship.

Career planning is fundamental to success. Managers guide clients' careers. A&R executives and producers are directly responsible for artists' recording careers.

Artists must maintain an image. Some artists might reason that since a current album is successful the subsequent project should be in the same musical direction. That is not necessarily accurate. The audience might become bored and think that the artist's creativity has declined. This is an inherent problem with popular music. If an artist's career is based on current musical trends, there is a great probability that they will not be able to sustain their popularity unless the artist remains musically current.

Staying current means that a producer must have the production skills to maintain the essence of the artist and produce music in a contemporary style. That is a difficult task. For instance, if an artist's primary audience is teens, it is difficult to appeal to that demographic as the artist matures. Young artists, such as Justin Bieber, must grow musically to sustain a career. Artists should continually evolve, as demonstrated by The Beatles and The Beach Boys.

Conclusion

The second album, referred to as the "sophomore jinx" in the record industry, is considered the most crucial album in an artist's career. One of the reasons that artists' second albums are often not as successful as their first album is because they are usually touring and promoting their first album, which limits the time they have to prepare for their follow-up effort. All of their time is devoted to rehearsing and recording their first album. Artists who achieve both critical and financial success with the second album have an improved chance of achieving career stability. The albums that follow are crucial and require strategic planning. The people who surround an artist's career are both artistic and business advisors; consequently, the choice of advisors is crucial to achieving continuing success. Many promising careers have been destroyed by poor planning and misguided advice.

The success of an artist depends on many factors: choice of record company, choice of producer, choice of songs/instrumentals, performance ability (charisma), personal management, booking agent, choice of musicians or band members, but most important is the artist's commitment to sustaining a career. A career is a potpourri of ideas and ideas emanate from people. If artists' advisors have a cordial and professional working relationship, the artists have an improved chance of achieving success. Artists should maintain a professional attitude and conduct their careers as a business. Partaking of irresponsible activities is certain to cause unwanted publicity.

Recording royalties and performance fees can be lucrative, and the business aspects of artists' careers must be scrutinized. *Guiding an artist's career is analogous to playing chess. One wrong move, and you lose!*

Assignment

Choose a popular solo artist (or band), and write an essay that analyzes the artist's career. Include discussions on the subjects covered in this chapter. Incorporate answers to the following questions:

- What is unique about the artist?
- What is the artist's image?
- If the artist is also a songwriter, what "message" is the artist trying to deliver to the audience? Cite examples.
- As a producer, why would you want to produce the artist?

4

Songwriting

> Too many pieces of music finish too long after the end.
>
> —Igor Stravinsky

Some composers consider songwriting the most difficult form of composition. Composing a simple, memorable, and seamless melody coupled with evocative lyrics is a difficult task. Some composers prefer to set melodies to lyrics, and some lyricists prefer to write lyrics to melodies. Songwriters who write melodies and lyrics generally write both simultaneously. A melodic line might trigger a lyric idea and vice versa. Many songwriting teams write together, feeding on each other's ideas. Rewriting almost always occurs after the basic song has been written. There is no answer to the colloquialism, "What comes first, the chicken or the egg?"

♫ The words *song* and *instrumental* are used interchangeably.

The foundations of recorded-music productions are the songs, and a considerable amount of time and consideration should be devoted to the process of writing and/or choosing songs. Some producers have an instinct for selecting commercial material, and others specialize in editing and shaping existing material. Producers are artists, and gifted producers are generally skilled song analysts and/or songwriters.

This chapter addresses the basics of songwriting. All producers, regardless of the their musical training, should study and analyze well-crafted songs as well as past and present hit songs. It is also advisable to study music theory and poetry. Answer the following questions while listening to a song:

- How is the lyric expressed? Are the lyrics poetic or conversational?
- What is the melodic contour of the melody?
- Does the melody complement the lyric? If so, why? If not, why not?

Producers should become familiar with harmonic, rhythmic, lyrical, and melodic structure. That will enable them to communicate to the songwriters in musical terms and make specific suggestions. The importance of this process cannot be overstated. *Songs are the foundation of most popular-music albums.*

Many record label A&R executives have musical backgrounds. Their job is to sign artists and creatively guide and oversee the artists' recordings. They are in constant contact with "song pluggers" who work for music publishing companies and are also in contact with successful songwriters who often control publishing rights. Songwriters want successful artists to record the songs they write and generally offer major labels or popular artists the A-list material before shopping the songs to less commercially successful artists.

Clive Davis, the legendary record executive, built the creative aspect of his career based upon his innate ability to pick hits. Whitney Houston, Aretha Franklin, Carlos Santana, and Alicia Keys are artists who have benefited from his inborn talent.

A socially conscious artist-songwriter must be contemporary. Bruce Springsteen exemplifies a socially conscious artist who has maintained both credibility and a faithful audience, while changing with the times. Many artists are not songwriters, but they select songs that are socially relevant.

Socially relevant does not necessarily mean writing about political issues. Country-music lyrics generally reflect everyday values and concerns of ordinary people. Many hip-hop lyrics are political in nature, while pop lyrics often deal with relationships that change with the evolving mores of society.

Do not disregard songs that are written merely as entertainment. Many novelty songs have sold millions of records and were worldwide hits. They are entertaining and should be considered a part of the popular-music lexicon.

The majority of popular-music producers vie to produce artistic records by choosing to work with artists who are serious about developing their craft and by using cutting-edge technology to achieve sonic proficiency. Producing sheer entertainment is also perfectly acceptable. Most youth-oriented records are designed to be entertaining and to achieve profitability. Producers and A&R executives want to capture a large segment of the youth market, and successful youth-oriented recordings are as skillfully produced as recordings that are intended to be artistic and reach an older demographic. The early recordings of Britney Spears and 'N Sync are fine examples of expertly produced records that achieved massive worldwide commercial success. (Britney Spears' latest album, *Femme Fatale,* is an example of how a young artist matures musically.)

If an artist writes songs, the producer's job is to shape the material. The audience must relate to the songs. The production may be immaculate, the engineering superb, the performance brilliant, but if the foundation—the composition—is weak, the "house will fall."

Below are some suggestions and guidelines for analyzing songs.

The Songwriting Process

The songs must fit an artist's musical persona. Obviously that is not a problem if the artist is the songwriter, but it becomes a major concern when choosing songs submitted by music publishers, songwriter/producers, or independent songwriters.

Most artist-writers demo a large selection of songs. The producer and A&R people are concerned not only that the material is well conceived and commercial but also that the songs suit the concept of the album. Most albums emanate a mood—a musical feeling—that offers an "experience" to the listener. Albums should be designed so the music flows in the same manner as words in a well-written book. Novelists hope that readers cannot put their book down; producers and recording artists hope the audience listens to their album in one sitting. Their goal is that the audience experiences a "musical novel."

The song sequence helps create the proper musical mood and maintain a listener's interest. Sequencing the song demos—before recording final versions—can be helpful in selecting the proper song order as well as determining if the song selection works as a unified entity.

Producers and artists must make difficult decisions. If an artist-songwriter writes a song that sounds like a hit but it is out of character with the other song selections, the choice should be to eliminate the song from the album. Remain true to the album concept. The other danger might be that the song is out of character with the artist's image and may damage the artist's credibility. When listeners become fans, they expect a consistency to the artist's musical output. A hit record that is out of character with an artist's persona can be more harmful than beneficial.

Song structure is important. Popular music normally emulates traditional musical formats. The study of music history teaches us the importance of musical form. Form means structure, and form exists in all styles of music as well as the other fine arts.

When listening to music of the classical era, we experience sonata, rondo, and scherzo forms; the symphony developed during the baroque period, expanded in the classical period, and took a major leap when Beethoven composed longer and more complex symphonies. During the Romantic period, new forms developed as well as new harmonic structures, which included lush melodies and inventive orchestrations. In much of the music of the twentieth century—in addition to the development of tonal music—we experience dissonance and atonality. What will be the main characteristics of the music of the twenty-first century? It is too early to determine. Music, in all forms, keeps evolving.

Since the beginning of the rock 'n' roll era, a variety of song forms have remained popular with the public.

In all forms of music, melodic lines, called *sentences,* are divided into smaller sections called *phrases.* The flow of a lyric must correspond to each *phrase.* If the accents or the word emphasis does not complement the melody, the song will sound awkward.

To analyze musical form, and specifically song form, an identification system was designed. (Song form is our focus, but the same principles apply to instrumental compositions.)

Most popular songs are written in a 32-measure format. Each section, on average, is eight measures. This basic format varies. The musical format is expressed in letter names. The following is the key to understanding the system:

♫ *The majority of hit songs follow a variation of the following formats:* In popular music, a chorus can be defined as a section that is usually memorable and easy to sing. A "hook" can be either a chorus or a catchy instrumental or vocal section used in an arrangement. This system does not indicate the introduction, prechoruses, or repeats. Sometimes small sections, referred to as interludes, separate various sections.

- A represents a verse.
- A1 represents an alternate version of the A verse. For example, if verse 1 is eight bars and verse 2 is four bars, verse 2 would correspond to A1. This lettering system would continue with A2, A3, and so on. The concept applies to all letters.
- B represents a new harmonic and melodic section; for example, a bridge or a chorus.
- C represents a new melodic section.

Format: ABABCB

- Introduction (four or eight bars)
- Verse 1 (A)
- Prechorus (leads into the chorus and is also called a *build*)
- Chorus (B)
- Verse 2 (A)
- Prechorus
- Either one or two choruses (B)
- Sometimes a new section referred to as a C section or a bridge (C)
- Chorus and fade-out or an ending (B)

Format: AABA

- Introduction
- Verse 1 (A)
- Verse 2 (A)
- Bridge (B)
- Verse 3 (A)

Format: ABABA

- Introduction
- Verse (A)
- Bridge (B)
- Verse (A)
- Bridge (B)
- Verse or variation (A)

Formats work in various combinations. Some additional popular formats are as follows:

- ABAB
- AAB
- ABCABCA
- ABAC
- B (chorus) A A B C A

Some songs end each section (stanza) with the same lyric, which is called a refrain. The refrain becomes a hook since the lyric is repeated in much the same manner as the hook of a chorus.

Songwriters often have a kernel of an idea that could develop into a viable song. Artists often play a "work in progress" for the producer. Producers make suggestions and guide songwriters until the song is complete. If the artist and the producer have a congenial artistic and personal relationship, the process can be fruitful.

Instinct plays an important role in the song-editing process. It is commonplace for inexperienced songwriters to compose songs that are not in the proper musical form. If the audience loses concentration when listening to a song, the problem generally lies within the form of the song or its basic structure.

The following are suggestions for solving some common formatting problems:

In popular music, the chorus or hook is often the section of the song that attracts the audience. Some songwriters do not reach the chorus quickly enough, presenting a lackluster experience to the listener. (Thus the popular music publisher's phrase, "*Don't bore us, get to the chorus!*")

The following are some suggestions:

- *Experiment by rearranging sections of a song.* A bridge or C-section, rather than the traditional second chorus, could follow the second verse or the second chorus. The second chorus could be followed by a repeat of the chorus, but with the addition of some alternate lyrics.
- *A section might sound too long.* If the second verse sounds too long, one solution is to use half of the verse—four measures rather than the traditional eight measures—followed by the prechorus. The lyric might have to be rewritten or condensed so that it flows into the next section. The same solution may apply to a bridge or a repeat of a bridge.
- *If the introduction sounds too long, try cutting it in half or possibly eliminating it.*

Introductions can serve a practical purpose. Radio disc jockeys talk while the introduction is playing. On some stations they announce the artist and song title. A number of station managers do not want the audience to know the song title or artist; they want the listener to call the station and inquire. That gives the station manager a barometer for judging the popularity of a song. When "going on" a new song and the phones do not ring, stations consider not playing it as often or deleting it from the station's playlist. Research is often used to select the records played on a station.

The Web has greatly increased the potential to get exposure. YouTube has become the most popular site where listeners discover new music and listen to established artists. (There are many other websites devoted to exposing new artists.) The videos have become a crucial component of achieving success, especially for new artists.

If the ending feels awkward, there are several solutions:

- *Write a definite ending to the song.*
- *Write a definite ending, but decrease the tempo near the very end.*
- *Try a fade-out ending* (the engineer gradually decreases the volume level while the music continues to play).

Some songwriters take offense when a producer suggests that some of the songs need rewriting or editing. The artist's usual counterargument: "When the song is arranged, the perceived problems will be solved." The we'll-fix-it-in-the-mix theory should not be the proposed cure for inherent compositional and lyric problems. Once trust has been established between the songwriter and the producer, the songwriter will—at the least—listen to the producer's suggestions.

The following are examples of possible changes that a producer might suggest for improving a song:

- *Lyric changes:* The tenses should match, and the manner in which a thought is stated should be clear. In most popular music, the audience's first reaction is the lasting one. If the lyrical message is not clearly stated, the listener will lose interest.
- *Melody changes:* If the melody does not blend with the lyric, the emotional intent of the song may be compromised. The melody might ascend rather than descend, the durations of the notes in melodic phrases could vary, or the notes' sequential melodic lines could vary. A seamless blend of lyric and melody creates well-crafted songs.
- *A section could be repeated or deleted:* For example, when the second chorus enters, repeating the chorus might help solidify the hook's appeal to the listener. The more often something is repeated, the easier it is for the listener to remember the phrase. Too much repetition can also cause boredom. These are both common problems with simple answers. Deleting or adding a section might improve a song's format.
- *A higher or lower key might better suit the lyric and/or the singer.* Many inexperienced songwriters, producers, and artists do not select the proper key. A half step, in either direction, can make the difference between a good performance and an excellent one. Ask the singer if the key is appropriate. If the singer says that the key is fine or he or she can sing the song in various keys, experiment and choose the key that not only sounds best from a musical perspective but also enables the singer to give a better interpretation of the lyric. The key helps the artist "sell the song."

- There is an additional consideration when choosing a key. If the artist is planning to ad-lib above or below the melody, there must be enough musical space to do so. In R&B music and pop music, ad-libbing is a common technique and should be considered before the rhythm tracks are recorded. The best test is through experimentation. It is a simple problem to solve, but if the issue is not addressed it can be both costly and time consuming.

The best solution to compositional problems is rewriting or reformatting. If the artist is recording "songs" as opposed to creating a "record" (technical tricks and a focus on rhythm are more important than the song), the song should sound complete when accompanied with only a piano or guitar. That is the concept of the television program *MTV UNPLUGGED.* The artists use no electric instruments or mixing technology other than reverb: "The song stands on its own."

The proposed solutions to common formatting problems are merely suggestions. There are no definite rules when dealing with the craft of songwriting. The songwriter's instinct is usually correct. *Without structure there is musical chaos.*

If a melody is problematic, the following suggestions offer possible solutions:

- *Experiment with the rhythmic values of the melody.* Some examples: Two eighth notes might sound better notated as a dotted eighth note followed by a sixteenth note. Adding a rest or deleting a rest creates variation. Syncopation generates movement especially in up-tempo songs. Anticipating a note creates rhythmic variation.
- *Experiment with the tempo.* If the tempo is 120 bpm and a song is played at 115 bpm or 125 bpm, the feel of the song will change. Tempo affects melodic flow. If the tempo is too fast, the song will sound rushed; if the tempo is too slow, the song will drag. On certain songs the tempo is crucial to the overall feeling. Some songs will work played in various tempos. If there is a problem with tempo, it is best to demo a small section of the song in several tempos and listen repeatedly. Generally, one tempo will feel better than the others.

Repeatedly listening to a song demo helps to determine if the song will have a lasting impression. The goal of songwriters is to keep the listener's interest in a song after repeated listening. The songs will be greatly enhanced by the final arrangement and production values, but the best test of a song is to hear it in its simplest form.

- *Experiment with alternate chords.* Chords known as substitutions (alternative chords) offer the composer an opportunity to make a melody more interesting. The first verse might have the original chord structure, and the second verse could contain some substitutions. If the harmonic structure remains stagnant, experiment with new chords throughout the song but keep the essence of the original song.
- *Experiment with inverting melodic phrases.* Inverting a phrase, but keeping the same note values, creates variety and rhythmic continuity. For instance, the eighth notes *CBA* would follow eighth notes *ABC* and so forth.
- *Experiment with sequential melodic phrases.* If the melody seems to ramble, try a series of phrases that modulate but keep the same relative interval structure. If the notes of the first phrase are *GAB*, the second phrase might be *ABC* and so forth. Sequential phrases are a standard compositional technique.
- *Experiment with changing the duration of notes.* Some examples: A whole note might be changed to a half note, a quarter note changed to an eighth note. The diminution or expansion of phrases greatly affects the melodic contour. Varying durations creates variety.
- *Experiment with various forms of modulation.* An effective technique that has been used in popular music for many years is modulating the chorus at the end of a song. Raising the key by either a half or a full step is standard. Modulating in the middle of the song or modulating sequential phrases is also a useful technique. Modulation creates musical excitement and reinvigorates the listening experience.
- *Experiment with conjunct melodic motion.* Conjunct melodic motion is more conducive to popular melodies than disjunct motion. It is easier for the average listener to remember melodies constructed with close intervals while remaining within the space of an octave.

The structure and form of the lyrics are as important as the musical form. Well-conceived lyrics are always clear and keep the audience interested in the message throughout the song. (The use of the word *clear* in this context does not necessarily mean that each thought has an obvious meaning but rather that the lyric has a defined direction.) Some songwriter-poets, such as Bob Dylan or Jim Morrison, expect the audience to think about the meaning of their songs. Certain lyrics are meant to trigger a subjective interpretation, and others are meant to be conversational. The principles of lyric writing apply to all styles.

Conversational lyrics are often the most effective. The test of a skillful conversational lyric is to read it and feel as though the author is speaking to the reader. Having a vocalist recite the lyric before singing it has proven

♫ Singers are actors; singers interpret lyrics, and actors interpret words. Great singers and actors generally choose well-crafted material, and part of singers' or actors' success is due to the artistic choices they make. Most singers are concerned with the message contained in the lyrics. It is difficult for a singer to deliver a great performance of a lyric when he or she does not empathize with the meaning.

to be an effective technique. The lyric should sound as natural as a conversation.

The audience must relate to the lyric of a song. If listeners do not find the subject matter of a song interesting, they will not want to listen to it repeatedly. Songs that become standards have artistic merit, and artists in different musical genres usually record the song in a variety of arrangements.

Enticing the listener can be accomplished in several ways:

- *The song title must catch the attention of the listener.* Most thoughtful titles either explicitly tell the audience what the song is about, such as the Lennon/McCartney song "Eleanor Rigby" (obviously about the woman) or conjure up an image, like Bob Dylan's "Like a Rolling Stone," which speaks of how fragile life is. Hit songs with clever and/or meaningful titles have a chance to become standards. They are licensed for use in films, commercials, and television programs, and numerous artists record the songs (called *covers*). Songs can also become *evergreens*, which is the goal of songwriters. Countless song titles are taken from either slogans or well-known phrases, such as James Taylor's "Fire and Rain" (written about the death of a loved one). Not only are the best titles easy to remember, but the titles also project various images. A title can conjure up an array of lyric ideas. Many lyricists arrive at a title and then write the lyric. Movie storylines have been inspired by song lyrics. The film "Sweet Home Alabama" was inspired by the classic Lynyrd Skynyrd song. "Sweet Home Alabama" is an example of how a lyric—a mini story—can be expanded into a full plot.
- *A lyric must have a central idea that continues to develop without repeating the same concept.* The exception is songs that have choruses. Although a hook line repeats, the answer lines can change. A chorus in an average pop song repeats at least four times. The hook line within the chorus becomes embedded in the listener's mind.
- *The hook often contains the title of the song.* After hearing a song several times, the audiences will (songwriters hope) sing along. The lyric and melody of the repeated line have to catch the listener's attention immediately.
- During the chorus of The Rolling Stones' "You Can't Always Get What You Want," the title line repeats three times ending with a

different lyric. The repetition drills the hook into the listener's mind and—due to ad-libs by Mick Jagger—does not become boring.
- Lyric writing requires great thought; without a significant idea the audience will lose interest.

Writing lyrics can be taught; "how to say something" cannot be taught. This is the "talent factor" and is analogous to the talent needed to compose music. Students can learn music theory, but they must apply their creative juices to composing music that will have originality. The same concept applies to writing lyrics. A skilled lyricist writes about subjects that people can relate to and does so in either a poetic or a conversational manner.

A variety of styles are used in lyric writing:

- Storyline songs
- Chorus or hook songs
- Verse-only songs with a refrain
- Message songs
- Novelty songs

♫ The implication is not that a songwriter "sit down and write a standard." That, of course, is absurd. Standards are rare and happen as a result of a hit song that is recorded by numerous artists. Quality songs have a chance to become standards. The goal of any artistic endeavor is to create something that will last. The rewards emanate from quality work.

All lyric forms work if the lyricist has a point of view and a well-developed craft. It can be accomplished by getting to the point without using too many extraneous words. Compress the lyric as much as possible.

Storyline Songs

Many country songs have *storylines*. A story lyric is analogous to a condensed short story. The lyric must have a beginning, middle, and end, and a subject that appeals to a target demographic. A musical and lyrical hook reels in the listener. The hook could be a chorus, an instrumental phrase, or riff, a refrain, or even an unusual technical effect, such as the long delay used on John Lennon's voice in "Imagine."

Story lyrics work in a variety of musical forms:

♫ If a writer has an idea for a lyric but cannot express it artistically, the lyric is not necessarily a *lyric*. That problem is widespread in the advertising industry. Copywriters, who are not traditionally lyricists, write lyrics for jingles, but most of what they write is not constructed in the same manner as a song lyric. The composers generally rework the lyrics so the words scan musically.

Chorus or Hook Songs

The chorus or hook of a song is what catches the audience's attention. Repetition with variation is one of the foremost lyric and musical techniques.

The *entire* chorus should catch the listener's ear. If the repeating hook lyric is "Can you feel the street?" followed by the answer line, "feel that body heat," followed again by, "Can you feel the street beat?" and a new answer, "comin' from the street," the audience will remember the words and melody to "Can you feel the street beat?" Since a chorus repeats three or four times in most popular songs, change the answer lines to avoid boredom. The lead singer's interpretation of the lyric, with the inclusion of tasteful melismas, plus variations in the instrumental and vocal arrangement, adds interest and variety to a song.

Verse-Only Songs

Songs written in verse-only form are also referred to as AAA form (each A represents a verse). Popular songs written in this style usually include a *refrain*, which is a catchy phrase at the end of each verse. The *refrain* is analogous to the hook line of a chorus. The writer hopes the audience remembers it and is able to sing along.

The Beatles classic "Eleanor Rigby" is written in verse-only form. Some AAA songs have more than three verses. The melody and the lyric must keep the audience's attention, or the song becomes cumbersome after repeated listening. If a verse has four lines, the last line or the refrain might be, *"If we knew then what we know now, we would still be together."* With a catchy melody, the refrain would become the hook of the song.

Message Songs

The problem with *message songs* (having an obvious or hidden message) is that they can become too preachy. Message songs that are written with care can be effective with the audience. The song "War"—about the horrors of war—although somewhat preachy, is a message song that became a hit. "Abraham, Martin, and John"—about assassination—is also a hit message song but is less preachy. Most lyricists who are trying to say something want to deliver a valid message. Skilled lyricists do that without alienating the audience.

Novelty Songs

Some of the most commercially successful singles are novelty songs. Most novelty songs are all hook, and many become worldwide hits. The audience is usually capable of singing back the *entire* song after listening several times. Writing and recording novelty songs are sheer entertainment and from a production standpoint should be approached as a track that will be fun and catchy. Some classic novelty songs are "The Chipmunk Song," by the Chipmunks, "Disco Duck," by radio host Rick Dees, and "Barbie Girl," by Aqua.

Novelty songs can be lucrative but are rarely followed by another hit in the same genre.

> ♫ The success of "The Chipmunk Song" is based not only on the song but also the use of recording technology. The voices were manipulated to sound like chipmunks.

The main objective of a songwriter is to keep the listener's interest throughout a song. Some of the basic problems that all songwriters and producers encounter have already been mentioned. If a song is basically well constructed, there are solutions to most problems.

A producer should provide concrete suggestions to songwriters so they can rewrite or reformat the sections of a song that are problematic. When the song form and the production are complete, envision listening to the final mix on the radio. The producer, the engineer, and the artist experience a feeling of satisfaction when the mix sounds final. Unfortunately, the feeling occurs only after an unearthly amount of frustration and hard work, but the results are worth the effort.

Familiarity with the songs of the past and the songs of the present aids producers in their role as critics. Choosing or recognizing hit songs or hit recordings is not teachable. Most producers who successfully choose hit songs to record have an innate talent or instinct. In the music business, this talent is referred to as "having good ears." Trends can be analyzed, and although it is not wise to imitate the current market, the overall feel of current music gives producers a general idea of the music listeners are reacting to.

Generally, it is best to choose songs with an interesting message and a catchy melody. That is not to insinuate that each song on an album has to sound like a commercial hit; quite the contrary. Producers should be concerned with the quality of the songs and remaining true to an artist's image. Artists who establish a musical persona automatically project an image. The audience expects high-quality productions and entertaining performances. When James Taylor or Elton John releases an album, the audience anticipates a certain sound. The audience may hope for musical surprises and innovative production values, but the overall quality of the production and the songs will remain at a very high creative level. It is important for producers and artists to grow so that their music and productions do not become stale and boring. The public can easily lose interest in artists who do not take creative risks.

Criteria for commercial success differ with musical genres. In country music, the songs are paramount. In R&B and hip-hop music, the feel of the rhythm tracks, the production values, and the songs are equally important to the success of a production. In rock 'n' roll music, the production values and songs are equal. When listening to heavy metal music, the listener has to feel the power of the rhythm track and the excitement of the lead vocal. In some instances, the song becomes secondary. The repertoire and the artists sell classical music. The success of popular-music recordings generally depends on a combination of all of these factors.

The same basic rules that apply to song structure apply to most instrumentals in the popular-music style. The composition must flow and keep the audience's attention.

Instrumental compositions are popular in the smooth-jazz genre. If lyrics were added to most of the compositions, the arrangement would basically need very little adjustment.

Many smooth-jazz hits are instrumental arrangements of popular songs. Within the format, using bits of the lyric is a common device; not only does it add variety to the arrangement, but it also reminds the audience of the original song. Many instrumentals contain the chorus of the original song, usually sung by background singers.

"The Lonely Bull" and "Taste of Honey," by Herb Alpert & The Tijuana Brass, and "Songbird," by Kenny G, were instrumental hits that produced sales equivalent to song hits. Both of these instrumentalists have sold many millions of albums.

Videos play an important role in song promotion; consequently, some lyricists are concerned that the lyrics lend themselves to visual images. Most songs can easily be transformed into videos. A lyric that does not have an obvious meaning can still conjure up some abstract and interesting visual images.

Author's Opinion: A lyricist should be concerned only with writing a lyric that works best as a song. Lyrics are supposed to trigger the listener's imagination. If a lyricist is concerned about creating a visual image, the lyric could become too literal, and some of the poetic content might be diluted. A lyric can succeed in both a song form *and* visually.

Conclusion

Producers and artists discover songs from numerous sources. Publishing companies are in the business of placing songs with artists. When an artist is planning to record his or her first album, major publishers might not want to submit A-list material. Publishers are interested in sales and have a better chance of selling large numbers of albums with artists who have had past successes.

Publishers and writers will agree to license "A" material to unknown artists for several reasons:

- A major label is committed to promoting the artist and assures the publisher that the song will receive attention.
- The artist or producer might have a personal relationship with the songwriter.
- Producers who are "hot" (producing hits) can usually acquire the best songs.

It is wise for a professional lyric writer to study grammar. This is not to imply that all lyrics have to be grammatically correct. The majority of popular songs are written in the vernacular of the target audience (e.g., hip-hop). The expressions used in lyrics of most songs are effective because the lyricist is talking directly to the target demographic; conversational lyrics are generally the best means of communicating with audiences.

Other styles of music require lyrics that appeal to a general audience, and proper grammar crafts a more literate and successful lyric. Regardless of the format, a lyric that is confusing or that rambles is not acceptable.

Most successful producers do not necessarily go into the studio to "record a hit." Their goal is to produce artistic recordings; the hits will follow. That means proper song selection.

Author's Note: I know successful artistic people working in various fields, and they all share the same goal—to produce creative work.

Artists in various genres climb into the top of the *Billboard* charts. Among them are some highly unusual artists whose music does not fit the mold of the general marketplace. Singers such as Michael Bublé, Josh Groban, and Andrea Bocelli appeal to a mature demographic and do not receive the same amount of airplay as artists who cater to a younger demographic. That suggests two scenarios: (1) The older demographic is buying adult music, and (2) The albums are not driven by a hit single. The albums are selling in the millions and are a testament to the importance of song selection. (Michael Bublé has been including at least one pop song on his latest releases and has had pop hits as a result. This has increased his demographic as well as increased the sales of his albums.)

Many songwriters are also producers. They have a musical vision and consequently want to produce the first recorded versions of the songs they wrote. The copyright laws provide the songwriter(s) with the right to assign the first recording of a song to an artist of their choice. After the first recording has been released, any artist can record the song as long as he or she applies for a compulsory license. (This subject will be covered in the chapter dealing with music publishing.)

Songwriters are not necessarily good producers. Songwriting is certainly a good training ground for production because of the detail and thought that must be applied to writing songs. Songwriters understand musical structure, but many are not necessarily skilled arrangers; they find it difficult to guide or write arrangements of the songs. It is wise for songwriters to study orchestration, arranging, and recording technology if they want to become artful producers. Songs are the backbone of any production.

Assignment

Choose 3 popular songs (in the styles listed below), and analyze the lyric and the musical form. Include in your answer the following:

- The musical form (example, AABA): Why is the melody holding the audience's interest?
- The lyric format (example, Verse A, Chorus 1 or A, etc.)
- The style of lyric (example, message song)

If you choose the third option, explain the content of the lyric and why you feel the audience will remain interested in the lyric, then choose songs in three of the following styles to analyze:

- Storyline song
- Chorus or hook song
- Verse-only song with a refrain
- Message song
- Novelty song

5

Arranging and Orchestration

It's easy to play any musical instrument: all you have to do is touch the right key at the right time and the instrument will play itself.

—J. S. Bach

This chapter is not intended to teach arranging but rather to discuss arranging concepts that will aid producers.

To gather an understanding of arranging and orchestration, listen to all genres of music and study scores. Reviewing the classics as well as the best of commercial-music scoring (recordings, film scores, commercials, etc.) provides the groundwork that leads to learning how to arrange and orchestrate. It also provides a foundation that will help producers guide arrangers and orchestrators. Knowledge of arranging and orchestration is essential to producing music.

Compositions are the foundation of music productions, and the arrangements and orchestrations are the interior walls. If the foundation (songs/instrumentals) is weak, the house falls—if the compositions are "strong" and the interior walls are weak (arrangements), the house stands, but it is dangerous!

Arranging is the process of choosing a musical environment for a song or instrumental. One song can be arranged in many styles (e.g., R&B, pop, and rock 'n' roll). The arranger sets the tempo, the chord structure, and the feel (mood), usually in conjunction with the producer and the artist. *An arrangement is a detailed piece of music often first written as a condensed score, such as a piano part. Orchestration is the process of choosing the instruments to play the notes within the arrangement. Painters choose colors and orchestrators choose instruments.*

Following the selection of songs (instrumentals), conceptualizing the arrangements and the orchestrations is—arguably—the most important function of music producers. Producers must communicate their creative visions to artists and arrangers. A thorough understanding of the musical personality of an artist is essential to accomplishing this goal. An arrangement sets the mood of a composition, and an inappropriate arrangement and/ or orchestration will project the wrong emotion. Arrangements and orchestrations make significant contributions to the creative concepts of overall projects.

Most band members arrange the band's music and the producer helps to *rearrange* the music for the studio recording. The main difference between arranging for the recording studio and arranging for a live performance is the length of the arrangement. Artists usually expand the compositions when performing. There is more room for improvisation and spontaneity during a live performance. The audience's reaction usually dictates the length of the arrangement. Extended arrangements heard on a recording can sometimes become tedious due to the lack of visual excitement; listeners can easily become bored. Also, for practical purposes, most radio stations playing popular music will not play tracks longer than 3 1/2 minutes in length, which is the average time of a radio single. (If the original recording is over 3:30, record labels usually offer radio stations one or two shorter radio edits, which are assembled to accommodate the needs of radio stations.)

In addition, it is easier to feature certain instruments in a studio recording. For example, a harmonica can be recorded on a separate track and the sound can sail above an orchestra. To replicate that during a live performance, the sound engineer has to be familiar with the arrangement and raise the level of the harmonica at the proper time. Also, effects processing is easier to apply in a recording studio. Both of these examples can be reproduced during a live performance, but it is more difficult.

It is generally easier for an arranger to use studio technology as an intrinsic part of the arrangement when specifically arranging for a studio session. For instance, repeated eighth notes generated by a synthesizer can be created through the use of a digital signal processor (DSP), such as a *tap echo*, rather than writing out the notes. The DSP gives the pattern a better groove. This effect is heard in techno music. The creative use of reverberation creates an ambience, which directly affects the manner in which the arrangement is written. Studio arrangers (of popular music) think of technology as a part of the arrangement. Technology is easier to apply in a studio than during a live performance, although modern technology has made it simpler to re-create the effects while performing.

The primary objective of an arranger (and producer) is to craft innovative arrangements that capture the musical persona of an artist. Producing music is making choices. Musically trained producers can communicate in musical terms, which is valuable when steering an arranger in a specific artistic direction.

Producers must understand the concept and flow of an arrangement in order to guide or "produce" the arrangement. They should have the ability to choose the most appropriate instrumentation, which is the basis for the final orchestration. The instrumentation, or synthesized sounds, creates a musical soundscape for an artist. Producers must also be certain that the format of the arrangement is appropriate. For instance, producers might suggest a musical interlude after the first chorus and prior to the second verse; they may also suggest that the second chorus repeat before the next section begins. These suggestions are also usually discussed with the artist.

Consider these ideas, which build on concepts presented earlier, when addressing the arranging process:

- When a band records, the arrangements will be consistent because they are the "sound" of the band. If a solo artist hires an arranger(s), the producer has to be concerned that a coherent sound is present throughout the album. The artist and the producer must agree on the style of the arrangements as well as the instrumentation.
- *Using the same instrumentation, musicians, engineer, and studio throughout an album helps achieve a coherent sonic image.* That is not always possible and most likely not probable. To achieve sonic unity, at the least, it is best to hire one engineer to mix the album. An engineer can create a consistent sound through the use of a particular recording console (e.g., SSL or Neve), equalization, reverberation, compression, and additional signal processing. If this is not feasible, the executive producer's job is to guide the various producers and engineers so that the album has sonic unity throughout.
- *The arrangement should complement the lyric.* A skilled arranger captures the emotion of a lyric. That is accomplished in both the arrangement and the orchestration. A producer should guide an arranger before the arranger begins work. Certain sections of a lyric might suggest interesting harmonic variations or obvious accents that will make the arrangement and orchestration more interesting. Competent producers have definite arranging ideas, which can be crucial to achieving the album's overall sound.
- The arrangement should complement the lead vocal. If a lead singer does not have a powerful voice, the arrangement and orchestration should not overpower the vocal. If the vocals are strong and rhythmic, the arrangement and orchestration can be more flexible. The choice of instruments must be based on the quality of the vocals or lead instruments (and also the budget).

The Instruments

The understanding of the range and tessitura (the most effective range of an instrument or voice) of musical instruments is essential to the study of arranging. It is necessary to think in terms of the generic sound of each instrument and write the parts accordingly. Without understanding the fundamental problems and restrictions of each instrument, an arranger cannot create a well-defined arrangement. One of the foremost problems with novice arrangers is that they do not understand the breathing problems and additional physical concerns inherent in the playing of wind and brass instruments. For example, brass players cannot continuously play high notes. Their lips cannot sustain that kind of abuse. It might sound acceptable played on a synthesizer or sampler but will certainly not be playable by a musician. Understanding the physical limitations of all instruments provides a composer with the necessary knowledge to write parts that will sound generic to the instruments.

It is necessary to understand music theory and harmony before studying arranging. In addition to traditional training, it is advisable to also study jazz theory and harmony. That provides a solid background, which enables a student to tackle almost any arranging style. Without a foundation in the essentials of music, it is difficult to become an accomplished arranger.

The following are condensed descriptions of the various sections and instruments of the orchestra and studio bands. The study of arranging and orchestration is a lifetime of work. At minimum, producers should have the ability to intelligently guide arrangers and orchestrators.

Orchestrators are used extensively in film scoring and for Broadway shows. In most instances, time does not permit the composers to also orchestrate. (Low budget film scoring requires the composer to also orchestrate.)

Strings

The string section is the foundation of the orchestra. It comprises violins, violas, cellos, and double basses. The string section is designed to emulate the traditional range of human voices: sopranos are the first violins, altos are the second violins, the tenors are violas, the bass/baritones are the cellos, and the basses are the double basses. (The double basses usually double the cellos an octave lower in traditional orchestral orchestration.) The string section provides the bed for the orchestration. The strings also blend well with the other sections of the orchestra.

Professional string players have remarkable technical dexterity and can perform virtually anything that is written by a schooled orchestrator. If an arranger feels a passage might not be playable, he or she is well advised to consult with a string player who plays the instrument in question.

The string section is the most flexible section of the orchestra. Strings can sound warm as well as strident and raucous. A large variety of effects can be achieved through the use of various bowing and fingering techniques. The following is a list of some techniques; consult an orchestration book to study the symbols used to indicate the effects.

- **Arco:** Playing with a bow.
- **Pizzicato:** Plucking the strings with the player's fingers rather than using a bow.
- **Up-bow:** Moving the bow in an upward position.
- **Down-bow:** Moving the bow in a downward position.
- **Slur:** A bow marking that connects a series of notes while the bow moves in one continuous direction.
- **Staccato:** The bow moves in very short strokes, creating a jagged effect.
- **Spiccato:** The bow bounces off the strings.
- **Jeté:** The bow bounces off the strings with the addition of bow markings, which indicates the direction of the bow.
- **Detaché:** Detaché means detached. Each note that is underlined indicates that the note must be held for its full value. The bow alternates between up-bow and down-bow.
- **Louré:** Each note is underlined with the same marking used in detaché. The difference is that there are slur markings over the desired notes. The player must briefly pause between notes while keeping the bow in one direction.
- **Tremolo:** The bow moves up and back in rapid succession creating a shimmering effect. Tremolo is indicated by putting a series of lines through the stem of a note.
- **Sul Ponticello:** The bow is placed in close proximity to the bridge of the instrument. The technique produces a thin, shimmering sound.
- **Sul Tasto:** The bow strikes the string near or over the fingerboard. A very thin tone is produced. *Sur la touché* is the French phrase used for the same bowing.
- **Col Legno:** The player strikes the strings with the wooden part of the bow rather than traditional bow hairs. The effect is similar to the sound of staccato bowing.
- **Portamento:** The fingers smoothly slide from one note to another.

The following are descriptions of string effects:

- **Mute:** A small piece of wood that is placed on the bridge of the instrument. Mutes produce an almost muffled effect. The orchestrator marks *sordino* to indicate the insertion of the mute; *senza sordino* means to remove the mute.
- **Vibrato:** The finger vibrating quickly, slightly below a note and quickly returning to the note produces the most frequently used sound on a stringed instrument. Vibratos vary between players, and the actual sound can sometimes help the listener identify the performer. Sometimes a composer does not want to hear vibrato. That is indicated by *N.V.* or the words *no vibrato* on the score.
- **Trill:** A quick movement of the fingers between two notes achieves a trill. The trilled notes are usually indicated above the note with the symbol *tr.*
- **Harmonics:** Harmonics produce a very thin and sparkly effect. There are two kinds of harmonics: (1) *Natural harmonics* are played on the open strings by barely touching the string a fourth above the open string. That produces a sound two octaves above the note. (2) *Artificial harmonics* are created by placing a finger a fourth above the desired note, which already has been chosen or stopped by another finger. The resulting note sounds two octaves above the stopped note. To indicate an artificial harmonic, the orchestrator/composer places a diamond-shaped note a fourth above the chosen note. Placing a small circle above a note indicates a natural harmonic.

It is necessary for producers to understand the number of string players needed (in a studio session) to achieve the rich and lush sound expected of a string section. Budget restrictions mostly dictate the number of players. This must be established before arranging a song (instrumental) because the number of musicians dictates the manner in which the parts should be orchestrated. For example, if there are only six violins playing high divisi (divided) parts the section will sound very thin. If the parts are played in the midrange with close harmony, the section will sound full. It is best for a producer to consult with the orchestrator/arranger before contracting a string section.

String players have the ability to play chords. Since navigating through each stringed instrument is different, the orchestrator must study each instrument and learn which chords can be played and how long it takes to change from one chord to another. Chords are mostly used as an effect rather than as a common compositional tool. Orchestration books cover this subject in detail.

♫ String samples are available for both synthesizers and samplers. Because of budget restrictions, string parts are played on synthesizers or with string samplers. The programmer must be aware of certain restrictions. For example, some of the bowings are difficult to achieve with samples. If the arranger is not familiar with scoring for real strings, the parts might not sound generic. The string writing will sound like the work of a keyboard player trying to emulate a live section without understanding the limitations and/or technical dexterity available with live string players. Arrangers also combine live strings with synthesized or sampled strings to enrich the overall sound.

Violin

Violins are divided into two sections: first violins and second violins. The remarkable technical ability of the players enables a composer to write almost anything that comes to his or her imagination. Evocative string writing can project virtually any human emotion. The violin is one of the most popular solo instruments.

Range: The violin is a nontransposing instrument. Notes are written in the treble clef and sound where written. The highest note is E two octaves above the treble clef. The lowest note is G below middle C.

Open strings for violin

Figure 5.1. Violin Open Strings

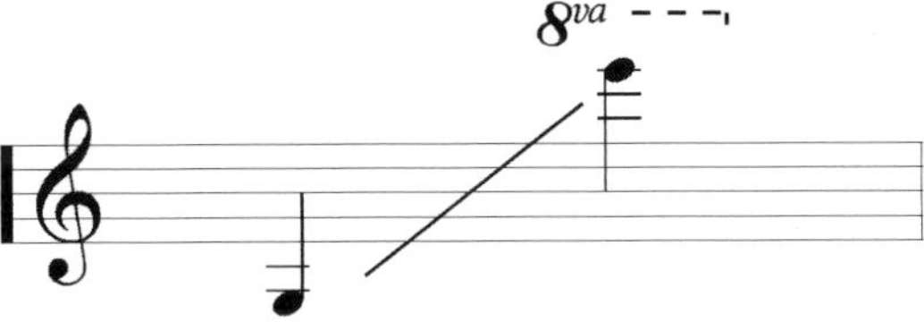

Figure 5.2. Violin Range

Viola

The viola is a little larger than a violin, and parts are generally written below the violin parts. Some orchestrators occasionally write viola parts in the middle of the violin parts. The viola has never achieved the same popularity as the violin because the sound is not as rich, and the instrument is not as versatile. The sound of the violas blend well with the cellos. Moving counter lines, sometimes written in unison with the cellos, is a signature sound of the violas.

Range: The viola is a nontransposing instrument. Notes are written in the alto clef and sound where written. The highest note is E one octave above the treble clef. The lowest note is C one octave below middle C. When the notes are high, the treble clef can be used.

Open strings for viola

Figure 5.3. Viola Open Strings

Figure 5.4. Viola Range

Cello (Violincello)

Cellos are the basses of the string section while the double basses are the sub-basses. Cellos have a rich and beautiful sound and can provide both sweet-sounding passages and deep and dark passages. The instrument is large, but the players have remarkable technical agility on the instrument. Cellos blend well with the violas and are capable of playing beautiful solo passages.

Range: The cello is a nontransposing instrument. The notes are written mostly in the bass clef and sound where written. The highest note is A above the treble clef. The lowest note is C two octaves below middle C. When notes are played on the D or A string, parts can be written in the tenor clef; higher parts can be written in the treble clef.

Open strings for cello

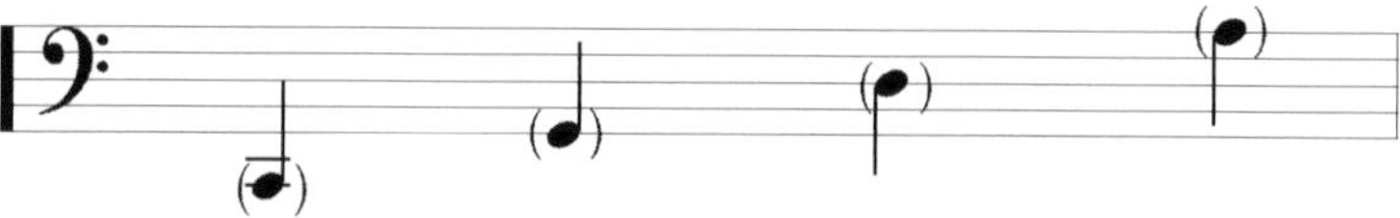

Figure 5.5. Cello Open Strings

Figure 5.6. Cello Range

Double Bass

The double basses play the lowest notes in the string section. In certain musical styles (e.g., baroque) the basses play in octaves with the cellos. Although the parts are notated the same as the cellos, the double basses sound one octave lower, creating a deep bass, while the cellos provide the clarity to the sound. Since double basses are larger than other string instruments, additional strokes are required when bowing.

In traditional jazz performance, pizzicato (finger-plucking) is the most common method of playing. Rock bass players play electric basses, which look like guitars but are tuned the same as a four-string double bass. (Some electric basses have more than four strings.)

Range: The double bass is written in the bass clef, tenor clef, and treble clef, and sounds one octave below the written pitch. The highest *sounding* note is B♭ above middle C. The lowest *sounding* note is E, four ledger lines below the bass clef; some basses have a low C.

Open strings for 4-string bass

Figure 5.7. Double Bass Open Strings

Figure 5.8. Double Bass Range: This Staff Indicates Where the Parts Are Written

Harp

The harp is a unique and complex instrument. It is tuned in the key of C♭ and is played by plucking the strings. Maneuvering seven pedals, one for each scale note, can change the open notes upward by two semitones; all octaves of the same note change when a pedal is depressed. The harp has a

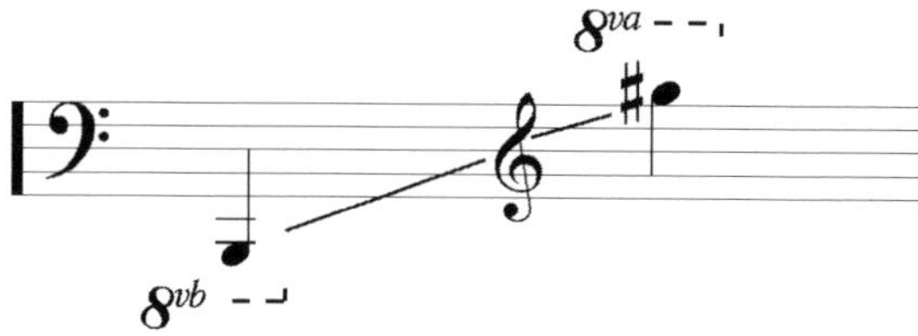

Figure 5.9. Harp

range of six octaves (forty-seven strings) and blends especially well with the strings and woodwinds. The signature sound of the harp is a *glissando* or *gliss*. The orchestrator indicates the beginning note and ending note of a *gliss* (and the notes in between or a chord symbol is indicated in place of the interior notes), which the harpist plays by moving his or her fingers rapidly through the strings. The harp also plays single notes and chords, but the parts must be written with a minimum of chromatics. If the tempo is too rapid, the harpist cannot change the pedals quickly enough to play chromatically.

Range: The harp is a nontransposing instrument. Harp notation is written in the treble and bass clefs; the notes sound where written. The highest note is G♯ (8va) above the treble clef. The lowest note is C♭, one octave below the bass clef.

Woodwinds

Woodwinds introduce numerous musical colors to the orchestra. The birdlike sounds of the piccolo and flute, the "humorous" and haunting bassoon sound—familiar to many in Prokofiev's *Peter and the Wolf*—the open, hollow sound of the clarinets, and the beautiful nasal sounds of the English horn and the oboe all contribute to the traditional orchestral woodwind section. Woodwinds blend particularly well with the strings.

Piccolo

The piccolo is a baby flute and is primarily used to create special effects and to play the highest parts in the orchestra. Flute players double on piccolo. The piccolo is commonly known for the obbligato parts written for marches.

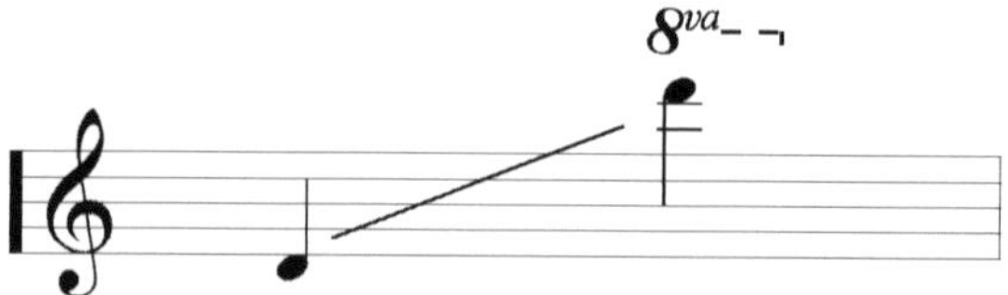

Figure 5.10. Piccolo: This Staff Indicates Where the Parts Are Written

Figure 5.11. C Flute Range

Range: Piccolo parts are written in the treble clef and sound one octave higher than the written pitch. The highest note is D two octaves above the treble clef. The lowest note is D, notated directly above middle C.

Flute in C

The C flute plays the highest woodwind parts in an orchestra (piccolo is used sparingly). The flute has a three-octave range. The low notes are difficult to hear and should therefore be used only if the orchestration is quiet and sparse; the highest notes can be played only with force and should be used sparingly. The highest notes are traditionally used when doubled with other instruments (or played in octaves). The additional instruments lend support to the flute, which is generally piercing in the upper octave. Flutists have great technical agility, which is analogous to the technical prowess of string players.

The flute is a popular solo instrument in traditional classical musical styles and is also popular in jazz and Latin music.

Range: The C flute is a nontransposing instrument. The notes are written in the treble clef and sound where written. The highest note is C 8va above the treble clef. The lowest note is middle C.

Alto Flute

The alto flute is a popular instrument in commercial music. It is used sparingly in traditional orchestral music. The alto flute produces a warm sound, but because it is inherently quiet it must sometimes be doubled with an additional alto flute to be heard. The player must force more air into the instrument than into a C flute; therefore parts should not be writ-

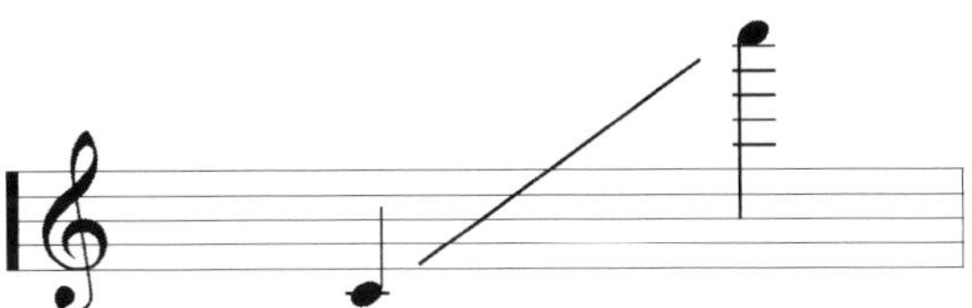

Figure 5.12. Alto Flute: This Staff Indicates Where the Parts Are Written

ten that require the same technical dexterity as the C flute. The high range of the alto flute is a poor imitation of the C flute and should be used cautiously. The rich tones are found in the midrange.

Range: Alto flute parts are written in the treble clef and sound a perfect fourth below the written pitch. The highest *sounding* note is G, four ledger lines above the treble clef. The lowest *sounding* note is G below middle C.

Bass Flute

The bass flute produces a beautiful low sound, which is similar in timbre to that of the alto flute. The performer must produce a substantial amount of air in order for the instrument to be heard. Bass flutes are soft; therefore several performers playing in unison might be required to hear the part in an orchestral setting. The orchestrator should not write technically difficult parts because of the physical limitations of the instrument; the orchestration surrounding the bass flute should be sparse for the instrument to be heard. The bass flute is not a traditional orchestral instrument. It is often used in film scores, where it can be amplified.

> ♫ Most cultures have endemic flutes made of various materials and containing a variety of tunings. Many film composers are familiar with the various sounds of ethnic flutes because they can bring a unique quality to an orchestration, when used effectively.

Range: Bass flute parts are written in the treble clef and sound one octave below the written pitch. The highest *sounding* note is F on the top line of the treble clef. The lowest *sounding* note is C one octave below middle C.

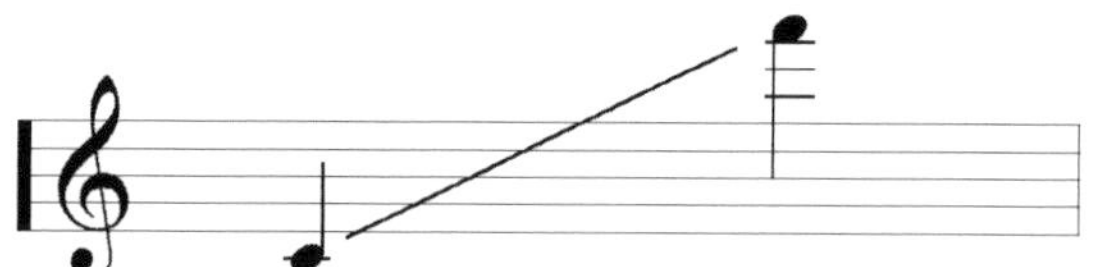

Figure 5.13. Bass Flute: This Staff Indicates Where the Parts Are Written

Double Reeds: Oboe

The oboe uses a double reed as a mouthpiece.

Oboes have a beautiful nasal, expressive quality, and they are often used to play solos in an orchestral setting. The double-reeded mouthpiece is made of cane. The nasal sound played with vibrato can be one of the

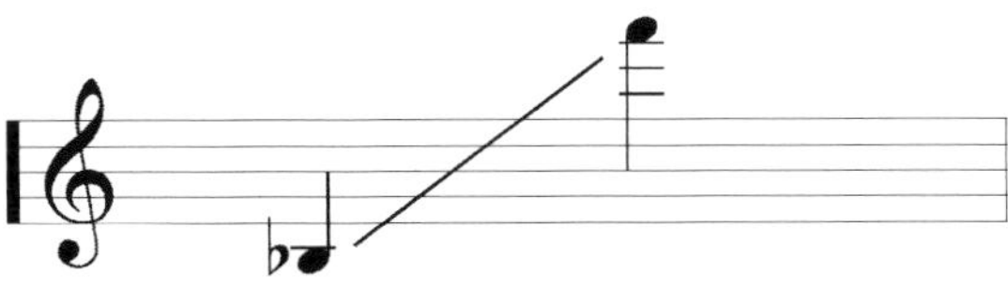

Figure 5.14. Oboe

most effective sounds in the orchestra. Oboists have impressive technical dexterity, and the sound of the oboe blends perfectly with the other woodwinds and also with the strings. Flutes and oboes played in unison or in octaves produce an especially lovely sonority.

Oboists spend endless hours making reeds, which is an art form. Many oboists make reeds for certain purposes. For example, some reeds are used for parts played primarily in the upper registers, while other reeds work more effectively in dry weather.

> ♫ Traditionally, the oboe player sounds the concert A, which is used as a benchmark by which the other orchestral members tune their instruments. The oboe is the only orchestral instrument that cannot be tuned.

The oboe is a unique instrument because reed making enables a performer to produce a unique sound rather than one produced by instruments with standard mouthpieces. (A performer's embouchure and training also contribute to the final sound of the instrument.)

Range: The oboe is a nontransposing instrument. The notes are written in the treble clef and sound where written. The highest sounding note is F one octave above the treble clef. The lowest sounding note is B♭ below middle C.

Double Reeds: English Horn

The English horn uses a double reed as a mouthpiece. The English horn is a tenor oboe and is fingered the way an oboe is. The lower range of the instrument produces a rich and warm sound that is unique to the instrument. It is frequently used for soloing.

Range: English horn parts are written in the treble clef and sound a perfect fifth below the written note. The highest *sounding* note is B♭ directly above the treble clef. The lowest *sounding* note is E below middle C.

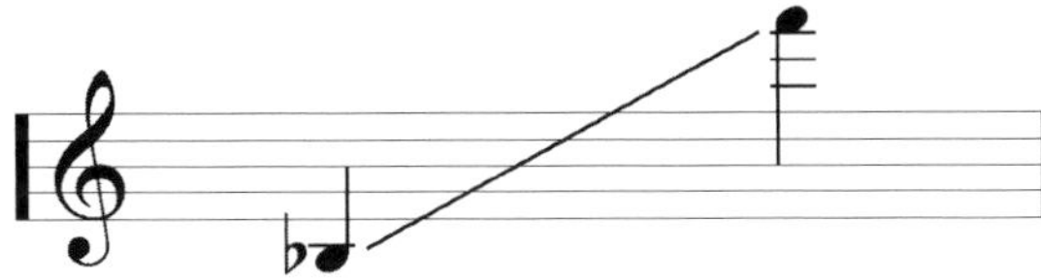

Figure 5.15. English Horn: This Staff Indicates Where the Parts Are Written

Double Reeds: Bassoon

The bassoon uses a double reed as a mouthpiece.

Bassoons produce what could be characterized as the happiest and most playful sound in the orchestra; they can also sound warm, sad, or dark. The low, beautiful, and unique sounds blend beautifully with the low strings. The high sounds are weak but can be useful in specific circumstances. They can produce an almost comic quality and are often used to create that effect.

Range: The bassoon is a nontransposing instrument. The notes are written in the bass clef and sound where written. The highest *sounding* note is E♭, notated on the top space of the treble clef. The lowest *sounding* note is B♭ below the bass clef. Some players can reach a high E natural. The tenor clef is often used if notes are high.

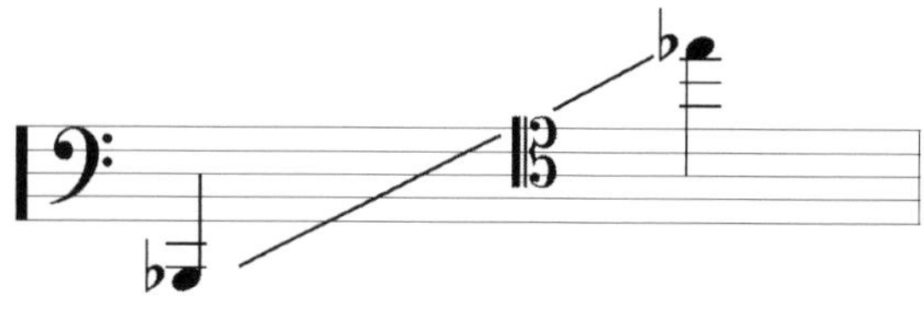

Figure 5.16. Bassoon

Double Reeds: Contrabassoon

The contrabassoon uses a double reed as a mouthpiece. The sound can generate a distinct low-end sonority. They are rarely used in popular music but can be very effective when used prudently.

Range: Contrabassoon parts are written in the bass clef and sound one octave below where written. The highest *sounding* note is F, notated on the third line in the bass clef. The lowest *sounding* note is B♭, notated one octave below the B♭, which is notated directly below the bass clef.

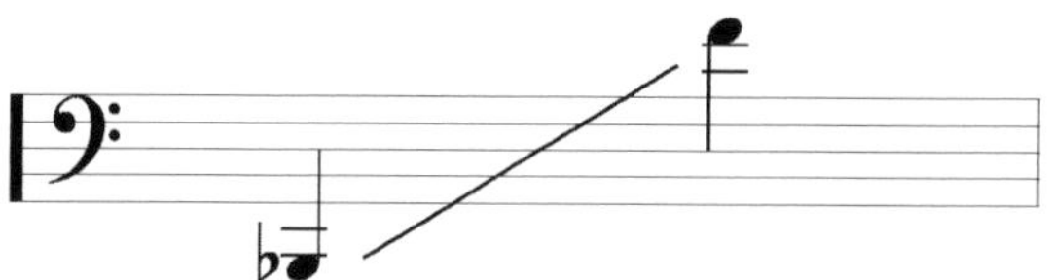

Figure 5.17. Contrabassoon: This Staff Indicates Where the Parts Are Written

Clarinets

Clarinets use single reeds and a hard rubber mouthpiece. Because of the round and warm sound, clarinets blend well with the other woodwinds, as well as with the string section. They are used equally in classical music, jazz, and all forms of popular music. From the wonderful obbligatos played in Dixieland music (B♭ clarinet) to the lead clarinet harmonized by saxophones in the 1940s Glenn Miller Band, the clarinet has proven to be a versatile instrument.

Most traditional orchestrations contain two clarinets. Generally, it is not wise to have clarinets play in unison. Intonation problems can occur, and the sound is not particularly pleasing. Clarinets are built in various keys.

B♭ clarinet is the most common clarinet used in commercial music. The players have marvelous technical dexterity and can play almost anything that is generically written for the instrument. Parts are written in the treble clef and sound one full step below where it is written. The highest *sounding* note is F, notated above the treble clef. It is possible to play higher. The lowest *sounding* note is D below middle C.

Clarinet in A parts are written in the treble clef and sound a minor third below where written. The highest *sounding* note is F♯, notated on the third ledger line above the treble clef. It is possible to play higher. The lowest *sounding* note is D♭ below middle C.

Clarinet in E♭ parts are written in the treble clef and sound a minor third above where written. The highest *sounding* note is C, notated one octave above the treble clef. It is possible to play higher. The lowest *sounding* note is G below middle C.

Alto clarinet in E♭ parts are written in the treble clef and sound a major sixth lower. The highest *sounding* note is G, notated on the first space above the treble clef. The lowest *sounding* note is G, notated on the lowest line of the bass clef.

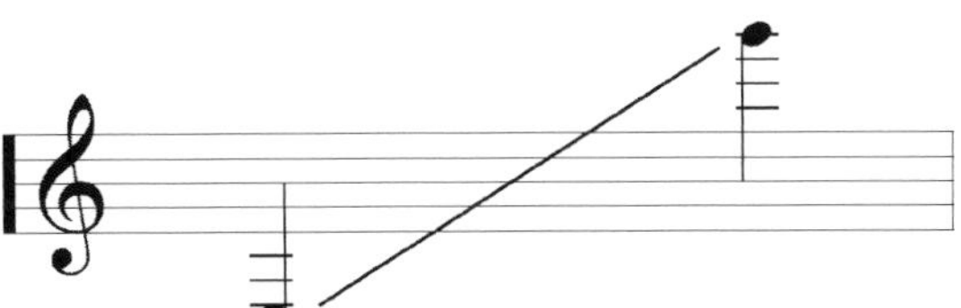

Figure 5.18. B♭ Clarinet: This Staff Indicates Where the Parts Are Written

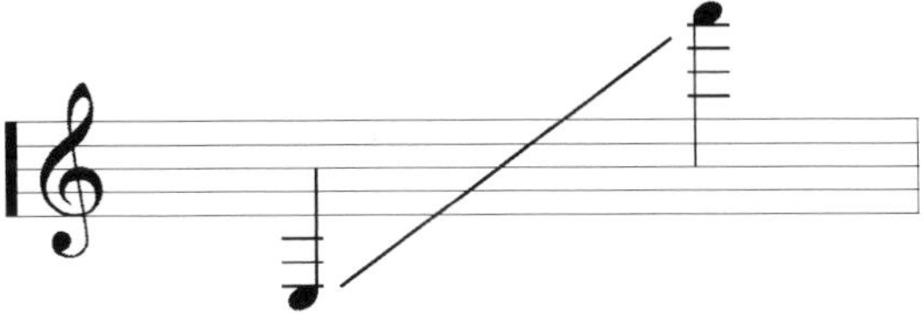

Figure 5.19. A Clarinet: This Staff Indicates Where the Parts Are Written

Bass clarinet in B♭ sounds one octave below the B♭ clarinet. It produces a beautiful low and resonant sound. The bass clarinet blends well with other low instruments. Bass clarinet parts are written in the treble clef and sound a major ninth lower. The highest *sounding* note is F above middle C. The lowest *sounding* note is D below the bass clef.

Figure 5.20. E♭ Clarinet: This Staff Indicates Where the Parts Are Written

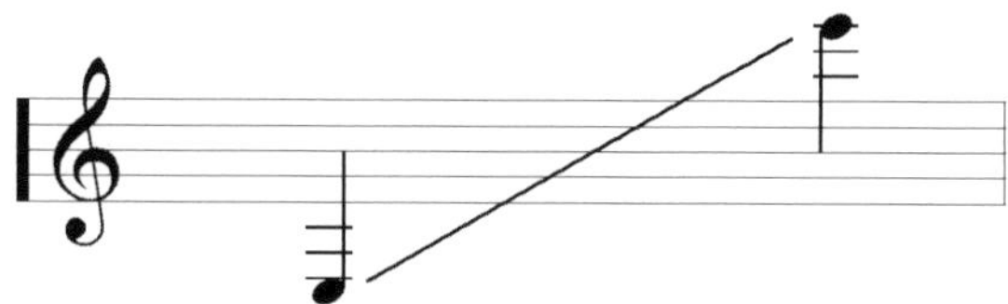

Figure 5.21. Alto Clarinet: This Staff Indicates Where the Parts Are Written

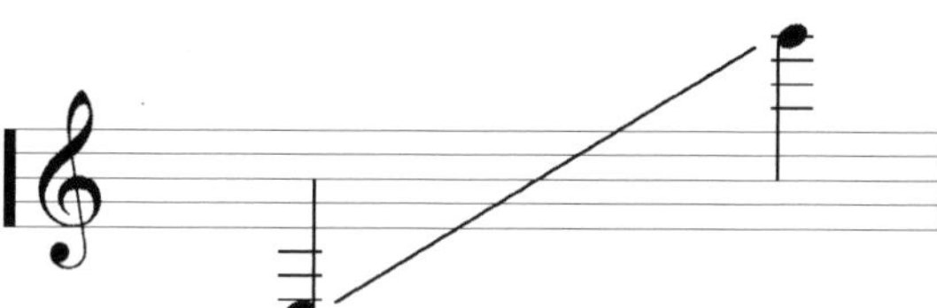

Figure 5.22. Bass Clarinet: This Staff Indicates Where the Parts Are Written

Saxophones

Saxophones are made of brass but are still considered woodwinds. They are played with a single reed that is attached to a plastic or rubber mouthpiece.

Traditionally, saxophones have not been extensively used in orchestral music. Some of the romantic composers, such as Bizet and Richard Strauss, incorporate saxophones in some compositions. They are widely used in band music and small ensembles and are periodically used in compositions by modern orchestral composers.

All forms of popular music have traditionally incorporated saxophones. Jazz musicians have showcased the saxophone more than any other musical genre. The big-band sound of five saxophones (two altos, two tenors, and one baritone—the bass saxophone is rarely used) is the traditional section. The smooth and expressive section sound was showcased during the swing era. The raw and expressive sound of the tenor saxophone has long been heard in rock 'n' roll and R&B bands.

The saxophone is not considered a traditional orchestral instrument, although some saxophone parts were written in concert music (mostly during the twentieth century). Saxophones are used in traditional band music and wind symphonies.

The saxophones, as a section, are most recognized as the backbone of a traditional jazz big-band sound. The players have remarkable technical ability. The saxophone is the most popular solo instrument in all forms of jazz and popular styles of music (with the exception of the electric guitar in rock 'n' roll).

Saxophonists are able to perform music written for virtuosos. Professional players can perform very difficult passages requiring amazing technical dexterity. Most saxophonists who play commercial music also play additional woodwinds. Traditional doubles are flute and clarinet; some saxophonists also play oboe and English horn. Playing multiple woodwinds affords the instrumentalist more job opportunities. Saxophones blend well with all sections of the orchestra.

Range: Saxophones are built in various keys, and they all have a *written* range from B♭ or B below middle C to E or F above the treble clef.

Soprano saxophone in B♭ has been a popular solo instrument in jazz music. The alto saxophone is generally used as the top voice in most saxophone sections, but the soprano saxophone is sometimes added to achieve a higher range. Parts are written in the treble clef and sound one step lower than where written. The highest *sounding* note is E♭ above the treble clef. It is possible to play higher. The lowest *sounding* note is A♭ below middle C.

Alto saxophone in E♭ is traditionally the top voice in a saxophone section. Many jazz saxophonists (e.g., Charlie Parker, Paul Desmond) play alto as their primary instrument. Since a traditional saxophone section has two altos, the second harmony part is usually played by the second alto, although the tenor saxophone is sometimes written to play the second

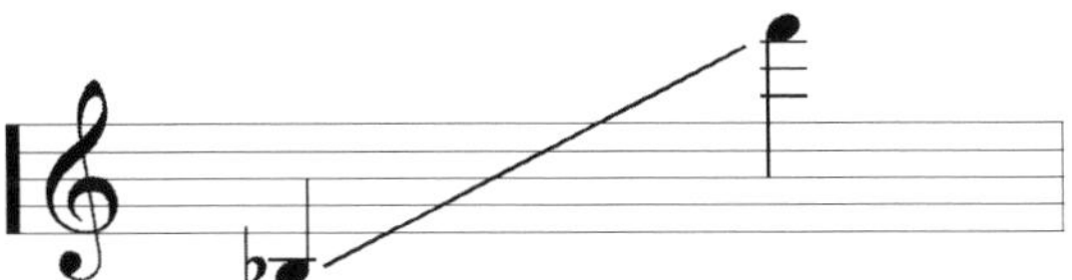

Figure 5.23. Saxophones: This Staff Indicates Where the Parts Are Written

♫ Soprano saxophones are built in two different shapes. The most common shape looks like an oversized clarinet but is longer and wider. Some sopranos have the same shape as the other saxophones. Both versions sound the same. (Some soprano saxophones are built in E♭.)

harmony part. In this case the second alto plays the part directly below the tenor saxophone. Parts are written in the treble clef and sound a major sixth below the written note. The highest *sounding* note is usually an A♭ above the treble clef. It is possible to play higher. The lowest *sounding* note is D♭ below middle C.

Tenor saxophone in B♭ is a solo instrument in rock 'n' roll, rhythm & blues, and jazz, and has achieved even greater popularity than the alto saxophone. The traditional saxophone section has two tenors. Parts are written in the treble clef and sound a major ninth below where written. The highest *sounding* note is usually an E♭, notated on the top space of the treble clef. The lowest *sounding* note is A♭, notated on the lowest space of the bass clef.

Baritone saxophone in E♭, referred to as a bari sax, is traditionally the lowest member of the commercial saxophone section. Although not normally used as a solo instrument, there have been some stellar jazz solo performers, such as Gerry Mulligan and Pepper Adams. The baritone sax was widely used in early rock 'n' roll, especially in the 1950s. Parts are written in the treble clef and sound an octave and a major sixth below where written. The highest *sounding* note is usually A♭ above middle C. The lowest *sounding* note is D♭ notated below the bass clef. It is possible to play higher.

Bass saxophone in B♭ is the largest of the saxophones and is rarely used. It produces a very low and resonant sound. The bass saxophone is a huge, bulky instrument and difficult to play. It produces a very low and grand bass in any musical setting. Parts are written in the treble clef and sound two octaves and a full step below where written. The highest *sounding* note is usually E♭ above middle C. The lowest *sounding* note is A♭, notated below the bass clef.

Brass

The brass adds both fire and richness to the sound of the orchestra. From the blaring, call-to-action trumpets to the all-encompassing hunting calls of the French horns and the deep and full-sounding tubas and the slide trombones, the brass fulfill an array of orchestral duties. Brass adds excitement and also provides a rich background to the most sensitive passages.

The French horns blend flawlessly with the strings, as do the trombones. The tubas in unison with the basses provide a perfect blend that enhances the bottom end of the orchestra. Open trumpets (without mutes) add midrange to high-range passages with a timbre that no other instrument can provide. Brass instruments are able to incorporate mutes, which change the sounds of the instruments; mutes are inserted into an instrument's bell. The orchestrator indicates when a mute should be used. Muted trumpets are particularly popular in commercial music. French horn players use the right hand as a standard mute in addition to a traditional physical mute.

> ♫ When a mute is inserted the player has more difficulty inserting air into the instrument. That must be considered when a composer is writing a passage because the extra air affects the player's technical dexterity.

In addition to playing the traditional fanfare parts written by many composers, brass players have the ability to double- and triple-tongue, creating a sound unique to brass. Brass instruments also sound good playing in unison, unlike most woodwinds.

Since the embouchure of brass players greatly affects the sound, the composer must be certain that the player receives enough rest between long passages. When a brass player's lips are fatigued, they cannot play, or the intonation might be compromised. The composer should write within the tessitura of the instrument. Writing long passages that are too high or too low often causes great fatigue for the performer.

Trumpet in B♭

The B♭ trumpet is the leader of the brass section in most commercial musical settings. Traditionally, a big band has three to four trumpets. The B♭ trumpet is the most common kind of the instrument, although throughout history trumpets have been constructed in many keys.

The cup mute, the harmon mute, and the straight mute are the most common mutes. Sometimes a rubber plunger is also used as a mute. The arranger/composer should be familiar with the timbres produced by various mutes.

> ♫ Orchestration books provide details on additional trumpets, such as the piccolo trumpet, which produces a high and unique sound.

Trumpets sound best playing in close harmony, in octaves, and in unison.

Range: Trumpet parts are written in the treble clef and sound one step below where written. The highest *sounding* note is C above the treble clef. The lowest *sounding* note is E, notated below the treble clef. Most professional players can play much higher. (Low E can be played but is generally not practical unless the composer is trying to write a pedal tone effect.)

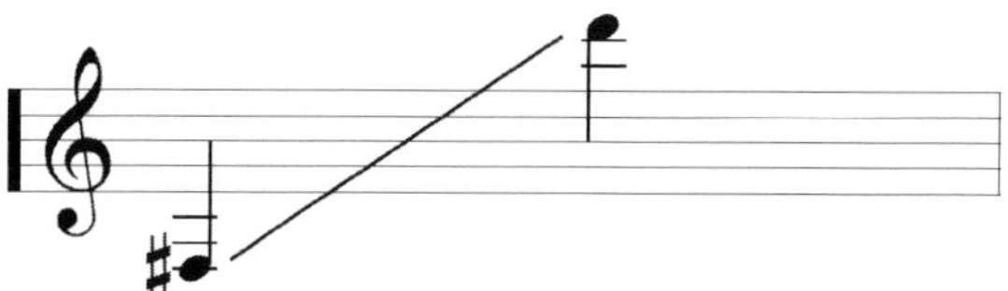

Figure 5.24. Trumpet Range: This Staff Indicates Where the Parts Are Written

French Horn in F

The modern French horn is pitched in the key of F. (Some symphony players prefer to use the horn in B♭.) As with other brass instruments, the French hornist changes the natural overtones of the instrument by changing her embouchure. French horns have three valves, which enable the player to achieve chromatic tones.

The majestic sound of French horns playing in unison or in fifths cuts through an orchestra with an important and sometimes soothing sound.

The sound of the instrument is unique. The room seems to be filled with a magnificent sound. Most orchestras have 3 or 4 French hornists. (Some film scores contain 8 horns.)

French horn players use cup mutes and straight mutes; unlike trumpeters, they cannot use a harmon mute. Players usually keep one hand over the bell in order to achieve a muffled, distant sound; they also play with an open bell. Do not write high parts for the French horn that last a long period of time. It is difficult to perform, and the sound of the horns will seem overused.

There are numerous solo French horn pieces written for orchestra and chamber music. Jazz French hornist soloists are rare, but French horns are used in jazz orchestras. They blend with all sections of the orchestra. Arguably, they are best used for legato passages, although staccato and sforzando passages are part of their signature sound. Arrangers must allow the players space to rest because the instrument is difficult to play and the performers' lips can easily become fatigued.

Range: French horn parts are written primarily in the treble clef and sound a perfect fifth below where it is written. If notes are written in a low

Figure 5.25. French Horn: Historical Notation, Although Most Contemporary Arrangers Use Key Signatures.

register, the bass clef may be used. The lowest written note is F, below the bass clef, and the highest written note is D, the fourth line on the treble clef. Some hornists can play higher.

Many arrangers do not write a key signature and notate the accidentals.

Tenor Trombone (Slide Trombone)

The tenor slide trombone section of a commercial jazz band usually consists of either 3 or 4 players. The bass trombone plays the lowest part.

Trombones are unique because of the ability to play portamento passages, which are achieved by using the slide. Trombones are also known for open and closed individual notes and musical passages played with plunger mutes. The sound is unique to trombones. They blend well with strings and also support upper brass passages.

Accomplished trombonists play with remarkable technical dexterity. An arranger must know the ability of a player before writing parts that are not typically written for the instrument.

Range: The tenor trombone is a non-transposing instrument. Notes are written in the bass clef and sound where written; parts written in the upper registers are usually notated in the tenor clef. The highest *sounding* note is B♭, notated in the tenor clef. The lowest *sounding* note is E, notated below the bass clef. Many professional players can play higher.

> ♫ Valve trombones are rarely used, but some jazz players enjoy playing them because they afford the performer more opportunities to play with the same dexterity as other instruments with valves. Not all slide trombonists know how to play valve trombones. Many trumpet players play valve trombones.

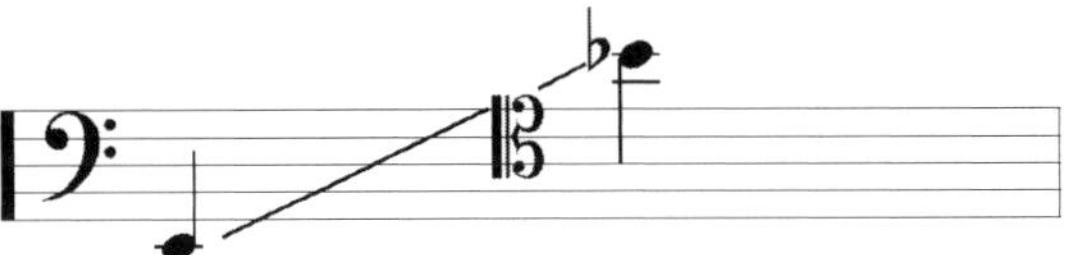

Figure 5.26. Tenor Trombone

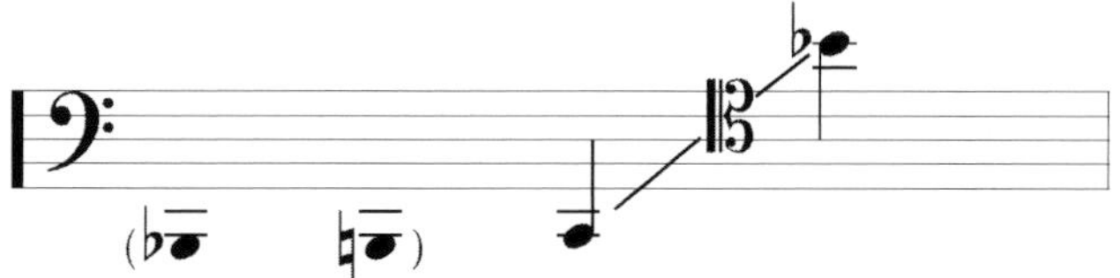

Figure 5.27. Bass Trombone

Bass Trombone

The bass trombone is one of the most all-consuming sounds heard in both an orchestral setting and a commercial band or orchestra. It blends well with virtually all of the low-end instruments. Other orchestral instruments cannot duplicate the bass trombone's low, resonant sound.

Range: The bass trombone is a nontransposing instrument. Parts are written in the bass clef and sound where written. The highest *sounding* note is usually B♭, notated in the tenor clef, and the higher notes are written in the tenor clef. Professional players can play higher. The lowest *sounding* note is B♭, notated below the bass clef.

Tuba

Tubas blend well with the double basses, bass trombone, cellos, and additional low instruments. Tubas rarely use mutes because mutes are cumbersome. Tubas are made in various keys. The most popular tuba, which is used in popular music, is a nontransposing instrument. Most tubas have four valves, but some have six.

Range: The tuba is a nontransposing instrument. Parts are written in the bass clef and sound where written. The highest *sounding* note is usually G above the bass clef. The lowest *sounding* note is F, notated one octave below the bass clef. (Some players can play a low D.)

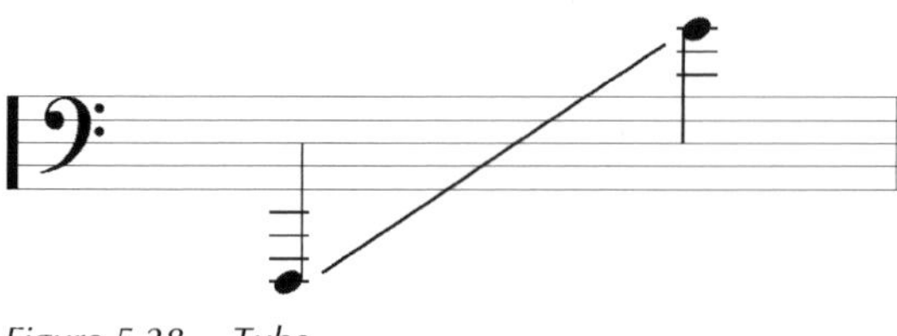

Figure 5.28. Tuba

Percussion

Percussion instruments are either struck or shaken. Some have a tone, and others do not. Since most cultures have indigenous percussion instruments, the instruments are too numerous to mention.

The orchestral percussion instruments add spice to an orchestration. From the jingling of a tambourine to the deep roll of the timpani, these special sonorities are unique.

In popular music, congas, tambourines, shakers, and the standard drum kit have been the backbone of the rhythm section. Mixing real percussion with synthesized percussive sounds is commonplace in commercial music.

Timpani

Timpani drums are played by hitting the drumheads with mallets of various sizes and shapes. Each drum can be tuned by tightening screws; modern timpani can be tuned by using a foot pedal and by tightening one screw. The pitch can be changed through the use of foot pedals, which either raises or lowers the pitch. The heads are made of either plastic or calfskin.

Timpani drums provide a unique contribution to the deep sound of the orchestra. Used sparingly, they provide a percussive bass and sub-bass component to the orchestra. Playing the same rhythmic patterns as the low brass and low strings is one of the most effective uses of the timpani. A soft roll provides an eerie or soothing rumble. No other orchestral instrument can duplicate the sound of timpani.

Although there are four timpani drums, usually only two are used—numbers two and four.

Range: The notes are written in the bass clef and sound where written:

- The lowest *sounding* note of timpani #1 is D, notated below the bass clef. The highest *sounding* note is A, notated on the lowest space of the bass clef.

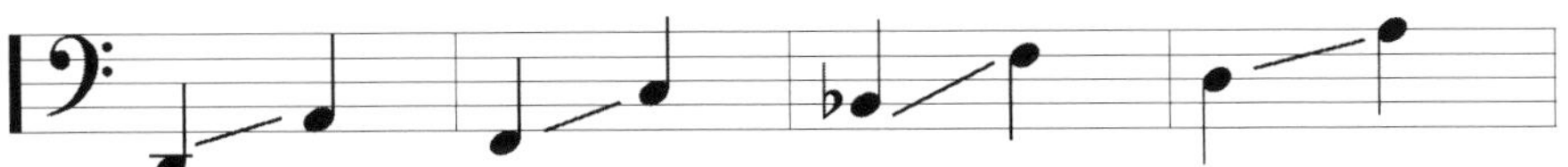

Figure 5.29. Timpani

- The lowest *sounding* note of timpani #2 is F below the bass clef. The highest *sounding* note is C, notated within the bass clef.
- The lowest *sounding* note of timpani #3 is B♭, notated within the bass clef. The highest *sounding* note is F, notated within the bass clef.
- The lowest *sounding* note of timpani #4 is D, notated within the bass clef. The highest *sounding* note is A, notated within the bass clef.

Drum Kit

The commercial drum kit is the backbone of the commercial music section. The drum kit consists of the following:

- Bass drum (kick drum)
- Snare drum
- Tom-toms
- Hi-hat cymbals
- Various ride and crash cymbals

Latin Percussion Instruments

Following are but a few of the Latin percussion instruments. They mix well with traditional drums.

- Conga drums
- Bongo drums
- Various shakers
- Tambourine
- Go-go bells
- Cabasa
- Claves

Traditional Orchestral Percussion Instruments

The following are the most common orchestral percussion instruments that do not have definite pitches.

- Concert bass drums
- Snare drum
- Tenor drum
- Wood blocks
- Castanets
- Tambourine
- Tuned boobam drums
- Temple blocks
- Triangle

Piano

In most traditional music programs, the study of the piano is a necessary component of a well-rounded music education. It enables a student to see (view the keys) harmony and hear harmony.

The piano has been popular in all forms of music for centuries. Being polyphonic makes it a stellar accompanying instrument for small instrumental combinations. Jazz pianists, pop pianists (Billy Joel and Elton John), and the great classical pianists demonstrate the all-encompassing versatility of, arguably, the greatest instrument ever invented.

In commercial music, keyboard skills are necessary to play synthesizers. Most commercial keyboard players have the ability to program synthesizers and engineer productions. It has become a matter of musical survival in the business of popular music.

Range: The notes are written in the treble and bass clefs and sound where written unless indicated by a marking that indicates playing the part in a different octave. *For example, 8va means to play the note one octave above the written note. Writing it an octave lower makes it easier for the performer to decipher the note.* The highest *sounding* note is C (15ma) above the treble clef. The lowest *sounding* note is A, notated one octave below the bass clef.

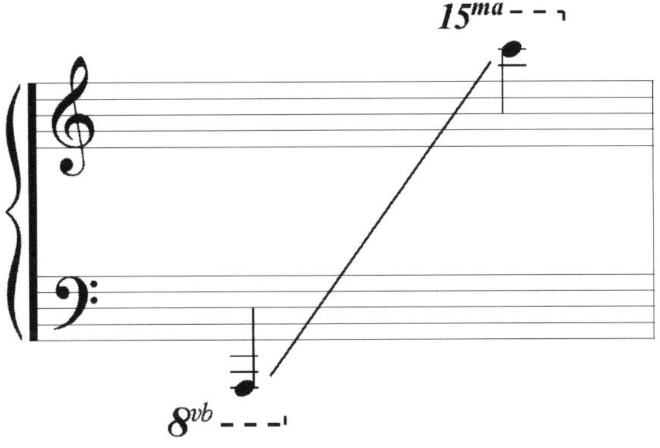

Figure 5.30. Piano

Celesta (Celeste)

The celesta is a small, bell-like keyboard that blends well with strings and woodwinds because of its ethereal sound. It must be used sparingly, or its effect will not be appreciated. The celesta provides an orchestral color that creates a soothing sonority.

Range: The notes are written in the treble clef and sound one octave above where written. The highest *sounding* note is C (16ma), above the C notated in the treble clef. The lowest *sounding* note is middle C.

Figure 5.31. Celesta: This Staff Indicates Where the Parts Are Written

Glockenspiel

The glockenspiel is a bell-like instrument containing two rows of metal bars that are struck by various metal mallets. The sound is reminiscent of a celesta but does not sound as delicate. It adds a sparkling "top end" to the strings and woodwinds and must not be overused. The glockenspiel does not usually sound good played in harmony or playing durations faster than eighth notes unless the eighth notes are used infrequently and to produce a desired effect. The glockenspiel's harmonics ring and cause a sound of confusion.

Range: The notes are written in the treble clef and sound two octaves above where written. The highest *sounding* note is C two octaves above the treble clef. The lowest *sounding* note is G, notated above the treble clef.

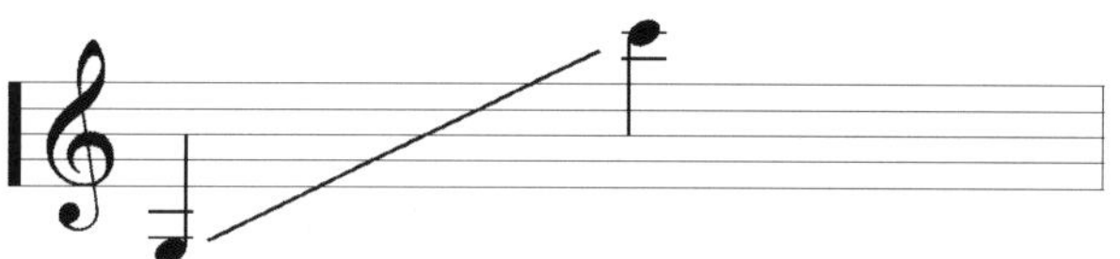

Figure 5.32. Glockenspiel: This Staff Indicates Where the Parts Are Written

Xylophone

The xylophone is an instrument constructed of tuned wooden bars that are hit with mallets. Xylophones sound percussive. When played in conjunction with various sections of the orchestra, the sound can be penetrating. The xylophone should be used sparingly to be effective.

Range: The notes are written in the treble clef and sound one octave above where written. The highest *sounding* note is C two octaves above the treble clef. (Some xylophones go as high as F or C above the treble clef.) The lowest *sounding* note is F, notated on the lowest space of treble clef.

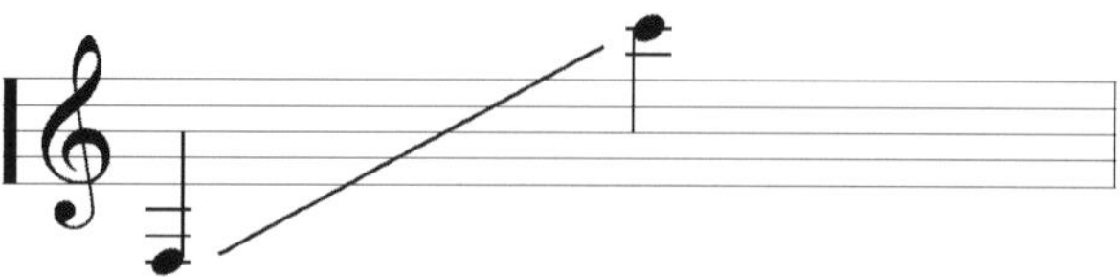

Figure 5.33. Xylophone: This Staff Indicates Where the Parts Are Written

Marimba

The marimba, struck by various kinds of mallets, is similar to a xylophone but does not sound as piercing. Made in different sizes, a marimba is played with one to four mallets. Chords are sometimes played with a rhythmic pattern, adding not only a percussive but also a melodic part.

Range: The notes are written in the treble and bass clefs and sound where written. The highest note is C two octaves above the treble clef. The lowest note is A, notated on the bottom space of the bass clef.

Figure 5.34. Marimba

Vibraphone

The vibraphone is essentially an electric marimba except that the bars are made of metal and played with mallets made of various materials. Depressing the sustain pedal on the vibraphone holds notes, as it does on a piano. The vibrato can be adjusted by turning a switch.

The vibraphone has been widely used in jazz for many years by luminous vibraphonists, such as Lionel Hampton, Milt Jackson, and Gary Burton. The vibes blend well with both acoustic and electric pianos and morph into almost any instrumental setting.

Range: The notes are written in the treble clef and sound where written. The highest note is F above the treble clef. The lowest note is F, notated below the treble clef. (Vibraphones are made in various sizes and ranges.)

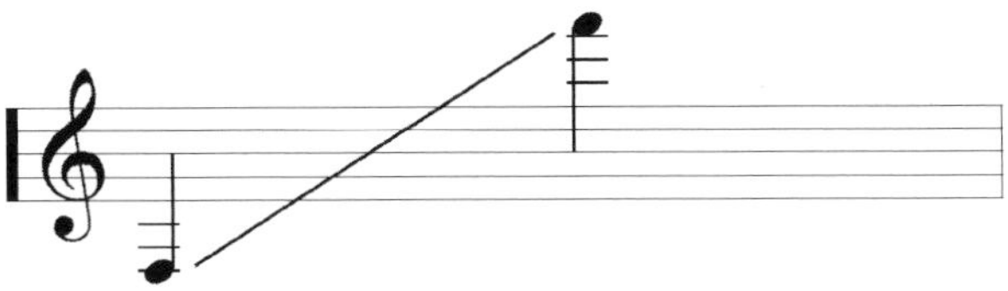

Figure 5.35. Vibraphone

Guitar

Guitars are either electric or acoustic. The electric guitar is the most popular instrument in rock 'n' roll and other forms of popular music. Some acoustic guitars are amplified.

Acoustic guitars have either nylon or metal strings. The choice of strings greatly affects the sound of the instrument. Some guitars have six strings, while others have twelve; the number of strings affects the sound. Guitarists use guitar picks or fingers to strike the strings. The use of a metal or glass bar sliding along the fretboard is the signature sound of the blues.

The sound of electric guitars can vary with the addition of effects through the use of various guitar-effects units. A large variety of guitar amplifiers and effects are built into certain guitars. From the pure sound of most jazz guitarists to the raucous sound of heavy metal guitarists, the instrument can produce a wide range of sounds and effects. A wide variety of guitars are available.

Register: The guitar is written in the treble clef and sounds one octave below where written. The highest *sounding* note is E, notated on the top space of the treble clef. The lowest *sounding* note is E two octaves below the treble clef.

Open strings for guitar

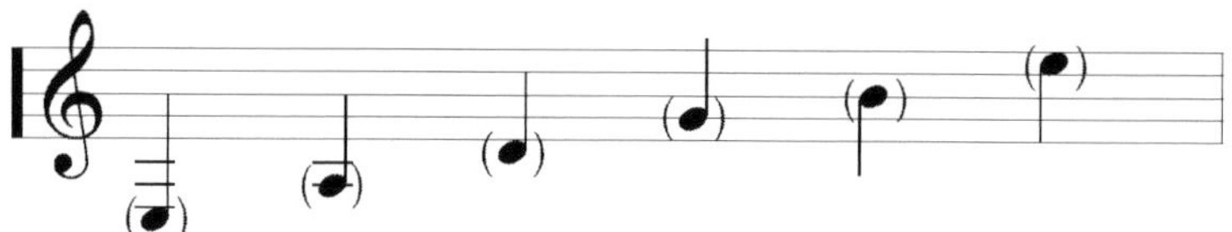

Figure 5.36. Guitar Open Strings

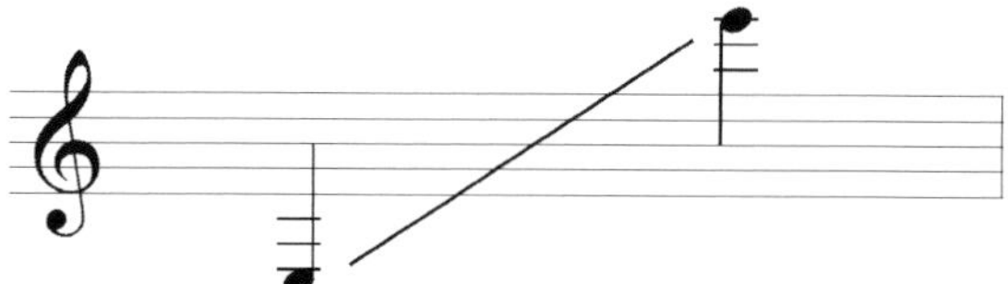

Figure 5.37. Guitar Range: This Staff Indicates Where the Parts Are Written

Voices

Voices are not traditionally included in orchestration books, but because of the extensive use of voices in commercial music, the vocal ranges are included for reference.

Soprano I

Range: The notes are written in the treble clef and sound where written. The highest note is C above the treble clef. The lowest note is B♭, notated below the treble clef. Some singers can sing higher or lower.

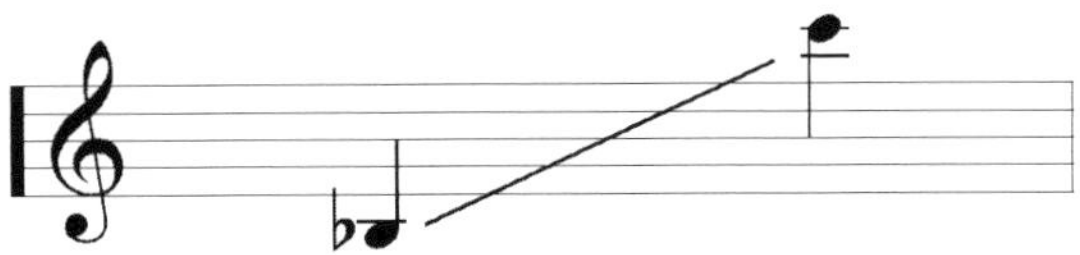

Figure 5.38. Soprano I

Soprano II

Range: The notes are written in the treble clef and sound where written. The highest note is G above the treble clef. The lowest note is A, notated below the treble clef. Some singers can sing higher or lower.

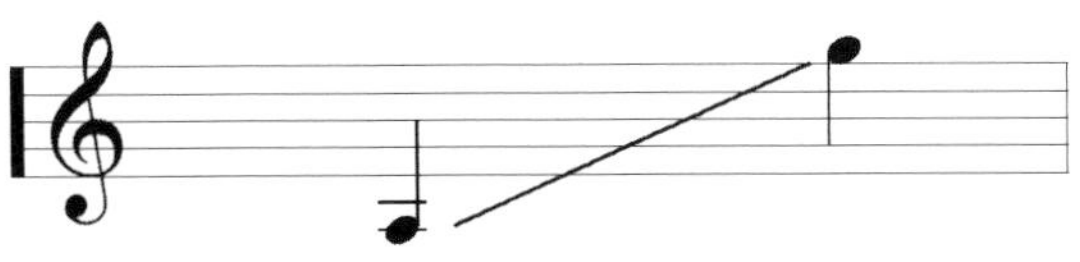

Figure 5.39. Soprano II

Alto I

Range: The notes are written in the treble clef and sound where written. The highest note is F, notated on the top line of the treble clef. The lowest note is G, notated below the treble clef. Some singers can sing higher or lower.

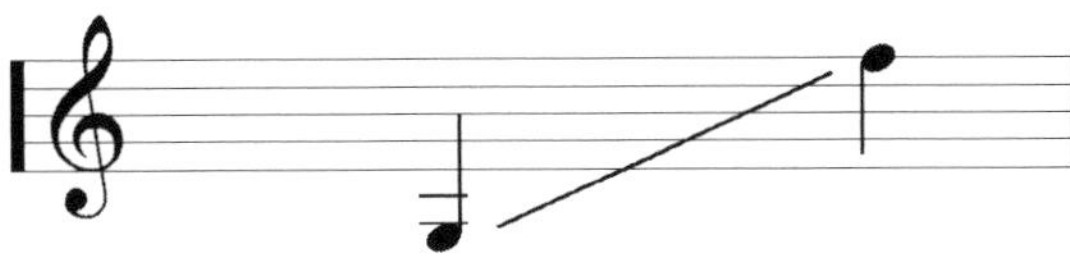

Figure 5.40. Alto I

Alto II

Range: The notes are written in the treble clef and sound where written. The highest note is E♭, notated on the top line of the treble clef. The lowest note is F, notated below the treble clef. Some singers can sing higher or lower.

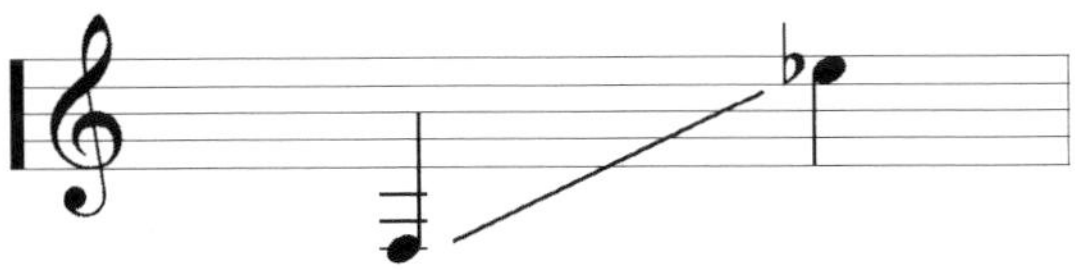

Figure 5.41. Alto II

Tenor I

Range: The notes are written in the treble clef and sound one octave lower than written. The highest *sounding* note is C, notated within the treble clef. The lowest *sounding* note is middle C one octave below middle C. Some singers can sing higher or lower.

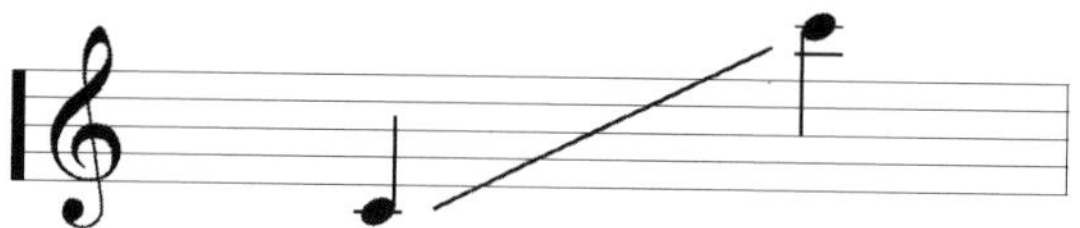

Figure 5.42. Tenor I: This Staff Indicates Where the Parts Are Written

Tenor II

Range: The notes are written in the treble clef and sound one octave lower than written. The highest *sounding* note is A, notated within the treble clef. The lowest *sounding* note is A, notated on the last space of the bass clef. Some singers can sing higher or lower.

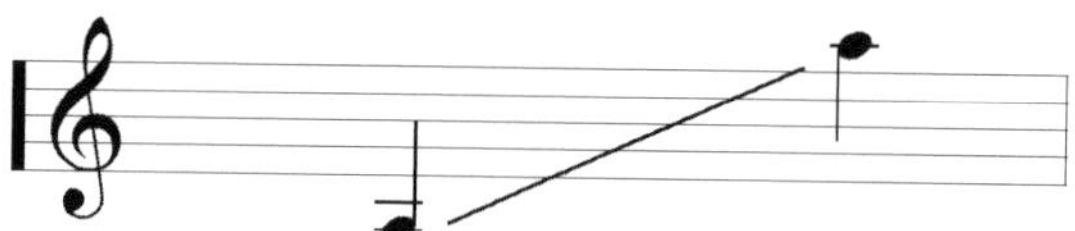

Figure 5.43. Tenor II: This Staff Indicates Where the Parts Are Written

Bass I

Range: The notes are written in the treble clef and sound where written. The highest note is F, notated on the bottom space of the treble clef. The lowest note is F, notated on the bottom space of the bass clef. Some singers can sing higher or lower.

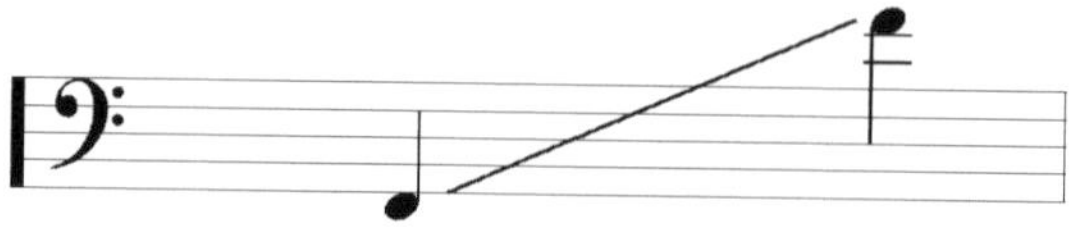

Figure 5.44. Bass I

Bass II

Range: The notes are written in the treble clef and sound where written. The highest note is E♭, notated on the first line of the treble clef. The lowest note is C, notated below the bass clef. Some singers can sing higher or lower.

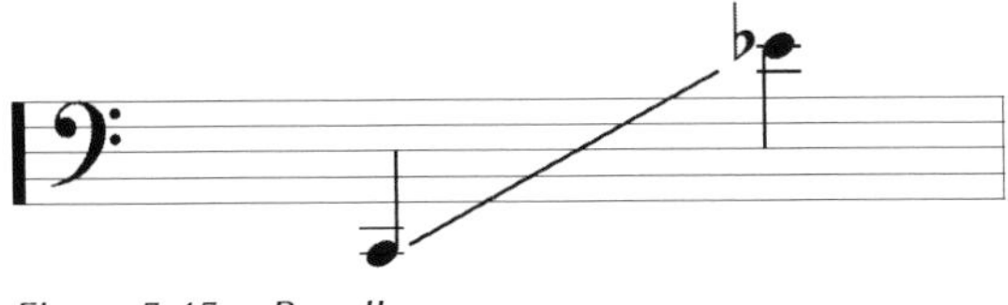

Figure 5.45. Bass II

Synthesizers and Samplers

The public has become familiar with the sounds of synthesizers and samplers and the innovative ways in which they are used. Synthesizers and samplers became popular partially because they are "chameleons." Tailors tailor custom suits, and programmers tailor custom sounds. Synthesizers and samplers are reasonably priced; consequently, producers and artists are able to produce music inexpensively. If a project has a low budget, producers and artists can create original music (records, film scores, television scores, commercials, etc.) using synthesizers and samplers for a fraction of the cost of using all live musicians.

> ♫ Virtual synthesizers and samplers are software versions modeled after analogous hardware devices. The virtual devices can produce basically the same sounds as their counterparts and also have the same editing functions. Generally, it is easier to program a virtual device than a hardware device.

- Synthesizers have changed the music industry. A synthesizer is an electronic instrument containing a keyboard or a rack-mounted version (containing no keyboard and is triggered by an external keyboard or another device, such as a guitar), which is capable of producing and editing both analog and/or digital sounds. *Analog* in music means that a synthesizer produces sounds that either are analogous to real instruments or can be programmed to produce innovative sounds. (It is accomplished by creating algorithms.) Samplers are devices that record and play back digital audio. Some samplers only play back.

- Techno dance music is an example of a musical style that contains mainly analog synthesis. Programmers specializing in this style are masters of creating sounds. Programming sounds is artistic more than it is technical.
- Tracks containing sampled oboes, flutes, and violins are generally played on synthesizers or samplers and are usually sampled sounds of real instruments.
- Third-party manufacturers record and sell samples of orchestral instruments, band instruments, percussion grooves, individual percussion instruments, drum kit grooves, individual drum kit instruments, sound effects, analogue synthesizer sounds, a variety of loops, and subcategories of all of the above. The sounds can be loaded into synthesizers and samplers (both hardware versions and software versions).

When synthesizers first became popular, clients viewed the ability to create popular electronic music as a means of cutting production costs. Since synthesizers were not meant to replace live musicians, the musicians' union incorporated new laws by which employers were required to pay the same union scale that a live player would have received had he or she played each part that was now performed by a synthesist. For example, if a synthesist played a synthesized piano part, a synthesized drum part, and a synthesized bass part, in theory, he or she was supposed to be paid for playing three separate parts. The theory was that a live musician had lost work. Therefore, if the employer had to pay the same wages to a synthesizer player, the employer would hire additional musicians to play the parts. The purpose of the mandatory scale payments was to help curb the loss of employment for live musicians.

In reality, synthesizer programmers negotiated (with employers) fees to play all parts required for either double or triple union scale; it became too costly to pay for each individual part. Eventually, the musicians' union made concessions and adjusted the pay scale. The popularity of synthesized music obliged the union to make concessions.

There are several ways to rationalize the union concessions:

- The recording label, or production company, might have a small budget and cannot afford to hire additional musicians; therefore, musicians are not losing work.

- When synthesis became popular, the audience became accustomed to listening to the electronic sounds. Live musicians playing traditional instruments, ironically, cannot duplicate many of the sounds (e.g., electronica or techno dance music).
- The problem escalated with the advent of sampling. Sampling, in lay terms, enables a programmer to sample (record) real instruments or other sounds and play them back in the same manner one would play a real instrument. If the instrument is programmed properly (and the synthesizer sounds or sampled sounds are of a professional sonic quality) it can be difficult to tell that the instruments (or the entire track) is synthesized or sampled.

Sampling has caused a drastic loss of income for instrumentalists in most musical genres. Club date bands used to contain 6 to 8 musicians. Now 3 can almost duplicate the same sound. For smaller affairs, a synthesizer player who also sings often replaces an entire band.

Synthesizer programming can never replace the feel that live musicians bring to the music. Many of the technical skills used by live musicians (e.g., various bowings used by string players, the sounds created by live brass players by varying embouchures) are difficult to reproduce on a synthesizer or sampler. Even when a skilled musical facsimile of a live band is reproduced, it does not sound completely realistic. Some instruments, for instance brass and some stringed instruments, do not sound real on most synthesizers and samplers; often, the sound is thin and piercing.

Musicians who are not trained can create music by learning a music-sequencing program, such as a computer-based system (e.g., Pro Tools) or recording in self-contained hardware units (e.g., digital workstations that contains a sequencer). Many novice musicians do not know the notational ranges of the instruments or the technical capabilities and limitations of the instruments.

> ♫ The most obvious example of sampling is the realistic string parts that can be played on synthesizers and samplers. A skilled programmer can combine digital samples with analog synthesis and create a lush background (a bed) that produces a beautiful timbre. In the United States, other than in film music, string players, brass players, woodwind players, and percussionists, who were previously employed as studio musicians, have experienced a drastic reduction in studio work. A select number of rhythm section players are still working because most synthesizer programmers use some live rhythm players to make productions sound *human.*

Thus they use the instrumental samples in the most basic manner or the samples are not used generically. For instance, if an arranger does not remain in the tessitura of the real instruments, the instruments will not sound authentic. If the goal is to replicate an orchestra, the arranger should write an orchestral arrangement that could be played by a real orchestra. This means that the arranger-programmer must know the playing style and technical capabilities of each instrument. It is difficult enough to replicate the sound and feel of authentic instruments on synthesizers and samplers, but when a novice attempts it, the results are usually substandard.

If an arranger is creating an arrangement using only electronic sounds, it is advisable to think of the electronic sounds as real instruments. A high-synthesized sound could be associated with violins, and a low synthesized sound might be equated with a contrabass. *Paint a mental picture of an electronic orchestra.* That helps an arranger conceive of the orchestration just as if he or she was approaching a traditional orchestration performed by a band or an orchestra.

Author's Opinion: When music industry executives complain that there is nothing musically new to present to the audience and sales are suffering as a result, the lack of musical knowledge by a majority of pop musicians is partially to blame. (The main reasons for a diminution of worldwide sales are illegal peer-2-peer file sharing from the Web and physical CD piracy.) When musical knowledge is limited, it lessens the creative options available to the music maker. It is analogous to a carpenter's having only half the tools necessary to complete a cabinet; yes, the carpenter can find a shortcut in order to complete a job, but the cabinet will not look as good or be as sturdy as if the correct tools were available and the cabinet was built by a master carpenter. The availability of a full tool chest of knowledge is always advantageous. The more tools available, the more options available.

MIDI and Digital Audio Computer Sequencing

Sequencers have become the mainstay of the contemporary music business. Music-sequencing programs, of which there are many, contain both a MIDI program and a digital audio program.

MIDI is an acronym for Musical Instrument Digital Interface. MIDI is an independent platform that sends information to both analog and digital devices. A computer-sequencing program such as Digital Performer, Logic Audio, or Pro Tools contains not only MIDI capabilities but also a digital audio program. The program records in the digital language, which converts information into a digital code, composed of ones and zeros (the digital language). The information is displayed by viewing sound waves, which can be edited and processed in infinite ways.

Most MIDI sequencing programs have notation programs, which enable programmers to view and edit the musical notes in manuscript form. The notation program helps a programmer edit in a more musical environment. Notes can be moved to new locations either by grabbing them with the mouse or by playing in new notes from a keyboard (or other input device) while viewing the notation window; notes can also be added by selecting notes from a notation template and dragging them to desired locations.

Editing MIDI can also be accomplished by using a graphic editing system, which is unnatural from a musical perspective. The graph has lines that correspond to the notes on a keyboard. There is usually a picture of a miniature keyboard on the side of the graph, and when the mouse is used to depress the lines, the corresponding note on the keyboard is simultaneously depressed. Grabbing the graphic lines with a mouse and moving them to other parts of the graph is a simple way to edit; the duration of the notes can also be altered by shortening or elongating the graphic lines. Many synthesists use the graphic editing system.

Since almost all commercial-music composers and arrangers (programmers) use synthesizers and samplers, the producer must have a thorough understanding of the capabilities of MIDI and digital audio. Numerous manufacturers have developed not only synthesizers and samplers but also software and sample CDs containing sounds such as orchestral strings, world music instruments, sound effects, orchestral brass, and more. They can be loaded into the sequencer.

Plug-ins are digital effects used in music sequencing–audio programs. They replicate hardware effects such as compressor/limiters, reverberation, echo, mastering programs, and many additional processors. Producers should become familiar with available plug-ins.

The audience is accustomed to listening to electronic music and, accordingly, accepts the sounds as a part of the modern musical litany. When producers guide arrangers and/or synthesizer programmers, they will probably discuss the desired effects they would like to incorporate in a final mix. The use of plug-ins influences the manner in which an arrangement is written.

Conclusion

It is advisable for producers to study arranging and orchestration and to also analyze scores. Listen to a variety of orchestral and synthesized music. Understanding the principles of arranging greatly enhances a producer's ability to "shape" music. Experimenting with sampled orchestral sounds as well as synthesized sounds can also help producers understand musical sonorities and musical concepts that can be directly applied to productions.

Assignment

Choose three popular songs and write a paper describing some of the concepts discussed in this chapter. Submit a recording of each song. For example, a track might include numerous plug-ins, reverb, delay, and so forth. At least one track should be an orchestral track. Site examples of various bowing techniques.

6

Approaching an Arrangement and Orchestration

Step by Step

The intention of this chapter is to offer suggestions on how to approach arranging and orchestration, primarily from a producer's perspective. Understanding the process is necessary for producing music.

Arranging *is* composition. Compositions must have form, and arrangements must also have form. When beginning the process of arranging a song (instrumental), the song format has already been established, but the form of the arrangement has not been created. The same principles that apply to composition apply to arranging.

The following is a list of tools arrangers use to help keep an arrangement interesting:

- **Variation:** Without variety, an arrangement will become boring. For instance, in a song structure, the first verse and the second verse should differ. If the second verse is exactly the same as the first, there will be no "surprises" for the listener. That is not meant to suggest that the second verse has to be drastically different than the first. The first verse might have only the rhythm section playing behind a lead vocal, and during the second verse a high string line is added to the same rhythm-section arrangement. Simple additions add variety. An example of an extreme change would be to begin the third verse with only an acoustic guitar playing behind the vocal and then build the arrangement in small increments: The bass enters, followed by the drums, followed by the strings, and so forth.
- Variation can be accomplished in multiple ways. If a basic instrument such as a kick drum is eliminated for several beats, there will

be a noticeable difference in the sonority of the arrangement. If the kick drum reenters, there will be a decisive difference in the feel of the track. When problems occur, which includes "writer's block," experimentation triggers the best solutions.

- **Harmony:** The basic harmony of a composition is indicated on a lead sheet (a melody line with chords). Most skilled arrangers use the basic harmonies, but test various substitution chords, which can add more interest to the harmonic landscape. Since harmonic change can dramatically alter a composition, an arranger should discuss the planned substitutions with the producer, artist, and possibly the songwriter. Not all harmonic substitutions radically change the basic harmony. Subtle changes can add enough variety to keep the arrangement interesting.
- **Modulation:** One of the most effective harmonic changes is to modulate from one key to another within a song. For instance, the arranger might suggest that the last chorus modulate up a half step. The change of key will instantly gain the audience's attention. Modulating can be effective if used in moderation. An arranger should not modulate without permission from the artist and the producer.
- **Instrumentation:** The selection of instrumentation is vital to the creation of an overall soundscape. If an arrangement is designed to enhance the basic sound of an established band (e.g., Linkin Park), then the choices are, obviously, less. A typical arranging assignment might be to write a string or horn arrangement, which will enhance a group's rhythm track. If an arranger is creating a complete arrangement, the producer and the artist must convey the desired emotional impact—what the arrangement should "say" to the listener.
- If the assignment is to write an orchestral arrangement, the arranger must consider the budget before choosing the instrumentation. If the budget is too small to hire enough musicians to accomplish the preferred sound, most arrangers add synthesized parts or sampled sounds of real instruments to enhance the arrangement. If an arrangement is orchestrated properly, it is difficult to notice that synthesized parts or sampled instruments have been added to the live instrumentation.
- **Orchestration:** Orchestration is assigning notes to individual instruments. In most forms of popular music, the arranger also orchestrates. In some instances, the arranger's duties are split between arranging and orchestrating. Some rock bands (e.g., The Moody Blues and The Who) have performed with symphony orchestras. The band's basic arrangements are orchestrated, and the arrangements are also augmented. An arranger/orchestrator will most likely hear a demo of a song. Ideally, the demo will have the basic feel the artist and the producer are envisioning for the final

arrangement. The arranger will then discuss an orchestration concept with the artist and the producer. For example, the arranger might suggest using, in addition to the basic rhythm section, a full string section, three trumpets, two trombones, three woodwinds, orchestral percussion, a tuba, three French horns, and synthesizer parts. If the instruments are enhancing a band's basic arrangements, the arranger/orchestrator will most likely describe specific orchestration ideas. For instance, an oboe and a flute will play in unison with a lead guitar line, or the strings will double a specific keyboard part. The orchestration will most likely contain live instruments plus synthesizers and samplers. Most orchestrators working in popular music are familiar with the use of electronic instruments in a primarily live orchestral setting.

> ♫ It is important to note that synthesizers and samplers are not necessarily used in large orchestrations to fill in parts because of budgetary restrictions. Many arrangers and orchestrators use these instruments to create sounds that can be created only on electronic instruments—often the best use of synthesizers and samplers. Film scores and Broadway shows use orchestrators because the composer usually does not have the time to orchestrate.

- **Rhythm:** Popular-music arrangers must be adept at writing rhythm-section arrangements. Certain styles of music (e.g., hip-hop) traditionally use synthesized rhythm sections (sometimes mixed with live musicians). Other styles of music, such as jazz and rock 'n' roll, traditionally use live musicians.
- **Repeated patterns and sequential patterns:** Commercial-music arrangers must be familiar with rhythm patterns, including steady kick drum patterns (rhythms), bass patterns, keyboard chord- and single-line patterns, and single-line guitar- and guitar chord patterns. Sequential rhythmic patterns have always been incorporated in all styles of music. They help to create continuity, and well-designed patterns also develop into hooks (catchy sections) within the arrangement.
- **Tempo:** To achieve the proper ambience of a song, a suitable tempo must be selected. Rehearse with the artist and experiment with tempos. The tempo has a direct effect on the sound of the arrangement.

> ♫ Arrangers who primarily arrange synthesized (sampled) tracks are usually referred to as programmers. Programmers must be aware of the most current sounds and rhythms used in cutting-edge popular music. Traditional music arrangers are usually more adept at orchestral writing than programmers.

- **Time signature:** In some styles of music, such as jazz, varying time signatures can be effective. Time-signature changes can make a dramatic difference in the flow of a song (instrumental). Therefore, unless time signature changes are endemic to a song, arrangers should not vary time signatures without first discussing the proposed changes with the artist and the producer.

♫ For the purpose of this exercise, the discussion will focus on how to approach a fully orchestrated arrangement that is specifically arranged for the recording studio. Arranging for a live performance often requires a different method.

There are numerous ways to approach an arrangement. The following process will provide a guide:

Step 1

Be familiar with the marketplace. Study the arrangements and orchestrations heard on successful albums that are similar in style to the music being produced.

- *What is the instrumentation? Make certain that it fits the style of music.* Instrumentation varies according to music style. A traditional orchestral arrangement suggests live musicians playing, primarily, acoustic instruments; hip-hop, pop, and contemporary R&B call for a mix of live musicians, samplers, and synthesizers; heavy metal is performed, mostly, by live musicians. These are generalizations. The arranger must choose the most suitable instrumentation for the style.
- Is the recording a mix of synthesizers, samples, and real instruments, or did the arranger only use real instruments?
- Do the arrangements sound dense or sparse?
- *Are background vocals included in the arrangement?* If background vocals are included, study the vocal arrangement. Are the background vocalists singing in harmony? Are the background vocalists singing countermelodies? Are the background vocalists doubling the lead vocal? Are the background vocals doubled or tripled?
- *Make certain that the arrangement is written in the most appropriate key for the vocalist.* A vocalist (or instrumentalist) can often sing a song in several keys. The artist, producer, and arranger should determine the final key. Leave room for improvisation; if the song is too high or too low, the singer's improvisational range will be limited.
- *Make certain that the tempo is appropriate.* One metronome marking in either direction can affect the mood of a song. An artist has to feel comfortable with the tempo or he or she will not find the "pocket" (the most comfortable rhythmic groove) of the song.

Vocals are an integral part of any vocal arrangement. When writing a song arrangement, at a minimum, the arranger should hear a demo of the vocals. Ideally, an arranger should have a copy of the lead and background vocals, which can be imported into a computer-music-sequencing program. That enables him or her to listen to the vocals while writing the arrangement.

Vocals sung without words, singing vowel sounds—called *vocalese*—is effective when used with orchestras. The technique is often used in film scores and sung by large choruses. Solo voice, also singing vocalese, can be very effective. In most popular music, background vocals incorporate both techniques. Background vocals are a fundamental ingredient of many arrangements. The arranger might also suggest adding additional vocal parts.

The arranger should be informed if the lead singer is going to sing harmonies with the prerecorded lead vocal. The additional harmony can affect contrapuntal parts within an arrangement as well as general orchestral harmony.

If possible, the arranger should have a version of all recorded vocals.

♫ The final movement in "The Planets" by Holst, contains a wordless women's choir. This is an example of vocalese.

Signal processing can affect an arranging concept. If vocals and instruments are going to be processed with delays, reverberation, echo, or additional processing, the studio arranger will write fewer notes within the arrangement so that the processing can be heard. For instance, if a lead vocal is processed with a long delay and feedback, the producer will want not want the delay to be masked; if a snare drum is processed with a tap echo—creating a rhythm pattern through the use of in-tempo timing delays—the producer will want the listeners to experience the effect. Signal processors should be considered "instruments."

- *What "sounds" are currently popular?* In hip-hop, R&B, and pop music, certain synthesized or sampled sounds (e.g., kick drums, snare drums, basses, and assorted effects) become popular for a short period of time. When producers and arrangers (programmers) notice that certain sounds are being overused, new ones become popular. This is an important consideration since most albums are not released immediately upon completion of a project. Consequently, the sounds used on cutting-edge productions could be outdated by the date of release.

- *What average tempos are currently popular?* Tempos become trends. For example, at the beginning of the disco era, the average dance tempo was 120 beats per minute. Contemporary dance (club) music has a variety of tempos that range between 130 BPM to 160 BPM, depending on the musical style. Hip-hop and R&B tempos are much slower. The producer and artist have to agree on tempos.
- *What instruments or vocals are featured in the mix?* That depends on the style of music. For instance, R&B and hip-hop records typically feature the kick drum and bass parts. Many productions feature a sub-bass and a sub-kick drum, as well as a traditional bass. Pay particular attention to the choice of sounds (samples) and rhythm patterns played by instruments or samples.

Rock recordings feature guitars, and the vocals are generally mixed lower than the vocals in hip-hop, R&B, and pop records.

If an arrangement is more traditional, such as the arrangements written for Andrea Bocelli or Harry Connick Jr., the rhythm section is not generally featured in the mix. The mixes are comparable to mixes heard on classical recordings.

This is not to imply that all mixes should be clones of other mixes. It is difficult to be completely innovative, so the ideal approach is to attempt to forecast the future—easier said than done. Experiment; try innovative approaches. Some ideas will work, and others will not, but one unique arranging and mixing idea can help make a recording creatively and commercially successful.

> ♫ This discussion encompasses a variety of styles; some arranging techniques, such as developing grooves, will not necessarily apply to all genres of music.

Step 2

Before beginning an arrangement (or guiding an arrangement) read the following:

- *Make certain that the artist and the producer have agreed on a song (instrumental) format.* Listen to a demo prior to writing the arrangement. If possible, the demo should be in the exact format that has been approved by the artist and the producer. If there is no demo, ask the artist to record a simple demo. It is important for the arranger to understand the artist and producer's artistic vision. Hearing the artist sing (or play) the song will trigger many arranging ideas.

- *If an arrangement is going to be synthesized, the choice of a synthesizer programmer is crucial to the success of the arrangement.*

Most programmers specialize in certain styles of music. They must have current sounds and samples and have the ability to achieve authenticity within a style.

Some traditional arrangers write out their arrangements on score paper and then work with a programmer. If the arranger is writing a part that is not supposed to sound like a traditional instrument (e.g., trumpet), specify the characteristics of the desired sound. For instance, the arranger might indicate that the sound should be percussive, filtered, and resonant, with an eighth-note delay or a smooth and rich "pad" (chords) that will flow throughout the track and blend with strings.

♫ Most synthesizer programmers are also arrangers. They own a computer-music-sequencing program and an array of synthesizers, samplers (software and hardware), and signal processors. Arrangers who are not programmers hire programmers to program their arrangements. This is common practice in film scoring.

♫ Listen to demo reels before hiring a programmer.

- *When arranging for synthesizers, the arranger should be familiar with the sounds he or she wants to use.* If the arranger is synthesizing the sounds of a real orchestra, the choice of samples is vital to the final sound of the track. There are literally thousands of samples available to purchase, and the arranger (and programmer) should listen to demonstration CDs offered by manufacturers. Many of the manufacturers' Web sites contain listening samples.

A synthesizer generally offers sounds that are unique to that particular instrument. (Many manufacturers produce traditional sounds—analog pads, kick drums, cymbals, and so forth.) Individual sounds become trends, and the sounds included in certain synthesizers (samplers) also become trends. With cutting-edge music produced to appeal to the contemporary youth market, certain synthesizers become overused; the audience begins to hear the same electronic sounds on numerous recordings, and the producer must be aware of and try to avoid this trap. Become familiar with the new synthesizers that are released every year. Ask colleagues what is going to be hot. (Many programmers primarily use software synthesizers and samplers.)

The use of vintage synthesizers has remained popular for many years, and they are still sonically effective. Because a synthesizer is not the "flavor of the month" does not mean it should not be used.

Step 3

The Rhythm Section

This section discusses one approach that is useful when writing an arrangement grounded by the rhythm section. It is advisable to work on a sequencer so that melodic, harmonic, and rhythmic ideas are recorded.

A producer who is not a musician should hire a keyboard player to perform the parts.

- *Setting the groove establishes the feel of a rhythm-oriented arrangement.* Create a drum and/or percussion loop (a repeated section) that can serve as an anchor for the rest of the arrangement. This can be a 2- or 4-bar loop.
- Not all grooves are created by drum or percussion patterns. For example, ostinatos programmed on synthesizers create grooves; catchy background vocal phrasing also creates grooves.
- *If a loop feels appropriate, start to play (and record) either a keyboard or a guitar part along with the loop.* It is best to keep looping (repeating) one section of the song to gain the benefit of this technique. When working on most popular songs, it is often wise to first begin work on the chorus because the chorus is the section that appeals to the audience. The following are some suggestions: *Compose keyboard or guitar riffs (short repeated sections) that will become instrumental hooks within the arrangement.* This can be accomplished by using chord patterns or single-line patterns. Sequential patterns *are* hooks. Sing the melody (internally or physically) when arranging patterns. Some riffs fit the groove, but when heard with the melody the riff might sound busy or not match the arrangement.
- *Instrumental or rhythmic hooks do not work on all songs or within all arrangements.* Even if repetitive patterns are not appropriate for a song, the keyboard, bass, and drum parts must still have form. That can be accomplished by developing a pattern that continues throughout the verse. Let us assume that the kick-drum rhythm is a quarter note followed by an eighth-note rest, followed by 2 quarter notes. The rhythm will anchor the drum part throughout the verse. The bass may also play the same rhythm pattern, but by adding "tasty" fills the part will not sound too "stiff" (rigid). The snare drum might play a quarter note on the second and fourth beats, and the hi-hat might play eighth notes. Although this example

> ♫ It is helpful to record a pilot vocal into an audio-sequencing program. Hearing the vocal makes it easier to program an arrangement.

is simple, it shows the importance of repetition within an arrangement, as long as it does not become monotonous. Adding fills and other forms of ear candy helps keep repetitive patterns interesting.

Step 4

String, Woodwind, and Brass Parts

Once the rhythm section has been arranged, begin arranging the string, woodwind, and brass parts. Since recording budgets do not always allow the arranger to hire a full complement of musicians, the arranger will most likely enhance the live musicians by writing synthesized and sampled parts. The arranger will have to program, play, and record the parts into a music-sequencing program.

The parts should be played in the generic style of the real instrument. That task will be relatively easy for an arranger who arranges for live musicians and knows the capabilities of professional musicians. Understanding bowing techniques used by string players and methods used by horn players to attack notes and breathe properly, writing parts within the tessitura of the individual instruments, and composing passages suited to the instruments are all necessary for an arrangement to sound exceptional.

When arranging for the studio, it is not unusual to wait until after the final vocals and rhythm tracks have been recorded to write string, woodwind, and brass parts. That enables the artist and producer to have creative freedom and to experiment when recording the basic tracks. If the entire arrangement is complete—depending on the style of music—prior to recording the vocals, the artist might feel too restricted.

It is wise for arrangers to own a sequencing program, a sampler, and orchestral samples so they can hear the arrangement before hiring musicians. That not only helps the arranger but also enables the artist and producer to preview the sound of the arrangement and make revisions. It can also be a catch-22! If the samples are of poor quality, the arrangement might not sound good, and the arranger must convince the producer and artist that with real musicians the arrangement will sound superb.

- *Sequence the arrangement prior to recording, even if live musicians will perform on the final recording.* Hearing the synthesized and sampled parts makes it easier to write string and horn parts or any additional parts. The arranger must be concerned that the writing is generic to the style of music. Generally in popular music, the string and horn parts are not complicated, and they complement the rhythm arrangements.

- That is not to imply that the writing should be trite and uninteresting. In traditional arrangements the approach is more orchestral, as in the arrangements on a Charlotte Church or Josh Groban album. A traditional orchestral arrangement sounds much better with live musicians than on synthesizers and samplers, especially if the arrangement is not rhythm section–oriented but relies on the sound of the orchestra.
- *The budget dictates the number of hirable live string players.* For a string section to sound rich and full in the studio, it is best to use approximately 16 violins, 4 to 8 violas, 2 to 4 cellos, and 1 or 2 double basses. Most budgets do not allow for a full section. The missing parts can be played with samples.
- Use of string samples will directly affect the types of bowings that can be used. Sophisticated string samples offer a programmer a variety of bowings for each stringed instrument. A problem occurs when trying to play certain bowings on a keyboard. The keyboard and the samples do not necessarily sound like real musicians. Arco, legato, marcato, and pizzicato passages sound real when mixed with real strings. Therefore, in that scenario it is wise to program the parts into a sequencing program and overdub the real strings while the musicians listen to the sampled strings. If the producer and the arranger are careful to match the live performance to the prerecorded samples, the results will be gratifying.

> ♫ It is wise to solo the sampled and real strings while both recording and listening back. That gives the producer and the arranger the ability to fix all mistakes while the musicians are in the studio.

- *The budget dictates the number of hirable live brass and woodwind players.* If the arrangement requires a small traditional horn section (such as 2 trumpets, 1 tenor saxophone, and 1 trombone) the budget will most likely be large enough to absorb the expense. If the budget is small and allows for only 1 or 2 musicians, program the horn parts using samples, and then add the live horns. As with strings, horn samples offer the programmer a variety of dynamic markings, a selection of mutes, and other variations and effects. Some sound real, and others sound thin and obviously not real.
- *If using a combination of traditional orchestral woodwind and brass instruments and samples, choose the best samples available. Record the samples first, and then record the live musicians while they listen to the prerecorded tracks.* Fortunately, there are many well-sampled traditional orches-

tral woodwind and brass samples. Oboes, English horns, flutes, clarinets, French horns, and tubas can sound remarkably real if programmed properly.

- *There are many well-sampled traditional orchestral percussion instruments.* If the arranger is writing an arrangement for a full orchestra and the budget does not allow for all live musicians, using samples in place of orchestral percussion will generally sound real if realistic samples are selected. Timpani, cymbals, snare drums, world percussion, and Latin percussion are all represented with fine samples.

Step 5

Recording additional overdubs. Step 5 could easily be step 4. Recording additional overdubs (additional parts) can take place before recording strings, woodwinds, and brass.

Overdubs generally include additional guitar, percussion, keyboard, solos (e.g., saxophone, guitar), vocals, or other parts that will enhance the final track. Overdubs do not necessarily have to be recorded during any particular segment of the production process. Most producers record additional parts, as they are needed. For instance, if the basic rhythm section sounds incomplete, the producer and arranger might suggest recording a conga part and an additional guitar part. Quite often a keyboard player is brought in for experimentation purposes. In fact, it is wise to experiment because the process usually produces usable parts.

General Information

Hire the most qualified musicians for a project. A competent music contractor hires musicians who are proficient in the style of music being recorded. Being versatile is necessary when performing film scores and commercials. Some generic musical genres do not necessarily need musicians who specialize. Some studio musicians become known for specializing in one or two musical genres—rock guitar players, R&B guitar players, Latin percussion players, Indian percussion players, and so forth.

Brass and woodwind players also specialize in certain styles, such as jazz or classical. Most musicians who play classical music usually play too "stiff" (rigidly) to perform on popular music recordings. All forms of popular music require musicians to feel the groove and to play in the pocket (playing within the feel of the rhythm section). Studio string players can play in any style because the parts are written and the playing style is basically the same for most musical styles. An experienced conductor can guide string players to play with any feel.

Instrumental Combinations for the Recording Studio

The following paragraphs, which are dedicated to instrumental combinations for the recording studio, are taken from my book *Writing Music for Television and Radio Commercials (and more)* (Scarecrow Press 2008).

String Combinations for the Studio

Since it is unusual to receive a budget large enough to hire a full string section for most commercial projects, the arranger must have options. The choice of instruments usually depends on the demands of the arrangement. Below are some suggestions:

- *6 first violins, 5 second violins, 4 violas, 2 cellos, and 1 double bass (if needed.)* This is a large section for most records. Most of the time, the budget does not allow for so large a section.
- *8 violins, 2 violas, and 2 cellos will sound good in the studio as long as the violins are not written too high.* Experimentation and experience help the arranger learn which studio combinations sound best for certain types of arrangements.
- *Some arrangers only use violins, violas, or cellos.* In the heyday of disco, almost all of the records had live violin parts. Many arrangers would use only 6 or 8 live violins augmented by synthesizers.

> ♫ There are several nontraditional uses of strings. The fiddle (violin) has been a mainstay of country and Irish music for many years. The style is very specialized. Many of the players cannot read music. In this case, the producer guides them. The solo violin has also been popular as a jazz solo instrument. The solo cello is used in rock 'n' roll bands as well as with pop and folk artists. The arranger should be aware of the various styles and techniques and learn how to write in these styles.

Brass Combinations for the Studio

Budget is a consideration in choosing the right instrumental combination. With a modest budget, 2 trumpets, 1 tenor trombone, and a bass trombone will sound full if scored properly. If the assignment requires a small orchestra, try to budget for one or two French horns. No other instrument can produce its sound.

The tuba is usually the last to be added. Most of the time a tuba player is hired because the arrangement specifically needs that sound, as in Dixieland. A tuba cannot replace the job of a double bass in a typical orchestra setting.

Woodwind Combinations for the Studio

Many woodwind combinations work well. The following are some suggestions:

- Flutes and clarinets playing in octaves
- Clarinet, oboe, and C flute playing in unison
- C flute and oboe in unison and/or playing harmony
- Flute, oboe, clarinet, and bassoon or bass clarinet playing in harmony
- Oboe and clarinet in octaves
- Clarinet with bass clarinet or bassoon playing one octave below
- 2 flutes playing in harmony
- 2 oboes playing in harmony
- 2 bassoons and 2 clarinets playing in harmony
- Flute playing the highest octave, oboe playing one octave below, and a clarinet one octave below the oboe

Almost any combination will sound good. Many of these instruments blend well with other sections of the orchestra. For example:

- Flutes with violins
- Bassoons with cellos
- Bassoons and bass clarinet with bass trombone and tuba
- Clarinets are compatible with almost any instrument.
- Muted trumpets and flutes

Saxophone Combinations for the Studio

If there is a limited budget, 1 alto and 2 tenors or 2 altos and 1 tenor will have a good blend. Generally, a baritone will be the last saxophone to be added unless that particular sound is generic to the style of arrangement, such as with '50s rock 'n' roll. Saxophones are pliable instruments and work with almost any orchestral or band combination.

General Combinations for the Studio

Some budgets only allow for a small horn section. The following are some examples of sections that blend well.

- 2 trumpets, 1 tenor sax, and 1 baritone sax
- 1 trumpet, 1 tenor playing in octaves or in unison
- 2 trumpets and 2 trombones
- 1 trumpet, 1 alto sax, and 1 tenor sax
- 3 trumpets, 1 tenor sax, and 1 tenor trombone

If a part is well written, various combinations will sound good.

Conclusion

All producers should listen to—and study—arrangements and orchestrations of all musical styles. Following the scores and listening to the music of the great composers, arrangers, and orchestrators, in all musical genres, is the preeminent learning tool. Some of the premier jazz and popular-music arrangers have written arranging books, including Nelson Riddle and Don Sebesky. Many traditional orchestration and arranging books are also worthy of study.

♫ Students should attempt to hear their work performed by live musicians. If that is not possible, they should use synthesizers and samplers.

A producer must be concerned that an arrangement is not over-arranged. Arrangements that are cluttered destroy the feeling of a song. Arrangements should breathe, so the listener can hear all of the parts. In rhythm-oriented arrangements, *nothing* should mask the rhythm.

Assignment

Choose a song or instrumental.

- Write and program (in a music-sequencing program) a rhythm-section arrangement.
- Add string parts.
- Add brass and woodwind parts.
- Add additional overdubs, such as percussion, guitar, and keyboard parts.
- Balance the parts and mix and burn a CD for review.

7

Coaching Singers and Musicians

The thing that influenced me most was the way Tommy played his trombone. It was my idea to make my voice work in the same way as a trombone or violin—not sounding like them, but "playing" the voice like those instrumentalists.

—Frank Sinatra

Coaching Singers

Music producers have to be amateur psychologists. Coaching singers can be a difficult task. Most singers have inflated egos and do not want to be corrected or coached, but with mutual respect between singers and producers, the coaching process becomes easier.

A producer and a singer generally have the same creative goals for a song, and most experienced singers welcome a producer's suggestions. It is rare that a producer and an artist disagree when a quality performance has been achieved.

In popular music, the most important goal of a producer is to capture the essence of a song. Technical mistakes have to be corrected, but some producers push a vocalist to achieve technical perfection while ignoring the emotional impact of a performance. That is a formidable task, and producers should attempt to capture both creative goals.

Music producers are not singing teachers. Singing teachers work with vocal exercises, interpretation, and vocal health; producers help singers interpret songs in the recording studio. Naturally, they also want the performer to achieve technical excellence. A recording is a permanent record of a performance and it is a producer's responsibility to coax the performance from the artist.

> ♫ It is wise for singers to attend ongoing coaching lessons for vocal-health reasons. Professional singers can easily damage their vocal chords if they are not properly trained. Vocal training is analogous to athletic training. Without training, performers cannot be in shape.

Lead Singers

The vocal and tone quality of a lead singer should be considered when selecting songs. This is easily discernible by hearing the singer sing a song. The singer will tell the producer if a song feels comfortable, but the producer must also decide if a song fits the singer. If there is a conflict of opinions, it is best to record a simple demo and then make a decision.

When the artist is also a songwriter, this problem is usually not an issue. If a group has multiple lead singers, the singers usually decide which singer or singers will sing or share the lead vocal. If the group is undecided, the producer usually suggests who should sing the lead vocal.

The key is crucial to the final success of the production. In popular music, singers must have enough room to improvise. If a key is too high or too low, the ability to improvise will be limited; if a key is too low, the song will sound dark and lifeless, and if a key is too high, the vocal will sound too strained and unnatural. One half step raised or lowered can affect the outcome of a performance. A singer will often be able to determine the most comfortable key. Recording a simple demo in several keys can sometimes be the best method of choosing the proper key. A singer might consider several keys vocally comfortable, but one key will generally sound best overall.

Coaching begins in rehearsals. Once songs have been selected and the arrangements have been solidified, it is time to schedule vocal rehearsals. Since most singers are involved in the song-selection process, the producer knows that the singer can identify with the message of the song or the song would not have been selected. During the rehearsal process, the singer's interpretation of the lyric and the vocal performance are the primary concerns of the producer. Singers will most likely achieve the best performance if they memorize the lyrics. It allows them to concentrate on the performance.

It is important not to overrehearse. Overrehearsing can take the freshness out of the final recorded performance and also strain the singer's voice. Look for spontaneity in a performance. It is the unexpected that brings excitement. Record all performances, including the warm-ups. A surprise can occur at any time, and if the record button is not on, it is too late to capture the moment.

If a singer recites a lyric in a conversational manner, the meaning of the lyric should become immediately clear. Lyrics are meant to communicate a message, and a producer's goal is to help a vocalist interpret the message. Directors direct actors, and music producers direct singers. A lyric can be sung in numerous ways just as an actor can interpret a speaking line in various ways. A singer has the advantage of a singing voice, which aids in the interpretation. The use of a melisma, a change in tone quality, breathing methods, and a variation of the dynamics all affect a vocal performance. If a vocal performance is conversational, the listeners will generally become more involved in the performance.

A producer might suggest that a singer listen to Broadway cast albums, not because actor-singers are necessarily fine singers, but because they are trained to further the story of the show with song. Broadway songs are direct extensions of the dialogue, and an actor goes from a speaking line directly into singing a song, which is merely an extension of what the actor has been saying. This is not to suggest that a popular singer use the same singing techniques that are used in musical theater, which often can be overly theatrical. What can be learned is *how* to interpret a lyric.

Producers must be concerned that singers do not abuse their vocal chords. Some singers have extraordinary technique and tend to engage in vocal acrobatics. The technique is often heard in R&B music. Most R&B vocalists have roots in church music, where expressive singing is part of the curriculum. Singers must be concerned with vocal health. Serious physical problems can occur if vocal chords are abused. It is wise for singers to study with teachers who assign vocal exercises, which help to keep the voices healthy.

Vocal acrobatics must be limited, or the listener will not bond with the melody because it can be covered by the excessive use of improvisation. Vocal acrobatics are overused in all styles of popular music and producers must carefully guide singers to apply this technique only when it is most appropriate.

A producer can coach a singer in the studio, and the singer will accomplish a well-crafted performance. That is done in several ways:

- *Record multiple versions of a song.* Surprisingly, the first performance often becomes the final version. When singers are warming up, they are frequently relaxed and not aware that the performance is being recorded. That is one more reason to always record the warm-up.
- *After recording multiple performances, if one overall version is excellent but can be improved, "punch-in" the lines that need improvement.* The producer instructs the engineer to hit the record button in certain sections. The singer should sing along with his or her recorded vocal prior to the punch-in so that the flow of the vocal continues after it. The producer must also tell the engineer where to punch-out so that the remainder of the performance in not erased.

- *Create a composite vocal.* Some producers select the best lines from various vocal performances and create a final *composite vocal track.* If the performances were recorded on different days, the tone quality, volume levels, and energy of the performance must be adjusted to match. This can be accomplished in a couple of ways: Adjust the levels when automating the tracks during the mixing process or normalize the waveforms. Normalizing (which may have other names) increases the volume levels to peak levels without causing distortion. Normalizing is an automatic process that can be selected in most digital-sequencing programs. The engineer may still have to adjust levels during the mix. Not all engineers or programmers normalize.

> ♫ One advantage of using a digital-sequencing program is that all performances are kept unless the programmer erases the parent, also referred to as the original, file. Even if the engineer erases part of the vocal because of a misguided punch-out, the remainder of the performance can easily be restored.

- *Ask the lead singer to double the entire vocal or sections of the vocal, or add harmonies.* Since the goal is to record the best possible performance, it is important to understand that certain production techniques can enhance a performance. Doubling a lead vocal can create the feeling of a more powerful performance. It is rare to double the entire lead vocal, but selective doubling will emphasize certain lyrics.

> ♫ In rare instances, vocals of the same song are created in different studios. Make certain that the same microphones are used. If the performances are recorded with different microphones and the overall sound of the vocals varies, it is possible for an engineer to equalize the performances and adjust the volume levels so that the vocals sound as if they were recorded during one performance. This is a difficult task, but it can be accomplished.

The following are ways to double the lead vocal:

- Ask the singer the desired earphone balance between the recorded vocal and the live doubling vocal being recorded. Some singers do not want to hear the live vocal and others want to hear an equal balance of either vocals or a variation thereof.
- The producer should solo both vocal tracks to make certain that the phrasing and the intonation match. Some producers solo the vocals while the singer is recording the double or solo the vocals after the doubled performance is complete. It is most important that the doubled vocal has the same feeling as the

original vocal. If the intonation on certain lines does not exactly match the original vocal, it may not affect the mix. Vocals sound doubled because of a slight variation in the intonation, which adds depth to the final vocal sound. Make certain that the intonation does not vary excessively. Using the plug-in auto-tune, or a similar pitch-correction program, can repair certain intonation problems.

- When blending the doubled vocal into the final mix, consider lowering the level of the doubled vocal and making it a shadow of the lead vocal. If the double sits behind the lead vocal, it may not be noticeable unless the double is muted. The producer is trying to add depth to the vocal sound by using this technique.
- Adding signal processing to the doubled vocal can also be effective. Reverberation, echo, filtering, and delay are some of the effects that enhance the vocal sound.
- Doubling or tripling a lead vocal can also create "stiffness" to the performance. A vocal that is conversational and sometimes emotional will relate best to the listener. Any production techniques that detract from that bonding are detrimental to the overall production.
- It is rare to double a vocal that contains vocal acrobatics or that has a non-metered vocal interpretation. The vocals will tend to sound overproduced.

♫ Some producers add additional unison or octave parts. It depends on the desired effect, and the technique should be used selectively.

Background Singers

Producers hire the most appropriate background singers for a project. In major recording markets, background vocalists usually specialize in musical genres. Only hire singers who sing competently in a particular style. The singers' voices must blend with one another and have flawless intonation, interpretation, and phrasing. Background vocalists work as a group, and individual voices should not stand out. Some are not solo singers but blend well with other singers. Solo artists and producers treasure seasoned background vocalists. They are specialists and deserve more recognition than they are generally afforded. A producer who does not know whom to hire has several choices:

- *Hire a singing contractor.* Most singing contractors are professional singers and know how to mix and match background singers. Certain background singers tend to regularly work with particular singers because they have developed a blend. This saves rehearsal time in the recording studio and they achieve better results than a group of random singers trying to achieve a blend.

- *Use a large chorus who performs for film scores.* Many choruses perform as professional organizations, led by choral conductors. To achieve the proper sound, it is best to hire professional choruses because it will save time in the studio, and their voices will automatically blend with each other. Large choral parts are written for sopranos, altos, tenors, and bass/baritones. To achieve the best balance, each part should have an equal number of singers. It is wise to plan rehearsal time if the score is complicated. The producer should inform the contractor that all of the singers must be proficient in sight-reading, especially if rehearsal time is not possible.
- *Ask background singers for recommendations.* Most background singers readily recommend singing colleagues. They know singers who will blend well with the other singers and also use vibrato selectively. If one singer has a vibrato that does not blend with the other singers, the overall sound of the background vocals will be awkward; if singers do not feel the music in the same way, it will be impossible to attain an excellent performance. Personalities also play an important role. Not blending on a personal level can affect the final performance. If a problem occurs, the producer must change hats and become an amateur psychologist. Solving problems is part of the producer's responsibility.

Some instrumental arrangers also arrange the background vocals. Many background singers in popular music do not read music but learn the parts quickly. The arranger teaches the singers the arrangement during the recording session. If a score is complicated and the background singers are required to read music, the contractor should, obviously, hire singers who cannot only read music but also *perform* the parts with a minimum of rehearsal.

If the background arrangements are not written, the background singers, in tandem with the artist and producer, arrange the parts. This is the norm in popular music. Often the background vocal arrangement is part of the song, and the background part is written on the lead sheet or heard on the song demo. The background part is usually expanded during the recording session. It is wise to leave time for experimentation. Professional background singers bring innovative ideas to a session. In popular music, as in acting, the performers are innovators as well as interpreters.

Most popular music recordings use 3 or 4 background vocalists. The percentage of male to female singers depends on the song. The producer and the artist usually have a sonic concept for the sound of the background vocals. Smooth and silky or hard and funky, professional background singers will deliver the proper performance. Several methods are used to record background vocals:

- *Most background vocals are, at the least, doubled.* Doubling the vocals not only creates a rich sound but also offers the producer an opportunity to create an effective stereo image in the mix. (A surround sound mix leaves room for a more enhanced sonic image.)
- *When doubling, the singers will sometimes exchange parts.* For example, the lead background singer might sing the second harmony part on the overdub rather than doubling his or her original vocal; the second background singer might sing the third background part during the overdub, and so forth. This process creates a more interesting final blend than having each singer double his or her original part.
- *In addition to singing harmonies in the choruses, singing counter lines, with and without lyrics, creates new colors within an arrangement.* Not all singers necessarily sing in all sections of a song. They can be divided by gender or mixed in various combinations, which will achieve various sonorities.
- *Some producers record one part at a time, and each singer in the group sings the same part in unison.* Each harmony part is usually doubled or tripled. Recording with this method creates a distinct blend; singing group harmonies simultaneously also creates a unique blend. Both recording methods are acceptable.
- *Doubling instrumental parts with vocals can be very effective.* The technique is used frequently in film scores. For instance, the baritones might double a cello or viola part; the altos might double the second-violin part. The producer should feature the instrumental section (being doubled) in the headphone mix so that the singers can clearly hear the part they are doubling. Before concluding the recording session, solo the vocal and instrumental sections to make certain that the blend and the intonation is correct. It can be difficult to hear mistakes when listening to the full track.
- *After the initial background vocals have been recorded, an individual singer might add a very high or very low part.* This part is not usually doubled. A very high vocal line can add brightness to the overall sound, and a low part can add resonance to the low end.

Some instrumental arrangers do not complete arrangements until all of the vocals have been recorded. The vocal counter lines and harmonies are a part of the final arrangement, and arrangers prefer to surround the vocals with instrumental parts rather than expecting the vocal parts to accommodate the final instrumental track.

Additional Concerns

A producer must be concerned with the intonation of all vocal performances. Intonation problems occur when recording vocals. It is best for a producer not to stop the *take* (performance), or recording process, because of faulty intonation. Producers have the option to punch-in and ask the vocalist to re-sing a section. They may also choose to use a signal processing device that pitch-corrects (e.g., auto-tune), although it is preferable to correct intonation problems by rerecording the section that is problematic. (There are numerous plug-ins that can be used to correct intonations problems or create innovative effects.)

Select a suitable microphone(s). Some experienced singers prefer to use a specific microphone. It is best to select a series of microphones and listen to each before making a choice. The microphone(s) used on one song might change on the next.

♫ Microphone cost should not be an issue. Some of the least expensive microphones sound best for certain singers.

Miking techniques affect the sound of the vocalists. The following are some of the engineering techniques:

- *The figure-8 pattern.* A figure-8 enables the vocalists to stand on either side of a microphone, and the sides will not pick up any undesired sound. The producer and the engineer decide on the position of the singers around the microphone. The positioning depends on the desired sound. For instance, to hear room ambience, the singers are placed further back from the microphone(s) than if a closer, more intimate sound is desired. Assuming there are 2 male and 2 female singers, the 2 males might stand on one side of the microphone and the 2 females on the opposite side.
- *The XY pattern.* The XY pattern looks like 2 microphones creating an X, and the microphones are positioned in front of the singers. Placing the microphones in that position creates a stereo image. Most engineers record each microphone on a separate track.
- *MS (midside) miking, similar to XY miking.* One microphone has a cardioid (heart-shaped) pattern that is pointed on-axis; the other microphone has a figure-8 pattern and faces sideways picking up the ambient sound. The engineer can create various sounds by mixing the two microphones together.
- *Stereo microphones contain two diaphragms housed in the same case.* One diaphragm can generally rotate by 180 degrees.

♫ When the microphones are placed as close together as possible, they are called coincident microphones or a coincident pair. The engineer must be aware of any phase cancellation.

- *For large groups, the microphones are usually omnidirectional.* The microphone is opened all around, and the vocalists can stand in a circle.
- *Each singer might have a separate microphone.* This technique is normally used if the engineer is having a difficulty blending the sound. Each singer is recorded on a separate track, and the tracks are mixed together to create a blend. That is not usually the preferred miking technique when recording group singers. To create an appealing overall sound, professional background singers or professional choruses blend by adjusting tonal quality.
- *In addition to the techniques just mentioned, a way for a producer to create an ambient sound is to hang ambience microphones from the ceiling or place microphones on very high microphone stands.* During the mixing process, the ambient sounds are mixed with the direct sound.
- *Some background vocalists record ad-lib parts after the initial background parts have been recorded,* a common technique in R&B records. A producer might ask for ad-libs sung with words, or without words using vowel sounds. Most of the ad-lib tracks are not used, but a producer might select certain ad-libs to be used sparingly. (Sometimes, certain phrases are repeated throughout a song, creating a hook.)

♫ Background singers who sing additional solo parts receive additional compensation.

Musicians

Coaching musicians is analogous to coaching singers. Producers are more apt to experience ego problems coaching bands than when coaching hired studio musicians. Creating a relaxed and creative atmosphere in the studio relieves tension; tension establishes a negative creative environment. As mentioned, successful coaches are amateur psychologists.

A producer engages a musicians' contractor to hire large ensembles for recordings. Contractors know which musicians will collaborate well. The producer describes the desired sound and the contractor hires an appropriate orchestra or band.

♫ In states that require musician's union membership, a contractor must be hired if the ensemble exceeds a certain number of musicians. (Read the American Federation of Musicians agreement for detailed information.) Contractors are paid double scale.

Most producers who work with studio rhythm sections develop relationships with rhythm-section musicians. In major recording markets there is a large selection of musicians who perform in specific styles. In smaller markets it will be more difficult to find musicians who perform in esoteric styles. In this scenario, it might be necessary to seek out musicians in major music markets.

Technology has solved the potential problem of not finding the most appropriate musicians for a particular project, such as an Indian tabla player. Send a MIDI and/or audio file(s), in a specified format (e.g., Pro Tools or Logic Pro) to the musicians. The musicians record and send the MIDI and/or audio files back either by mail or over the Internet. The collaborators make comments and revisions can be instantly made. (One of the disadvantages with this system is that there is no interaction during the session.)

> ♫ If the file is being sent via the Internet, it must be sent on an FTP site, which can hold much more data and a better-quality digital file than regular e-mail. Professional-quality audio is too large to be attached to a regular e-mail account.

Producing studio musicians is analogous to producing studio singers. The producer has to "get" an acceptable performance. There are several methods used to record basic tracks:

- *If the basic track is synthesized, the synthesizers and sampled parts are recorded prior to overdubbing live musicians.* The producer approves the overall feel of the track before beginning the overdub process. The overdubs are usually recorded with one musician at a time unless instrumental sections perform the overdubs. This enables the producer to experiment and not feel pressured.

Overdubbing Guitar Parts

Guitar players usually record multiple parts. All parts are not necessarily used, but portions of the performances can be utilized. The following are examples of playing styles used in most popular-music recordings:

- *Rhythm-guitar parts.* The basic rhythm part is usually recorded first. The producer must be concerned that the feel of the part fits with the rest of the track. The best performances are usually achieved through experimentation. Once a performance is acceptable, the producer might choose to double the part. That enables the mixer to create a stereo image in the mix. Doubling is not always beneficial because the track might sound too cluttered and could mask other instrumental parts.
- *Single-line guitar parts.* Single-line hooks are effective. The parts are usually constructed by inventing sequential passages that will catch the listener's attention. For instance, guitar players use a muted sound for this style because it provides a hook that is not only me-

lodic but also percussive. The plucking sound usually blends with the drum and percussion patterns.

- *It is wise to record more guitar tracks than will actually be used in the final mix.* Recording three or four extra tracks enables the producer to choose patterns and hooks that can be placed in various sections of the track. For instance, a guitar pattern performed in the first chorus may be copied and pasted each time the chorus is performed. Sometimes the final track comprises a combination of all tracks. Experimentation is usually beneficial.

Overdubbing Bass Parts

- *If the producer plans to overdub a live bass player, it is helpful to record a synthesized bass when designing the basic track.* That helps the programmer get the feel and serves as a demo for the live player. The reason for hiring a live bass player is to obtain a "human" feel. Bass players, like guitar players, have individual styles, and each musician will bring something unique to a track. If the basic feel of the synthesized bass is appropriate, the producer will generally ask the live player to play a similar part, but with a looser approach. Bass players can use a thumb for a percussive effect, slide up and down the strings, bend strings, and adjust their sound, in addition to creating numerous intangible subtle effects that only a live musician can achieve.
- *A live bass is sometimes added in addition to a synthesized bass part.* Once again, a live player is added to play "licks," or fills that not only add a live feeling but also enhance the final track.
- *Studio bass players usually offer the producer a selection of basses to choose from.* There are many manufacturers of basses, just as there are numerous manufacturers of guitars. The various basses produce a variety of tonalities. If the producer is not familiar with the differences in sounds, it is best to ask the player to send a sample CD or MP3 or ask him or her to demonstrate the differences in sounds. Some bass players bring 2 or 3 instruments to the studio, offering the producer choices.

Overdubbing Percussion for Popular-Music Tracks

- *Overdubbing live percussion on a synthesized or sampled drum track can make the entire track sound live.* In general, adding live instruments to a track humanizes the sound, if that is the desired result (techno music is intrinsically robotic). Hire a percussionist who specializes in the style of music being recorded. Some percussionists specialize in Latin music, while others play R&B, rock, and so forth. It is advisable to record more overdubbing-percussion tracks than will actually be used. That affords the producer an opportunity to add additional parts during the mixing process.

- *Inform the percussionist which instruments to bring to the session.* Studio percussionists bring a large variety of instruments to sessions. If a specific instrument is required, the producer should inform the percussionist prior to the session. If the instrument is unusual, rent the instrument from an instrument rental service.

Instrument-rental services are located in all major recording markets.

Most percussionists want to record a solid, steady groove that mixes well with the rest of the rhythm track. It is usually the first part recorded. Instruments such as conga drums, bongos, tambourines, and shakers are traditionally used to accomplish that. Additional parts are then added. The producer should request fills and ear candy that can either be used or deleted after the track is completed. Unusual sounds—doctored with such signal processors as EQ, delays, etc.—make unique contributions to the final mix.

If extra percussion is planned, make certain the original trap-drum part leaves room for additional parts. It is best to advise the trap drummer or the drum programmer that percussion will be added; the objective of the trap drummer or drum programmer is to record a solid groove.

Overdubbing Keyboards

- *Keyboards can be programmed to accomplish almost any musical goals, ranging from string pads to the most complex rhythmic sonorities.* It is wise to book an extended session so that the programmer has enough time to edit and create the desired sounds. It is beneficial for the programmer to have a copy of the basic track prior to the session. That enables him or her to prepare sound patches or at least to know what is expected at the session. (The programmer will also know which synthesizers and samplers to bring.)
- *Because of budget restrictions on most recording sessions, synthesizers and samplers have become intrinsic parts of the recording process.* Electronic instruments can fill in missing parts. The producer must make certain that the proper sonorities are used and that they blend with both the real instruments and the other electronic sounds.
- *When recording contemporary popular music, the producer should be aware of the current sounds being used.* The production must not sound dated. Kick drums, basses, and percussion are most often the trendiest timbres. (This can be a double-edged sword: If an album is in production for a year or longer, those timbres might be replaced with the new flavors of the month by the time the album is released. This is not meant to discourage programmers

and producers from being creative, but a producer must be aware of the marketplace and cannot ignore what listeners are reacting to.)

> ♫ It is important to state that if a part would sound better played by a live musician, it is always preferable to hire the musician rather than play the part on a synthesizer or a sampler.

Overdubbing Strings

- *The producer should know the string sound that will match the track.* The selection and placement of microphones have a profound effect on the overall ambience that the string section will have when mixed with the final track. Strings can sound piercing or warm and mellow. Most producers opt for the strings to sound "real."
- *Excessive equalizing can create a harsh sonority; accordingly, it is critical to achieve a natural sound during the recording process.* Some engineers specialize in recording live instruments, and it is wise to hire an engineer who is experienced in recording strings.
- *Record the violins, violas, cellos, and basses onto separate tracks.* (If the section is large, the producer may suggest recording some of the individual sections, like violins, on stereo tracks.) In addition, request that ambience microphones be placed in the room so that the room sound is recorded. That offers the producer an opportunity to use as much or as little room ambience as needed in the final mix.
- *Prior to overdubbing strings, carefully scrutinize the entire track, searching for harmonic or rhythmic mistakes.* When overdubbing strings—either during the recording or before completing the strings session—solo each string part, solo the entire section, and also listen to the string parts soloed only with either a keyboard or another chord instrument. That is the only method of catching the subtlest mistakes. It is very difficult to hear certain mistakes when listening to the entire track.

> ♫ Most independent recording engineers travel with an array of microphones and racks of electronic equipment, such as compressor/limiters, preamps, and so forth. The equipment, plus musicality, contributes to the final sound of the recording. Listen to engineers' strings recordings. They have individual styles, and selecting the proper engineer is subjective.

> ♫ If the studio has a pleasing natural reverberation and echo, that sound is preferred to using a signal processor to create a room ambience.

> ♫ If the budget allows, double the strings playing the exact same parts. The overall sound will be richer.

Overdubbing Horns (Trumpets, Saxes, and Trombones)

- *Producing a horn section is analogous to producing background vocals or a string section.* The producer must be certain that the overall "feel" of the performance matches the ambience of the track. Each player can use many subtle techniques to create sounds. Brass and woodwind players can "scoop" a note up or down by manipulating their embouchures. Muted brass instruments create new sonorities; the choice of mute also alters the timbre of the instrument.

  We have discussed how important it is for background singers to blend with each other. The same principle applies to horn sections. Some horn sections have become famous, such as the Tower of Power or the Memphis Horns. Because they perform as a unit, they have created a unique sound. It is best to hire a horn contractor—usually one of the section members—to hire the additional horn players. That person knows who will blend well with the rest of the section.
- *Use the same process as for recording strings.* When recording popular music, doubling small horn sections creates a powerful sonority. Pay particular attention to possible intonation problems. Overblowing can affect intonation.

  If, for example, a section consists of 2 trumpets, 1 tenor saxophone, 1 tenor trombone, and 1 baritone saxophone, the producer might choose to record each instrument on separate tracks and later combine the tracks to create a stereo mix. Producers generally use this method so they have control of the blend during the mix. For instance, during the chorus sections, the baritone saxophone might sound better if the level is louder than in the verses.

Overdubbing Solos

- *Solos are generally overdubbed.* Working with soloists should be approached in the same manner as working with lead singers. A performance is the same, whether it is instrumental or vocal. Recording multiple solos helps the player feel relaxed and contributes to recording a better performance. It is most desirable to record a solo during one performance, but a final track can be edited together if there are multiple performances to choose from.

  The producer normally has a creative vision of what the solo should accomplish within the context of a song. With that in mind, the producer should hire a musician whose past work displays the ability to achieve the producer's creative goal (e.g., saxophonist Clarence Clemons, who played

> ♫ Once a solo has been chosen, consider overdubbing some harmonies and/or doubling certain sections of the solo.

in a rock 'n' roll style, or Kenny G, who plays in a smooth jazz style). Most accomplished musicians offer the producer a variety of performances, one of which will be used on the final track.

- *Choosing the most appropriate microphone(s) is an important consideration.* When recording singers, it is difficult to determine which microphone(s) will sound best without experimentation. The same is true of recording an instrumental soloist. Select a variety of microphones, and have the soloist record a small section of a solo. It is usually obvious which microphone sounds best. If several microphones sound good, record the solo simultaneously on a number of microphones, and make a choice during the mixing process.

Dan Warner Interview

Dan Warner is a studio guitarist who has played on recordings by Barbra Streisand, Timbaland, Celine Dion, Shakira, Cristina Aguilera, Pink, Madonna, Justin Timberlake, Barry Gibb, Alicia Keys, Kelly Clarkson, Enrique Iglesias, and many more. He is also a record producer.

MZ: What skills are necessary to become a studio musician?

DW: Reading music is helpful, having a great ear, being musically flexible . . . being able to adapt to any kind of track...find a spot were you can make the track better . . . knowledge of styles and past styles . . . find your space where you are going to be valuable and not get in the way [of the vocals]. Know what kinds of sounds work [for various styles] . . . for a guitar player, know what sound [choice of guitar and effects] works on a certain kind of track. Now [unlike the past], you also have to be an engineer. I'm [had to become] a great engineer when it comes to recording guitars. A lot of the young engineers [even in major studios] don't know how to record a drum set, much less even seen [drums] recorded . . . or guitar amps. Everything is either plug-ins or plug in directly [to the console or sequencing program]. [It is necessary to have technical skills.] Being a great player is not the most important thing. It's figuring out how you fit on a song.

MZ: What percentages of tracks are sent to you via the Internet so that you can record the guitar parts in your studio rather than going to a major studio?

DW: I rarely leave my studio. I don't leave my studio unless (I have to). About 60–70% of the tracks [I work on] are sent to me online. Many people, even those that live locally, upload files and never [come to the session]. . . . Frequently [I receive] an MP3 and a BPM [tempo marking], I play my part [with the proper quality such as 24/48 WAVE], and the producer [just] adds my tracks to the original session. The quality of their tracks doesn't matter for what I'm doing.

MZ: Do you normally send back several guitar tracks for the producer or artist to choose from?

DW: I do not. Maybe with guitar solos, I will give 2 or 3 options. I try to get as much information before I start. . . . I try to find the direction the producer or artist is going for . . . [do they have any] specific references [where they want a specific sound]. Sometimes I get very specific references and [often] no direction . . . sometimes [a client] will ask me to add an extra solo for a reintroduction or add something to a little part or something like that. I don't have a problem doing that . . . if there is something I can do kind of easily, I will do it. [He tells his clients to send the finished track before he plays on it. Otherwise, it is too time consuming.]

MZ: With the decline in music sales, have the record labels reduced their budgets, and if so, how does it affect you?

DW: I think it's affected everybody. I am fortunate enough to have a lot of work. Because the budgets have gotten smaller, I think the people are a lot more careful about whom they hire . . . and that's actually helped me. They don't have a lot of money or time so they want to make sure that it's as good as possible right off the bat. As a player, I've stayed static. In a lot of instances, I'm charging what I was charging 10 or 15 years ago to play on a song or an album. The difference is now I have a studio, I'm the engineer, I have a mortgage on the studio . . . so I'm making the same money, on average, per song as I may have made 10 years ago. I've managed to maintain some high-end clients where the money is great, which it should be but for [average work] the [clients] are just getting a lot for their money. It is [now] necessary to wear a lot more hats [being able to arrange, produce, engineer, edit, etc.]. We are maximizing our budgets even when they are not great.

MZ: How often do you receive music from producers?

DW: 10% (of the time). . . . I write a chart about 90% of the time. I literally write about 500 plus charts a year.

MZ: Have you been playing live?

DW: Very rarely. I would say between 5 and 10 (gigs) a year. Half of them are for charity.

MZ: How many guitars do you have in your studio?

DW: Somewhere around 25.

MZ: Out of the 25, how many do you actually use?

DW: (I use) about 12 to 14 that are in heavy rotation.

MZ: So, you can get any sound that a client requests?

DW: Yes. I only buy guitars that would make my job easier . . . sometimes the artist or producer says that, "They have never heard anything like that before." . . . they are getting something unique.

MZ: Do you have any final words of advice?

DW: Hard work. Nobody's going to make your bed. Learn how to be a professional. Know what to bring to a session . . . show up on time . . . one of the most important things is being a good guy. People want to be around people that they like.

Conclusion

A music producer is a coach. If a producer has a clear artistic vision, he or she will convey confidence to an artist; that is beneficial when coaching performances.

Prepare to experience problems with multiple egos and the subjective opinions of the performers. If an overall production concept is not solid, problems will arise, making it difficult for all artistic collaborators to be satisfied. Preproduction preparation and respectful personal relationships contribute to creating a successful project.

Coaching singers and musicians requires practice. The best training ground is producing demos, which affords a producer an opportunity to experiment and apply the studio techniques discussed in this chapter.

Assignment

Choose a song for the exercise. Design a full arrangement:

- Assume you will hire 4 background vocalists. Record and arrange a background vocal part. Experiment with the various recording techniques discussed in this chapter. In writing, explain the various techniques applied.
- Assume you will be working with a small horn section. (If you cannot use real horn players, use samples.) Record and arrange a horn-section part. Use the recording techniques discussed in this chapter. In writing, explain the various techniques applied.
- Assume you will be working with a small string section. (If you cannot use real string players, use samples.) Record and arrange a string-section part. Use the recording techniques discussed in this chapter. In writing, explain the various techniques used.

8

Mixing and Mastering

> You do not want to hear the following phrase: "We'll fix it in the mix!"
>
> Mastering is a process-Not a magic box of some sort. It doesn't come in a bottle or a set of plug-ins. If it did, everyone's recordings would sound the same.
>
> —John Scrip (mastering engineer)

Note: Audio engineering and the engineering terms used in this chapter are explained in the technology section.

Mixing

Mixing is the penultimate stage of the recording process. After all of the tracks have been recorded, the producer and the engineer begin the long and arduous process of creating the final sonic image—*the mix*. Just as a film director and editor sculpt the final film during the editing process, the music producer and audio engineer create the final album during the mixing process. Since the purpose of a mix is to create a sonic picture, it is suggested that student producers and engineers attend live concerts. Observe the stereo image heard during a live concert. Bands position themselves in a variety of ways, but an orchestral setup is mostly traditional. When producers and engineers are trying to recreate a live performance in the recording studio, attentive listening will help them develop a realistic sonic image.

What is the album going to "say" to the listener? That is the question that should be asked at the beginning of a production. *Did the producer and the artist remain true to the original creative and sonic concept?* A music producer's goal is to enhance an artist's creative vision and must be the primary objective of producers and engineers during the mixing process.

Each stage of the mixing process is essential to the final sonic picture. Is the album supposed to sound intimate (as if the artist is performing in a small club) or live (as if he or she is performing in a concert hall)? Is the album supposed to sound like a studio creation, with the help of technology for the purpose of creating an electronic soundscape? Can the sound of the final mix be reproduced during concert performances? That might be of concern to the artist. Each scenario must be taken into consideration before mixing.

Most of these considerations have been addressed for the prerecording stage, but the concepts must once again be discussed. *Mixing is the blending of technology and art, and art is ever changing.* Accidents constantly occur during the mixing process, and many of them remain on the album. *The actual creation of the album continues throughout the mix.*

It is relatively easy to physically describe the elements of a mix, but it is not easy to describe the *art* of the mix. Obviously, a producer's knowledge of recording technology, discussed in the next section of the book, must become second nature, just as music theory is second nature to musicians. A musician has to know how to play his or her instrument before being able to interpret music and create a performance. The manner in which a producer uses studio technology is a creative decision and a matter of taste. If a musician randomly plays myriad fast passages, the audience hears groups of fast notes with no structure. If the notes are carefully selected, however, the audience is rewarded with an interesting surprise when the passage occurs. The producer and the engineer have to make choices analogous to the example just cited. If the producer adds excessive reverberation and feedback to every part, the listener will experience nothing but a cloud of sound. The mix will have no definition. If the producer and engineer selectively add reverberation and feedback, the listener will experience a well-thought-out ambient effect. Painters choose colors and decide how to blend them; orchestrators color arrangements with instruments; producers must decide how to blend an infinite variety of signal processing to color the final sonic image.

The minutest change in any form of signal processing or level control shapes the entire mix. When does the producer complete the final mix? In my view, the answer is never! If that statement sounds ridiculous, ask most producers whether they are ever satisfied with their final mixes or, in general, with the creative content of an album. They will most likely respond by saying, "If I had only..." That is the nature of most artists and also the healthiest attitude an artist can have. Producers are artists, just as movie directors are artists. They must continually seek new ways to improve and create artistic visions. It is not creatively healthy to feel completely satisfied with anything that is artistic, and it is the excitement of the *process* that encourages an artist to create. There is a time when the artist, the producer, and the engineer must approve the final mixes and deliver the album to the record label for distribution. Creative people sometimes experience the equivalent of postpartum depression. The baby has been delivered and, along with a feeling of exhilaration, the creative team realizes that the process is complete and that it is time to move on to a new experience.

Before beginning the mixing process, listen carefully to each track, and eliminate any audio problems. Subtle distortion can be difficult to hear when listening to an entire track. If working in a digital-audio program (e.g., Pro Tools), listen to each track soloed, simultaneously viewing the waveform. If the sound is distorting, first see if the waveform is too "hot" (industry term for too loud). If the waveform is peaking, rerecord the track. An effects processor can cause a normal-looking waveform to distort. For instance, over-compressing a track will distort the sound; the same is true of using a *trim,* which increases the level of a track. Almost any effects processor, used in excess, can cause the audio signal to distort.

Unwanted material can be on tracks when the main audio signal is not playing. For example, the space between electric guitar parts can sound noisy. The noise can emanate from multiple sources: The amplifier might have a hum; string noise might be recorded while the guitarist is resting before making an entrance; quiet talking might be on the track. There are two ways of eliminating these and similar problems: Erase the unwanted noise, or use a noise gate on the guitar. (The function of a noise gate is described later in this chapter.)

The producers and engineers should scrutinize the tracks before beginning the mixing process. Preparation in the analog domain is similar. Solo each track and erase the unwanted material. That is sometimes not a suitable option because once a track has been erased on audiotape it cannot be recalled. There are two options:

- *Automate the track.* Automation enables the engineer to mute the unwanted portions of the track.
- *Make a safety copy of the tape before attempting to erase the unwanted material.*

Before mixing, the producer and the artist should make certain the performances and arrangements are acceptable. When listening back to a rough mix, the producer and the artist may decide to add, delete, or rerecord tracks. Try not to initiate the mixing process until all tracks are acceptable.

When working in the digital domain, which is the preferred format by most producers, the process of preparing for the mix is much simpler than working with audio tape. Digital editing allows recalling material that was eliminated, if the audio is properly saved; editing is also simpler than editing audiotape. Always backup your files at least 2 times. It is common to experience problems.

Engineers and producers have individual styles of working, but the common goal is to create a sonic image!

The following are the main elements of a mix:

- Balancing levels
- Equalization
- Panning (spatial relationships)
- Signal processing

Balancing Levels

Balancing the levels of the vocals, the instruments, and the effects processors is vital to the design of a mix. Most genres of popular music have distinct mixing styles. Producers are attuned to the marketplace and know the sound of the current musical trends in the genre of the music they are producing. That knowledge applies directly to the *balancing* process. For instance, in R&B music, the kick drum and the bass are important elements in most mixes. Therefore, the loudest instruments in the mix are the kick drum and the bass. Guitar is the most prominent instrument in rock 'n' roll mixes.

Producers and engineers try to be innovative when mixing, but competing in a contemporary marketplace requires the mixes to sound competitive. The audience might not accept anything that does not conform to the style of music currently being played on the radio. For example, most hip-hop records are mixed with loud bass and drum parts; if the producer did not create the typical hard-driving rhythm heard on most hip-hop records, it is possible that the listeners might not react to the record because hip-hop recordings are designed to be rhythmic. If the public accepts an inventive mixing approach, other producers and engineers might emulate the style of mixing, and a new trend could emerge.

Most music productions contain numerous tracks, and balancing them is a difficult task. That becomes a complicated subject because each new element that is introduced into the mix affects the *balance.* If a bass has a desirable sonic quality and three new instruments—in the middle and/or lower registers—are added to the mix, not only will the *balance* of the bass change, but the engineer will also most likely have to re-equalize, or change the sonic quality of the bass so it can be heard. That is but one example of complications that occur during the mixing process.

Most producers begin the mixing process by listening to the vocals and the basic rhythm section. That gives the producer a basic balance to build on. In most vocal mixes, the vocals are the most prominent element. The remaining tracks surround the lead vocal and most likely the background vocals as well. After achieving an acceptable balance, most producers and engineers begin to process the tracks with EQ (equalization), level, reverberation, and additional signal processing for the vocals, kick drum, snare drum, hi-hat, tom-toms, percussion instruments, keyboards, guitars, and bass. It is the foundation of the recording. The producer hopes by the time this process has begun that he or she is already satisfied with the basic sounds of the individual instruments and the vocal tracks. If a producer is working with samples, any of the sounds can be changed quickly. When working with live musicians, it is vital that the producer communicate to the engineer the technical objective of the session. The engineer must plan how to capture the producer's sonic goal (most engineers have a sonic plan prior to the mixing session). Because it is costly to rerecord live musicians, problems should be repaired during the recording sessions, not during the mixing sessions.

Equalization (EQ)

Equalizing (EQ, or equalization) is usually the next step in the mixing process. EQ enables the producer and the engineer to boost or cut the frequencies of each audio track. Equalization can dramatically affect the sound of each instrument and vocal. The producer and engineer have to be careful not to either distort a sound or use excessive equalization on an audio signal. Excessive equalization can make a recording sound unrealistic, piercing, dark, lifeless, heavy, light, or basically any other negative adjective that can be applied to sound. Using equalization carefully can accomplish just the opposite. EQ can enhance certain audio frequencies that sound too dark and make them sound more pleasant; it can add clarity to a vocal or an instrument; applied to a completed mix, EQ can help achieve an overall well-balanced sonic image. Equalizing is probably the most effective form of signal processing because if the basic sound is not right, adding additional processing will not be as helpful to the final sound. Used properly, EQ is a *creative tool.*

It is the unwritten code of most audio engineers to record the most natural sound during a recording session and try not to rely on using EQ. Engineers would rather not use equalization to fix sonic problems, although it is rare when EQ is not used to some degree. Sometimes, it cannot be avoided. As instruments and effects are added, most sounds need some signal processing to help achieve a blend, but a producer always hopes for limited EQ.

In some instances, the drastic use of EQ is planned. For instance, there might be a section of the vocal where the singer is supposed to sound as if he or she is talking on a telephone. A drastic filtering process is used to achieve the sound. The kick drum might not sound "punchy" enough—even during the recording process—but the engineer knows that adding EQ to certain frequencies will accomplish the desired sound.

Most engineers who record live orchestras or bands use a minimum of equalization. It is achieved through the proper selection and placement of microphones, the acoustics of the studio, the selection of the recording console, and additional elements used in the recording process. Keep in mind that although we are talking about the individual components of the recording process—both technical and creative—they all blend together when the mixing process begins.

Engineers and producers think about the mix while they are recording. If any sound (e.g., synthesizer) or part (e.g., guitar, bass) is not meeting the standards of the producer or engineer during the recording session, an attempt to fix the problem is made during the mix. The one phrase that is *not* welcome is this: *"We'll fix it in the mix."* Certain problems *can* be fixed in the mix, but studio time should be devoted to recording the best possible performance—creatively and technically. Fixing it in the mix is a last resort.

Most engineers do not record using EQ, for once equalization has been added to the recorded signal, it cannot be deleted. Equalization, like additional signal processing, is generally added during the mix. Add signal processing during the recording only if the processing will not be available during the mix. That will not occur in professional recording studios, but many home-studio computers have limited memory and cannot process numerous signal processors simultaneously.

A variety of equalizers are discussed in the technology section of the book.

Panning

Panning is the process of creating spatial relationships. Decorators look at an empty space and decide where the furniture will look its best. If the job is to place furniture in a bedroom, the dresser will normally be against the wall with a painting or a mirror above it, a chair farther out and to the side. On the opposite side of the dresser might be the bed with paintings above it, a bookcase on one side wall, and a long table on the opposite wall. Each piece of furniture and decoration has a place in the overall decorative plan.

Decorators deal in spatial relationships, and music producers deal in sonic decoration. Placing each instrument and effect in the stereo image is called *panning*. Not only does panning an instrument to the left, center, or right (or in between) in the mix create a place for each vocal and instrument, but the level (volume) of the sound contributes to the overall effect experienced by the listener as well. The producer and engineer must *decorate* the empty sonic canvas.

Once again, we are dealing with the *art* of the mix. *Panning* is a creative function of the mixing process. A producer and engineer have many choices when deciding where to place certain instruments in the stereo image, and in most instances it is a matter of taste and not a question of right or wrong. It is helpful to think of the musical canvas as a clock. The producer and engineer can plan where to place each vocal, instrument, and effect within the sonic image, which can be thought of as a clock. For instance, the kick drum is placed at 12:00; the background vocals are spread from 11:45 to 12:15; the snare drum is placed at 11:55 and so forth. Once the assignments have been made, it is relatively easy to make slight changes without disrupting the entire mix. Panning a signal slightly left or right on the clock can make a dramatic difference in the sonic image. For instance, if the lead vocal is not placed at 12:00 but is placed at 12:10, the relationships within the entire sonic image will change. Just as level adjustments (volume) are a difficult task within the process, so is panning. Each time a new element is panned, the entire mix is affected. Experimentation is the only means of arriving at an acceptable sonic image.

One strategy is to think of the orchestra or band as being on a stage and to pan the instruments so that they resemble the positioning of a live performance (e.g., violins on the left at 11:45, cellos on the right at 12:15, trumpets coming from the right rear at 12:20). When dealing with electronic sounds, the producer and engineer have to invent an imaginary image of a live orchestra since the sounds do not really exist as instruments.

Certain practices are standard in specific musical genres. The following are standard:

- In rhythm-oriented tracks, the kick drum and the bass are usually panned to twelve o'clock.
- The snare drum might be slightly to the right of the kick at 12:05, with the hi-hat panned slightly to the left at 11:55, and so on.
- Percussion is usually spread throughout the sonic image. Bongos might be on the left at 11:50, the shaker might be at 12:00, and the claves at 11:45.
- If there are 2 guitars, they will usually be placed on opposite sides of the clock; 1 guitar might be at 1:45 and the other guitar at 12:15. The positioning of additional guitar parts is usually arrived at through experimentation.

- Do not spread the stereo image of keyboards to the extreme left and right; for example, the left side of the keyboard placed at 11:35 and the right side of the keyboard at 12:35. They will not sound realistic. As the panning is being adjusted, listen carefully to the stereo image until the spread sounds natural.
- Strings are normally spread in a realistic live performance image. Imagine viewing the stage from the audience's perspective: violins to left (11:50), violas slightly right of center (12:10), cellos to the right (12:15), and double basses on the far right (12:25).
- A small horn section, playing in harmony, should have a realistic stereo spread. If the section is playing mostly unison lines, the stereo image does not have to be as wide.
- When recording an orchestra, try to place the instruments in a realistic live-performance setting. Draw a diagram of the orchestral setup and sonically reproduce it. The producer and engineer should envision themselves in the audience, sitting directly behind the conductor. That will help determine the correct sonic image.

Signal Processing

Signal processing helps create an ambience for the overall sound. Most signal processing is accomplished in the digital domain and is referred to as *digital signal processing,* or *DSP*. Producers and engineers use hardware or software versions of either the same processors or processors that accomplish the same sonic goal. Some engineers use a combination of DSPs and *analog* processors. During analog processing the signal remains in the analog domain without being converted to the digital domain.

Many forms of processing can affect a chosen sound(s). It is the producer and engineer's mission to selectively choose from the tool chest of processors. *Signal processing* is complex, since each added processor can change the overall ambience of the track.

Working *in the box* (in the computer) has become the most widely used recording method. Most engineers either work exclusively in the computer or use a combination of a computer and a recording console. If the signal processing is accomplished in the computer, the signal processors are referred to as *plug-ins.* Plug-ins (used to enhance digital audio programs) are virtual signal processors and are made by a variety of third-party manufacturers. Most digital-sequencing programs provide the user with a basic set of plug-ins (e.g., reverbs, compressors). Buying plug-ins can be pricey, but not nearly as costly as purchasing hardware. The quality of virtual signal processors is equal to most hardware versions, and in general plug-ins are easier to edit. The processing is automated, which affords an engineer the unlimited ability to change the sound, and the edited sound will be perfectly reproduced by the computer. With hardware, once the settings have been chosen, the engineer has to physically change the settings in order to edit the sound. Most professional recording consoles have some built-in signal processing, but it is limited when compared to DSPs available for a computer. Plug-ins can be easily loaded into a computer and are available with one click of the mouse.

We have discussed achieving relative balances prior to incorporating signal processing. It is important to note that adding processing can affect the overall balance of the mix. As processors are added, balances have to be adjusted. Relative level balancing, equalization, and panning are continually adjusted throughout the mixing process: Mixing is making a sonic stew. You keep adding spices until the taste is acceptable, and processors are the producers' and engineers' spices. It takes years for a cook to become a chef; it takes years for a fledgling producer to become a *producer* and for an assistant engineer to become an *engineer.*

Producers and engineers have recipes for sound, and it takes years to develop individual mixing styles. Some engineers do not record tracks but mix only. Producers should carefully listen to their recordings before hiring them. Engineering styles vary, and so do their artistic abilities.

The basics of signal processing include equalization, reverberation, compression, limiting, and gating. They are the most frequently used signal processors. (It is advisable to study audio engineering as a separate subject.)

Reverberation. *Reverberation (reverb) creates a special ambience.* It is generally defined as the sound heard within 30-50-milliseconds after the direct sound has occurred. Without either natural reverberation or reverb created with a reverberation device, all recordings would sound dry and most likely lifeless. Reverberation communicates *space* to the listener. It is the most important factor in *psychoacoustics*. A large room, a concert hall, a small room, or variations thereof can be created with a twist of a dial. DSPs (plug-ins) are generally the most popular devices used to create reverberation. Various reverb settings can "transport" listeners to an environment. There is a large selection of hardware and software reverb devices. An engineer can edit a device's parameters to create both interesting and complex algorithms. Choosing standard or newly created reverberation algorithms is a creative decision. Because most mixes are composed of multiple tracks, the producer and the engineer mix and match various reverb settings. If not handled properly, that can create musical chaos. Too much reverb will wash out a track, causing no definition between instruments, and too little reverb can cause a track to sound dull and lifeless. Experimentation is the only method of arriving at the correct blend.

Echo. *Echo* is an extreme form of reverberation. After the direct sound hits, echo is the sound that occurs after at least a 30-50-millisecond delay. *Echo* is used to create a cavernous effect, such as the echo heard in the Grand Canyon.

Compressor. *In lay terms, a compressor (also referred to as a compressor/limiter) is used to lower a signal when it reaches a threshold, which is set by the engineer.* It enables the engineer to raise the overall level of the track without experiencing distortion. For instance, if the producer wants the bass and kick drum to be prominent in the mix, a compressor is used to reduce the dynamic range of the signal and enable it to be pushed to the limit.

Overloading a compressor can cause distortion. In popular music, vocals are often compressed, as are bass, guitar, and drum parts. Many producers and engineers compress an entire mix. It is risky if the music contains dynamics, such as pp, ff, crescendos, diminuendos, and the like. *Compression reduces the impact of dynamics.* For that reason it is rare to use compressors in classical music.

Limiter. *Limiting is an extreme form of compression.* It is normally used to avoid high peaks, which can cause distortion. Limiting should be used judicially and is often applied during the mastering process.

Noise Gate. *A noise gate is used to allow selected signals to pass through a threshold determined by the engineer.* For instance, *noise gates* are normally used on snare drums or guitar tracks. A properly set noise gate will attenuate the noise between audible information. Scenario: A guitar plays (records) for 4 bars, rests for 2 bars (e.g., unwanted guitar noise is heard during the 2 bar rest), and continues to play for another 4 bars. If the recorded signal is gated properly, the noise gate, eliminating the unwanted noise, will attenuate the 2 bar rest. Gating is also used to create interesting effects. Excessive gating will cause signals to be cut off.

Delay Units. *Most delay units are digital and, therefore, referred to as digital delay units.* Delays, which are calculated in milliseconds, are added to audio tracks to let a signal "trail off" over a selected time period. Delays help create an illusion of space. They are often used on vocals, snare drums, solo instruments, and so forth. A delay administered at the end of a phrase is referred to as a "tail" because the sound of the delay trails off to infinity. Slight delays used on certain instruments create a "live" sound similar to a slight echo in an auditorium.

Delay units afford a producer and an engineer the opportunity to choose a delay that is based on a musical duration. For example, an engineer can place an eighth-note delay on a snare drum. Listeners will hear a slight delay on the snare drum, but they will probably not realize that the delay is in perfect time with the remainder of the track. Creative uses of delays create complex rhythm patterns.

Chorusing. Adding a chorus (hardware or software processor) makes an instrument or instrumental section, or vocals sound doubled. *The device creates delays of the original signal, which are manipulated to slightly alter the frequencies. The resulting effect is a unique sound, which has been popular for many years.*

♫ *Flanging* was partially developed by John Lennon and used on The Beatles' albums.

Flanging. *Flanging* is the process of mixing 2 identical signals and adding a minimal delay to the original signal. *This creates a doubling effect without creating a need to rerecord the original track.*

Microphone Modeling. *Microphone modeling* is used to recreate the sound of a particular microphone, although that microphone was not used to record the original audio. For instance, the signal from a dynamic microphone could be modeled to sound like a ribbon microphone.

Auto-Tune. *Auto-tune helps pitch-correct a track.* For example, if a vocal performance has intonation problems, place the audio signal through *auto-tune* and (with the proper settings) the intonation will be corrected. (*Auto-tune* is very sensitive and must be carefully programmed, or the vocal will sound unnatural.) There are other pitch-correctors.

Monitoring

Make certain that the control room has a flat frequency response. (A flat frequency response is when none of the frequencies are enhanced or attenuated.) This helps assure the producer and the engineer that the music played on the control room monitors (speakers) will sound the same on consumer sound systems.

Many mixes are not recorded in professional studios. If recording and mixing in a home studio, the producer and the engineer must adapt to the sound of the room. The most efficient way to accomplish that is to listen to recordings that have been tested on a variety of speakers and compare the sound outside the studio to the sound in the studio. It is best to use recordings that have been produced by the producer. It is also advisable to listen to mixes on headphones because the sound of the room will not color the sound of the earphones. The producer and engineer must be familiar with the sound characteristics of the earphones, for all earphones differ.

After a mix has been completed, listen to the mix on various speakers—car radio, inexpensive portable CD player, iPod, midline home system, computer, and so forth. The mix should sound relatively the same on all systems, or there is a problem with the mix. If the producer and the engineer are not familiar with the mixing room, anticipate remixing tracks several times. It is difficult to become familiar with the sound of a room without experimentation.

The selection of studio monitors affects the mixing process. Many engineers bring signal-processing devices and personal speakers to the mix. If the producer or engineer does not bring monitors, become familiar with the studio speakers. All professional studios have *far-field monitors* and *near-field monitors. Far-field monitors* are large and mounted on the wall in front of the recording console. *Near-field monitors* are small speakers that are mounted on a shelf that usually sits directly in front of the engineer above the recording console. As the name implies, the speakers are close to the engineer. Near-field monitors are preferred when mixing most musical styles because they closely replicate home speakers. Far-field monitors are used primarily for mixing dance music, film music, or any music that will be played on large speaker systems. If the producer and the engineer prefer to mix and record on far-field monitors, it is advisable to also listen on near-field speakers. Large monitors generally enhance almost any recording, but when the mix is played on a home system, it might not sound the same.

With either monitoring system, the producer and the engineer should sit in the center of both speakers and listen at a medium to low volume level. Listening at excessive levels can contribute to hearing loss and hearing fatigue.

Surround Sound Mixing

Surround sound mixing, also called 5.1 surround sound, has been the standard in the film industry for many years. In recent years, record labels have been remixing popular surround-sound versions of popular archived recordings. Some new albums are being mixed in surround sound, but sales have not warranted a general attraction to the process. (More advanced surround sound formats exist but are rarely used.)

Surround sound comprises five speaker outputs: left, right, center, surround left, surround right, and subwoofer (bass speaker). The producer and engineer must choose how to pan (distribute) the sound, and the choices are usually made based on the general concepts used in stereo mixing. Surround mixing can become complex because it is not as natural as mixing in stereo.

> ♫ Some surround-sound mixes are created artificially, and although they give the listener a sense of surround sound, it is not the same effect as actually mixing in the medium.

Automation

Mixing requires a complex series of adjustments and editing within the workings of an audio console, whether the console is virtual or physical. Automation enables an engineer to automate panning, EQ, level, signal processing, and so on. Most consoles allow an engineer to automate all parameters of the mix. For instance, panning, reverberation, levels, and equalization can be adjusted throughout the mix, and the automation program memorizes the changes and plays them back. The engineer also has the option of adjusting the levels of all audio information, including plug-ins, which avoids having to use the faders to automate the mix. *Automation* is one of the most important functions of a recording console and is indispensable to the creative process of mixing. Automation enables producers and engineers the opportunity to experiment with multiple mixes and never erase a mix. *Updates* can be infinite. The process also affords a producer and an engineer the luxury of taking several days to complete a mix without resetting the console each time parameters are updated.

Just slightly adjusting the volume levels, one fader at a time, can make a dramatic difference in the sound of the mix; increasing and decreasing reverberation levels can also dramatically affect the ambience of a track.

Some producers submit stems to the mastering engineer. Stems are individual tracks (stereo or mono) such as brass, drum kit and percussion, strings and so forth. If the mastering engineer adjusts the level of the stems, he or she becomes a "second mix engineer." Many producers and engineers do not like to submit stems because the approved final mix will change. If the producer(s) and mix engineer(s) submit stems, many prefer to attend the mixing sessions so that their mixes are not changed without their approval.

Conclusion of Mixing

Prior to booking a mixing room, request a list of the equipment that will be available. Normally engineers prefer to mix in a studio they are familiar with and feel certain they will achieve the best results for their clients. The use of non-traditional equipment may not be included in the quoted studio rental fee. The producer must be aware of this, for budgetary reasons.

Some studios gain reputations for having superior-sounding mix rooms. For example, studios specialize in dance mixing because the sound of the room is designed to simulate an average club. Mixing studios become popular when hits are mixed in the room.

Countless effects processors are available, and they are mostly variations of the processors discussed. Plug-ins, designed for digital-audio programs, are popular and have become standard signal processors. It is surprising that a minimum of processing is needed for certain styles of mixing. Home (project) studio recording is popular, and many hits have been created using basic equipment. *Pro Tools is the most popular digital-audio program.* An array of high-quality third-party plug-ins is available. When working in a Pro Tools room, ask which plug-ins are included in the rental fee.

It is preferable to use one mixing engineer so that the album has a consistent sound. Many albums have multiple producers who record in different studios. Choosing a mixing engineer is usually the decision of the executive producer, who often works for the record label. The executive producer is responsible for the producers and must also communicate the production concept and the sonic image to the mixing engineer. The final mixes are crucial to the success of the album. It is often necessary to either completely remix tracks or to update mixes.

Mastering

Mastering is the final step before manufacturing. Mixing is the final creative endeavor in music producing, but it would be unfair not to include *mastering* as both a creative and a technical process. Digital audio editors are the most used devices for editing.

After the producer and the record label have accepted the mixes, the producer books a *mastering session,* which is conducted by a *mastering engineer.* The final *mastered sound recording* goes to the manufacturer for replication or is uploaded for digital distribution and streaming.

Mastering is a creative process since the sound of the album can change during the process. The following are some responsibilities of a mastering engineer:

- *The mastering engineer assembles an album in the correct listening order.*
- *The producer tells the mastering engineer the number of seconds to leave blank between songs.* The average is 2 to 3 seconds. The concept of the album might be to not have space between songs, e.g., some tracks on The Beatles *Abbey Road* album.
- *During the mixing process, the producer and the engineer are concerned that the mixes sound the same on speakers of all sizes.*
- *The level (volume) of each song must be evenly matched.* It is rare that the levels on an album match; one song might be very loud and another 25% softer. If the levels are not adjusted, the album will not sound as loud as it should when played at low levels. The engineer carefully adjusts the level of each track.
- *Pops, digital errors (distortion), and clicks are removed.*
- In the world of popular music, producers and mastering engineers always try to make the master recording sound as *hot (loud)* as possible. "Hot" means that at a low level, the recording still projects a feeling of being energetic. The mastering engineer often pushes the levels just short of distortion.
- *If the tracks are mastered in different studios, the sampling rate and bit rates of the recording could vary.* The *mastering engineer* converts all tracks to a sampling rate of 44.1 and 16 bits to meet CD standards. A variety of parameters exist for DVD mastering. (Bit rates and sampling rates affect the sonic quality of a CD.)

- *If the dynamics of the music are not important, the producer and/or mastering engineer might suggest compressing the overall album. Compression* will help make the album sound "punchy" (louder). *Mastering engineers* use multiband compressors and limiters to adjust the overall sound.
- *Adjusting EQ is also a possibility.*
- *The mastering engineer listens for any extraneous noises.* Listen for clicks, pops, and other forms of distortion. Software programs can eliminate some forms of distortion (digital error) and extraneous noise. The engineer must have the ability to adjust the parameters of the software properly, or the software can cause additional damage to the existing problems. The problems should not occur if the producer and the engineer are careful during the recording and mixing process. If a *mastering engineer* is assembling an array of tracks from different producers working in various studios or if the tracks are old and have to be remastered, the engineer will most likely experience some of these problems.

> ♫ Classical-music recordings use the least compression—if any—because hearing the dynamic range of the music is important. Compression creates less dynamic range, which, in most forms of popular music, is not as important as in classical music.

- *Some mastering engineers equalize each track.* There are several reasons to apply EQ to the final tracks: *The audio quality of each track must match so that the tracks relate to one another sonically. Adding high or low frequencies will either make the track "sparkle" or add extra bottom end.* Adding low end is almost standard when mastering tracks designed for dance clubs. High end is added mostly to tracks that sound too dark. *Some mastering engineers add overall EQ to the album.* This is a rare occurrence and should be used only if there is no other way to solve a problem.
- *Mastering can be engineered in a multimillion-dollar mastering studio (lab) or with software designed for use in a home (project) studio.* The choice usually depends on the budget. Inexpensive software programs can produce favorable results. Unfortunately, using mastering software designed for a project studio does not include the talent of a mastering engineer.

The mastering process is complex, and producers should listen to the work of numerous mastering engineers before choosing one. Many recording engineers specialize in one or two musical styles, as do mastering engineers. They must be familiar with the general sound of the marketplace and know how to master an album with the proper sonic quality. For instance, mastering engineers who specialize in dance music (club music) know that the CD or the vinyl record will be played on very expensive loudspeaker systems, that the bottom end of the record has to "jump out," and the tracks, in general, have to sound energetic. In this musical genre, the mastering engineer can literally be responsible for making the record a success or vice versa. In some instances, the sound of the final recording can be as important as the mix. (Naturally, the song has to be well produced.)

Some labels master special albums for distribution to the radio stations, and the albums are not for sale to the public. Mixes are also designed only for the radio. Since radio signals change the sound of recordings, the mastering engineer and mixing engineer tailor the recordings to meet the sonic restrictions. Engineers and producers of popular music address the sonic needs of the medium.

Some producers plan on adjusting certain parameters during the mastering process and design the mixes with mastering as a part of the overall sonic plan.

Conclusion

Mastering is not generally considered the most exciting step in the recording process, but it certainly is equal in importance to any event within the process. Mastering engineers are creative artists. The choices of a mastering engineer and a mastering studio are crucial to the final stage of any recording project. Make certain that the mastering studio has state-of-the art equipment and also that successful recordings have been mastered in that studio. A mastering studio has a sound, just as recording studios and control rooms have individual sonic qualities. Listen to recordings mastered in several studios before contracting with a studio. Mastering engineers also produce a sound; listen to an engineer's work prior to hiring him or her.

Many classical-music listeners are audiophiles and enjoy high-quality digital surround-sound recordings. The DVD (Digital Versatile Disc) and SACD (Super Audio CD, a high-resolution, multichannel audio format) audio formats have become popular with audiophiles because of the exceptional clarity of sound. Although the market is small for these formats, most record labels distributing classical and jazz music reproduce some of the recordings using cutting-edge technology. Many older classic recordings have been remastered and converted to the above-mentioned formats so that the listener can enjoy an enhanced audio experience.

Assignment

Program 32 bars of a song or instrumental:

- Mix the track applying signal processing and automation.
- Write a detailed report on the process. For example, "balanced track levels, panned the snare drum slightly to right of center, applied X percent of reverberation to the violins, etc."

Call several mastering labs and compare prices and equipment included in the mastering fee. Devise a budget detailing the differences in equipment and costs. There may be extra charges for the use of certain equipment.

> ♫ The mastering engineer could be hired as an independent contractor. That means the budget must include a fee separate from the studio fee and supplies.

9

Music Videos, Video Games, and Film and Television Trailers

Music Videos

Music videos are first and foremost promotional tools. They are played on a variety of television stations (mostly cable stations), some specializing in a musical genre—country, rock, R&B, and so forth. The Internet is also now the primary source for viewing music videos, e.g., YouTube, MySpace, Hulu, and more. YouTube has become the number-one source for discovering new music. MTV started the craze in the United States but in recent years has concentrated on original programming geared to its core youth-oriented audience. MTV affiliated stations play music videos and live concerts. Music videos have, once again, become necessary promotional tools, even for unsigned artists.

Record labels have lowered production budgets. Labels have spent millions of dollars for certain superstar videos, and the income generated has not warranted the return on investment. Approximately 50% of a video budget is charged against an artist's record royalties. Since music videos have generated traditionally poor sales but are essential for exposure, most artists would prefer to receive higher artist's royalties on record sales and produce videos for a reasonable budget.

♫ As discussed in chapter 3, 13-year-old singer Rebecca Black, an unknown artist, has received 153,653,217 hits on YouTube as of the writing of this book (2011). This is a remarkable example of the power of social networking. Current technology affords artists the opportunity to produce music videos at a reasonable cost. Black's video was produced for $2,000.

Music videos enable artists to solidify images with the public. Cutting-edge contemporary film directors direct music videos. They

♫ Music videos can be costly to produce and traditionally have not been a profit center for the labels. There is an effort to reverse that trend and generate a profit from sales. Universal Music Group is charging online companies for the use of its videos. In the past videos were supplied as promotional tools, but once again they are considered essential to marketing and promoting an artist. (Product placement in videos by high-profile stars can garner substantial revenue.) Cable stations such a Palladia, owned by MTV Networks, show live performances as well as music videos. They also program interviews with notable artists. This format provides audience members with further insight into their favorite artists.

specialize in reaching the youth and young-adult audiences. Videos provide artists with visual exposure and the exposure helps record labels sell albums. Touring artists usually perform in a city once a year or once every several years. Radio airplay exposes their music but does not expose an artist's persona. A combination of music videos and radio play is the ideal promotional tool.

Video subject matter can produce a negative effect. Madonna's "Like a Prayer" is an example of a video that caused criticism—in that case from the Catholic Church. "There is no such thing as bad publicity" is not necessarily true. Many careers have been ruined because of controversy, for example Michael Jackson. (Although his record sales catapulted after his death in 2009.) Artists must be concerned with how artists' songs and visual images are portrayed.

Established artists usually work with directors to develop video concepts. New artists, who are signed to labels or production companies, rarely control the video content. If the content is offensive or can damage the artist's image, an artist can refuse to appear in the video. Video production is most effective as a collaborative process.

Videos have been popular for many years in foreign territories, especially in Europe. Websites, MTV Television Networks, and independent stations play music videos throughout the world. The videos provide exposure for artists who are not touring. A video is the fastest and most effective means for an artist to create a public image. A video can instantly reach a worldwide audience.

Although artists have generated hundreds of millions of Internet video impressions (e.g., YouTube), a formula for determining how to fairly distribute the income has not yet been determined. On average, one million streams will produce $1,000 to $5,000. Advertising rates for video ads online are determined on a cost per thousand impressions (views). This helps to establish the revenue. Advertisers pay more to advertise on a superstar's video than for an artist who has not achieved the same level of success.

The website presenting the video usually takes 30% of the gross revenue, and the label and the site receive the remaining 70%—out of which the label pays the artists' and mechanical royalties. The performance royalties for *official videos* are paid by the performance rights societies, BMI, ASCAP, and SESAC in the U.S.

Depending upon an artist's contract, the act either receives a 50%/50% split or the artist receives a standard artist's royalty, which averages around 12%. A proper formula for how to distribute this revenue stream will most likely take several years to sort out.

Conclusion to Music Videos

Music-video directors have influenced feature-film directors. Fast editing, unique camera angles, and interesting storytelling have had a lasting effect on segments of the movie industry. MTV-style direction is also popular in commercials. When films are being made to appeal to the younger demographics, the expression "It should look like MTV" is analogous to asking for Kleenex (a brand name) when actually referring to a generic tissue. The Beatles' feature film *A Hard Day's Night* is essentially a long-form music video. In addition to promoting the music, the popular *MTV Music Awards* promotes awareness of the craft of producing and directing music videos. Used properly, music videos can help create careers.

Assignment

Select 3 hit songs and their accompanying videos. Compare the storyline of each song to its video portrayal. Answer the following questions:

- Does the storyline in the video accurately portray the song lyric? If so, why? If not, explain.
- Does the video complement the persona of the artist? If so, why? If not, explain.

♫ Parents' organizations have objected to the use of alcohol, sex, tobacco, and violence in some music videos. Many social-science studies have investigated the effects of music videos. These organizations have little effect because the Internet, the primary source for viewing videos, cannot, in general, be controlled.

Video Games

Video-game content sales were $15.4 billion to $15.6 billion for 2010 (market researchers NPD Group Inc).

Video game music has become a major source of income for music producers, composers, arrangers, recording engineers, and Foley artists. Games are played on video game consoles, computers (social networks), handheld game devices, and mobile smart phones (apps).

- Video games are interactive and, obviously, have to be entertaining.
- They are often developed to target a specific demographic.
- Game developers are concerned about the price-point of a game. (It is costly to develop a video game and this cost is passed on to the consumer.)

Video game music is as essential to video games as film scoring is to films. Music, for both mediums, should have a common tone that connects the score and makes it a *cohesive score*, rather than random compositions without a musical thread. This can be accomplished through orchestration, the tone of the music, theme and variation, and other traditional compositional techniques.

Although there are similarities, conceiving video game scores differs from approaching film scores. Film composers view a film while composing the music. In most instances, game composers receive sketches of the game characters and/or storyboards (cartoon-like characters), a description of the characters and how the game will be played. Game companies employ music supervisors who oversee the sound designer(s) (sound effects). As in films, the composer is also the music producer; therefore, the information in this book applies to producing music for games.

Versatility is an asset for a game composer. One game might require music composed and arranged in numerous musical genres. The ability to compose memorable thematic material and motifs in addition to arranging and orchestration skills are essential to achieve a successful career.

The executive producers and music supervisors usually play musical examples of the style(s) of music that will appropriately accompany the game. Some composers begin the process by composing thematic material. After recording a mockup (synthesized version) of the material, the supervisors will, hopefully, choose one or several themes. Game music must be composed so that the themes and motifs can be "dissected." If a theme is composed in musical phrases (sections), those phrases can be extracted from the complete theme and the phrase can use the basic material to develop a new section. This process is effective because the game player will still associate the music with the theme.

Since games are interactive, the player can manipulate the direction of the game. This means that the music will change as the game progresses. From a compositional viewpoint, the music should make a seamless transition between scenes. One technique is to keep a theme or motif in one key or a related key, e.g., A minor and C, so if the game player quickly changes scenes the musical transition is not jarring. Using musical motifs is also a skillful technique since composers can easily modulate, change the duration of the notes, and invert the notes, as well as use other compositional techniques, while the motif(s) keeps its basic musical character.

Another approach is for the composer to create a theme and/or motif for each character in the game. The audience will subliminally associate the theme or motif with that character. A common technique is to create various mixes of the themes and motifs. For example, one mix consists of a full orchestra, in the 2nd mix the strings are deleted, in the 3rd mix only the rhythm section is used, in the 4th mix the theme or motif is removed, and so forth. This technique creates multiple options for the music director.

Creating a musical loop, which is a section that keeps repeating, is a compositional technique that keeps the musical momentum without sounding disruptive. Composers have the option to overdub new parts while keeping the loop as the underlying element that "sews" the musical section together.

Some composers create a music library comprised of multiple moods. For instance, a number of compositions create the following moods: *sadness, triumph, humor, tension,* and so forth. The composer and sound designers can choose the proper moods to fit the various situations created in the game.

Sound Effects

As in film sound, sound effects are crucial to creating an ambience to the complete soundtrack, which includes music, dialog, and sound effects. Games that have substantial budgets hire synthesists or Foley artists who specialize in sound effects, called *sound designers,* to create the effects. If a game's budget is relatively small, the composer is required to construct the sound effects. Most composers either create an original sound effects library or purchase sound effects libraries. A composer must understand that in most games, the sound effects are going to be loud; therefore, the composer must include the sound effects as an integral part of their compositions. This is a difficult task because the sound effects might not be added until after the music is composed. Ask the executive producer or music producer of samples of effects they plan into the game.

Games are mixed in 5.1. surround sound so the final mix is crucial to the overall ambience of the game.

Voice-Over Actors

Voice-over actors are usually auditioned and chosen by the game's producer. Obviously, the character of the voices is crucial to a game's success. In low-budget games, the composer might be asked to audition and record the actors. Make certain that the game producer approves the actors.

Scoring Time

Developing games is time consuming; hence, it might take a composer for a game several years to complete composing the music. This does not imply that the game is the only project a composer works on during the development period. He or she might work for several months, be off for 3 months, work for 2 months, and the cycle continues. The amount of time a composer devotes to composing the music is included in the composer's contract. He is permitted to work on other projects during this time period with permission of the production company.

♫ Some video game companies have music budgets which allow composers to use 70–90 piece orchestras.

Game music is a substantial source of income for music producers, record labels, composers, music publishers, arrangers, recording engineers, and sound designers. Songs are licensed for use in video games and certain games allow the player to replace the existing music by downloading new music.

Conclusion to Video Games

Music production provides a good background to become a video game soundtrack supervisor. The position entails licensing songs for the company's games, licensing original music composed for the company's games for use in motion picture trailers, commercials, etc., and supervising the sound design and original music for the company's games. Game development is an involved undertaking and also requires a large financial investment by the developer. The music, sound effects, and actors, as well as the graphics are equally important in achieving success with consumers.

Assignment

Select a game, mute the sound, and compose multiple themes and motifs that will appropriately accompany the game. Use the musical techniques discussed in this chapter to create several versions of each theme and motif.

Film and Television Trailers

A film (video) trailer (aka theatrical or movie trailer, or television program trailer) is an advertisement for a motion picture or television program. Film trailers are viewed primarily in movie theaters but are seen on television, the Internet, DVDs, airplane entertainment systems, and mobile devices.

Basically, they can be seen in any format that supports video advertising. (HBO creates exceptional trailers for their miniseries presentations as well as their weekly programs.)

The reason this subject is addressed is because trailers usually contain a considerable amount of music; most often there is continuous music and sound effects throughout most trailers. This requires music supervision and music production skills. There are producer/composers who specialize in this discipline.

Clearly, the purpose of a trailer is to attract an audience for the film. Since a trailer is a commercial, the visual content and sound must maintain the audience's attention. The trailer can be crucial to the success or failure of a film or television program. (Social networking (word of mouth) is, most likely, even more essential to a film's or television program's success.)

The trailer film/video editor must create footage that will "whet the appetite" of the audience, yet not reveal too much about the plot. The same is true of the music and the sound effects.

Multiple trailers are created for films with a generous marketing budget. There is always a "general audience" trailer. In addition, trailers are also designed to appeal to a specific demographic. For example, one trailer might appeal to a young male demographic while another is edited to appeal to a mature female demographic. Since as many as 30 trailers might be created for a big-budget feature film, the music differs on many of the versions. The music is designed to appeal to the targeted demographic.

Most trailer music is licensed from music libraries or record companies. Some of the music is used from other films. It is rare to use music from the actual film unless there is a known theme, or theme that will be used repeatedly in the film, such as the theme from *Star Wars*. Approximately 10% to 20% of a trailer contains original music. The music supervisor (discussed later in this book) chooses the library music, or music from other sources, and also supervises the producer/composer who writes the original music. Executives at the studio who specialize in creating trailers supervise the editing of the film and the selection of music. Television networks often create their own trailers. Sometimes advertising agencies are hired to create television trailers.

The average feature film trailer is between 2 and 2.5 minutes and is released just prior to the film's release. Major studios usually release shorter trailers, referred to as "teasers," 3 to 6 months prior to a film's release; they are usually 60 to 90 seconds.

Theatrical trailers created for television are usually 30 seconds, with 15- and 10-second versions. For a "blockbuster" film, the studio may create a 1-minute version. The music for the television versions usually differs from the music used in a theatrical trailer unless there is an identifiable theme such as the theme from *Superman*. If a film is successful at the box office, the studio might create new trailers, which are called "refreshed" trailers. For instance, the trailer might promote the fact that the film was nominated for certain awards or that the DVD is being released.

Trailers designed for the international market generally contain music that differs from the music used in the U.S. The music usually fits the "culture" of the market. This concept also applies to the film clips; some clips used in the U.S. might not be acceptable in another culture.

Conclusion to Film and Television Trailers

Music production is an excellent background for producing music for trailers. It is essential for trailer music producers to become familiar with creating and/or choosing sound effects that may not be provided by the studio. Most producers have extensive sound effects libraries or they create the effects.

Assignment

Compare a 2- or 2 1/2-minute theatrical trailer to a 30-second trailer for the same film. In your analysis, include the following information:

- Does the music differ?
- Describe the target demographic.
- How is the same interest in a film generated in 30 seconds as compared to the long 2 1/2-minute version?

Include any additional pertinent differences.

10

The Production Process

Assignment

We have discussed the concerns producers must cope with before signing an artist to a production agreement and/or agreeing to produce an artist. This section is intended to serve as a practical exercise. Answer the following questions in detail.

- You have just been hired as an A&R executive at a record label and the label is considering signing an artist. Describe the process of signing an artist, and compile a list of questions that pertain to understanding the artist's persona and artist's artistic intentions.
- Describe the preproduction process.
- Describe the production process.
- Describe the mixing process.
- Describe the mastering process.
- Design and produce a project, which is based upon all areas studied thus far.

11

Producing Music for Film and Classical Recordings

When I am, as it were, completely myself, entirely alone, and of good cheer—say traveling in a carriage, or walking after a good meal, or during the night when I cannot sleep—it is on such occasions that my ideas flow best, and most abundantly. Whence and how they come, I know not, nor can I force them.

—Wolfgang Amadeus Mozart

Music for Film

Producing music for films differs from producing music for records. There are no "producers" of movie music. The composer is the producer. It is helpful for a composer to study music production and the basics of audio engineering.

The majority of film scores are orchestrated for large orchestras; therefore, recording the ambience of a live room becomes a primary consideration. Recording in the proper studio—called a *scoring stage* when recording film music—with an experienced engineer—called a mixer or sound mixer—who specializes in recording film music is essential to capturing the proper sound.

♫ On December 28, 1895, the Lumiere family of France used music to accompany several films produced by the family's film company. The score, performed on a piano, was presented at the Grand Café, in Paris. That is the first known use of music accompanying films. The event was so successful with the public that theater owners began hiring orchestras to accompany the films.
In 1908, the noted French composer Camille Saint-Saens composed the first film score for the film *L'Assassinat du Duc de Guise.*

There are a number of differences between recording music for films and recording music for records:

- *Since most film scores are written for a full orchestra the engineer must have a thorough knowledge of microphone placement and selection.* Very few pop records are recorded with a large orchestra; therefore, engineers who specialize in pop recording may not be familiar with miking techniques used for recording large ensembles. Record engineers are primarily concerned with being on the cutting edge of recorded sound and consequently become masters of current recording and mixing techniques. They use the latest effects devices and are concerned about the most contemporary overall sounds popular at a particular time. Generally, a film engineer has recorded more orchestral music than studio-oriented popular styles of music. (Some engineers are proficient in both styles.) Their orientation is that of a more classic approach to recording. They try to recreate the sound of a live orchestra as opposed to recording a track guided by signal processing and synthesizers.
- *Film music is mixed so that it will sound spacious and has an impact when heard on a surround sound speaker system in a movie theater.* Films are mixed in *5.1 surround sound*; therefore, the composer and the engineer must assign the instruments within the sonic image of the surround-sound format.
- Speaker outputs in surround sound: left, right, center, surround left, surround right, and subwoofer (bass speaker).
- When an audience listens to a symphony orchestra, the violins are on the left, the cellos on the right, the percussion in the rear left, and so forth. That is generally the blueprint for panning a surround-sound mix. Sometimes the composer will ask for an unusual sonic placement of instruments or instrumental sections. Experiment with panning positions to determine the most effective sonic results. For instance, if the first and second violins are separated instead of remaining in their traditional live orchestral seating position to the audience's left (facing the stage)—the first violins panned to the left speaker and the second violins panned to the right speaker—the orchestral balance will be disrupted, and the orchestra will not sound balanced.
- Experienced film engineers are aware of the problem and convey potential drawbacks to the composer prior to the recording session. It is costly to make changes while in the studio; therefore, the sonic plan should be decided before the session.
- *The engineer usually records ambient tracks, which helps create a feeling of space when they are mixed with the traditionally recorded tracks.* Am-

bient microphones are usually hung very high above the orchestra and are used to record the natural room sound of the orchestra. The ambient tracks help create the sound of a concert hall. Most film engineers and composers are attempting to replicate the sound of a live performance. When sitting in a concert hall, the audience experiences the natural ambience in the hall. The sound of an orchestra will vary in different venues. The composer must have a sonic image, which the engineer will be asked to replicate. For instance, the composer may request the sound of a large concert hall, a medium-size venue, or an intimate, small orchestral sound, such as that of a classical orchestra.

- When working on major films, the final sound engineer(s) is not usually the music engineer. There are usually 3 engineers in a dubbing session, which is the process of blending the music, sound effects, and dialogue. For independent films and films with limited budgets, there will most likely be one engineer.
- *Mixing film music differs from mixing a record.* Scoring mixers (recording engineers) record and mix film music. They must consider that the final mix will consist of music, sound effects, and dialogue. These elements affect the manner in which the music is mixed; the sonic image must leave space for dialogue and effects. All of the elements are combined to form the final 5.1 surround-sound theater mix.

The following information should clarify some of the differences between record production and film music production.

Music Supervision for Film

Music supervisors, in the film industry, perform a pivotal role shaping the final musical landscape of a film. In the past, their primary function was to select songs for a motion picture; their role has since been greatly expanded. Independent music supervisors and in-house studio music supervisors provide a myriad of services for both major studio productions and for independent production companies. They help directors develop a musical concept for a film, assuming that the director does not have a clear musical vision, which would be unusual. Even if a director has a clear musical vision, a music supervisor might help the director expand his or her vision. The job requires supervisors to be knowledgeable in both the creative and business areas of the film and music businesses.

In addition to helping select a composer to write a score, a well-versed musical supervisor must also have the aptitude to select a song that is appropriate for a scene and to possess the business acumen to negotiate the rights to license not only the song from the music publisher(s) but also the master sound recording from the rights holder(s) such as a record label(s) or an independent artist(s). (Each song and master sound recording might have multiple rights holders.) The negotiations can become rather complex because each usage has to be negotiated separately with each rights holder. For example, negotiating the right to use a song and the master sound recording during the opening (main) title of a film differs from using that same song in the trailers, during the closing (end) title, or in a specific scene. Also, a song cannot be used on a soundtrack album without a separate negotiation. The negotiations are referred to as *clearances*: "clearing the song(s) and/or sound recording(s)."

Music supervisors can hire composers to write songs specifically for a film. Since some music supervisors are also record producers, they might produce the original songs and also help the composer produce the score music. They attend *spotting sessions*, which is the process of choosing the scenes to be scored or scenes that might require songs. Another responsibility is to oversee the entire music budget, which is an intricate process. Unexpected occurrences, such as a publisher increasing the cost of a licensing fee, must always be considered when assembling a music budget. Supervisors attend *dubbing sessions*, which is the process of combining the dialogue, music, and sound effects. They assemble *cue sheets*, which list the background music and songs, the composers, music publishers, performance rights societies, and timing of each musical cue.

Licenses

To use a song or master sound recording in a film, music supervisors must obtain 2 types of licenses. The first is a *synchronization license*, commonly referred to as a "sync license." A synchronization license means that the song can be used with a timed visual image. Music publishers grant synch licenses. It is not unusual for a song to be published by multiple publishers and written by several writers. This requires negotiating with each entity. If a master sound recording of a song is used, the supervisor must negotiate a *master use* license. This grants the film company the right to use the master sound recording in the film. Both licenses are required if the song and the master recording are going to be used. *Transcription licenses* are issued to use a song on the radio for commercial purposes, e.g., a radio commercial. (This does not refer to radio play of a sound recording that is used to promote an artist.)

Clearing and licensing music is a time-consuming effort. The following is a list of some of the usages that require licenses:

- Use of non-profit and for-profit documentaries
- Short subject films
- Trailer music
- Source music
- Corporate and in-house videos
- New technology projects
- All digital media projects
- Soundtrack licenses
- Compilation album
- Video licenses, e.g., YouTube and Hulu
- All mobile phone content
- Theatrical productions
- Commercials
- Television programs
- Feature films
- In-store promotions
- Infomercials
- Film festival rights

The only music that does not require clearance is music in the public domain. Determining if a composition is in the public domain often requires hiring a qualified musicologist. A composition may appear to be in the public domain but it is actually an arrangement of a public domain composition and the arrangement is copywritten.

The most efficient means to identify the music publisher and/or copyright owner of a song is to contact the performance rights societies, which are BMI, ASCAP, and SESAC in the U.S. Enter the name of the song and other pertinent information and the publisher's information should appear.

> ♫ Some publishers request a "most favored nation clause," which means that all licensees receive the same terms. This might be difficult to negotiate if a film company is willing to pay a substantial fee for a popular song and not pay the same fee for other songs.

To find master sound recording information, read CD covers or search websites such as Amazon.com. Most information can be found on the Internet. They want to know all information that is connected to the project; for instance, the territory, length of the agreement, the quote, and so forth. Most often, if a song is being used in a scene, the script of that scene is sent to the potential licensor for approval.

To obtain a synchronization license and a master use license, contact the publisher and the owner of the master sound recording (if the sound recording is being used). All publishers and labels (copyright owners) have departments, or an independent music supervisor, that negotiates licensing.

Music Samples

Music samples are sections of existing recordings, or other sources, which are included in a new sound recording. It can be a drum sound, a portion of an entire recording, a voice, and so on. Both the sampled sound recording and the publishing rights to the composition have to be cleared to legally use a sample.

Darren Higman Interview

Darren Higman is the executive vice president of music at Warner Bros. Pictures

MZ: What are the responsibilities of a music supervisor?

DH: The main responsibility is to oversee all of the music in the film. If there are songs to be written, you go to songwriters and/or artists. If there are songs to be licensed you oversee the process of licensing. You spot the film with the composer and director. [Spotting is choosing the scenes to be scored or where source music should be licensed such as a popular song.] You are responsible for gathering composer choices and presenting them to the director if they don't already have a composer that they work with. You work along side of a music editor to temp the score, as well. [A temp/temporary score is adding existing underscoring and/or songs against a film to offer the director and composer a musical direction.] That is when you experiment and find the tone and the voice of the music in the film. This is probably the most creative part of the process. Then you can publicly start showing the film. [Many films are shown to audiences with temporary music tracks, which will be replaced by original scores. These screenings are called *recruited audience screenings*. After analyzing the audience's reaction, the editing might change, song choices might change, the composer begins to write the score, etc.] There is an administrative side to music supervision, which is a lot of details. You are licensing songs, adhering to a music budget, which includes a composer fee, recording costs, and all of the songs whether they are newly written or licensed. When you temp the film, you have to be careful not to put in songs you can't afford . . . songs that can't be cleared. You deal with music publishers, lawyers, record labels, and managers. In the recording process, there is a thing called the *final dub*, which is where all of the final music is placed into the picture. The score is generally handled by the composer, who records the music, mixes the music, and then has a music editor of his own cutting the score into the movie. The music supervisor will be working with another music editor who will primarily be cutting the songs . . . making sure that you have the correct versions of the songs . . . , [the correct] masters [sound recordings], and the right mixes. [Original mixes recorded specifically for a film are mixed in 5.1 surround sound.] The final dub process is about a two-week period. [The final dub process is mixing the music, sound effects, and dialogue together.] [Sometimes] a music supervisor is involved from the time a script is written because if there is anything that is written into the movie that is performed on camera or if a particular song is being listened to on the radio (called source music) . . . all of that needs to be figured out and finished before the film shoots, particularly if they perform anything on camera. It is called prerecords.

MZ: How close should the composer's score sound like the music in the temp track?

DH: It really depends on the project. The music of the composer is often used for the temp track. So it is in a style that they are probably familiar with. But sometimes, the actual score is wildly different. Composers do mockups (synthesizer demos) of different cues because it is hard sometimes to imagine what the score will sound like. They want to hear stuff before it is actually recorded.

MZ: Is the music supervisor generally involved in the spotting sessions?

DH: I've experienced both. If there is an emphasis on songs or source cues, it is a good idea to have a music supervisor involved. However, the flip side of that is that composers sometimes think that supervisors try to jam too many songs into a movie. I always think the spotting session is helpful because it is pretty apparent where songs would go. But sometimes, when you do the entire spotting session and then you attempt to temp the movie in that fashion, in many cases I've found there are way too many songs. I firmly believe that if the music in the film is good, and part of the fabric of the film, it will make an impression on people who will want to experience that via a soundtrack (album).

MZ: Does the music supervisor usually go to the dub mix?

DH: Generally, yes. The music supervisor usually goes to the playback [after the dialogue, music, and sound effects have been added to a reel]. And then all of the different departments would have their say . . . the director would be there, the producers would be there, the film executive, the music supervisor, the sound people . . . [they all make suggestions]. [After all the reels are complete] there is a final playback of the film. [This is the last opportunity to suggest changes.]

MZ: Are you involved with administering the cue sheets? [A cue sheet is a list of compositions or songs used in the scenes of a film.]

DH: Cue sheets are sometimes done by music supervisors but generally for smaller independent films. Our licensing department and our legal team mostly handles the cue sheets. It is the last part of the process. They will watch the film with a stop watch and time every cue [scene] and generate the cue sheet. Cue sheets are also generated from music editors.

MZ: What is the difference between a music executive and a music supervisor at a film studio?

DH: As time goes by, there is less and less difference at all. [Most music executives are also music supervisors. Most music executives oversee many projects and do not have the time to also supervise the music.]

MZ: What percentages of directors have a clear vision of what the tone of the music should be for their films?

DH: I would say most. Directors have an idea of what they want in all aspects of the film. Even if they have a clear idea of want they want, and you don't agree [the music supervisor], then you have to sort of persuade them that there may be a different approach that might work better.

MZ: Are most directors open to suggestion?

DH: Yes, by and large. Films, in general, are a big collaborative effort. Sometimes, it is just an execution of what they [the directors] want. Helping them execute is exactly what we want to do.

MZ: Are most of the music publishing rights owned by the studio?

DH: Yes. Composers stand a better chance of retaining part of their publishing, if not all of it, with an independent film. They [independent film makers] don't have a lot of money to pay you [the composer], so they are not gonna insist on ownership.

MZ: Do you ever view the dailies? [Each day's filming.]

DH: We get *digital dailies*. It is on your computer. In dailies you might find that they had a great idea on the set to sing a song or they had a great idea to play back something or perform a dance to a song. For us it is more informational to make sure there aren't any big music things being done that we are not necessarily aware of.

MZ: Do you attend most of the scoring sessions?

DH: Yes. We attend most of the recording sessions of all the movies we are overseeing. [During a] recording session, in theory, the music should be to such a state that there shouldn't be a lot of changes during the scoring session. It should be straightforward recording. Occasionally, certain cues are not working in the way they imagined. [The director and composer discuss the cue.] As a music person [supervisor], you are there to represent the interest of the music and any kind of decision-making that would go along with that . . . i.e., extra recording sessions.

MZ: Do composers generally have 6 to 8 weeks to compose a score?

DH: Sometimes it is less but sometimes it is a lot more. Like in animation, not that it is a complete full-time job, but is not unusual for a composer to be on a film for 3 years. They do demos . . . it is a work in progress.

MZ: What percentages of songs that you license are from unknown artists?

DH: I would say 25 to 30 percent. [From a financial standpoint, it saves the studio money to license music by unknown artists and the artists gain exposure.]

Doug Frank Interview

Doug Frank is the former president of music operations for Warner Bros. Pictures. He is currently a consultant in the film industry.

MZ: What does a music supervisor do? Is the job similar to that of a record producer?

DF: The music supervisor at one point, going back ten, fifteen years ago, was the go-between [for] the film industry and the record business. That person would explain to the record business how the film business operates and vice versa. They served a very useful purpose of marrying the film company and the record company and having one goal, which is for the music to (1) enhance the film and make it a better picture; (2) promote the film, by way of a single on the radio, music video on MTV, and advertising; and (3) add additional revenue with record royalties and publishing income. As the years have gone by, record companies have become more sophisticated in the ways of film companies, and film companies have learned about record companies, and they have hired their own in-house people. The independent music supervisor isn't a dinosaur per se but doesn't necessarily perform the same function they used to. Now they are more of a babysitter or hand-holder of directors and producers. I often hire them because they serve as buffers. I don't have to necessarily deal directly with the filmmakers 100 percent of the time, especially when you have a large volume of films that you are responsible for on a daily basis. The independent music supervisors will be attached to one project and should be working on one project at a time. Again, they are functioning in this liaison role, where they are bringing music to the film, suggesting songs, suggesting composers, and dealing with whatever soundtrack label is releasing the record.

MZ: Do music supervisors produce film scores?

DF: There are a few that are qualified to do so because they were music producers in a previous career; but generally speaking, no. Producers are producers, and supervisors are supervisors. Most of the time the score is produced by the composer. Some composers actually work with people to produce their score in a more of a record fashion.

MZ: How much actual mixing is done with a film score?

DF: You may record the orchestra for five days and then mix (music) for a day or two. But the other term *mixing* may refer to dubbing the various elements into the film, and those elements are music, effects, and dialogue. That process goes on for several weeks.

MZ: What are the differences between a record engineer and a scoring mixer (engineer) who specializes in recording film scores?

DF: Many record engineers have never had the experience of miking a full orchestra. They haven't had the experience of working with room sound, which is an art in itself. So there is a big difference. Sometimes you want a record sound for your score, and you may opt for record-type mixing.

MZ: Do you mix only in 5.1 surround sound?

DF: Yes.

MZ: Have you been hiring record producers to work with composers on scores?

DF: It's been a fascination of mine to combine people to score a film. We have done this successfully at times because you want certain flavors. You may want the uniqueness of a certain recording artist. I can recall on all the *Lethal Weapon* movies, when Michael Kamin was the chief composer, but he also brought in David Sandborn and Eric Clapton. You got some unique artistry adding those kinds of sounds on that score. Since then, and this is not in any kind of chronological order, we did a film called *Queen of the Damned,* where we had the lead singer of the band Korn, Jonathan Davis, work on the score and songs on the film with his writing partner, Richard Gibbs. That was a very successful project. It starred Aaliyah. Unfortunately, she died before the film came out. The album went gold. With the collaborations, we put DJs with the composers. We are coming up with different ways of approaching film scoring. In my mind there are a couple of different ways of looking at a film score. One is "*What you see is what you hear.*" The musical underscore of the action and the picture change, and things happen on screen; the music will change with that. Another approach is just an environmental approach to film scoring, where you don't deal so much with the action itself. You create an environment of music that goes along with the look and sound of the film. That puts you in the frame of mind. And some filmmakers like this approach because you are not leading the viewer that much. The music score can tell the viewers exactly how they are supposed to feel: Be afraid, don't be afraid, laugh, don't laugh. Somehow when the score is just environmental the viewer treats the experience as seeing the movie on a very personal level. We put Paul Oakenfold (DJ) together with a composer named Christopher Young. We put Stanley Clark, the bassist, with Timberland, the hip-hop producer. We come up with all different types of combinations: Some work, and some don't work as well.

MZ: What is the ideal background for a music supervisor?

DF: Music supervisors, for the most part, were people that came from record companies, and the truth of the matter is the best music supervisors have the best Rolodexes in this business, which is built on relationships. The ability to deliver people is really what is crucial. People think music supervisors sit with the film all day long and they keep throwing songs up against the picture, and they do that, but that's not where the job is. The job is: Can you get me Bruce Springsteen? Can you get me an artist that matters?

MZ: Would you advise a young person to get a job in a record company before applying for a music supervisor's job at a film company?

DF: Young persons just need to get into the flow. The flow refers to the flow of information (they receive) if they are working for a music publisher, record company, or a film company. Who are they talking to during the day? Are they talking to the movers and the shakers, regardless of the industry? They are able to establish a relationship with these people, and they are in a flow of information. They see what is going on. In Hollywood, people started in the mailroom. The reason they started people in the mailroom is because when you deliver their mail you get to know whom everybody is, and more important you get to know what everybody does. That's how you learn how the business functions. So any job that puts you in the flow of information, that gets you in a position of dealing directly with creative types and executives, is a good job to have.

MZ: Is there anything else you would like to mention concerning the production of music for film?

DF: Be knowledgeable about editing systems, software, and try to stay very current. I think that colleges and universities really need to look at that in their communications programs and music programs, to invest in the kind of equipment that will allow their students to be armed and equipped for the real world when they get out of school. Most of the major universities are seeing the wisdom in this. My pet peeve in life is that students and graduates come to me, and they don't have a clue how to approach this business, either as a composer, orchestrator, arranger, or executive. They just have no idea. To sum it up, there is the old joke about the five stages of your career. I'll use myself: "Who is Doug Frank? Get me Doug Frank. Oh, Doug Frank's not available; get me somebody like Doug Frank. Get me a younger version of Doug Frank. Who is Doug Frank?" I know for me in this job, it's the time I spent with you [DF was signed to my music publishing company as a songwriter] and other things that I did helped me enormously in this job, in my ability to relate directly to the writer and producer—having an understanding for the process and not just being a businessman. It's like building blocks, everything you do in your life. You do this now, and you'll do something else, and you'll take from those experiences and build upon them.

Additional Comment by Doug Frank

The downfall of the record industry has made the film business more creative . . . we're not looking for the hit single as much or looking for the major artist to cover . . . radio has gone away for a lot of people . . . unless you're a major artist radio is not available . . . I think we're in an age of discovery . . . the audiences for our motion pictures, for the most part, are the same people that congregate at different websites . . . it's a community of people out there . . . I don't want to say there's a backlash if we have a soundtrack featuring major artists but we're more better off with that than we are with a soundtrack of emerging artists. It's all about making these films as good as we can make them with music. Because radio has gone away for so many people, we're experiencing a time where we've never had so many artists come in to see us with hopes that we would use their material in film . . . these are major artists, emerging artists . . . everyone is trying to hitch a ride on this vehicle known as film or television and engage in lots of Internet strategies . . . that's pretty much of what the effect of the music business has been. Also, (film studios) are much more into ownership of the songs and the recordings and not necessarily licensing so much. I think the soundtrack business is fairly healthy. When people want to live the experience of a motion picture . . . you get that with *High School Musical*, you get that with *Twilight*, you get that with *Juno* when there is a deep appreciation for the music and an even deeper appreciation for the film itself. I think if you have the right product, you will sell some records and get some downloads. It's nothing like it was 10 years ago and it will never be that way again . . . but at least it's somewhat healthy. If you look at the top 40 albums—the top 100 albums—there is always some representation as far as soundtracks are concerned . . . studios don't depend on music . . . we are looked upon as a service division. Publishing income is up because of performance royalties (from television and film).

Kevin Gershan

The following information is based on an interview with Kevin Gershan. Kevin Gershan is a television music supervisor at Paramount Pictures, in Los Angeles.

- *Music supervisors supervise original-soundtrack music and license recordings for motion pictures and television programs.* Many have backgrounds in the record business. Some music supervisors also produce or coproduce the music with the composer.

Music supervisors should have extensive knowledge of music history. It is helpful to be a musician and to be technically savvy. They supervise the following:

- Union payments
- Contracting musicians
- Planning recording sessions
- Music-publishing issues
- Music clearances
- Master recording clearances
- Synchronization licensing
- Music-production issues
- Legal issues

Television is a "one-composer" medium. Most television composers record primarily with synthesizers; not many television programs have a budget to hire a small orchestra. They build cues (music pieces of various lengths) beginning with the first episode; they create a music library that will be used in numerous episodes. The composers edit and produce the music. Some music supervisors also produce or coproduce the music.

Music jobs at film companies: A *music coordinator* is a clerical person who logs the *cue sheets,* which are music selections used on television programs or in films. Cue sheets are submitted to the performance-rights organizations so that composers and music publishers can receive proper performance royalties. *Music clearance supervisors* are liaisons between production companies and music publishers. They process the cue sheets. The *vice-president in charge of music* oversees all programs at a studio or production company. Part of the job is to hire the composers.

Conclusion: Music for the Film Industry

The film industry offers opportunities for music producers interested in film music. Skills learned as a composer, music producer, music publisher, and recording engineer are applied in creative and executive positions. Working in any area of the record industry serves as preparation.

Music supervision is the closest position linked directly to music production. Some music supervisors—especially those working for independent filmmakers—produce soundtrack music; they also often coproduce soundtrack albums with the composer.

Classical Recordings

Producing classical music is similar to producing film music. Producers who produce classical music are called *classical record producers*. In most traditional film music, the composer, music supervisor, and engineer are trying to capture a live performance. Classical-record producers are also striving to capture a live performance. It is rare that overdubs are requested. In place of overdubs, *inserts* are recorded and edited into the preferred overall performance. For instance, if mistakes are made between bar 20 and bar 30, the artist will rerecord only those bars. The newly recorded section is edited (inserted) into the selected performance.

> ♫ In this context, the term *classical music* is being used as a generic term meaning concert music, not music from the Classical period.

Classical record producers should be trained musicians. The prerequisites for classical production are familiarity with the traditional music repertoire and familiarity with the scores. In addition to musical training, it is necessary to understand the engineering process. A classical producer's knowledge should equal that of a popular-music producer. Specializing in live recording techniques, having extensive knowledge of microphones, microphone placement, recording systems, and recording consoles is a necessary skill.

Classical record producers are critics. Most popular music albums contain new music, and the producer is generally creating a new product. Most classical music has been recorded numerous times; therefore, the producer's job is to help the artist and/or conductor interpret the music and achieve a high performance level. Most musicians adhere to unwritten standards when interpreting historical genres of music, and the producer must be familiar with those practices. Some artists experiment with unusual interpretations, and they are either criticized or praised by the critics.

A producer follows the score and points out possible discrepancies between the score and the performance. It is less costly and less time consuming to fix problems during rehearsals than during the recording sessions. The artist must have a clearly defined understanding of the music and how he or she wants to interpret the music, before rehearsals and recording commence.

Interpreting music is subjective. Question: If interpretation is subjective, how do a performer and a music producer determine the proper interpretation, especially in the traditional Baroque, Classical, or Romantic repertoire? One answer is for the performer and producer to understand the historical time period during which a composition was written. For example, if a composition was written during Bach's or Beethoven's time, the instruments on which the pieces were performed sounded differently than when they are played on modern instruments; consequently, what is reflected in the score (e.g., dynamics) might not sound the same when played on a modern instrument. For instance, pedaling on an old keyboard instrument would not necessarily translate to a modern keyboard. In this example, the performer must choose an interpretation based on historical knowledge of how the music sounded. One might ask, "How is it possible to know how music sounded when performed on period instruments?" The answer is that many serious musicians play the composition(s) on period instruments (instruments of a historical period) and then translate the sound to a modern instrument by adjusting the various musical indications on the original score. An additional answer is to carefully listen to recordings of critically acclaimed performances and then compare the newly recorded performance. This is not to suggest that the artist copy another artist's interpretation, but that it can be used as a guideline.

A producer is always listening for something unique within a performance. Without a distinctive interpretation, the recording will not be considered worthy of competing in a highly competitive market.

There are differences between recording performances in a concert hall and a studio. A producer has one or two performances to choose from when recording a live performance. Studio recordings enable a producer to record multiple takes and edit sections together.

Editing classical music is more difficult than editing most popular music. The majority of popular music has a definite tempo, which eases the process of creating acceptable edits. Most classical music has variable tempos, which makes the editing process more difficult; producers and engineers are skillful at performing difficult edits.

Recording live performances has inherent problems. There is usually unwanted noise from the audience, page turning, foot tapping, and myriad other acoustical distractions. Some of the issues can be corrected by using special miking techniques and various forms of noise reduction. It is often difficult to filter out unwanted noise. The audience has become accustomed to listening to live recordings, and unwanted noise is expected. Some producers believe that the noise adds to the ambience of a live performance.

Author's Opinion: Some classic recordings (in all genres) have been "cleaned up" to the point of losing the excitement of the original performance. An attempt should be made to eliminate any distracting noises but not to make the recording sound unnatural.

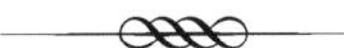

Work with an engineer who specializes in recording classical music. Engineers generally own an array of microphones and other recording equipment. Their goal is to record the instruments so that they sound realistic. Inferior microphones used for recording classical music are generally not adequate.

Since recording quality is important, the choice of a recording console is significant. Selecting a console is a matter of taste, and the choice is usually the decision of the producer and the engineer. Producers and engineers usually have working relationships and work as a team. Their sonic personalities are normally compatible.

Most classical music is recorded digitally at a sampling rate of 96kHz and a sampling width of 24 bits. Most classical record producers value the clarity of digital recording and the ease of editing in the digital domain with a program such as Pro Tools.

Conclusion: Classical Music Production

Students interested in producing classical music should be proficient in score reading, the concepts of audio engineering, and musicology. Study the performances of the great concert artists and conductors, and analyze the reasons their performances are considered exceptional.

Some classical music producers specialize in opera, orchestral works, or chamber music. Most producers are capable of producing all genres of concert music, but they are usually more familiar with the repertoire of one style.

The following is a statement by Edward Turgeon, who earned a Doctor of Musical Arts Degree (D.M.A.) from Yale University. He is a performing artist and a member of the piano faculty at Florida Atlantic University.

> Through various techniques, a production/engineering team can determine in advance the sonic personality of the musician(s), e.g., What kind of recorded instrumental sound they prefer.

I have often thought that before beginning a recording, it would be interesting for the production/engineering team to confer with the musician(s) as much as is feasible. A possible procedure might be for the musician(s) to provide three CD examples, which, in their opinion, feature unacceptable instrumental sonority, as well as three example CDs which feature ideal sonority. In each case, the musician(s) would explain why, and through this process, the production/engineering team could identify the artists' sonic sensibility before recording actually begins.

I have noticed that the more post recording communication between producer/engineer and musician(s), the better. This is perhaps most crucial and intense in the case of classical recording, since there are often many takes, with only the most subtle differences between good and bad takes. The musicians' likes are often very different compared to those of the production/engineering team. Therefore, all parties must effectively manage different artistic visions, in order to come up with a final product that meets the satisfaction of all involved.

Assignment

Watch a film of your choice. The director wants to add 3 songs to 3 scenes. Each song must relate to the storyline of that scene.

- Choose 3 scenes from 1 more film. Select a song for each scene. Write an explanation of why you chose each song.
- Select a title song (opening) and a closing song. Write an explanation of why you chose each song.

The director wants your input on how the film music should be scored.

- Watch a film of your choice and write an outline of suggestions you would make to a composer. (The direction of the music should not be the same as the score composed for the original film.)
- In addition to the question above, select 3 scenes and write detailed comments to the composer. These comments should include the placement of musical "hits" ("hits" are musical accents), and where specific mood changes should occur.

Record a simple piano sonata or trio multiple times. *Produce* the recording; make interpretative suggestions to the pianist.

- Correct mistakes.
- Experiment with various miking techniques.
- Edit pieces together.

Submit a CD and a written outline of the assignment.

12

Producing Library Music

Library music, also called production or needle-drop music, is specifically composed and arranged with the intention of licensing it on a nonexclusive basis. Often it is designed to enhance visual and audio productions, such as television programs, television and radio commercials, documentaries, training videos, low-budget film productions, and additional multimedia formats. The licenses are generally issued as synchronization licenses, which means the music must be used in an audio and/or visual project and cannot be used without negotiating a synchronization fee. The advantage to the consumer is that the licensing fees are reasonable because they are nonexclusive. The disadvantage is that the music is not specifically composed for a particular project, and the music does not match the action as well as customized music. It is rare to hear an extensive use of library music in high budget projects.

♫ Some directors and editors edit the film to the music.

Many of the large music library companies hire composers to write music in almost every style. Some of the companies hire music producers to produce numerous hours of *production music* per year. The company generally markets thousands of titles that are filed under album names; the album titles describe an emotional response expected from the audience. *Jazz, Smooth Jazz, Traditional Jazz, Pop, World, Novelty, Dramatic, Horror, Lush,* and *Emotional* are examples of album titles. Many of the companies also produce sound-effects albums.

Producing *library music* is a competitive business. The music can be costly to produce, advertise, and promote. Production music is a niche business and can be lucrative for a versatile composer/producer. Many composers also produce their music. Some large companies hire music producers to act as both producers and executive producers. Executive producing for a large *music library* company can be a complex job. Versatility, for both a producer and an executive producer, is an advantage because of the variety of music most companies produce.

The larger library companies produce albums with orchestras and small combos, as well as synthesized music. The musicians and singers are normally paid on a work-for-hire basis, which means they do not receive mechanical- or performance royalties (under the terms of a work-for-hire agreement, the company becomes the author). Some composers are able to negotiate a mechanical royalty (a percentage of albums sold). If the author is the production company (e.g., under a work-for-hire agreement), 100% of the income generated by performances will be paid to the music library production company. If the composer shares in the royalty split, the composer receives 50% of the performance royalties. In the United States the performance royalties are tracked, collected, and paid by BMI, ASCAP, and SESAC.

For a fee, a composer agrees to write and record a predetermined number of minutes of music. A majority of the music is produced in states or countries (U.S.) where union membership is not mandatory. (The company usually establishes session fees for the musicians and the singers.) The production company owns the music in perpetuity and has no further financial obligations to the composers, musicians, or singers.

The Business of Library Music

The licensing of *production music* (library music) varies according to use. Each company requires the licensee to sign agreements that specifically cover the usage of the music. The following is a description of some of the terms and agreements used in negotiations:

- Buyout—Some companies offer a "buyout" (a one-time fee for the nonexclusive, worldwide, unlimited use of the music in perpetuity); however, those rights are non-assignable to a third party. The contractual agreements specifically detail the rights of the licensee but also detail the restrictions on the licensee.
- Audio-Only—Certain companies license music to be used only on audio productions. Any additional usage requires permission from the licensor and usually an additional fee. The music must be used without alteration—most licensors do not allow the licensees to alter the music in any way. For example, many hip-hop producers use prerecorded tracks, add drum and percussion parts, add lyrics, and alter the tempo of the original track. These changes are not allowed

without permission from the licensor and most likely would require an additional fee, if permission were granted.

- Additional fees are charged if the music is used for motion pictures, television programs, or commercials.
- *The fees (U.S.) for commercials are usually based on the size of a territory.* For instance, if a commercial were broadcast in the southeast United States, the fee would be lower than if it were broadcast nationally.
- *The usage might be granted for a specified period of time and not in perpetuity.* For example, if a composition were licensed for a one-year usage in a commercial, the licensor might agree to pay additional fees if the licensee decided to extend the time period. Most extensions and additions are negotiated at the time of the initial agreement.
- *The music cannot be sold or licensed to a third-party.* For example, the track cannot be included on an album that is for sale; it cannot be licensed to a third-party through a Web site, and so forth.
- *A derivative work cannot be created using the licensed music.* For instance, a composer cannot write a saxophone melody, record it with the licensed track in the background and rename the track. However, the music can be edited to fit the purpose of the music, assuming the work remains the licensed work.
- *The music can be used in music videos that can be viewed on Web sites such as YouTube and Hulu.* If the licensed music is used, the title of the composition, the composer, and the publisher must be credited when completing an information form provided by the website.
- *The author(s) should receive credit unless it is not possible.*

Conclusion

Licensing *library music* is a multifaceted business. Carefully read the licensing agreements, and make certain not to use the music in any unauthorized manner. If necessary, retain an entertainment attorney to review the contract.

Assignment

Contact several music library companies to request demo reels; most demo reels can be found online. Licensing information can be obtained on Web sites. Write a report based on the following:

Scenario: You plan to use 5 pieces of library music in a corporate video. The video will be used as a non-broadcast training tool and shown to employees of a corporation for 1 year. Select the music you plan to use. Also assume that the length of track 1 has to be 34 seconds, track 2, 2 minutes, track 3, 1 minute and 47 seconds, track 4, 3 minutes and 4 seconds, and track 5, 2 minutes and 50 seconds. Answer the following questions:

- What type of license will you request?
- Determine the cost of the licensing fees for a 1 year period.
- Do you have the rights to use the music in perpetuity? If not, how much will it cost to extend the use of the music for 6 months?

♫ Create an intricate scenario so that you are able to practice "negotiating" a complex agreement.

Your report should include any possible extenuating circumstances (e.g., the licensor might want to extend the agreement for an additional year).

13

Producing Advertising Music, Television Music, and Corporate Music

> It's taken me all my life to learn what not to play.
>
> —Dizzy Gillespie

Advertising Music

Television Advertising

Advertising is a major source of revenue for composers and music producers. Some major advertising agencies retain staff music producers who oversee the production of the music. All advertising music companies have either a staff music producer or the composers (music company) produce the music. The average television commercial is 30 seconds, usually notated as :30. In addition, some commercials are :45, :15, :10, and in rare instances 1:00. Working in short form is difficult and requires composers to give the illusion that the music is written in long form. Creating a smooth transition between scenes and addressing the emotional impact of a commercial is both the job of the composer and the responsibility of an advertising music producer.

In addition to traditional production skills, advertising music producers must understand the specific needs of advertisers. The production of advertising music differs from record production in the following ways:

- An understanding of the advertising business is essential. Clients are only interested in selling their products. For most clients, the artistic value of the commercial is second in importance. The music designed for each commercial must, therefore, appeal to a target audience.

- The writer, art director (the creatives), and advertising producer convey to the music producer the musical direction for either a commercial campaign or an individual commercial.
- The music producer asks music houses (companies) to submit demos containing material similar in nature to the style of music required for the commercial. Most music houses assemble special demo reels specifically geared to the needs of the assignment. In addition, a general reel is submitted to show the quality of the work.
- The music producer "spots" the film with the music company representative. The style of music is discussed and the placement of the musical hits (accents) are determined.

> ♫ Hits are actions or emotions that have to be musically emphasized.

- Large agencies usually hire 3 music houses to compete for a job. Each company submits at least 3 demos. When the final selection is chosen, the music producer suggests changes to the demo and arranges for the final recording session.
- Agency music producers must be familiar with the union agreements: AFM (American Federation of Musicians), SAG (Screen Actors Guild), and AFTRA (American Federation of Television and Radio Artists). The unions will be discussed in the business section of this book.
- During the recording session, the music producer makes certain that the timings are correct and that the music addresses all concerns of the creative team. The music producer is also responsible for the overall technical sound quality of the production.
- The message of the commercial is of primary importance. The music can never mask the sound of the actors and/or voiceovers. Mixing a record affords the producer and engineer more artistic freedom than mixing commercials. In commercial mixes, the vocals and dialogue are mixed louder than the music. The advertiser's message is paramount. The advertising music producer coaches the singers to enunciate each word and make the lyric believable. Agency executives make comments such as, "I can't hear the *T* in the word *the*!" They are literally that particular.
- The producer often hires the musicians and singers. In major markets, many musicians and singers specialize in performing commercials. They are versatile artists who have the ability to perform in many styles and at a high level of competency. Vocalists readily accept direction and understand the importance of *selling* the product. The musicians and singers work quickly. Studio time and fees are costly in major markets, and overtime sessions can be pricey.

- In major markets, budgets are affected by the residual payments that are paid to musicians and singers. If the payments will be high, the agency may restrict the number of musicians and singers who can perform on a commercial. This formula that determines the cost of paying residuals is based upon the amount of airplay, the region or regions in the United States that are covered, the number of months or years the commercial is played, and additional considerations. This can be difficult to calculate. Some agencies require the music producer to project future residual payments.

> ♫ Many engineers specialize in recording commercials. They have to work quickly and must have the temperament to deal with extraordinary pressure.

- Advertising music producers are not only producers but also music supervisors. Songs or other music (e.g., soundtracks) are licensed for use on commercials. Music producers, copywriters, and art directors might suggest songs or instrumentals that are suitable, and the music producer's job is to negotiate a possible synchronization and/or transcription fee. Licenses must be obtained from both the music publisher(s) and the rights holder(s) (e.g., record company) if the master sound recording is used. The negotiations can become complex; therefore, the agency attorney is always involved.

> ♫ The producer must be thoroughly familiar with the union agreements to perform these calculations.

- The music must end at least a 1/2 second before the picture ends. The music should not begin until between 5 to 7 frames after the picture has started. Each agency has different requirements. With digital technology, the composer may be able to compose music for the full length of the commercial.
- The producer should separate the effects from the music by keeping the elements on separate tracks. Make a Pro Tools (or another audio program) file. Lead and background vocals should also be separated. Separation gives the mixer more options.

Radio Advertising

Producing and composing radio music for commercials is, arguably, more difficult than producing music for television commercials. There are no visuals, which implies that the music has to "help" tell the story; possibly more so than when there are pictures. Many television campaigns are also designed for the radio. Often, the music is not the same, and if it is the same, it generally has to be expanded to 1:00. The music producer supervises all revisions and expansions.

The average radio commercial is 1:00, which allows the composer more time to develop a composition. (The music can run the full length of each radio commercial.) Some composers feel designing music for radio commercials gives them more freedom than composing for television commercials, which in turn makes it easier than composing music for television.

If the music is underscoring voices (actors and/or announcers), the music cannot mask the words. In some instances, the emotional impact of the music might have to be exaggerated since there is no picture for the audience to relate to. If the music is a song (jingle), the production is similar to a record production, with the exception of the volume level of the vocals. Each word must be clear and the vocals should always be the loudest element in the mix.

In addition to coaching the musicians and singers, some music producers also coach the actors' and announcers' performances. This is usually done in conjunction with the copywriter.

It is advisable for the music producer to give the composer a copy of the script and the actors' and/or announcers' recorded tracks. The composer uses the script and the audio tracks for reference while composing. If the final voice track is not complete, it can be helpful to ask the copywriter to record the script and make certain that the reading coincides with the correct timings. Hearing the copywriter read the script with the proper inflections illustrates the writer's intentions; merely reading a script will not necessarily convey the true intent of the writer. This makes it difficult for a composer to create the proper musical mood. Often, this process is used for the composer to compose a demo. The demo is then revised to fit the final script.

Conclusion: Advertising Music

Most advertising music producers have a background in record production. They should have eclectic musical taste and extensive knowledge of music history, particularly of popular music.

Advertisers generally want original jingles (songs written for advertising) to sound like hit songs. Underscoring (instrumental music) has to mirror the emotions of a commercial without being obtrusive. Music producers have to understand the advertising business and modern recording technology, as well as the technical requirements of writing to visual images.

Producing music for advertising agencies is a high-pressure business. There are almost always rigid time restraints. Time buys (airtime) on broadcast, Internet, Satellite, and cable stations or other outlets (e.g.,

Hulu videos) are usually made in advance of the production schedule; consequently, the commercials have to be sent to the stations and posted on the Internet within a specific schedule. (The delivery might be digital or physical.) It is common to revise the music, script, and video. It appears as though each job is completed at the last possible moment—standard operating procedure in the advertising business.

Advertising music production is a stimulating and exciting vocation. The music producers and composers work with the finest musicians, singers, and technicians. (Engineers are artists.)

Television Music

Most composers produce the music they write for television programs. The producer or director of the program usually serves as the executive music producer. The main differences between television music and film music are as follows:

- The producer of a television series makes the final music choices; in feature films, the director makes the final decisions.
- Television music has to be composed in shorter time periods, and the budgets are lower.
- More electronic music is used in television than in feature films.
- A studio music supervisor may coproduce or supervise the music.
- Music supervisors select songs and library music that is used on national and nationally syndicated television programs. Many music supervisors are also music producers.
- Music for situation comedies (sitcoms) is usually produced as a *music library,* which is specifically composed for a program. At the beginning of the season, the composer records and produces numerous cues (musical selections) of varying lengths. The music supervisor selects the music for each episode and synchronizes it with the video. Some episodes require newly scored music.
- Music for dramatic shows is usually created and recorded in 7 to 10 days. The composer writes and orchestrates the music. In feature-film writing, funds to hire an orchestrator are usually included in the budget. Some national television programs have a budget to hire a small orchestra. Some small orchestras are used in addition to synthesized tracks.
- Individual television stations use music for local news programs, station

> ♫ Small-budget feature films usually do not have funds to hire an orchestrator.

identifications, and similar presentations. Television networks also commission music to help create a musical identity, such as the "NBC News Theme" by John Williams. Music houses (companies) that primarily record advertising music also provide music for television stations and television networks. Music producers who work for music houses guide the process.

- Mixing music for television and radio differs from mixing music that will be heard on a theater or home audio system. The music has to sound its best on a television speaker or on a radio being played through average car or home speakers. The low frequencies and some of the very high frequencies will generally not be heard (unless the transmission is in the high-definition digital domain). That affects not only how the music is mixed but also how the music should be composed. For example, very low or very high notes should be avoided.

Conclusion: Television Music

Most flourishing composers have been weaned on electronic music and also have the ability to produce and engineer their own projects. These skills are necessary for survival in the competitive television music industry.

Music for Corporate Videos

Advertising agencies and independent production companies produce corporate videos. A music house or individual composer who mostly produces music for commercials usually produces corporate music. Advertising-agency music producers oversee agency projects and film producers oversee the music produced by independent companies.

Corporate video is an umbrella term because of the wide range of subjects covered in the videos, everything from training to in-house information to in-store promotions. The music producer analyzes the needs of the client and suggests the most appropriate music. Often, the music has to appeal to a wide demographic, which implies that the music cannot "offend" any particular group. Most corporate videos have wall-to-wall music containing a variety of musical moods.

Corporate videos vary in length. The music producer or composer usually *spots* the film with the producer and/or director. The important musical hits are targeted, and the overall mood of the music for each cue is chosen. The process is similar to working on a television program, except that most corporate videos are trying to sell something, such as enticing a prospective job recruit to work for a certain company. The music producer must be aware of the scenes that require a sell musically. There might be a musical logo at the beginning and end of the video or there might be product shots throughout the video that have to be addressed musically; it is analogous to composing and producing music for commercials.

The budgets are relatively small compared to the budgets for commercials or television programs; consequently, the music is primarily synthesized, possibly involving 3 or 4 live musicians.

Conclusion: Corporate Videos

Advertising-music producers apply the same skills to overseeing corporate videos as they do to guiding commercials. Understanding a client's needs, selecting the appropriate music, and completing the project on time and within a budget are part of a music producer's responsibilities. The music must clearly define the corporate message and depict a corporation's image. Poorly conceived music can damage the image of a corporation.

Music for Infomercials

Infomercials are long-form commercials, which are viewed primarily on cable stations and on broadcast stations at off-peak hours. Infomercials can also be viewed on the Internet. The average length of each program is 30 minutes; some are 1 hour and some are quite short. (Short-form infomercials can be viewed on YouTube.) Infomercials are produced by advertising agencies or by production companies that specialize in infomercials.

Infomercials are designed to generate immediate viewer response. The producers expect viewers to call in and order the product. If a program does not test well, the airplay schedule is usually cancelled immediately.

Direct Response Television (DRTV) is a short form of an infomercial, averaging 1 to 2 minutes in length. DRTV is also designed to generate immediate viewer response.

The music is produced by an advertising music producer, the producer of an independent production company, or by the composer. The composer spots the video, and the producer and/or music producer decides on the style of music and where the musical hits should occur. Infomercials follow a format, which must be addressed musically.

- The host is usually a celebrity or someone associated with the product—the inventor, for example. The host must be believable. Host celebrities often share in the profits generated by the infomercial.

- The music producer should direct the composer to write a memorable theme for the opening and closing of the program. The closing is normally shorter than the opening and requires the composer to compress the thematic material. The opening and closing parts of the video usually contain a logo, which should be addressed musically, since the logo music also helps to establish the product.
- Call-to-Action (CTA) segments, repeated numerous times throughout the program, are the actual sell—the "pitch." The phone number is displayed on the screen and an announcer or the host reads the copy, which is designed to encourage the viewer to call in and order the product.
- The CTA is actually a commercial within the infomercial. The music producer generally directs the composer to approach the CTA as a separate commercial. Each time the CTA appears, the music is usually a variation of the first CTA music, or it may be a direct repeat of the original music. CTA music generally is a variation of the original theme because CTAs vary in time and content, so the audience does not lose interest. It is wise to direct the composer to write something memorable so the audience subliminally relates the CTA theme to the product.
- Testimonials—Testimonials from satisfied customers are sprinkled throughout the program. The testimonials should be addressed musically. The composer may possibly write a testimonial theme and vary the orchestration and tempo for the various testimonial sections. The music producer's job is to encourage the composer to write music that will help entice the audience to order the product. Uplifting music is usually most appropriate.
- Bumpers—Bumpers are short interludes that normally run 3 to 5 seconds and are designed to separate the various sections of the program. Bumpers are usually catchy, and the bumper music is often repeated throughout the program. The length and orchestration of the bumpers may vary, but the basic theme remains the same.

♫ Some infomercials are produced for the radio, but that is rare.

Conclusion: Infomercials

Infomercials are designed to create the illusion that viewers are watching an entertaining television program. When the Call-to-Action appears, the advertisers hope, the sales begin. Composers who write music for commercials and advertising-music producers are usually the best people to produce music for infomercials, since the ultimate goal of an infomercial is to sell a product.

Music for Documentaries

The composer usually produces the music for documentaries. Either the producer and/or the director serve as the executive music producer. Documentaries usually contain music throughout the entire video, and the scoring procedure is similar to the one for scoring television programs. The budgets are normally modest; therefore, synthesizers and samplers are extensively used. The budget might allow for 2 or 3 live musicians. In unusual circumstances—such as for IMAX productions—documentaries have budgets sizeable enough to hire an orchestra.

The composer spots the video with the producer and/or director. The style of music is chosen and the musical hit points established. Documentaries can be as dramatic as a scripted drama and require the composer to possess the same musical sensibilities. Unless a documentary is targeted to a specific demographic, most documentaries require generic music because the music must appeal to a diverse audience. The composer is often the music producer, arranger, and engineer.

Conclusion: Music for Documentaries

In 1952, famed Broadway composer Richard Rodgers wrote the music for the television series *Victory at Sea*, which encompasses 26 episodes about World War II. The RCA Victor Symphony Orchestra performed the score. It was an unusual project for the 1950s, and it remains uncommon. Major documentaries, such as some of the films shown in the IMAX theaters, might contain scores performed by live ensembles, but the scores are more likely to be performed on synthesizers and samplers and supplemented by live musicians.

Composing music for documentaries can be a rewarding and interesting experience. A composer/producer should have eclectic taste and the ability to compose in various musical styles.

* * *

For detailed information on this subject, read *Writing Music for Television and Radio Commercials (and more) Second Edition by Michael Zager*. (Scarecrow Press, Inc.)

14

A Brief History of Popular Music, Part I

The Blues had a baby, and they called it rock and roll.

—Muddy Waters

Pop, country, dance, gospel, R&B, hip-hop, rock, world music, and jazz are the main genres of popular music today. Each of these categories has subgenres: contemporary country (Taylor Swift), smooth jazz (Kenny G), traditional jazz (Miles Davis), modern rock (Green Day), hard rock (Led Zeppelin), alternative rock (Kings of Leon), and heavy metal (Metallica).

It can be helpful to understand the background—the roots—of musical genres. It can be especially beneficial when producing music for film. If a film calls for a re-creation of music from a historical period, an accurate musical interpretation is necessary. The importance of musical authenticity, in all styles, cannot be stressed enough. Understanding the history of the music is essential when producing film music, advertising music, or various genres of listening music.

> ♫ Many interesting books have been written about popular music, and one intention of this book is to encourage readers to do further research, if needed. This chapter is simply a brief overview.

Production Elements

An understanding of historical musical styles and recording technology helps expand a producer's creative palette. Producers can benefit from past ideas, which may be updated and applied to contemporary music production.

The expression *everything old is new again* applies to music production. The production techniques used on landmark albums, such as The Beatles' *Sgt. Pepper's Lonely Hearts Club Band* and *Pet Sounds* by The Beach Boys, are still used. Eric Clapton currently represents the original style of blues guitar playing, and the original nuances of blues vocals are still heard in the vocals of Mick Jagger.

Several important general observations can be made about the historical aspects of all popular styles of music:

The lyrics of many popular songs reflect historical time periods, as well as the mores of the societies. Further research into each genre could, for example, help a music supervisor select music for a film or aid a music producer in authentically re-creating a style and sound. Playing Baroque instruments to perform music from the Baroque period, performing on instruments used during the Civil War to re-create marching-band music of the period, or writing lyrics that simulate the syntax of a historical time period are helpful production techniques.

Below is a brief timeline of the general lyrical content of some historical periods:

♫ "Corn Ditties," sung at the end of the 1700s, preceded Negro Spirituals.

- Negro spirituals reflect on the life of slavery in the U.S.
- The blues, developed after the Civil War, reflect primarily on black southern rural life, but went urban when blacks moved to Chicago, mostly after World War II.
- The roaring '20s is depicted with "good-time" dance music, such as the Charleston dance style and the development of jazz. The Great Depression of the 1930s is portrayed in songs such as "Brother, Can You Spare a Dime," while the wartime songs of the 1940s were patriotic, e.g., "Boogie Woogie Bugle Boy."
- Beginning in the late 1930s, jazz ballads echoed sexuality and sensuality; torch songs are sexy and fun, and rhythmic virtuosity is portrayed in the more upbeat songs sung by artists such as Lambert, Hendricks, and Ross, a 1950s vocal group that emulated big band instrumentalists with lighting-fast rhythmic lyrics and inventive harmonies.
- Country music has always reflected the American southern rural lifestyle. Beginning with hillbilly music, the lyric content of country music has dealt with rural life and/or the common problems and mores of everyday people. This is the predominant reason for its continued popularity. People can associate not only with

♫ Rock 'n' roll played an eminent role in the civil rights movement. The races united in a love of "the devil's music" and remain united. This angered southern (and northern) racists.

specific situations and emotions described in lyrics but with the demeanor of most of the performers as well. Many country-music performers have credibility with the public, since many of the fans come from similar backgrounds. As pop/country became popular, the lyrical content, in many songs, became more "suburban" in subject matter.

- The rock 'n' roll music of the 1950s reflects the mores of young people and also a cultural rebellion. The young audience wanted a musical identity that differed from the music listened to by their elders. The lyrics reflected freedom, fun, and love.
- In the middle 1960s, rock 'n' roll developed into rock. The message (lyric) became significant. Escapism, countercultural ideals, and violence were depicted in the various subgenres of rock music.
- Some heavy metal music has been, arguably, highly destructive. Suicides have been blamed on listeners' reaction to lyrics. This is a controversial issue among psychologists.
- Folk artists, such as Bob Dylan and Joan Baez, reflect the times and generational mores. Anti–Vietnam War songs were reflective of an unpopular war.
- Popular culture was permanently changed not only by the lyric content of The Beatles' music (which became popular in the United States in 1964) but also by the lifestyle of The Beatles. Their long hair was a sign of nonconformity. A fascination with Indian culture, and specifically with Indian music, introduced world music to popular music audiences. Their use of the sitar, an Indian guitarlike instrument, was the first use of an ethnic instrument in popular music that received global acceptance. The Beatles' lyrics run the gamut from silly to thoughtful.

♫ When studying the evolution of rock 'n' roll, one element that performers share is their admiration, and in some cases idolization, of the artists who preceded them. Many also greatly admire their contemporaries.

The most revered artists, who have had the greatest influence on rock 'n' roll, are the classic blues singers. Since popular music is a direct descendant of the blues (and black music in general), it is rare not to hear the originators of rock refer to popular blues singers such as Howlin' Wolf and John Lee Hooker. Music has always evolved from one musical style to another. Rock 'n' roll continues in that tradition. New names and subgenres are given to various musical styles but the underlying basis of the music remains the same.

Author's Opinion: There are only two kinds of music—*good and bad.*

- *Hip-hop is the most socially relevant and influential music since rock 'n' roll.* The roots of hip-hop originate with the Griots (storytellers) of West Africa. Much of their culture entered the United States with the slaves.
- Hip-hop (rap) is based upon music from Jamaica called *dub*. The dub artists kept repeating the "hottest" sections of records because dancers reacted. They also began repeating short vocal phrases, which morphed into rapping. *Scratching* (rhythmic record turntable manipulation), DJs, breakdancing, and graffiti art became a part of the hip-hop culture.
- Rap surfaced in the South Bronx, New York, in the 1970s and was originally recorded by small independent labels. These boutique labels were trying to appeal to the "street culture." The music eventually spread globally and is now performed and recorded in almost every language.
- Hip-hop lyrics reflect lifestyle, violence, and entertainment. A variety of lyrical messages has had a profound influence on the listeners and has made a major sociological impact on society.
- A hip-hop producer must be aware of evolving trends, both from a technological standpoint and from the ever-changing mores of the hip-hop community.

> ♫ The Berklee College of Music, in Boston, Massachusetts, offers a course called Turntable Techniques. The students learn the craft of rhythmically scratching vinyl records to create percussive effects.

- In the middle to late 1970s, disco music triggered a lifestyle change for the gay community. The disco (nightclub) became a prime meeting place not only for gays but also for the Hispanic community and other party people of all races who loved to dance in a glitzy and exciting atmosphere.
- Most disco songs reflected the club scene or love, or espoused social commentary. Songs such as Gloria Gaynor's "I Will Survive" and "Ain't No Stoppin' Us Now," by McFadden and Whitehead, became anthems. The Bee Gees' soundtrack album *Saturday Night Fever* was

an international sensation and brought disco to the forefront of popular music.

♫ Punk music originated in the UK and reached its popularity between 1976 and 1981.

- During the late 1970s, punk was disco's nemesis. Many punk lyrics were political in nature, and some were racist, associated with common use of the swastika (Hitler's logo, which symbolized Nazi Germany). The music never gained mainstream acceptance in the United States.
- The year 1981 marked a transformation in the music industry, with the introduction of MTV (Music Television) in the United States. (Music videos had been popular in Europe prior to the introduction of MTV.) The audience was now able to *see* an artist's visual conception of a recording. Music videos were considered promotional and marketing tools and did not generate profits for the labels. Video airplay became almost as important as radio airplay. Listeners heard songs more often on the radio than they viewed videos because of the amount of time they spent in cars. Music became a benchmark for a new breed of film—video direction. The directing style became popular and inspired many feature film directors to capture an MTV look. Some examples:
  - Michael Jackson's album *Thriller* became the largest-selling album in history. The exposure of Jackson's music videos on MTV was crucial to the album's success. The songs were in the black-pop genre (funky rhythms with pop vocals). Jackson continued the Motown concept of black music that appealed to all races.
  - Whitney Houston is another example of an artist who became a superstar partially due to her ability to crossover to a universal audience. (Here music videos allowed the world to see her.) There was a backlash from the black community since she recorded pop songs rather than R&B–based material. Her future attempts to sing more R&B–oriented songs never gave her the same level of success as her pop songs. Singing love ballads made her one of the greatest stars in the history of commercial music.
  - Madonna, a disco diva, achieved worldwide popularity. The forerunner of the Britney Spears style of pop, Madonna's career is based on her brilliant marketing abilities and her controversial lyrics, represented by songs such as "Like a Prayer." ("Like a Prayer" was a groundbreaking video and caused much controversy.) Her dancing and sexy image is pure entertainment and she continues to be an international superstar.

  - Bruce Springsteen represented (and still represents) blue-collar workers. His socially conscious lyrics have helped politicians attract voters. His persona is clearly visualized in his music videos. He performed and campaigned for John Kerry in the presidential election of 2004.
- Hip-hop (rap) continued to develop. When the "genre barrier" was eventually broken on MTV, hip-hop videos became a staple.
- During the 1980s, musicians used celebrity status to raise money and awareness for causes, such as Live Aid and Band Aid.
- During the 1990s, hip-hop grew in popularity and remained, primarily, socially conscious music. The alternative bands, such as Nirvana and Pearl Jam, were popular; the dance music market also continued to grow by dividing into multiple subgenres. The Latin market crossed over to the pop market with artists such as Santana and Ricky Martin; country music also crossed over to the pop market.
- Political and lifestyle lyrics remained popular but the decade was not as distinctive as some others.
- From the turn of the century to the present, the music industry has experienced a rebirth and reformation by having to address major issues, such as illegal peer-2-peer file sharing, the Internet as a major source of revenue, substantial income from music used as ringtones and ringbacks, artist controlled sound recordings, and the consolidation of major record labels.
- Hip-hop has consistently populated the top 10; adult contemporary artists, such as Andrea Bocelli and Josh Groban, achieved top 10 successes and country artists are continually represented on the top 10 pop charts. The music business is more amalgamated and it is difficult to indicate a specific cultural trend in the first decade of the 21st century. Country musicians continue to sing about blue-collar issues, hip-hop artists continue to rhyme about socially relevant issues, and many artists have continued to provide unadulterated entertainment.
- The public has varied tastes, which are reflected in the diverse range of musical genres represented on the sales charts. As the primary point of purchase switches to Internet stores, the public can select a greater variety of music than in most brick-and-mortar stores; consumers can also assemble personalized compilation albums on services such as iTunes. The Internet stores compile information on customers' buying habits and the information is analyzed by the industry. The music business is perpetually evolving and "*where it will stop, nobody knows!*"

Conclusion

Popular music continues to reflect the lifestyles of many performers. Therefore, be concerned with the images that artists portray to the public. This is not a reference to cookie-cutter acts but to performers who have the potential of achieving career longevity. Thoughtful career planning and artistic achievement and development are the best weapons against contracting "artistic antiquity." Attention to song choice, arrangements, stage performance, interview techniques, image building (including videos), artist management, booking agent representation, production achievement, and label commitment all contribute to artists' successes or lack of successes.

Overview of Musical Genres

The following is a brief overview of the various popular music genres. Numerous books have been written about each of the following subjects and it behooves a conscientious music producer to become familiar with the historical aspects of the genre of music he or she is producing. Not only should the history be studied but also the production techniques used to create the earliest recordings. For example, the simple technique of recording an orchestra with two microphones is still used (in conjunction with modern microphone techniques) by many classical and film-scoring engineers. The sonic images in many old recordings are benchmarks by which to judge modern recordings. Skilled producers are good listeners and observers.

> ♫ The following section discusses some of the major highlights of popular music.

A Brief History of Country Music

The musical roots of country music stem from the British Isles. The British, who immigrated to America in the eighteenth and nineteenth centuries, brought their musical culture with them.

Country music was defined by a style of fiddle playing and song lyrics. The fiddle (and later the banjo) was used to surround or replace the vocals. As the genre progressed and became popular in the 1920s, the lyrics became the property of the southern "working man" much the way hip-hop (rap) lyrics have influenced contemporary African-American society.

Country music was also influenced by the music of the American slaves and later by the American black culture. The black rhythms and the dancing had a direct effect on the development of the music.

Country music was initially most popular in the southern agricultural areas. The music spread with the traveling medicine shows, which were similar to vaudeville shows. With the advent of the railroad, music and culture were able to spread at a faster pace.

Country music has remained the working person's music. If the audience can empathize with the lyrics, songs will remain popular. The music is traditional American music. Since country music is tied to American southern culture, it has not achieved acceptance in other cultures. Only in the United Kingdom, and to a smaller degree France, has country music realized success out of the United States. Other European countries have a small country music market.

Subgenres of country music include country-rock, bluegrass, honky tonk, and Texas swing. Their roots remain deeply tied to traditional country music.

Country and pop music have much in common. Most of the songs contain simple, memorable melodies, which enable the audience to effortlessly sing-along. The repeated sections called hooks or choruses are catchy and 'hook' the audience into wanting to hear the songs again.

In the 1920s radio achieved popularity. *The Grand Ole Opry* (a country-music radio program) did more to help spread country music than any other source at that time. It was founded and hosted by George D. Hay, who said, "The principal appeal of the *Opry* is a homey one. It sends forth the aroma of bacon and eggs frying on the kitchen stove on a bright spring morning." Country music remains popular and has an ever-growing crossover audience.

A Brief History of Negro Spirituals

African-American slaves—brought to the United States mainly from West Africa—were mostly converted to Christianity. The slaves attended church services and also worshiped in "praise houses," which were makeshift, informal churches. They morphed African musical language with Protestant hymns to form what became known as Negro spirituals. The songs spoke of love of Jesus Christ who was looked upon as a savior from the miseries of slavery. Many of the songs were sad and referred to as "sorrow songs." Additional songs, called "jubilees," had faster tempos and the lyrics were not as depressing as the "sorrow songs."

At first the slaves were not permitted to sing and dance while working on the plantations, so they met in remote locations to do so. Eventually, they were allowed to sing while working. The songs were called "work songs" because the slaves sang to pass the time while working on the plantations. The lyrics dealt with enduring pain and suffering. "Pick a Bale of Cotton" was one of the most popular work songs.

Spirituals were sung in the call-and-response musical form, which is accomplished by alternating lines between a soloist and the congregation. The music was filled with improvised vocal lines called melismas, which are a group of notes usually sung around one syllable (later known as blue notes). Also included were hand clapping and syncopated rhythms, transplanted from African music.

The Underground Railroad was an organization that helped slaves escape to the North. This institution became a source of lyrical ideas for spirituals. To avoid being tracked by hounds, slaves periodically walked in water to interrupt the scent. The classic spiritual "Wade in the Water" deals with the plight of the slaves. Another classic spiritual, "Swing Low, Sweet Chariot," referred directly to the Underground Railroad and was considered a code for escape to the North. Spirituals were first brought to international prominence by a group of college students called the Jubilee Singers. In 1871, they began touring for the purpose of raising money for Fisk University in Nashville, Tennessee, an African-American institution.

Numerous recordings of spirituals were made between 1933 and 1942. They are housed in the Archive of Folk Songs in the Library of Congress. The archive is one of the most important historical documentations of the most shameful period in American history. *All American popular music stems from the music developed by the slaves.*

A Brief History of Gospel Music

At the end of the nineteenth century, spirituals were replaced by the singing of the gospel (the story of Jesus Christ), referred to as gospel music. The end of slavery propelled the decline of spirituals. The lyrics were no longer of interest in the black churches, although the music was performed in concerts, also called *revivals.*

Gospel music is a direct descendant of the spirituals. The lyrics praise God and Jesus in a more upbeat manner than spirituals. Each church had a choir that performed in the call-and-response tradition, a continuation of the basic musical style of the spirituals. Gospel developed at the same time as jazz, ragtime, and blues. The musical elements were incorporated into the gospel style.

Thomas A. Dorsey (this is not the famous Tommy Dorsey, a trombonist and bandleader who was a mainstay of the American big band era in the 1940s and 1950s) is considered to be the father of gospel music. He formed the first music-publishing company devoted to black gospel music. Traditional gospel incorporates hand-clapping, organ accompaniment, large choruses and harmonies, and lyrics that praise the Lord. Artists such as Mahalia Jackson and James Cleveland sang in the traditional style.

As the music developed, so did the form of accompaniment. A banjo, fife, and drums often accompanied spirituals. In the 1930s, the piano and guitar were the primary accompanying instruments for gospel music.

In recent years, contemporary gospel has become popular. Artists such as Kirk Franklin have proven that contemporary gospel music can sell millions of albums. This can be partly attributed to the close musical alliance that gospel has with the musical styles of contemporary R&B and hip-hop—especially the use of rhythm. The only difference is the content of the lyrics.

A Brief History of the Blues

The blues is an outgrowth of the music of the slaves in the United States. While working in the fields they sang songs called *field hollers,* which reflected the abhorrent living conditions and the horrific life of slavery. The songs were sung in a call-and-response style. A soloist sang, and the rest of the field hands answered. Singing served two purposes:

- It gave the slaves a way to communicate with each other. The slave owners were interested only in work and not social interaction.
- Working in the cotton fields and other fieldwork was boring and tedious. Singing helped to pass the time.

This music developed into spirituals and gospel music. At the end of the nineteenth century the blues, a direct descendant of spirituals and gospel music, was born. Rhythm & blues and rock music are direct descendants of the blues.

The blues (in some instances) mimicked the call-and-response of the field holler; a soloist was the leader and the guitar and/or banjo (sometimes harmonica) answered. The bending of the "blue notes" is the signature sound of the blues. Because the original blues singers actually lived the lives they were singing about, the music had an authenticity not found in many musical styles.

Author's Opinion: Rock 'n' roll is based on the blues, and rock guitar playing is blues based. Rock players play electric guitars instead of acoustic guitars, and they use electronic effects to alter the guitar sound. The Rolling Stones, The Beatles, Eric Clapton, and Bob Dylan are artists directly influenced by the old blues singers.

The Rolling Stones and Eric Clapton were directly influenced by bluesman Robert Johnson, who made his final recordings in 1937.

When Eric Clapton was in the rock group Cream, they recorded *Crossroads*, a Robert Johnson composition. (Clapton's album *Me and Mr. Johnson* is a tribute to Robert Johnson.)

Muddy Waters, Howlin' Wolf, John Lee Hooker, Robert Johnson, and BB King are some of the blues musicians who are revered by many great rock musicians. They set an example for young contemporary singers. The goal is not for younger singers to mimic the styles of those artists but to understand what made those artists iconic. The audience knows when a performer "lives" the music.

W. C. Handy is credited with being the father of the blues. His classic song "St. Louis Blues" was recorded in 1914, and it has been recorded numerous times since. He was the first person to codify the blues. In addition to being a musician and a songwriter, he owned a music publishing company that published sheet music.

Blues singers influenced many of the great jazz singers, notably Bessie Smith, Billie Holiday, and Joe Williams.

Blues: Essential Elements

Early recordings permanently documented live performances. Review the reasons blues was such a significant element in the development of popular music.

- In some of the earlier recordings, the singer played the melody while singing. The combination of a steel string guitar and voices singing in unison was a unique sound.
- Holding a "bottleneck" (a piece of a bottle's neck was worn on a finger) or a small, metal bar in the guitar player's left hand and sliding it across the strings often defined the sound of the blues acoustic guitar. This device, along with "blue notes" and call-and-response singing, gave the blues its signature sound. (Blue notes can be defined as notes that are slightly lower than, or flat of, the normal pitch, and produce a sliding effect. Blue notes can also "bend up"—mostly to a minor third or perfect fifth. This style of playing is still the most definitive element in any form of popular guitar playing.)
- The Mississippi Delta region was the home of many original blues musicians. Since most of them were black and lived a hard life, the authenticity of the lyrics provided the audience with an unusual musical experience. This was not just entertainment; it was "real life," and the audience related to the artists.
- This style of guitar playing and singing is closely related to country music. Country music, blues, and rhythm & blues are relatives.

Listen closely to the essence of some of the original blues artists. Classic blues performers, such as Muddy Waters and Howlin' Wolf, possessed believability, which translated into public acceptance.

Credibility is the one element shared by most superstars.

♫ There is a direct parallel between a truly gifted jazz musician and a gifted vocalist. Both "feel" the music.

The public will continue to support artists who "speak to them." Although this quality is rare, most successful music artists believe in their craft. (Their level of artistic skill may not be as distinctive as artists who reach legendary status.) Many cookie-cutter acts are highly professional and achieve substantial record sales. Since they are not unique, however, many cookie-cutter acts have a brief professional life span.

It is important to include recording engineers in the above discussion. Their contributions to recorded music are often overlooked. Exceptional recording engineers have a highly developed musical sensibility and an incredible ability to sonically reproduce and augment a performance in the most creative manner. Not only must they be sensitive listeners, but they must also have the technical knowledge and ability to achieve the sonic goals of producers and artists. Many engineers are also successful producers.

A Brief History of Jazz

Jazz, America's native art form, began to develop at the end of the nineteenth century. Jazz was born in New Orleans. The roots of jazz are found in spiritual and gospel music. African rhythms were combined with European musical influences—brought to the South by Creole musicians—to form the foundation of jazz. Jazz is a highly sophisticated, improvisational art form; it is *art created at the moment.*

♫ In 2002, Norah Jones, a Blue Note label artist, won the Grammy award for Best Album. Although Jones is not a traditional jazz artist, it is interesting to note that a jazz label signed her. Diana Krall, a traditional jazz artist, has experienced impressive international success. This is an indication that what many consider to be a dying art form is still a popular, viable musical genre.

Jazz became popular beginning with the great Louis Armstrong and has continued with the multitalented Wynton Marsalis and many other educator-musicians. Jazz has experienced an ever-changing development. From the minstrel shows—the first national form of entertainment—came Dixieland, blues, swing, bop, modern jazz, fusion, and the current crossover music, smooth jazz. Traditionally, musicians have drawn on the past to reach the future.

Many contemporary jazz producers have roots in R&B and hip-hop music. They combine the sophistication of jazz improvisation and harmonies with the rhythms of R&B and hip-hop. Herb Alpert has been credited with creating smooth jazz.

Author's Opinion: American universities should be credited with keeping Traditional Jazz alive. They offer jazz programs within the music departments, which include workshops with great jazz musicians. Exposing listeners to jazz music is essential to the historical preservation of American music.

Jazz album sales in the United States are minimal compared to sales of other musical styles, but the international market continues to flourish. Many jazz musicians perform and record in Europe and Japan, where jazz remains popular.

A Brief History of Rhythm & Blues (R&B)

R&B (soul)—originally referred to as "race music"—is an offshoot of the blues, which emanates from spirituals and gospel music. The African rhythms continued to develop. So did improvisational vocalizing, which has remained a defining trait of African American–based music. Rhythm & Blues, developed in the late 1940s, has continued to advance artistically and remain popular in the marketplace. Artists such as Ray Charles, James Brown, Aretha Franklin, and Prince are some of the most important proponents of traditional R&B and funk music. Contemporary artists Luther Vandross, Brian McKnight, Alicia Keys, and Beyoncé have continued the tradition.

Electronics have influenced all genres of popular music. Many contemporary R&B and hip-hop records contain hypnotic rhythm patterns and sounds that cannot be performed by a live musician. Combined with traditional R&B rhythms, the grooves have become more infectious and more inventive. Live musicians, mixed with synthesizers and samplers, usually perform on contemporary R&B records.

Motown

Traditional Rhythm & Blues was geared toward black audiences. Berry Gordy, the founder of Motown Records, had a different idea. He wanted to record R&B–oriented records that would crossover to the white audience.

Gordy lived in Detroit, which had a large black population and no major record companies. The church proved to be a gold mine of talent.

> ♫ From a sociological perspective, one might wonder why Detroit contained so many extraordinary musical artists. Detroit is the home of the automobile industry, and during the 1940s and 1950s labor was needed for the assembly plants. Southern African Americans relocated to Detroit from the South, where jobs were scarce. Attending church on a regular basis was part of the culture. Gospel music and participation in church choirs was, and still is, the training ground for many rhythm & blues artists.

The "Motown sound"—also called the "sound of young America"—comprised catchy melodies, universally accepted lyrics, and great R&B arrangements. The tracks were soulful but differed from the James Brown school of funk. The audience could dance and feel the backbeat but the sound and feel of the music appealed to all ethnicities. Many of Brown's original songs were designed around a repetitive rhythm pattern (mostly four-bar patterns) and rhythmic vocal lines. The Motown songs were fully developed pop songs but surrounded by the elements of soul music. This musical hybrid made Motown unique.

In 1960, Gordy founded Tamla Records, followed by Motown, Gordy, and Soul Records. He experienced unprecedented success in a short period of time. Motown was outselling the major labels. Gordy developed a formula that consistently worked. The Motown "creatives" worked for the record label.

- A core group of songwriters and producers wrote for and produced the artists. The staff personnel included Smokey Robinson, Norman Whitfield, and Holland, Dozier, and Holland. They created the Motown sound.
- Staff engineers recorded the records in the Motown studios. This gave the recordings a sonic consistency.
- The original studio was called Hitsville U.S.A, which is currently a museum in Detroit.
- The Funk Brothers were the in-house rhythm section. They recorded rhythm tracks that had the feel and sound that defined Motown.

> ♫ Booker T. and the MG's were the equivalent of The Funk Brothers for Stax Records in Memphis, Tennessee. Stax was a highly successful Rhythm & Blues label.

- Cholly Atkins choreographed every act. His unique choreography helped create Motown's visual image.
- Paul Riser, the principal arranger, complemented the rhythm tracks by also bringing a unique sound to the arrangements.
- The artists were taught etiquette, which included training in how to respond to the press and respect their fans.

- The performance wardrobes were carefully selected.
- Motown was not only a record label but also an *image*. The audience knew when they were listening to or watching a Motown artist. The sound of the records and the visual images of the artists were distinct.

Some of the Motown artists in the 1960s were as follows:

- Smokey Robinson and The Miracles
- Diana Ross and The Supremes
- Stevie Wonder
- The Jackson 5
- Marvin Gaye
- The Temptations
- The Four Tops
- The Spinners
- Martha and The Vandellas
- The Marvelettes

Berry Gordy and his staff literally changed pop music during that time period. The influence that the Motown sound had on pop music still continues.

Author's Opinion: The success of the Motown sound is unique in the music industry; very few labels before or after the heyday of Motown had their own identity. The Chess and Vee-Jay recordings were associated with R&B and blues, but the Motown records were produced in-house, creating a central musical identity. Herb Alpert, Louis Armstrong, Miles Davis, Frank Sinatra, and Nat "King" Cole are examples of artists who are or were so unique that after the first few notes of a recording, listeners recognized them. The same was true of the Motown artists during that historic time period.

Motown: Production Elements

- Gordy's approach to record production still remains *the* most important factor in the production process—*The song is the foundation.*
- Since the mission of Motown was to achieve crossover records (appealing to all ethnicities) the lyrics were not standard R&B lyrics, which dealt with the black experience in the United States. Motown lyrics dealt with subjects that had universal appeal.
- The songwriters generally produced the songs they wrote. They had a clear creative vision, which was the sound of Motown. Because the songwriters, producers, musicians, and engineers were part of the

Motown family, a mutual trust developed, which made the creative objectives easier to achieve. The production and writing teams were well-oiled creative machines. All parts worked smoothly.

- The backbeat of the rhythm section was featured in the mix. Nothing cluttered the strength of the rhythm section. The string and horn parts were most often sparse and complemented the arrangements rather than overcrowding them. The producers knew that the audience liked to "groove" to the beat, and the nature of the music enabled them to feature the basic feel on the records. This still holds true of most popular-music recordings. If the audience cannot get into the "pocket" of a rhythm-oriented recording, it is virtually impossible to achieve a hit record. (This concept applies to all styles of popular music.)

> ♫ Gordy's attention to the song helped him create one of the most successful publishing catalogues in the history of popular music. The company is called Jobete Music. In 1997, EMI Music publishing bought 50% of Jobete and Stone Diamond Music Corporation, Jobete's sister company.

- The background vocal arrangements made major contributions to the sound of the records. Most of the background vocals had a gospel feel. In fact, if only one Rhythm & Blues component could be extracted from the general sound of a Motown artist, it would be the background vocals.
- Vibraphone and a low baritone saxophone were signature sounds used on many Motown recordings. An example is Diana Ross and the Supremes' recording of "Where Did Our Love Go." Those instruments became associated with the Motown sound.
- The lead vocalists did not sing in a standard Rhythm & Blues style. (They did not scream and were not as powerful as many soul singers.) The melodies were clearly stated (not many melismas); therefore, the audiences could easily sing along. The typical improvisational style of most Rhythm & Blues singers did not exist at Motown. Some of the early records were remarkably close to the sound of the 1950s, such as "Mr. Postman," by The Marvelettes.

> ♫ Since Motown artists were recording and performing acts, dancing, appearance, and interplay among the members of the act made equal contributions to the ultimate success of the artists. All of the Motown artists during this time period can be cited as examples. If an artist did not fit the Motown profile, he, she, or they were not signed to the label.

- Hand claps were prominently featured. This was a remnant from gospel music. (Finger snaps frequently took the place of hand claps.)

♫ Listen to the early Stevie Wonder records compared to his later work. The melody was simply defined, allowing the audience to immediately grasp the song. He later sang with more melismas, some of which he wrote as part of his melodies. Diana Ross, Marvin Gaye, Smokey Robinson, and other Motown artists took the same approach.

- Piano tracks often resembled the honky-tonk style that was not only used on rock 'n' roll records but also displayed on many of The Beatles' recordings. The rock 'n' roll piano style, which developed from the gospel and boogie-woogie style of playing, continues to be emulated by many contemporary pianists, such as Elton John and Dr. John. (Boogie-woogie was a form of blues usually played with a shuffle beat.)
- The piano parts were prominent in the mixes. Most were gospel tinged and some tracks retained a 1950s pop feel.
- Signal processing aided in creating an ambience for the records. Extensive use of equalization, compression, and limiting shaped the recorded sound, which made the records sound exciting on the radio.

♫ Radio mixes are an essential element in the creation of hit records.

Motown's Success

The height of the Motown era was between 1964 and 1967. In 1 year, the company charted 5 records in the top 10. The following are some of the relevant statistics:

- 14 #1 charted pop singles
- 20 #1 R&B chart hits
- 46 additional singles were in the top 15 on the pop charts
- 75 additional singles were in the top 15 on the R&B charts

From a sociological viewpoint, such statistics prove that there were no racial barriers in popular music. Rock 'n' roll helped break down racial barriers and so did the sound of Motown.

Motown's Demise

In 1967 some of the performers were unhappy, and group members changed. Motown never agreed to certify records gold, which would have confirmed a minimum number of units sold and required royalty payments. The artists and the songwriters did not feel that they were being paid the proper royalties. The star songwriting team of Holland, Dozier, and Holland left Motown and sued the company for back royalties.

In 1971 Motown moved from Detroit to Los Angeles, which in my opinion also contributed to the downfall of the original Motown Records concept. Most of the talent signed to Motown was from Detroit, and Motown had a sound unique to the city, partially due to the geographical location and partially due to the family atmosphere that Gordy created within the company. The Motown ambience was destroyed. As the formula began to decompose, so did the Motown sound. The records were no longer distinctive. They lost the identity that Motown had established with the public.

In 1988 Motown was sold to Boston Ventures and MCA for a reported $61 million. Boston Ventures bought MCA's interest and in 1993 sold the company to PolyGram for a reported $325 million.

The publishing company, Jobete Music, has been valued at hundreds of millions of dollars. Some of Jobete's copyrights include the following:

- "Three Times a Lady"
- "I Heard It Through the Grapevine"
- "Stop! In the Name of Love"
- "Tracks of My Tears"
- "What's Going On"
- "Dancin' in the Streets"
- "Reach Out, I'll Be There"
- "My Girl"
- "Superstition"

Conclusion

The creativity of the producers, songwriters, and musicians was the key to Motown's success. One of Motown's major contributions to popular music was the universal appeal of the music. In the beginning of rock 'n' roll, Caucasian artists rerecorded black music. They attempted to make the songs more appealing to white audiences. Gordy's formula was to appeal to all groups, thereafter breaking down musical racial barriers. It is highly unlikely that another Motown will ever exist.

James Brown

James Brown virtually invented what now is categorized as funk. Called the "Godfather of Soul," and "the hardest-working man in show business," Brown had a concept of rhythm that made his recordings the most sampled in the music business. Funk and rhythm-based artists who have followed in Brown's footsteps have incorporated his musical feel in their styles. Just as jazz trumpet players credit Louis Armstrong as *the* innovator, James Brown has influenced artists who either consciously or subconsciously steeped their music in rhythm.

Author's Note: James Brown is another example of a unique talent. As a producer, one is always searching for artists who have "their own voice." Musicians I know who have worked with James Brown have all said that he knew exactly what he wanted and knew how to get it. Brown was musically demanding and was known for fining musicians who made mistakes during a live performance.

James Brown's influence on music is attributable to his distinctive interpretation of rhythm and also his exceptional performance skills. James Brown was one of a kind.

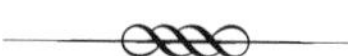

Songs

In 1956, "Please, Please, Please," by James Brown and The Famous Flames, was his first hit. It went to number five on the R&B chart. Among his numerous hits under his name only are these:

- "Papa's Got a Brand New Bag" reached #8 on August 7, 1965, on the *Billboard* pop chart.
- "I Got You (I Feel Good)" reached #3 on November 20, 1965, on the *Billboard* pop chart.
- "It's a Man's Man's Man's World" reached #8 on May 7, 1966, on the *Billboard* pop chart.

> ♫ "Papa's Got a Brand New Bag" reached #25 on the UK Charts on September 23, 1965

> ♫ "I Got You (I Feel Good)" reached #29 on the UK chart on February 24, 1966.

> ♫ "It's a Man's Man's Man's World" reached #13 on the UK chart on June 16, 1966.

James Brown: Production Elements

The most important element to analyze is James Brown's style of arranging. The components are as follows:

- A very strong backbeat, created by the drums and guitar.
- Infectious rhythm riffs are anchored in the guitar, bass, and drum parts, with catchy answers and fills from the horns. (Brown developed his rhythmic style by eliminating any parts that interrupted the rhythm. He wanted the audience to feel every beat.)

- Most of the songs do not have background vocals.
- He had a unique style of singing. (He began his career singing in a gospel group.)
- The recordings are not slickly produced. His voice is mixed louder than the instrumental tracks and the audience always feels the groove.
- There is limited reverberation. The tracks contain minimal reverberation.

Author's Note: It is important to consider the musical format of most of James Brown's hit songs. The funk songs have long passages that remain on one chord. This allowed the groove to develop and also allowed the audience to really feel the funk (rhythm). There is a musical relief by going to the bridge and then returning to the main groove. All R&B and hip-hop groove-oriented songs follow James Brown's example. Many hip-hop songs have only one chord and achieve variety by changing melodies, instrumental riffs, and background vocals, while riffing over the same basic groove.

Sly and The Family Stone

Sly and The Family Stone was one of the most rhythmically infectious bands in the history of popular music. They peaked between 1969 and 1971. There were no racial barriers with the audience, which contributed to Sly's enormous popularity.

The group was unique because of the cross-pollination of rock-pop and R&B. Since all rock is anchored in black music, the musical potpourri Sly created enabled the group to crossover to pop. They were not considered a Rhythm & Blues band but rather an "everyman or everywoman" act.

Sly was the next step in the development of funk, started by James Brown. (It is important to mention the stellar contribution to the genre from George Clinton & Parliament Funkadelic.) The main difference between James Brown and Sly was that Sly wrote pop songs with a funk/pop/rock rhythm section while James Brown wrote and recorded primarily groove-oriented songs. "I Want to Take You Higher" is the closest Sly came to a song that could be considered reminiscent of James Brown.

In addition to a string of hits, the band's live show was one of the best in the music industry. They sold out the largest venues in the United States. When the group began to perform, the audience stood up and never sat down.

Author's Opinion: The author was co-leader (with partner Aram Schefrin) of Ten Wheel Drive. TWD toured with Sly & The Family Stone. Sly performed the best live show of any band at that time and one of the best live shows in the history of pop music. "I Want to Take You Higher," a signature song in concert, reached only #38 on the *Billboard* chart.

The songs are a combination of message songs and entertainment. The audience connected with the universal messages, the catchy sing-along tunes, and the infectious rhythms. The combination of these elements made Sly and the Family Stone superstars.

Message Songs

- "Everybody Is a Star" reached #1 on January 10, 1970, on the *Billboard* pop chart.
- "Stand" reached #33 on April 22, 1969 on the *Billboard* pop chart.
- "You Can Make It If You Try" was a popular message song in concert although it never became a chart hit.
- "Everyday People" reached #1 on the *Billboard* pop chart on January 4, 1969.
- "Thank You" reached #1 on the *Billboard* pop chart on January 10, 1970.
- "If You Want Me to Stay" reached #12 on July 14, 1973 on the *Billboard* pop chart.
- "Life" was a popular message song in concert, although it never became a chart hit.

> ♫ "Everyday People" reached #36 on the UK chart on March 19, 1969.

Entertainment Songs:

- "Dance to the Music" reached #8 on the *Billboard* pop chart on March 2, 1968.
- "I Want To Take You Higher" reached #38 on the *Billboard* pop chart on June 20, 1970.
- "Hot Fun in the Summertime" reached #2 on the *Billboard* pop chart on August 30, 1969.

> ♫ "Dance to the Music" reached #7 on the UK charts on July 10, 1968.

- "Family Affair" reached #1 on the *Billboard* pop chart on November 13, 1971.
- "M'Lady" reached #32 on the UK singles chart on October 2, 1968.
- "Sing A Simple Song" did not chart but was popular with his audience.

♫ "Family Affair" reached #15 on the UK charts on January 8, 1972.

Sly & The Family Stone: Production Elements

- The vocals are rooted in gospel music and typical of the R&B singing style of that era. Instead of featuring one lead vocalist, the vocals were divided between members of the band, who sang antiphonal lines.
- As was typical of the time period, the vocals are mixed low in the track, although the lyrics are easy to understand. (The vocals in rock records of that time are mixed lower than Sly's vocals.)
- Sly & The Family Stone was unique because the backbeat—the primary rhythmic element in R&B—was not the driving force in Sly's music. The upbeat bass patterns, half-rock and half-funk guitar parts, and percussive background vocals, are the main rhythm section components.
- The background vocals resemble updated doo-wop parts. The parts are not typical of background vocals sung by Rhythm & Blues groups. The vocals are used to propel the rhythm—they can be considered additional percussion elements.
- The tracks are mixed in a clear stereo field. Each vocal is panned to a space in the stereo spectrum, while the bass and guitar are more prominent than the drums. Although the backbeat is not featured in the mixes, the simple drum parts fit perfectly and propel the band.
- The 2 horn players (trumpet and saxophone) play jazzy riffs mixed with James Brown's style of funk.

Aretha Franklin

Aretha Franklin is called the Queen of Soul and Lady Soul. Legendary producer John Hammond signed her to Columbia Records in 1960. She started her recording career as a pop artist but she was not successful. In 1966, Jerry Wexler signed her to Atlantic Records where she achieved legendary status by recording rhythm & blues music. In 1979, Clive Davis signed her to Arista Records.

Like many R&B artists, Aretha sang in her church, located in Detroit, Michigan. Her father, C. L. Franklin, was the preacher. Aretha's inspiration came from two great gospel singers who also sang in her father's church—Clara Ward and Mahalia Jackson. She developed a virtuosity paralleled by few commercial singers. Her singing style is steeped in tasty melismatic turns. (Many of her clones overuse this vocal technique, causing the audience to lose contact with the melody.) Her feeling for the lyric is expressed with her magnificent voice, which remains under control at all times. She uses her God-given talent in a refined and thoughtful way.

Aretha Franklin and Ray Charles are icons of Rhythm & Blues. Both artists crossed racial barriers to become international superstars and legends. Aretha is the recipient of 15 Grammy Awards and 39 nominations. She has reached the top 10 of the *Billboard* pop chart 17 times and has entered the *Billboard* top-200 album chart 22 times. She has achieved 21 R&B chart entries for hit singles and 10 #1 R&B albums.

Aretha Franklin: Production Elements

Atlantic Records, in many ways, had a production process similar to that of Motown. Atlantic's resident rhythm section played on most of the R&B tracks during the late 1960s through the 1970s. Richard Tee (keyboards), Bernard Purdy (drums), Cornell Dupree (guitar), and Jerry Jemmott (bass) were the mainstays of the rhythm section. These great musicians (and others) created a sound that defined Rhythm & Blues of that period. They performed on many of Aretha's recordings.

> ♫ Aretha had an unusual way of working. She played the song on the piano, and the rhythm section followed, working out and refining each individual part. She followed the same procedure with the background singers.

> ♫ "Respect," which was released in 1967, became a popular civil rights song and a song that also helped to promote women's rights. The legendary singing group The Sweet Inspirations, led by Cissy Houston, performed on many of Aretha's recordings. The Sweet Inspirations also performed with Elvis Presley. (The Sweet Inspirations did not sing on "Respect.")

- The rhythm section was very funky and did not attempt to appeal to a white audience, although all races embraced the records.
- *As a result of this process, the background vocals have a distinct sound.* They are based in the gospel tradition, which, in a secular setting, makes them funky. The background vocals were at all times prominent in her earlier records.
- Most of the songs Aretha chose to record have a message—"Respect," "A Natural Woman," "Think," and "Bridge over Troubled Water."
- Great singers would not have achieved success without believing in the message of the songs they recorded.
- Many of Aretha's records contain traditional R&B horn parts. The horns added excitement that was part of the signature R&B sound during that time period. Some of her recordings also contained strings.

Aretha's first album for Atlantic Records was recorded in Muscle Shoals, Alabama. Muscle Shoals was known for a specific southern soul sound, which was defined by what became known as the Muscle Shoals Rhythm Section. Many hits were recorded in Muscle Shoals. The famous Memphis horns also performed on her album. The album *I Never Loved a Man* reached #1 on the singles chart.

Philadelphia International Records

Philadelphia International Records was formed in the early 1970s by songwriters Kenny Gamble and Leon Huff. They had a close relationship with composer, arranger, and producer Thom Bell, who was in many ways a third partner.

They emulated Motown with the exception of distribution. Motown was independently distributed, and Columbia Records distributed Philadelphia International.

Similarities to Motown

- The music crossed all racial barriers. The artists were primarily African American, but even the music by the Caucasian artists was R&B oriented. This genre was known as blue-eyed soul.
- Staff writers wrote most of the songs. Many of the hits were written by Gamble and Huff (a team) and also by Thom Bell.
- Philadelphia International had the equivalent of a resident rhythm section, which gave the records a distinctive sound.
- Resident arrangers provided the label with an identity. For example, master arranger Thom Bell arranged the tracks for the artists he produced for other labels, such as The Spinners (Atlantic Records) and The Stylistics (Avco Records). The songs were richly orchestrated and performed by consummate musicians.
- Most recordings were tracked at Sigma Sound Studios in Philadelphia. (Motown recordings were recorded at Motown's Hitsville Studios in Detroit.) The recording and mixing process had a significant effect on the overall sound and feel of the records. The engineering—precise and clean—was a crucial element in manufacturing the Philadelphia Sound.
- Gamble and Huff maintained the publishing rights to the songs. The catalogue became extremely valuable and was eventually sold.

♫ When disco became popular in the middle of the 1970s, Philadelphia International was at the forefront of R&B disco.

Some of the artists signed to Philadelphia International Records were as follows:

- Billy Paul
- MFSB
- Jerry Butler
- The O'Jays
- Teddy Pendergrass

Differences between Philadelphia International and Motown

The artists were not controlled to the same degree as they were at Motown.

- The artists' performance styles were similar to those of the Motown artists, but they were not as homogeneous.
- Each act worked with different choreographers and bandleaders.
- Most of the Philadelphia International artists had separate managers and agents.

A Brief History of Rockabilly

In the early 1950s—before rock 'n' roll—rockabilly was popular. Most rockabilly singers were from the South or Southwestern part of the United States.

The music was based on rhythms taken from early race music, blues, and white southern rhythms used in country music, Appalachian music, and western swing music. Gospel influence can be heard in standard background vocal parts and hand clapping that accompanied numerous songs.

Many of the up-tempo songs were constructed in a standard twelve-bar blues pattern. Like most popular-music genres, rockabilly was dance and party music. During and after World War II people wanted to escape and music was a release. The lyrics and the music were entertaining. Rockabilly remained popular for only approximately two years. It had a great influence on rock 'n' roll, which started between 1954 and 1955.

Elvis Presley was one of the first rockabilly singers and is considered—along with Carl Perkins—the definitive rocka-

> ♫ Elvis Presley used background singers to help define his musical style. His background group was called The Jordanaires. Although The Jordanaires were Caucasian, the sound was derivative of traditional black gospel groups. It is interesting to note that one of Elvis's vocal groups, near the end of his life, was Cissy Houston's African-American vocal group, The Sweet Inspirations.

billy artist. Carl Perkins recorded "Blue Suede Shoes" before Elvis. Elvis developed into one of the first rock 'n' roll stars and the most successful and influential individual rock singer of our time. (Listen to Gene Vincent sing "Woman Love," Tommy Sands sing "The Worry Kind," and Bobby Lee Trammell sing "You Mostest Girl.") There is a remarkable similarity to Elvis Presley, in both production and vocal style. John Lennon, of The Beatles, said, "There would be no Beatles without Elvis Presley."

The first rockabilly recordings were produced in the legendary Sun Studios in Memphis, Tennessee. Sam Phillips, who originally discovered Elvis Presley, was directly responsible for helping to invent the sound of rockabilly, which was primarily defined by using a tape delay on the lead vocals and the guitar.

Bill Haley and Buddy Holly began as rockabilly singers and were among the first rock 'n' roll stars.

Rockabilly: Production Elements

Popular record-production techniques were an intrinsic part of the sound of rockabilly:

- The vocal styling was rooted in country music. In numerous recordings, a tape delay was applied to the vocals. The unique sound helped to define the genre. (Distinctive tape delay was used on several of John Lennon's records.)
- The twangy electric guitar sound, based on the blues and country style of playing, gave the music a distinguishing sound. Many of the guitar parts were processed with tape delay similar to the delay used on rockabilly vocals. Some guitar sounds were bordering on distortion, which became the predominant sound of rock 'n' roll. The almost nasal quality mixed with rhythmic playing helped to give the music a special feel.
- The hard, honky tenor saxophone sound, which had its roots in jazz, became part of the signature sound of many rockabilly recordings. (The tenor saxophone and baritone saxophone became more prevalent in the middle to late 1950s, when rock 'n' roll became popular.) The basic bluesy, raspy saxophone sound is still used today.
- The style of background singing was a direct descendant of the gospel vocal style.
- The slap-bass technique was heard on various rockabilly recordings. The bass player slapped the neck of the instrument after playing a note. The slap added a percussive effect and enhanced the rhythmic groove. This distinctive playing style helped define the backing tracks.
- Rockabilly piano parts often contained triplets, which became a signature sound on many 1950s rock 'n' roll recordings.

♫ Little Richard, Jerry Lee Lewis, and Fats Domino defined the rock 'n' roll piano style. It was based on the gospel style of piano playing, as is the piano style of traditional R&B. (Ray Charles was one of the greatest influences of the piano style used in rhythm & blues.) Elton John, Billy Joel, and Billy Preston are direct descendants.

- The bands generally comprised a piano, drums, bass, and electric guitar. The tenor saxophone and a limited use of the country fiddle were also included in rockabilly bands.

I'm the originator, the emancipator, and the architect of rock 'n' roll.—*Little Richard*

A Brief History of Rock 'n' Roll

Early Rock 'n 'Roll

Rock 'n' roll was born in the American south, in the mid 1950s; its roots are in "race music" (black music). The segregationists publicly denounced the music due to racial hatred. In their view, bringing black music to the general public was abhorrent. Throughout the country, many people thought the music was overtly sexual, and, therefore, denigrated society. Until the 1960s, rock 'n' roll was generally considered distasteful. This is probably the definitive reason for its success. The youth aligned themselves with a unique genre of music, as well as a culture. The music was raw and loose, mirroring a lifestyle that was appealing to a large segment of the adolescent population. Their parents were fond of a different style of music. Dress codes changed, mores changed, and the dances changed. *Rock 'n' roll was a cultural revolution.*

♫ Rock 'n' roll is a generic term for multiple musical styles. Some of the subgenres are doo-wop, heavy metal, punk rock, soft rock, and progressive rock.

Rock 'n' roll had as much to do with helping integration in the United States as did marching and protesting. That was the sentiment held by Chuck Berry and Little Richard. The segregationists hated rock 'n' roll because of the effect the music had on society. This was a revolution of the youth against adult mores. Racial barriers were broken and young people had their own music.

Elvis Presley and Jerry Lee Lewis were recording and performing black music, which brought race music to the general public. Chuck Berry is considered the father of rock 'n' roll and the first rock 'n' roll guitar player. Little Richard was also considered a founder of rock 'n' roll.

Little Richard, Fats Domino, and Jerry Lee Lewis were the first rock 'n' roll piano players. Rock 'n' roll piano playing is a combination of boogie-woogie and the blues. Chuck Berry incorporated the boogie-woogie piano style into his guitar playing. That became the basis for all rock 'n' roll guitar playing.

White artists began covering (rerecording) songs written and recorded by black artists and achieving greater success than the original recordings. For instance, Pat Boone's recording of "Tutti Frutti" outsold and garnered more airplay than the original record, recorded and written by Little Richard. Radio stations were segregated; some stations played race music and others played white music. Alan Freed, a popular Cleveland disc jockey, coined the name *rock 'n' roll*, which was a reference to sexual activity. Freed refused to play watered-down cover versions by white performers; he played the original recordings by black artists. This was a revolution for the music industry. There were no racial barriers in popular music. Rock 'n' roll belonged to the American youth. Adults publicly railed against what they referred to as sexual promiscuity, which they considered detrimental to society.

♫ Fats Domino hails from New Orleans and brought the true and distinctive New Orleans piano style to rock 'n' roll. He began as a Rhythm & Blues singer and pianist. His unique style catapulted him into the role of one of the most important and influential rock 'n' roll stars.

The rhythmic patterns Fats played with his left hand made his piano playing unique. It produced a distinct sound that became associated with other New Orleans pianists, who have emulated his style, notably Dr. John.

Young people were subjected to dress codes and mores that emanated from the music. Leather jackets and tight skirts were forbidden dress in some school systems. Movies such as *Blackboard Jungle* associated juvenile delinquents (called hoods) with rock 'n' roll. When Elvis Presley appeared on television wiggling his hips, thousands of letters were written in protest. *Rock 'n' roll was like a locomotive barreling down the tracks with no way to stop it.* It continued to grow by fueling its growth with the creative juices of the young musicians and singers who followed in the founders' footsteps.

Rock 'n' roll is the direct descendant of rockabilly music. In 1955, Bill Haley and His Comets recorded the first major rock 'n' roll hit, "Rock Around the Clock." It was the first rock 'n' roll hit published on the *Billboard Magazine* chart. When "Rock Around the Clock" was a hit, no other records on the charts resembled its sound. Rock 'n' roll was youth-oriented party music that offered relief from the horrors of World War II and the Korean conflict.

"Rock Around the Clock" has a shuffle rhythm, repeated melodic patterns (emulated in other records), a prominent electric guitar sound, and a slapped upright bass sound that is similar to the bass parts used in many rockabilly records.

Rock 'n' roll—like rockabilly—is rooted in black American music. The music is a combination of blues, boogie-woogie, and gospel, and influenced by country music. Rock 'n' roll was a natural progression from rockabilly.

Rock 'n' roll, jam-packed with sexual innuendoes, was designed as party or dancing music. The Everly Brothers, Elvis Presley, Little Richard, Fats Domino, Jerry Lee Lewis, Buddy Holly, and Chuck Berry were some of rock's first superstars, and all varied in style and performing presentation. Elvis, Little Richard, and Jerry Lee Lewis were energetic; The Everly Brothers, Fats Domino, and Buddy Holly were more subdued.

The guitar, piano, and saxophone were the prominent instruments used in rock 'n' roll bands. A distinct rock 'n' roll style of guitar playing was born. As the genre progressed, the overdriven (distorted) guitar sound became the norm and rock's defining "sound." Great saxophone players like Red Prysock and Louis Jordon developed a raw, honky, soulful tenor saxophone style, which also was indicative of the sound. That basic style is still used in all genres of popular music and contemporary jazz, with artists such as Kenny G and David Sandborn carrying on the tradition.

Rock 'n' roll was popular with all ethnicities. The music had a positive impact on the promotion of desegregation.

Many rock 'n' roll songs were based on the twelve-bar blues format and signature playing style of blues musicians. The bent blue notes have remained the most quoted and expressive playing element in rock 'n' roll.

Rock 'n' roll soloing techniques are based on the improvisational styling of jazz. It is interesting to note that music in the jazz era was technically difficult to play. Rock 'n' roll was much looser-sounding music and did not require the same technical ability. The simplicity of early rock 'n' roll is most likely what appealed to young listeners. They could relate to the basic feel of the music. Dancing and partying are antidotes to the stresses of daily strife.

Technology is an intrinsic part of the continuing development of popular music. The electric guitar was invented in the 1930s. Prior to the electric guitar, certain instruments masked the sound of the acoustic guitar. In 1951, Leo Fender invented the electric bass, primarily for the same reason.

The sound of the electric guitar became the most prominent instrument in rock 'n' roll. The invention of effects, which offered a player the opportunity to vary the tonal quality of the guitar sound, has enabled guitarists to create infinite musical moods. The sound of *distortion,* which started to become prominent in the 1950s, eventually dominated rock in the 1960s and continues through today's music.

American Bandstand and *The Ed Sullivan Show*

Dick Clark, host of the television program *American Bandstand,* played the latest hits while teenagers danced. Each day recording artists performed and also promoted new recordings. No other show had the hit-making ability of *American Bandstand,* with the exception of *The Ed Sullivan Show,* which was on the CBS Television Network on Sunday nights. Elvis Presley, The Beatles, and The Rolling Stones performed on *The Ed Sullivan Show.* The audience's reaction was staggering. The artists' careers soared after their appearances.

The business of rock 'n' roll flourished because of television exposure but radio airplay has always been, and remains, the best promotional tool for breaking a record. This now includes exposure on the Internet and Satellite radio

Radio's impact has expanded with the addition of Internet radio, streaming and Satellite radio, and video sites such as YouTube.

Elvis Presley

Elvis Presley recorded 30 #1 hits. "Heartbreak Hotel" (released on January 17, 1956) was his first rock 'n' roll hit, as well as his first record as an artist on the RCA record label. Elvis was the first artist to cross the racial musical barrier. He made his first recording in 1954 for Sun Records, in Memphis, Tennessee. Because his musical style was steeped in white and black gospel music, he musically represented both ethnic groups. His recordings sold in three markets: pop, country, and R&B. This accounted for his unprecedented success.

Just as Beethoven propelled classical music into the Romantic musical period, Elvis Presley not only was the bridge from rockabilly to rock 'n' roll, but he also became the genre's model pop star as well as a movie star. His appearance (sideburns and flashy outfits) and stage presence (hips wiggling and facial expressions) were as much a part of his success as his music. This was Elvis's natural way of expressing his musical emotions. Gospel music was his passion, and it is documented that the same body movements he made as a pop star were also used when singing gospel music before becoming a pop icon. Elvis received 3 Grammy Awards for singing gospel music.

Singers such as Frank Sinatra were pop idols in the 1940s, but they did not define a generation as Elvis did. (The only other pop artists to have the same sociological influence on society were The Beatles.)

In 1956, Sam Phillips—owner of Sun Records, Elvis Presley's first record label—sold Elvis's contract and his master recordings to RCA. His rockabilly-country-gospel style of singing developed into what would later be called rock 'n' roll. Elvis retained his country music and gospel roots, although his records for RCA were produced in a more contemporary style. Elvis was known for trying to achieve perfection and he recorded as many as 30 takes of a song before he was satisfied.

Elvis Presley: Production Elements

- Most popular music recordings of 1950s had a time length of between 2:00 and 2:30. Radio stations would not play a song that was too lengthy.
- The songs were recorded in mono and Elvis's voice was the loudest element on the track. (Stereo was not released to the public until 1958.)
- Elvis recorded songs that had commercial appeal. They were melodic and suited his vocal style. Dedication to his craft is evident in everything he recorded.
- Most of Elvis's hits were recorded with a basic rhythm section and background vocals. His band consisted of piano, bass, drums, and guitar. Later in his career, orchestral instruments were added; for example, "In the Ghetto" has a string section added to a basic track, which was dominated by acoustic guitar, a marching-style snare drum, and a sparse bass part. It is a simple arrangement that is effective because of Elvis's extraordinary delivery of a meaningful lyric.
- The arrangements and performances were tailored for each song. Much care was given to the structure of the arrangements, which included the carefully crafted background vocal arrangements.
- In rockabilly music, an excessive amount of delay was used on vocals. Not as much was incorporated into most rock 'n' roll records, although reverberation was a signature in most rhythmic tracks. Many of Elvis's ballads were mixed with less reverberation than his rhythmic songs.
- Elvis's background singers were a four-man gospel quartet called The Jordanaires. On many of his recordings the background vocals provided a cushion, endemic to most white gospel music. They sang few words but the harmonies were smooth and distinct. (Elvis spent most of his leisure time singing gospel music, which was his true love. "Crying in the Chapel," a gospel song became a hit.)

Author's Note: Cissy Houston, leader of the vocal group called the Sweet Inspirations, told me that Elvis would break into a gospel song (for fun) in the middle of rehearsals, when they were performing in Las Vegas.

- Some of his early hits did not sound like the new rock 'n' roll but retained the influence of the rockabilly style. Gone was the slap-echo delay prevalent in so many rockabilly recordings, although "Heartbreak Hotel" had a slight delay on the vocal, which was reminiscent of some of his earlier recordings.

- Surprisingly, many of Elvis's hits did not have a driving rhythm. The drums were mostly understated. The bass player slapped the bass, which created an additional percussive sound; Elvis often slapped his guitar to also help create rhythm. Much of the rhythm was created by Elvis's vocal inflections and the rhythmic patterns sung by the background vocals. (This technique is still used in contemporary popular music.)
- The bass and the left hand of the piano part often played the same notes. The piano parts were frequently patterned after the boogie-woogie style. The honky-tonk piano style was also prevalent in his rhythmic songs.
- "Hound Dog"—recorded in New York and released on July 13, 1956—was truly a rock 'n' roll production. The song has a strong backbeat (a defining element of rock 'n' roll), a distorted electric guitar, and a bass pattern used on many rock 'n' roll recordings of the 1950s. Elvis's vocal was usually powerful and driving.
- "Love Me Tender," released on September 28, 1956, was a simple, mellow acoustic guitar–driven production. Elvis admired ballad singers, such as Bing Crosby, and he wanted to be considered a competent balladeer.
- Elvis was not *one* singer. The production elements of each song changed according to what was appropriate for the song. Elvis's constancy was his individuality as an artist. He was dedicated and original. Elvis said, "I don't sound like nobody."

Although there could not be a more eclectic group, an uncanny similarity exists between the music and production techniques used by such diverse artists as Elvis Presley, The Beatles, The Rolling Stones, and Steely Dan. These artists are unique even within the musical genres they represent.

- No other popular rock 'n' roll artist sounded like Elvis or performed in exactly the same style. (Of course, there have been imitators, but imitation rarely brings equivalent success.) Compared to almost all other hits of that era, Elvis's records are unique. This is analogous to the raw, bluesy quality of The Rolling Stones, the distinctive and ever-changing style of The Beatles, who brought an unusual approach to each song (in their later recordings), and the extraordinarily clear and precise production techniques used on the Steely Dan recordings.
- The arrangements on The Beatles and Steely Dan recordings are meticulous and innovative. All parts fit together like a complex riddle. The Beatles and Steely Dan recordings illustrate the importance of scrutinizing the minutest arranging and production details.

- Creating a sonic ambience has much to do with forming an artist's musical image. The Beatles, especially on the *Sgt. Pepper's Lonely Heart Club Band* album, created an almost incomparable and idiosyncratic ambience to the recording. That was accomplished by months of experimentation, as well as the extraordinary creative ability of producer George Martin and engineer Geoff Emerick.
- The Rolling Stones have been able to capture a "live" quality on their recordings, which is a difficult task. Many artists need a live audience to keep adrenaline pumping. The excitement of a live performance partially accounts for the success of live concert recordings. The Stones have been able to transport this energy to the recording studio.

Trivia

- Johnny Cash, Jerry Lee Lewis, and Elvis Presley all recorded for Sun Records.
- Payola (illegal payment for airplay) almost destroyed the popular-music industry in the United States.
- Lieber and Stoller, two of the most successful songwriters in pop-music history, immersed themselves in the black culture. Their lyrics and songs reflected the roots of R&B and, therefore, the mores of African Americans.
- Eric Clapton's favorite singer was blues singer Muddy Waters.
- Chuck Berry sang "Maybelline," which is truly a country song. This shows the influence of country music on a gospel singer, who became a rock 'n' roll singer.
- There was an accordion in the Bill Haley and His Comets version of "Rock around the Clock."
- Joe Turner recorded "Shake, Rattle, and Roll" before Bill Haley recorded it.
- Louis Jordan was the first crossover R&B artist who became known as a rock 'n' roll artist.

15

A Brief History of Popular Music, Part II

Production

In 1930, guitarist Les Paul developed the first recording process that allowed additional music (sound) to be added to an existing recorded track; the process is now referred to as overdubbing. This was the beginning of multitrack recording and record production.

The above paragraph is a repeat of the same statement made earlier in the book. The A&R executives at record labels were responsible for discovering and signing artists, selecting songs, and guiding artists through the recording process. Since recording techniques were limited, the initial A&R executives acted similar to contemporary record producers without necessarily having the same technical expertise required of today's producers. Their goal was to capture a live performance. Prior to the invention of tape and multitrack recording, all recording was direct to disc (no overdubbing). With the invention of tape, producers were able to record multiple takes (performances) and edit them to assemble the best possible performance.

Preproduction is the most important stage of the music-production process. Selecting the songs, choosing an album concept and a sonic image, and crafting the arrangements are the basis of producing recordings. Without this foundation, it is irrelevant whether the performance is emotionally and technically proficient.

Achieving commercially and creatively successful recordings begins with the song or instrumental. Listeners react to music that causes them to experience an emotional reaction, such as in a love song or a dance song.

As recording technology became more sophisticated, its effect greatly influenced the sound of recordings, particularly of popular music. Hundreds of effects processors are available, and each one has an infinite number of settings that can affect the overall sound of each recorded track. The producer and the engineer use the devices to create an overall ambience, which ultimately affects the listener's response.

In the next section, we will discuss some of the artists and producers who pushed the envelope and influenced the development of contemporary record production. Listen to the songs and follow the analysis. The purpose of the analysis is to study how the recordings were musically arranged and sonically developed. The basic approach to production is timeless and the reader will benefit by listening to some of the classic recordings by The Beach Boys and The Beatles.

The Beach Boys and The Beatles

> If you had to give rock 'n' roll another name, it would have to be Chuck Berry.—John Lennon

The Beach Boys' album *Pet Sounds* and The Beatles' album *Sgt. Pepper's Lonely Hearts Club Band* are considered seminal albums in the craft of music production and classics in the history of rock 'n' roll. Both groups took a remarkable creative leap from their earlier albums. The Beatles' previous album was *Revolver* (released in 1966), which included "Eleanor Rigby," "Here There and Everywhere," "Yellow Submarine," and "Got to Get You into My Life." It is interesting to note that *Beach Boys Party* (released in 1965), the album prior to *Pet Sounds*, contained three Lennon/McCartney songs; "I Should Have Known Better," "Tell Me Why," and "You've Got to Hide Your Love Away."

Sgt. Pepper was recorded on a 4 track tape recorder. Brian Wilson, of the Beach Boys, recorded the instrumental tracks for *Pet Sounds* on 3 or 4 tracks and proceeded to create a mono mix. The instrumental backing track was recorded on 1 track of an 8 rack machine, which left 7 tracks to record vocals.

On both albums, the producers bounced tracks together, which allowed them to overdub additional parts over previously recorded tracks. Because they were working in analog technology, the more tracks that were bounced together the more hiss (noise) remained on the tape. Both albums have been "cleaned up" (using digital recording technology) for rerelease in the CD format and the Internet. It is remarkable that the quality of the vocals and the backing instrumental tracks remains clear and relatively unaffected by the bouncing process.

Three brothers and a cousin formed The Beach Boys in 1961. Brian Wilson was the main writer and arranger and also played piano and bass, and sang. Dennis Wilson played drums and sang; Carl Wilson played guitar and sang; cousin Mike Love also played drums and sang. Additional members were Al Jardine, who played guitar and sang, and Bruce Johnson, who joined the band after 1965.

♫ Trivia: During the 1960s Brian Wilson worked with Jan and Dean, who were also pioneers of surfing music. Also, The Beatles and The Beach Boys were on EMI-owned labels; The Beach Boys recorded for Capitol Records and The Beatles were signed to Parlophone in the UK (The Beatles were first released on Vee-Jay Records in the United States. They later switched to (EMI) Capitol Records.)

The Wilson brothers and Mike Love were born in California and were pioneers in the development of surfing music. At the beginning, their lyrics catered to the youth culture. "California Girls," "I Get Around," "Surfin' Safari," and "Surfin' U.S.A." were hits, along with many more. The Beach Boys were called the "American Beatles." The Beatles progressed artistically with each album, as did The Beach Boys.

Brian Wilson created The Beach Boys' vocal sound based on his admiration of the jazz vocal group The Four Freshmen. He also admired the production techniques of famed producer Phil Spector. Spector pioneered what is referred to as the "Wall of Sound." There was no separation of instruments in the studio; the instruments "bled" into the sonic space of the other instruments, creating a huge mass of sound. The Wall of Sound was enhanced by an unusual amount of echo and reverberation.

The following are some of the records produced by Spector:

- "You've Lost That Lovin' Feelin," by The Righteous Brothers, reached #2 on the *Billboard* pop chart on December 26, 1964.
- "River Deep, Mountain High," by Ike and Tina Turner, reached #3 on the UK charts on June 9, 1966.
- "Imagine," by John Lennon, reached #3 on the *Billboard* pop chart on October 23, 1971.
- "All Things Must Pass," by George Harrison, reached #1 on the UK charts on November 1, 1975.
- "Let It Be," by The Beatles, reached #1 on the *Billboard* pop chart on March 21, 1970.

♫ "You've Lost That Lovin' Feeling" reached #1 on the UK charts on January 14, 1965.

♫ "Imagine" reached #1 on the UK charts on November 1, 1975.

♫ "Let It Be" reached #1 on the UK charts on May 23, 1970.

The only track that George Martin did not produce for The Beatles was "Let It Be," which was produced by Phil Spector. There has been great criticism of this track because the production techniques used by Spector varied from the precise and tasty productions associated with George Martin. In spite of the criticism, "Let It Be" became a standard.

The Beach Boys combined jazz vocal harmonies with Spector's 'Wall of Sound' technique, coupled with the influence of surfing music. Earlier Beach Boys productions were also influenced by 1950s doo-wop music. Their background vocal arrangements resembled doo-wop backgrounds.

> ♫ The Beach Boys charted a #5 hit in 1976 with a remake of the Chuck Berry hit "Rock 'n' Roll Music." The Beatles were greatly influenced by Chuck Berry. It is interesting to observe that neither group had an R&B musical flavor, although both groups had a love for the music.

> ♫ Note: Ironically, the *Pet Sounds* album inspired The Beatles to write and create the album *Sgt. Pepper's Lonely Hearts Club Band.*

> ♫ Note: Brian stopped touring with the band in 1965, after suffering a nervous breakdown (associated with his use of drugs—primarily LSD). He completely devoted himself to working in the studio, which became his passion.

The Beatles' album Rubber Soul triggered Brian Wilson's creative juices. Brian was highly competitive, and although he admired The Beatles, his ambition was to top them.

Unusual circumstances surrounded the production of *Pet Sounds*:

- Brian Wilson wrote most of the songs with independent lyricist Tony Asher rather than writing with members of The Beach Boys or with writers he had collaborated with in the past. Tony was an advertising-jingle lyricist, which made the collaboration even more unusual. They worked for several months writing the songs. Brian wanted the lyrics to reflect his feelings and state of mind at that time. He viewed the project as a labor of love.
- In place of The Beach Boys playing on the recording sessions, Brian hired Los Angeles studio musicians.
- Brian's arrangements are orchestral, rather than the standard rhythm-section arrangements of the past.
- The vocal arrangements—their signature sound—remained consistent with their previous work.

The Beach Boys and The Beatles: Production Elements

The album *Pet Sounds*, by The Beach Boys, was released in May 1966. The Beatles' *Sgt. Pepper's Lonely Hearts Club Band* was released in June 1967. Both albums are universally considered to be two of the most celebrated pop albums ever recorded.

When listening to The Beatles' *Rubber Soul* album, it is difficult to hear much of the songwriting and production techniques used in *Pet Sounds*. It appears as though Brian Wilson was attracted to *Rubber Soul* due to the quality of the songwriting and the pristine production.

Sgt. Pepper was never intended to be a concept album. *Pet Sounds* was intended to be a concept album. Throughout the album, lyricist Tony Asher documented Brian Wilson's most inner feelings. (Asher did not write all of the lyrics for *Pet Sounds*.)

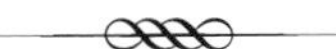

Author's Opinion: The quality of the melodies that Brian Wilson wrote for *Pet Sounds* was a major creative leap for him. Wilson's goal of making a better album than The Beatles influenced his melodic and production skills.

One of the main differences between The Beatles and The Beach Boys was that The Beatles' recordings were more of a collaborative effort. Brian Wilson was clearly the driving creative force behind The Beach Boys. The following are some similarities between the two albums:

- The Beatles' "You Won't See Me" has background parts similar to those used by The Beach Boys.
- "God Only Knows," on the *Pet Sounds* album, uses the signature quarter-note feel made famous by Ringo Starr (drummer) and The Beatles.
- The use of studio musicians was unusual for an established band. The Beach Boys did not play on *Pet Sounds*. The Beatles did not play on some tracks on *Sgt. Pepper*, and several tracks were greatly enhanced by studio musicians. Brian Wilson arranged *Pet Sounds*. The Beatles arranged the rhythm tracks on *Sgt. Pepper* and producer George Martin arranged the orchestral parts.
- The sound effects used on *Sgt. Pepper* were clearly influenced by *Pet Sounds*.

Author's Opinion: It was the overall quality of The Beatles' *Rubber Soul* that influenced Brain Wilson. Wilson was not trying to imitate The Beatles but rather to attain the same artistic quality.

Pet Sounds—*The Beach Boys: Production Elements*

The Beatles' *Rubber Soul* album was the inspiration for *Pet Sounds,* although the album is more reminiscent of the productions of Phil Spector. The use of the "Wall of Sound's" overabundance of echo and heavy use of timpani were production watermarks of Spector's.

Analysis

Pet Sounds reached the #10 position on the *Billboard* chart on July 2, 1966. On July 9, 1966, it attained the #2 position on the British chart.

Listen to the song being analyzed while reading the analysis. The following is an analysis of some of the songs from *Pet Sounds*:

"Wouldn't It Be Nice" reached # 8 on the *Billboard* chart on August 20, 1966. Brian said that the lyric was about "the need to have the freedom to live with somebody." (Brian guided almost all of the lyrics on the album, but Tony Asher wrote the lyrics.) The production is greatly influenced by Phil Spector's "Wall of Sound" production technique.

- The song starts with a short introduction featuring a harp surrounded by an excess of echo.
- During the first verse, the lead vocal is doubled, and the keyboard part is played in the triplet style of 1950s rock 'n' roll.
- The second verse continues with a lead vocal doubled, and the background vocals are performed in the standard Beach Boys style.
- The bridge reintroduces the harp from the introduction with the same ambient sound. The section has a dreamlike quality.
- The next section uses a Beatles' technique; the tempo slows down. It is unexpected and refreshing.
- There is a smooth transition back into the original tempo. The fadeout does not have lyrics but the signature Beach Boys nonlyrical vocal parts.

"God Only Knows" reached #39 on the *Billboard* chart on September 17, 1966. It achieved the #2 position on the UK chart on July 28, 1966. The lyric speaks of the importance of a lasting relationship. "God only knows what I would be without you" is the crux of the lyric.

- This track is the closest comparison to a Beatles' track. The introduction has the signature Beatles rhythm pattern with an emphasis on each quarter-note. The track is the sparsest on the album, which suggests a Beatles influence.
- The French horn melody in the introduction is suggestive of tracks on the *Sgt. Pepper* album.
- The unusual percussion track, which remains throughout the first verse, is reminiscent of The Beatles' "Looking through You," on the *Rubber Soul* album.
- A refreshing modulation creates a bridge leading into the second verse. The arrangement remains basically the same as the one in the first verse.
- An abrupt transition into a new section is reminiscent of The Beatles. The track remains the same as the preceding verse, but the chorus vocals (without lyrics) become more contrapuntal and interwoven.
- A reprise of the second verse leads to a vocal round. The song fades out with a simple snare drum pattern creating fills around the vocals.
- The vocal arrangement remains purely in The Beach Boys' style. The contrapuntal moving parts and the jazz harmonies remain throughout. (Listen to "You Won't See Me" on the *Rubber Soul* album. The Beatles' vocal parts were slightly influenced by The Beach Boys.)

"Caroline, No" reached #32 on the *Billboard* chart on April 23, 1966. This was the only record released from *Pet Sounds* under Brian Wilson's and not The Beach Boys' name.

Brian Wilson said that "Caroline No" is about growing up and the loss of innocence. Brian considers this song one of his best and contains one of his most beautiful melodies. The melody has interesting chord progressions and is well constructed. It sounds like a standard.

The instrumental arrangement remains consistent throughout the song. It is spiced with sparse percussion fills. (There are no background vocals.)

- The song opens with a short and unexpected percussive introduction. The drummer played an empty water bottle to achieve a unique percussive effect.
- The first verse features a doubled lead vocal singing against a mellow, pretty instrumental track.

- The second verse replicates the first verse.
- The bridge has standard jazz-oriented chords that move smoothly into the third verse. The instrumental background remains the same as the verses.
- A short third verse is followed by an instrumental verse with the melody played by a flute. The song fades out.

Sgt. Pepper's Lonely Hearts Club Band—*The Beatles: Production Elements*

> *Sgt. Pepper's Lonely Hearts Club Band* was a musical fragmentation grenade, exploding with a force that is still being felt . . . it changed the entire nature of the recording game for keeps.—George Martin

> ♫ The Abbey Road Studios became a landmark because of The Beatles' album cover for the *Abbey Road* album, which is a photograph of The Beatles crossing the street in front of the Abbey Road Studios.
>
> There is a similar story about the signing of the group U2 to Island Records. Label owner Chris Blackwell did not like them on first hearing. But he felt that they had something, so he signed them.

The masterful producer George Martin was The Beatles' producer and helped to shape their sound. Martin was the head of A&R for a small UK label called Parlophone, which is owned by the conglomerate EMI. Parlophone's biggest sellers were comedy albums, but Martin wanted to expand into the rock market. Virtually every desirable label had turned down Brian Epstein, the Beatles' tenacious manager. Martin thought the original demos were horrible but heard some potential. He auditioned the band in January of 1962. Under his guidance, they recorded new demos in the famous Abbey Road Studios.

The Beatles' original songs were the primary reason for their unprecedented success. Hailing from Liverpool, England, they began as a "copy band" (playing popular songs recorded by other artists). They were untrained musicians who had a great love for American rock 'n' roll and played the music of American artists they admired. After weeding out several members, the "Fab Four" that remained were John Lennon, Paul McCartney, George Harrison, and Ringo Starr.

Subsequent to achieving local success, they lived and worked in Hamburg, Germany. Between 1960 and 1962 they made 5 trips to Hamburg. Most evenings, they performed in a nightclub playing between 5 and 8 hours a night. During this period, The Beatles developed a sound. Their popularity grew throughout Europe, but it was not until 1964 that they toured America. They agreed not to cross the ocean until they had a #1 hit in America—and that is what they did. "I Want to Hold Your Hand" reached # 1 on the *Billboard* chart on January 25, 1964, and it reached #1 on the British chart on December 3, 1963.

The Beatles achieved remarkable creative growth. They began as a cover band and in a short time period wrote and recorded some of the greatest records in the history of popular music.

Author's Note: The Beatles' development, beginning with recordings such as "Love Me Do" (1962) to the concept album *Sgt. Pepper's Lonely Hearts Club Band* (1967), is a remarkable achievement in a relatively short period of time. A great deal of their success is due to "the fifth Beatle," producer George Martin. His guidance, both in the studio as a record producer and as a record executive, made him the 5th Beatle.

The Beatles' unparalleled success, both commercially and artistically could not be predicted. Viewing old film and video clips at the beginning of the band's public exposure merely shows an energetic young group of musicians who obviously had commercial appeal. Their artistic values matured, and The Beatles matured. Exploring new musical options was a modus operandi for the group. Creative curiosity and extraordinary songwriting—encouraged and nurtured by George Martin—are the primary reasons for the extraordinary artistic and commercial success they achieved. The audience tires of artists who do not continue to grow artistically. Many artists in popular music have short careers because they become artistically stagnant.

Artistic growth is necessary in all forms of creative endeavors. Most painters are judged by various artistic "creative periods" (e.g., Picasso). The same is true for writers, (e.g., Hemingway), composers (e.g., Mozart), and playwrights (e.g., Shakespeare).

From the simple production of their first hit single "Love Me Do" (released in the UK on October 5, 1962, and in the United States on April 27, 1964) to the much more sophisticated music contained in the album *Sgt. Pepper's Lonely Hearts Club Band,* the development of innovative production techniques and the unusual pop/rock arrangements helped keep the sound of The Beatles fresh to the public. Martin and the group continually experimented with unusual sounds and developed some production techniques that are still used today, such as *flanging*. Flanging (which creates

♫ Brian Wilson said, "In December of 1966, I heard the album *Rubber Soul* by The Beatles. It was definitely a challenge for me. I saw that every cut was very artistically interesting and stimulating. I immediately went to work on the songs for *Pet Sounds*."

almost a doubling effect) came about because John Lennon did not want to double his vocals.

Pet Sounds, by The Beach Boys (released on May 16, 1966, on Capitol Records), was the benchmark for The Beatles; *Pet Sounds* was Paul McCartney's favorite album. The Beatles were striving to reach that level of production. They were also greatly influenced by 1950s rock 'n' roll and the Motown sound of the 1960s.

Sgt. Pepper's Lonely Hearts Club Band *(Released in 1967)*

> We don't like their sound, and guitar music is on the way out.—Decca Recording Company rejecting The Beatles, 1962

Many music fans and critics consider *Sgt. Pepper's Lonely Hearts Club Band* to be the greatest pop album ever recorded. The album was not designed to be a concept album, even though one song leads directly into the next without a pause, lending the work a cohesive quality.

The Beatles had a sharp wit (as a group and as individuals) and they enjoyed having fun. Their sense of humor is revealed in the lyrics and orchestrations. The full band did not perform on each song; instead, a variety of arrangements and styles were used on many of the songs. *Sgt. Pepper* contains backing tracks with instrumentation as diverse as a string quartet, Indian instrumentation, and a brass band. That a rock band would take the musical chance of developing highly uncharacteristic, nonpop arrangements and orchestrations made The Beatles unique. In a musical climate made up of clones, no other band or solo artist sounded like The Beatles. Why did such an eclectic album hold together as a concept album and why is the album considered a landmark? Several observations follow:

- First and foremost, the superb quality of the songs. The nonrestrictive approach in the songwriting created highly innovative work. Their audience can either relate to the proprietary lyrics in a subjective manner or be curious enough to try to decipher the metaphors. Some of the songs leave interpretation to the listener.
- The Beatles progressed with each album, in both songwriting and production concepts. They were interested in the recording process, and along with producer George Martin and engineer Geoff Emerick, they continually experimented.

The following is a comment by Geoff Emerick from the liner notes on the digitally remastered version of the album:

> The Beatles insisted that everything on *Sgt. Pepper* had to be different . . . so everything was distorted, limited, heavily compressed or treated with excessive equalization . . . we plastered vast amounts of echo onto vocals and sent them through the circuitry of the revolving Leslie speaker inside a Hammond organ. We used giant primitive oscillators to vary the speed of instruments and vocals and we had tapes chopped to pieces and stuck together upside down and the wrong way around.

Author's Note: With digital technology and hard-disk recording and editing, the process Emerick describes could have been accomplished in a comparatively short time. Contemporary technology also enables an engineer and a producer to perform infinite edits without any loss of audio quality. The technical experimentation used on *Sgt. Pepper* was an unprecedented accomplishment at the time, and the quality of the production has continued to set an example for technical creativity.

- The Beatles achieved *creative individuality*. The album set a new production standard.

Author's Note: The album was so influential that The Rolling Stones recorded an album called *Their Satanic Majesties Request*, which was released in 1967. They were trying to record a landmark album; the album cover overtly resembled The Beatles' cover of *Sgt. Pepper*. Even though the album became an artistic success (there were many bad reviews), the audience did not accept The Stones' departure from their traditional R&B and blues-based music. Following this album, The Stones returned to the original musical roots that brought them success.

- The *Sgt. Pepper* arrangements are innovative. Each part fits the sonic puzzle; there is no clutter. The arrangements encompass the lyrics, which is the mark of fine arrangements.

♫ It took 700 hours to complete the album.

Analysis

Try listening to the album—with earphones—while reading the following analysis. It is not my intention to analyze the songs from a traditional musical perspective but rather to emphasize the production elements that contributed to making this album a benchmark in popular-music production. It is essential to understand how the record was built. All producers are not arrangers but they must understand the arranging process. One of the primary functions of a producer is to guide the arranger or artist. Without this understanding one cannot produce music.

"Sgt. Pepper's Lonely Hearts Club Band." The lyric sets up the album by introducing *Sgt. Pepper's Lonely Hearts Club Band* to the listener. "Sit back and let the evening go" is the lyric that informs the listeners what they are going to experience.

> ♫ Note: Allegedly, the real Sgt. Pepper was a Canadian police officer who met The Beatles while they were touring Canada in 1965.

- The opening track sets up the premise of the album. Crowd sound effects and marching-band brass parts are mixed with a rock rhythm section.
- The introduction contains a distorted lead guitar playing a melody, which leads into the first verse.
- The lead vocal is almost screamed, heavily processed, and low in the mix.
- As the brass "circus" band enters, a crowd is heard cheering. The band is playing a melodic line set in a circus-band arrangement. There are no drums; the bass is used to anchor the track.
- The chorus follows with the lyric, "We're Sgt. Pepper's Lonely Hearts Club Band," sung in harmony. The band track contains distorted rhythm and lead guitar, and the arrangement switches from a circus to a rock arrangement. Only one horn phrase is performed.
- The bridge contains a rock rhythm section and held sustained chords in the brass.
- The crowd reenters, and Paul McCartney's high-energy vocal carries the second verse.
- This is followed by what is expected to be a reprise of the brass-band section, but instead it segues into the next song, "With a Little Help from My Friends."
- "With a Little Help from My Friends"

> ♫ Note: Near the end of the song the lyric says, "so let me introduce to you the one and only Billy Spears, "who is going to sing a song." It is a mystery whether the Billy Spears character is supposed to be Ringo, who sings the lead vocal on "With a Little Help from My Friends."

The song is about relationships and love. Note: The song was originally going to be entitled "Badfinger Boogie." Ringo sings the lead vocal.

- The production has a very simple rhythm section arrangement, with the addition of a shaker part.
- The track has a strong backbeat. The rhythm section (including a piano part played by Paul) emphasizes the quarter note, which supports the signature quarter-note rhythm feel made popular by Ringo.
- The bass has a clear sound and plays an interesting and simplistic part. The fills and the rhythms work well within the framework of the arrangement.

Paul had a knack for playing simple but interesting bass parts. Having been primarily a guitar player, his unique style of bass playing probably developed from a guitarist's perspective, making his bass parts unique.

One of the reasons this song works well within a simple framework is that the song itself is well defined. That is not unusual. One of the tests of a well-written song is to sing it, or play it, using either a piano or a guitar; a well-constructed song will still sound great without a band arrangement.

- A segue from "Sgt. Pepper" into "With a Little Help from My Friends" replaces what would traditionally have been a standard introduction. (Ringo, although not a singer, has a believable quality.)
- The rhythmic feel of the chorus is the same as that of the verse, but with the addition of a tambourine.
- Background vocals enter near the end of the chorus.
- Following the backgrounds is a "tasty" electric-guitar fill.
- The addition of alternate background vocals adds variety to the second verse.
- Background vocals, in harmony, are added to the second chorus.
- The bridge continues with the same format as the second chorus.
- The third verse begins with the backgrounds singing in harmony, answered by the lead vocal (antiphonal singing prevails throughout the song).
- The third and second choruses are basically the same.
- The second bridge contains the backgrounds singing in harmony, answered by the lead vocal.
- The last chorus follows basically the same format as the previous choruses.
- The song ends with a short coda and a held chord.

"Lucy in the Sky with Diamonds." It would be logical to think that the lyric was inspired by The Beatles' well-publicized use of psychedelic drugs. Maybe some of the images were inspired by John Lennon's use of LSD, but the following are direct quotes from Lennon.

> "My son came in one day with a picture he painted about a school friend of his named Lucy. He had sketched in some stars in the sky and called it *Lucy in the Sky with Diamonds.*
>
> The images of "Lucy in the Sky with Diamonds" were from *Alice in Wonderland.* It was Alice in the boat. She is buying an egg, and it turns into Humpty Dumpty. The woman serving in the shop turns into a sheep, and the next minute they are rowing in a rowing boat somewhere, and I was visualizing that. "Picture yourself in a boat on a river with tangerine trees and marmalade skies." There was also the image of the female who would someday come save me—"a girl with kaleidoscope eyes" who would come out of the sky. It turned out to be Yoko, though I hadn't met Yoko yet. So maybe it should be "Yoko in the Sky with Diamonds." [Note: Lewis Carroll, author of *Alice in Wonderland,* is one of the people depicted in the famous collage used on the cover of *Sgt. Pepper.*]

- "Lucy In the Sky with Diamonds" is in 3/4 time for the verses and goes into 4/4 time for the choruses. This alternation of meter was unusual for a rock song.
- The introduction begins with a distant and processed (effects) harpsichord sound, which continues throughout the first verse.
- There is a solo lead vocal with no reverberation.
- A bass is the only other prominent instrument playing.
- Near the end of the section, effects are gradually added and the vocal is doubled. This section serves as a transition into the prechorus.
- When the lyric says "cellophane flowers of yellow and green," the entire ambience of the track changes. This section (prechorus) contains numerous effects, which creates a musical dreamlike state. The vocal melody is doubled with a processed electric guitar.
- A short, simple drum fill is used as a transition to the chorus, "Lucy in the Sky with Diamonds," which is in 4/4 time. The guitar has been routed through a Leslie speaker, which is normally used only with a Hammond organ.
- The second verse returns to 3/4 time. The harpsichordlike obbligato plays behind the solo lead vocal, which is doubled on the last line. There are no drums—only a simple bass part.

♫ This section alone was a remarkable technical achievement, considering the limitations of a four-track tape recorder and the limited effects available then compared to today's technology. With modern recording technology, these effects could be duplicated in a fraction of the time.

- The second prechorus is similar in effects and style to the first pre-chorus.
- The second chorus is similar to the first chorus (4/4 time).
- The third verse is similar to the first two verses (3/4 time).
- The third chorus, which keeps repeating to create a fade-out, sounds basically the same as the other choruses, with the addition of drum and guitar fills (4/4 time). The guitar answers following the word "diamonds," becomes a musical hook.

"Getting Better." The song is about the positive effect love has when helping to combat anger.

> ♫ Note: Paul used the phrase "it's getting better" to a reporter while talking about the weather. This triggered the idea for the lyric.

- Extraordinary production skills are displayed. The quarter-note-accented guitar pattern—mirrored in the drum pattern—is similar to "With a Little Help from My Friends."
- The 4 bar introduction is unusual.
- The first verse is 8 bars and sounds as if it should continue into a pre-chorus, but instead moves directly into the chorus.
- During the chorus, the quarter-note rhythm groove continues, and the background vocals answer the lead vocal, which sounds doubled.
- The second verse is similar to the first with the addition of claps on the back-beat. The lead vocal is sung in thirds.
- The second chorus is similar to the first chorus.
- A catchy vocal interlude leads into a new section.
- The C-section (new section) is defined by a radical change. A sitar, the Indian guitarlike instrument, enters. Additional percussion is added by including Indian tabla drums and finger snaps.
- The chorus returns and retains a processed sitar and tabla drums.
- During the end chorus, the bass changes to a reprise of a rhythmically free-sounding part introduced earlier.
- An unusual fade-out follows, with a highly processed sitar, guitar line, or a tabla drum beat (because of the signal processing it is difficult to decipher the instruments).

> ♫ There is an effect on the ride cymbal, which plays only on the upbeat of the third beat for the first half of the first verse. The influence of The Beach Boys is heard in the background vocal.

"Fixing a Hole." The lyric is self-analytical and leaves interpretation to the listener.

Note: Allegedly, the song is about drugs. Another theory is that the images emanate from an old house that Paul bought in Scotland. Some people think that the deeper meaning had to do with heroin addiction. Here is Paul McCartney's response:

> "If you're a junkie sitting in a room and fixing a hole then that's what it'll mean to you, but when I wrote it, I meant if there's a crack, or the room is uncolourful, then I'll paint it."

- The introduction features a harpsichord. The tempo of this short intro is faster than the first verse. A new hi-hat pattern introduces the first verse, playing a simple swing pattern.
- The first verse establishes the tempo for the remainder of the song.
- Electric-guitar fills tastefully interrupt the basic acoustic-guitar rhythm pattern.
- The bass plays a simple pattern.
- The solo lead vocal is doubled with the line "where it will go," which refers to character's mind. A smooth reverberation is set behind the voice.
- An effective use of silence introduces the beginning of the chorus.
- The basic rhythm and acoustic-guitar pattern continues until another surprise—the electric guitar plays an old 1950s rock 'n' roll riff.
- The lead vocal is doubled.
- The third verse is similar to the first verse.
- The same electric-guitar fill enters, but with the addition of the lead vocal singing on top of the line.
- A solo guitar enters.
- The backing track in the second chorus is basically the same as the one in the first chorus. To help build the production, vowel sounds are sung by the background vocals. The backing track basically mimics the first chorus.
- The fourth verse contains the continuation of the "oos" sung by the background vocals during the preceding chorus.
- A melodic variation in the last chorus is followed by a quick fade.

> ♫ The hi-hat rhythm pattern is an updated old jazz, swing rhythm. The rhythm eventually goes into the quarter-note feel heard on some of the songs already mentioned.

"She's Leaving Home." The lyric tells the story of a daughter leaving home after being lonely for many years, and the guilt and hurt felt by her parents.

Note: The content of the song comes from a newspaper article read by Paul.

> "That was a *Daily Mirror* story again: this girl left home and her father said, 'We gave her everything, I don't know why she left home.'"—Paul McCartney

This song runs almost 1 minute longer than the previous songs. Most pop records during that time period had an average length of 2½ minutes; the shorter length accommodated radio station formats.

- "She's Leaving Home" begins with a 2-bar introduction, featuring a harp with a slight delay. The harp part is notated with a traditional Beatles' quarter-note-accented rhythm pattern, also heard in "Getting Better" and "With a Little Help from My Friends."
- The song is performed in 3/4 time, similar to parts of "Lucy in the Sky with Diamonds."
- The first verse begins by telling a sad story, which is depicted musically with a poignant sounding background track, containing only a harp with the addition of a melodic cello line and a high, simple solo violin part.
- A staccato violin chord, containing three quarter notes, provides an abrupt transition.
- High, doubled falsetto background vocals enter in the chorus. The background vocals represent the sad thoughts of subject's parents.
- The second verse continues with the same instrumentation as the chorus. As the verse progresses, the strings play a more complex part, which complements the lyric.
- The second chorus is similar in feel to the first chorus, but with the addition of several background parts.
- The third verse and the following chorus provide a development in all sections of the arrangement, by adding additional strings and vocal patterns.
- The song ends with a coda.

The song is yet another example of a basically simple arrangement that completely envelops the lyric, as well as the delicate vocal performance by John Lennon.

"Being for the Benefit of Mr. Kite." In keeping with the music-hall ambience of most of the album, "Being for the Benefit of Mr. Kite" is a look into the circus world. Whether the lyric is a metaphor is difficult to determine.

- The short introduction sets up a circus atmosphere. An accordion is the dominant instrument.
- The first verse begins with an accordion background; the open-close hi-hat cymbal is playing on the second and fourth beats, and a simple but "tasty" bass part adds rhythm.
- The drums switch into a tom-tom rhythm pattern.
- A short, calliope-oriented, electronically processed, circuslike section transitions into the second verse.
- The arrangement of the second verse is the same as verse one.
- Vocal harmonies lead into the next surreal, calliope-style section, which is in 3/4 time. It is much longer than the first section, yet similar in style and sound, and contains many interesting effects. Various instruments are processed through a Leslie speaker.
- An abrupt transition catapults us into the third verse, where the time signature returns to 4/4.
- The third verse is once again followed by a surreal, calliope-style interlude, filled with a cacophony of circus-music references; the verse melody continues instrumentally throughout this section.
- At the very end, the circus music briefly continues at an increased tempo, and the song abruptly ends.

♫ Note: Most of the lyric was taken from an 1843 circus poster.

"Within You Without You." This is the only song on the album written by George Harrison. It is a landmark in popular music because the backing track, performed by Indian musicians, continued to promote world music to the popular-music audience.

World music—in today's vernacular—refers to elements of folk music from various countries, mixed with contemporary music. This can be a mixture of pop, jazz, or other musical genres. (*Billboard Magazine* publishes a world music chart.)

Note: The song is about meditation. The lyric is basically saying that the world would be a better place without self-indulgence.

Harrison wrote the Indian-based song "Love You To" for the *Revolver* album (1966). The level of playing was far below "Within You Without You." "Tomorrow Never Knows" (Lennon/McCartney), also from the *Revolver* album, has a hybrid of Indian and Western instruments in a pop-music setting.

"When I'm Sixty-Four" is an unconventional pop song. The lyric is whimsical and deals with aging. The subject is unexpected since The Beatles were a young band.

> ♫ Note: Paul said he wrote the melody when he was 15 years old. This was the first song recorded for the album.

- The simple orchestration is performed by two clarinets—including the low bass clarinet—an oompah bass part (circus), a processed piano (e.g., honky-tonk piano), a two-beat drum part, "oos" in the background vocals, short chime passages, and several guitar parts.
- The first verse is very simple. Clarinets outline the chord structure; bass and drums play on the second and fourth beats; the drummer plays with brushes instead of sticks. The song has an almost vaudevillian flavor.
- A 4-bar introduction leads to the bridge. The bridge introduces the backgrounds singing vowels and has a processed piano part. Chimes enter near the end of the section.
- A brief interlude introduces the second chorus.
- The beginning of the second verse is the same as the first verse. In the second section, the "piano-like" sound enters for several bars.
- The second bridge does not have an introduction, as does the first bridge. The addition of a filtered background part makes this bridge different from the first one. The chimes reenter near the end of the section; the character names his grandchildren, creating a humorous ending.
- The third verse is richer than the previous verses, by the addition of a country-flavored guitar part. A clarinet plays harmony with the lead vocal.
- The ending is a reprise of the clarinet melody used in the introduction.

"Lovely Rita" is a meter maid who awards parking tickets. The Beatles continue with whimsical fun.

> ♫ Note: Allegedly, Paul read an article about American parking meter maids.

- The introduction consists of a standard 4-bar instrumental, enhanced with a simple, doubled background part, sung without words.
- The band consists of a guitar with a chorus-type effect, a lead guitar, a piano (mostly honky-tonk style), bass, and drums.
- Following the introduction is a harmonized first chorus rather than the traditional first verse.

- The first verse, sung with a tongue-in-cheek attitude, has a doubled effect, which creates a slight delay. The bass is playing a stilted, quarter-note feel.
- The acoustic guitar plays a standard rhythm pattern.
- An electric guitar, with a playful effect, sounds almost like a pedal steel guitar.
- Vocal percussion enters near the end of the verse. After the lyric, "military man," there is a cartoonish, kazoo-type effect.
- The second verse, which contains just a portion of the first verse format, is enhanced by background vocals. This is followed by a completely different section of harmony vocals. This section leads into a honky-tonk piano solo.
- The second half of the verse format follows. This leads back into a harmonized chorus and lead vocal ad-libs.
- A new, bizarre section follows the chorus. It consists of playful and percussive vocal effects, and a piano part consisting of a harmonic pattern not before heard.
- The song abruptly ends.

"Good Morning, Good Morning." Continuing with the overall light-hearted ambience of the album, "Good Morning, Good Morning," is sprinkled with animal sounds. (This is clearly a reference to The Beach Boys' *Pet Sounds* album.)

The song is about a typical day in an apparently just "okay" life.

> ♫ Note: John got the idea from a Kellogg's Cereal commercial. The Beach Boys' *Pet Sounds* album probably inspired the animal sounds.

- The first sound is that of a rooster, which represents reveille, the traditional army bugle call to wake up.
- The introduction consists of a distorted rhythmic guitar, processed background vocals singing "good morning, good morning," and a disjointed, almost disoriented-sounding rhythm pattern.
- The first verse has an unusual meter: 2 bars of 3/4 time followed by a 4/4 measure. Variations of this quirky and jarring meter pattern continue.
- The distorted rhythm guitar continues but is periodically interrupted by a distorted lead-guitar line.
- Once again, the background vocals sing "good morning, good morning, good morning," as a transition to the second verse.
- The shortened second verse continues with the meter changes.
- The distorted rhythm guitar plays sustained chords, which complement the lead guitar lines.

- This leads to a rock 'n' roll section highlighted with a typical 1950s guitar and bass octave signature line. (Baritone saxophone, guitar, and bass parts in many '50s records typically played this pattern.)
- An abrupt drum fill is used as a transition to the third verse.
- The third verse is basically the same as verse one.
- A raw, distorted guitar solo follows.
- The next section is a repeat of the rock section but with the addition of lead guitar fills.
- The fourth verse closely follows verse one.
- The opening rooster sound effect begins the outro (ending).
- The song fades out.

"Sgt. Pepper's Lonely Hearts Club Band" (Reprise). The first time we hear this song (at the beginning of the album), the lyric introduces the band to the audience; during the reprise, the band thanks the audience for attending.

- The reprise starts with a voice counting off the song, crowd noise, and a faster tempo than the opening. The arrangement has a completely different feel and song format from the first "Sgt. Pepper" track; it is rockier and contains an active lead-guitar part.
- The first vocal entrance is during the chorus, and the vocals are sung in harmony. The chorus modulates.
- The song segues into "A Day In The Life."

> ♫ Note: This is the only song on the album that does not have a lead vocal; the vocals are in harmony and sung by a group.

"A Day in the Life." The lyric to "A Day in the Life" is a combination of 2 separate songs. John wrote one song, and Paul wrote the other. Paul's song refers to his school days, and John's song refers to the film *How I Won the War*. Included in the lyric are references to other events, which are represented in a fictional account.

- The introduction starts with an acoustic guitar, piano, and bass.
- During the first verse John's voice is processed with reverberation and delay. A shaker is the only percussion instrument, and the piano and acoustic-guitar parts continue playing.
- The second verse continues with the shaker keeping the rhythm anchored, and drum fills, which emphasize significant lyrics. The drums morph into a regular rhythm part.
- The third verse continues with the same feel and instrumentation as the first verse, with the addition of a full drum set playing with the shaker. Strategic drum fills continue.

- The next section is a completely bizarre grouping of tape loops and effects, containing everything but the kitchen sink. The main effect sounds as if a spacecraft is taking off.
- The next section is the second of the two songs that have been combined to make "A Day in the Life." The band begins by playing all quarter notes, relieved by a syncopated melody line. The rhythm feel is—once again—that of a vaudeville or English music-hall song.
- After Paul sings the lyric "I went into a dream," the background vocals answer with a highly processed dreamlike vocal line without words.
- The orchestration expands during the end of the dream sequence; strings and brass are added.
- The strings and horns drop out. The fourth verse melody is the same as the first verse, but the mood of the track remains the same as that of the previous section; the track does not return to the original rhythmic feel. The drum fills continue to emphasize important lyrics.
- The song proceeds to restate the space launch, by using the same basic effects.
- The section ends with a high orchestra octave hit (a powerful orchestral sound) followed by a processed piano chord with an endless echo delay.

Author's Opinion: Since most of The Beatles' early influences were African-American artists, such as Chuck Berry, Fats Domino, and Little Richard (John Lennon's earliest influence was Elvis Presley, who was influenced by black gospel music), it is puzzling that The Beatles' rhythmic feel was anything but loose and funky. Ringo's basic drumming style, plus the raw, untrained guitar playing (during the formation of the band) became a magical hybrid that probably developed accidentally. There were endless hours playing in clubs, which helped to form the sound of The Beatles. The "Liverpudlian" accents, of course, became a trademark.

The brotherhood that developed between the Fab Four greatly contributed to their artistic and commercial success. They became one artistic entity—*the sum of all parts equaled the whole.*

With the influence of George Martin (the 5th Beatle) a completely unique sound was born. The future of pop music was born with the unprecedented artistic growth of The Beatles.

Extra

The following is an analysis of some of The Beatles' greatest hits:

"I Want to Hold Your Hand," recorded in October of 1963, was The Beatles' first song recorded on a 4 track tape recorder. George Martin bounced tracks together to make room for additional overdubbing and experimentation.

> ♫ What is remarkable about these recordings is that it is difficult to discern any loss of audio quality, which is a problem when combining and bouncing tracks on analog tape. When listening to the remastered tracks, which have been cleaned up in the digital format, it sounds as if they were recently recorded.

"Eight Days a Week," recorded in 1964, is reminiscent of the vocal styling of the Everly Brothers, and retained a somewhat rockabilly sound. The hand clapping is directly related to the hand-clapping rhythms used in the records of the 1950s. (The hand clapping was taken from black gospel music.) The bass pattern, derived from early rock 'n' roll, differed from most early rock 'n' roll only because it was played on an electric bass. (The electric bass was invented in 1951 but was not popular in the earliest rock 'n' roll records.)

Ringo's drum playing was unique. He created a rhythm pattern and style that has been emulated on countless recordings.

> ♫ Ringo did not play on all of The Beatles' records. This was not divulged for many years. My colleague Bernard Purdy played drums on several of the hits.

"Yesterday," recorded in June of 1965, was recorded with acoustic guitar and a string quartet. The instrumentation was highly unusual for a rock group.

"Let It Be," recorded in 1969, had a church-music quality to the production.

> ♫ "She's Leaving Home," recorded on March 31, 1967, was recorded using only a string quartet and vocals.

- It begins with a tamed gospel style piano part and a solo voice. (The piano continues to set the church ambience throughout the production.)
- High, "angel-like" vocals enter with the chorus.
- A subdued bass and sparse drum part (playing a backbeat) enter as part of a buildup.
- The next chorus contains the "angel-like" background vocals in addition to a more pronounced bass and drum part. An organ pad is added to define the church image.

- An unusual rock-style electric guitar solo enters. The sound of the guitar is an excellent example of the painstaking attention both George Martin and The Beatles paid to experimentation. They were always striving to be fresh when approaching each song.
- The ride cymbal is used in place of the expected hi-hat. This becomes the height of the song rhythmically.
- The next verse is more subdued but builds in the next chorus, with the drummer once again playing the ride cymbal.
- The ending is composed of a riff-style figure. All musicians played the same rhythm pattern.

"**Come Together**," recorded in July of 1969, was released in the UK on October 31, 1969, and also released in the United States on October 6, 1969, and was an innovative production.

- The vocals are mixed relatively low in the track, and contain a slight delay.
- A vocal percussion part, composed only of a shush sound, adds a unique quality.
- Unusual percussive parts are added, including a distinctive and unexpected muted tom-tom sound.

The arrangement is divided into numerous sections, each with a unique quality:

- Throughout the song, the drums are interrupted with a repeat of the opening riff, which creates the signature sound of the production.
- A distorted guitar plays the same rhythm pattern as the bass.
- An electric piano part enters in the middle of the song, playing with an almost pedal steel–sounding guitar solo.
- A second, simple guitar solo has a lonely sound and is surrounded by a rhythmic pattern played by the electric piano, bass, and a new rhythm guitar part. The guitar melody line, also a signature sound, continues throughout the fade-out.

Extra

Excerpts from the following article written by David Dermon III should be of interest to any student fascinated by the music business. The story of The Beatles' breakthrough in the United States is not unusual. (Vee-Jay Records was a successful independent label based in Chicago.)

> EMI, the British record company with ties to the U.S. Capitol label, approached Vee-Jay in Summer 1962, after Capitol had used their right of first refusal to turn down a couple of artists EMI had offered. The Beatles

at that time had yet to record "Love Me Do," which was their first real British hit, and the decision to pass them up was made on the strength of several German recordings with Tony Sheridan, and a few items like "Ain't She Sweet" and "My Bonnie."

According to Calvin Carter (vice president of A&R and publishing), "At the time, we were pretty hot. We had the Four Seasons and we got a lot of airplay. There was a number one record over in England at the time, and our lawyer, who represented us in other countries, was Paul Marshall. Trans-Global (an EMI affiliate), a company over there had a number one record and they asked us if we wanted it, and of course we wanted it. It was 'I Remember You' by Frank Ifield. We took the record, and as a throw-in, they had a group and asked us if we would take them, too. The group turned out to be The Beatles, and we got a five-year contract on The Beatles as a pickup on the Frank Ifield contract."

The Rolling Stones

The members of The Rolling Stones are Mick Jagger (rhythm guitar, harmonica, and percussion), Keith Richards (lead and rhythm guitar, background vocals, and infrequent lead vocals), Charlie Watts (drums and percussion), and Ron Wood (guitar and background vocals). Former members were Bill Wyman (bass), Brian Jones (guitar), and Mick Taylor (guitar).

Their first recording contract was with Decca Records (UK) in 1963. They are essentially a blues band heavily influenced by American blues singers like Muddy Waters, 1950s rock 'n' roll, and American country music. The blues influence can be heard in tracks such as "Honky Tonk Women," and the country influence can be heard in "Wild Horses" and "It's All Over Now." Mick Jagger summed up the sound of The Stones in a song—"It's Only Rock & Roll."

Their musical style went through periodic transformations. The Rolling Stones released "Ruby Tuesday" in 1967, the same year The Beatles released the *Sgt. Pepper* album. "Ruby Tuesday" sounds heavily influenced by The Beatles. The album, *Their Satanic Majesties Request,* was a blatant attempt to compete with The Beatles' seminal recording of *Sgt. Pepper*. Even with forays into other styles of music, The Rolling Stones have always returned to their roots—and what the audience wants to hear—blues-influenced rock 'n' roll. Their first hit in the United States, "Tell Me (You're Coming Back)," reached number 24 on August 1, 1964, on the *Billboard* pop chart.

Their first #1 hit in the United States (*Billboard* chart) was "(I Can't Get No) Satisfaction." It hit the chart on June 19, 1965.

♫ "Come On" was the first hit in the UK. It reached #21 on July 25, 1963.

♫ "It's All Over Now" was their first #1 hit in the UK. It reached #1 on July 2, 1964.

The Rolling Stones: Production Elements

- Blues-oriented chord progressions.
- Distinctive guitar riffs set the harmonic structure and the groove for an entire song, as in "(I Can't Get No) Satisfaction." Keith Richards—lead guitar player and cowriter (with Mick Jagger) of most of the songs—has a unique guitar style. He plays catchy riffs combined with tasty blues-related fills. His rhythmic playing complements Jagger's vocals.
- Jagger sings in a raw blues style. He also plays blues harmonica with the feel of a traditional blues musician.
- Jagger, who is more a stylist than a singer, has the one characteristic that cannot be taught—charisma. He sings with an honesty that is conveyed to the audience on recordings as well as during live performance. His superb stage presence is one of the key reasons for The Stones' longevity. They created an image, which is portrayed on records and seen during concerts.
- Although their recordings have a live feel, some of the guitar parts are processed with additional reverberation, which is reminiscent of the sound of early rock 'n' roll.
- The audience relates to most of The Stones' lyrics. Many are clever, and the imagery is unusual.
- A number of songs are augmented with horn arrangements. (Horn sections are typical of 1960s R&B records.)
- Blues and early rock-oriented piano parts are featured on many of the songs.
- Some tracks have additional background vocals, performed by studio singers.
- Throughout the Stones' long career, the one element that has remained constant is the raw quality of their music. The "rawness" is captured on the studio recordings, as well as heard during their concert performances.
- Most of the vocals are mixed at a low level.
- The audience has witnessed an eclectic array of song styles, but The Rolling Stones have always remained "true to their roots," performing songs as diverse as "Jumpin' Jack Flash" and "Symphony for the Devil."

♫ Many bands, known as consummate performers, cannot capture the same performance energy in the studio. The Stones have been able to transfer a live feel to their recordings.

♫ Billy Preston played on some of the recordings. He also played on some of The Beatles' records, including "Let It Be."

♫ Horns, piano, and background vocalists augment the band during live performances. They also perform with a bass player, who is not a member of the group.

♫ In the 1960s and 1970s this style of production was heard on most rock 'n' roll records.

- The drum patterns are simple and strong and create solid grooves. This simplicity is the rhythmic foundation for each song.

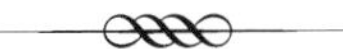

Author's Note: Drummer Charlie Watts is an example of an accomplished musician who never loses the basic groove of a song. Often, drummers with superior technique want to display their "chops" (technique). This quite often disrupts a groove. Simplicity creates grooves in pop music, and The Rolling Stones are a groove-oriented band.

When producing a group whose recorded presence should replicate a live performance, the producer must be concerned with maintaining the essence of the artist. The studio offers many opportunities to enhance recordings—*to a point of destruction*. (This refers to "sanitizing" the feel by trying to attain perfection.) For some bands, such as Steely Dan, perfection works and in fact has been a studio trademark. That style of production would not work for The Rolling Stones. Their signature sound is raw and bluesy, and the music is also based on retaining a "garage feel."

The Rolling Stones have become the most successful rock band in history. They perform to sold-out concerts throughout the world.

Bob Dylan

Many consider Bob Dylan the poet laureate of rock 'n' roll. He started as a folk singer and progressed into his own niche within the broader concept of rock. Dylan eventually used electric guitars and performed and recorded with rock-oriented musicians, but his style remained rooted in folk music.

Dylan has been a major influence for some of the premier artists in the music business, such as The Beatles and Eric Clapton. His innovative lyrics are thought provoking and original. His state-of-consciousness melodies sometimes seem to ramble, but with time and attention the audience is drawn into the messages and the songs begin to flow.

Dylan's limited vocal ability does not hinder his power to communicate. The production values of his recordings are minimal because the focus of the recordings is not technological but performance based. The surrounding elements of a Dylan performance are merely that—surrounding. His longevity is due to the substance of his songs. Some of the lyrics are difficult to analyze, but there is something intriguing that makes the listener want to understand his intentions. This mystery also adds to Dylan's appeal and his unique persona.

Analyze Dylan's work and other stylists. Why are they popular? In Dylan's case, it is more obvious than with other artists. It is also interesting to observe the audience's reaction to artists who are not musically proficient but who possess a raw artistic demeanor. In my view individuality is attractive to the audience. There is an audience for Bob Dylan and Bruce Springsteen, and there is also an audience for Take 5 and Barbra Streisand. Dylan and Springsteen sing from the gut, while Take 5 and Streisand are not only technically proficient but concerned with immaculate production values as well. An audience exists for both types of performers.

Dylan's move into electric music was not unusual. As a youngster, he was influenced by rock 'n' roll acts. His thought-provoking lyrics and vocal style fit perfectly into the folk movement of the 1960s, but as the folk movement dwindled, he had to change in order to survive in a business that continually evolves. He did not change his music; he altered the manner in which his music was presented. Incorporating electric instruments in the folk genre, which was rejected by most traditional folk artists, changed the manner in which alternative rock 'n' roll was presented. Dylan started a new form of rock—folk rock.

Some of Dylan's lyrics are accessible and straightforward, while others have hidden significance. Understanding the meaning of each song is essential for a producer/arranger because the lyric must be accompanied with the appropriate arrangement and production techniques.

A music production is a creative venture that contributes to the audience's perception of a song. A mood must be created for each song/instrumental, and an overall vibe is fundamental when trying to create a cohesive album.

Many artists have recorded Dylan's songs:

"The Times They Are A-Changing" (1963). The lyric speaks about the need to change with the times. People who do not understand change and the need for change become stagnant. Ignoring change is impossible. "The Times They Are A-Changing" is a protest song.

> ♫ Dylan's recording reached number 9 on the British charts on March 25, 1965.

"Blowin' in the Wind" was recorded by Peter, Paul, & Mary. It reached #2 on the *Billboard* chart on July 13, 1965. Stevie Wonder reached #9 on the same chart on July 30, 1966.

The lyric speaks of unconscionable sociological issues and deals with Dylan's frustration with bigotry and a lack of social consciousness. Dylan says that the answer (to these problems) is "blowin' in the wind." This song became associated with the civil rights movement.

"Like a Rolling Stone" was a hit for Dylan. It reached #2 on the *Billboard* pop chart on August 14, 1965. The lyric warns that anyone can fall from his or her position in life. Life is fragile, so do not look down on less fortunate people.

♫ "Like a Rolling Stone" reached #4 on the British chart on August 19, 1965.

"Mr. Tambourine Man" was a hit for the British group The Byrds. It reached #1 on the *Billboard* chart on June 5, 1965. Allegedly, this is a drug song. Mr. Tambourine Man is a drug dealer, and the images are psychedelic in nature. Dylan denied this allegation. Other analyses claim that Mr. Tambourine Man is the drug itself.

♫ "Mr. Tambourine Man" reached #1 on the British charts on June 17,1965.

"Lay, Lady, Lay" reached #7 on the *Billboard* pop chart on August 2, 1969.

♫ "Lay, Lady, Lay" reached #5 on the British charts on September 13, 1969.

Bob Dylan: Production Elements

- Dylan's earlier productions had few production elements that are worthy of study. Many of the tracks are shabbily performed. Dylan would basically begin playing in the studio, and the band followed. The production values of his latter recordings improved, but the productions are not worthy of discussion.
- Dylan has great influence as a songwriter with a social conscience. A producer or A&R person at a label continually auditions artists. Some artists have a dynamic presence and slick performance skills, and other artists are more artistic. A producer should concentrate on "what the artist has to say." It is easy to miss an artist, such as Dylan, who is not a dynamic performer. Singer-songwriters have always been a major force in the record industry and always will be. To find a talent as unique as Dylan's is rare. His career began in the early 1960s, and his concert performances still sell out.

1970s

In addition to the various artists who made a mark in the 1970s, there were two important factors that changed popular music. One was the advent of FM radio, and the other was the introduction of disco in the United States.

Receiving airplay on FM radio stations meant that artists could achieve popularity without realizing a hit single. "Underground" radio stations played album tracks containing meaningful lyrics and/or imaginative arrangements and inventive productions. The artists were concerned with recording an artistically acclaimed album rather than producing a top 10 single. Some artists were able to produce hit singles without compromising artistic integrity. Many of the artists became superstars.

Two examples of bands that defined the 1970s were Black Sabbath and Led Zeppelin; both were heavy metal acts, and both truly identified the genre. They achieved popularity because of FM radio airplay.

The English band Queen, formed in 1970, personified theatrical rock. Their concept was to sing tight harmonies over a heavy-rock rhythm section. They became one of the most successful bands in the world. Lead singer Freddie Mercury was a flamboyant dresser, and he kept "metamorphosing" his stage persona. Queen had a visual image that complemented their musical style.

Some of Queen's hits:

- "Bohemian Rhapsody" reached #9 on the *Billboard* pop chart on February 7, 1976. "Bohemian Rhapsody" reached #1 on the UK charts on November 8, 1975.
- "We Are the Champions" reached #4 on the *Billboard* pop chart on November 26, 1977.
- "We Are the Champions" reached #2 on the UK charts on October 22, 1977.
- "Another One Bites the Dust" reached #1 on the *Billboard* pop chart on August 30, 1980. "Another One Bites the Dust" reached #5 on the UK charts on November 14, 1998.

> ♫ Listen to Black Sabbath, Led Zeppelin, and Queen. Their songwriting ability and musicality define this time period. They were conscious of creating a defining sound on records and are instantly recognizable. Layered vocals, creative guitar playing, and unique songs made these bands distinctive.

Disco

Disco began in New York in the early 1970s. New York is traditionally a late-night town, and discos afforded the partygoer an opportunity to hear exciting and creative music, and to dance until the wee hours. Socially, it established the first opportunity for gays to congregate openly.

Discos helped create a gay and lesbian culture—a lifestyle. Additionally, discos were, and still are, popular with Latinos and African Americans.

From a sociological viewpoint, there was and still is a disco (dance) subculture. Many subgroups such as homosexuals, who were considered outcasts in traditional society, found a home—a comfortable atmosphere where they were not judged by their lifestyle. The audience related not only to the feeling of the beats—emanating from state-of-the-art sound systems—but also to some of the socially relevant lyrics, such as Gloria Gaynor's "I Will Survive," or The Village People's "Macho Man," "Y.M.C.A.," and "In the Navy." (The Village People's songs appear to be lighthearted but have deeper meanings.)

Today, disco is called dance/electronic music. The only difference between disco and dance music is the natural evolution of the music. The word *dance* is used because of the negative connotation that disco assumed. Many journalists and music critics defamed disco music, and, in addition, discos became known as "drugstores." Clubs were and often still are associated with drugs. This unfortunately has marred the creative aspects of the music, from a production viewpoint. Dance music has been dominating the pop charts, as of the writing of this book, e.g., Lady Gaga and Katy Perry.

Disco bashing became rampant within the music industry. The music was designed to be lighthearted, fun, and entertaining. What has rarely been touted is the extraordinary musicianship and creativity displayed in dance music. Many artists in other genres have borrowed the production techniques used in dance music.

The film *Saturday Night Fever* (1977) catapulted the genre into worldwide popularity and gave dance music legitimacy. The album is one of the best-selling of all time. The Bee Gees wrote the most popular songs from the film; many became not only hits but also standards: "Stayin' Alive," "How Deep Is Your Love," "Night Fever," and "More Than a Woman."

The popularity of the songs opened the doors of top 40 radio stations, which basically blackballed disco music from playlists. Radio stations, such as WKTU in New York, programmed disco music twenty-four hours a day. The trend was mirrored in dance-oriented cities throughout the United States. In general, there was always resistance from mainstream radio to playing disco music. The main cities in the United States with a large dance culture are New York, Miami, Chicago, San Francisco, Los Angeles, and Atlanta. Radio stations there played dance music on the radio, but

♫ Discos became so popular that patrons stood on line for hours just to be admitted into the hottest clubs in New York City. Studio 54, the most famous club, was the height of glamour. The most popular stars in all areas of entertainment sat in the VIP section each evening, and danced most of the night.

as with any trend that gains massive popularity in a brief period of time, the level of public acceptance waned, and most of the stations changed formats.

Today, numerous hip-hop and pop stations have weekend dance music (club music) programs called mix shows; they begin at midnight and broadcast throughout the night. Many emanate from local dance clubs, which adds to the excitement of the music.

The Remix

The club DJ's job is to keep the dancers on the dance floor, by sequencing records in a fluid rotation. "Playing" has become a craft because of the extraordinary skill developed by some DJs. A DJ's musical taste separates the superstar from the average spinner. The most popular DJs can attract an audience of 15,000 patrons in one night. They bring a unique perspective to the music, by mixing in new beats, combining several records by manipulating the recordings, and by choosing a selection of music that is distinctive. Successful DJs are popular artists and can command very large fees. DJing on a regular basis affords them the opportunity to observe dancers and their reactions to the production qualities of remixed recordings. They learn *what* makes people dance. For example, a track might build to a musical climax, break down to only a kick drum and vocal, and then slowly build to a full, throbbing groove; the dancers react to the changes. Many DJs become competent remix producers due to their exposure to the music in a club setting.

Since the average single ran an average of 3½ minutes, it was not long enough for the dancers to "get into the groove." The purpose of remixing a track was to extend the length to an average time of 6 minutes. This format became so successful that labels began remixing records that were not necessarily dance records. Rock records, for example, were remixed for the clubs to help expose an artist to a more diverse audience. A successful remix afforded a label additional sales opportunities and airplay on radio stations that normally would not have played the original record.

The cultivation of the remix was revolutionary for the craft of record production. New stars were born—the producers and the DJs. Many DJs became producers since the training of a DJ gave them the opportunity to reconstruct records, which taught them the craft of music production. The original multitrack recording was stripped down to only vocals. Under the guidance of a remixer, the arranger and/or synthesizer-programmer wrote and recorded a new arrangement, using only the original vocal parts; sometimes, additional vocals were added.

Many club records contain 4 to 6 different remixes. Each mix is usually geared to appeal to a different genre of dance-music audience, such as house, techno, garage, and so forth. Many records that debuted in the clubs became hit pop records. In fact, if a record did not achieve a strong audience reaction in the clubs, labels would sometimes not promote them to traditional radio stations.

♫ When remixes first surfaced, the remixer merely muted various sections of the original production and created essentially rhythm-oriented loops (repeated sections). The original kick drum rhythm pattern was replaced with four quarter notes, essentially creating a metronome for the dancers. As remixing progressed, the remixers generally began creating new tracks, using only the original vocals.

The "Death of Disco"

In the late 1970s, disco was a phenomenon. The "death of disco" never occurred. Disco music merely assumed a new name—*dance music*. In Europe, dance music and the dance lifestyle are a main part of the popular culture. A hit dance record in Europe can sell more than a million copies. The songs are continually on the pop charts, and dance compilations, containing classic songs, can sell several hundred thousand copies.

Disco: Production Elements

Disco was the first area of recorded music where the producer, arguably, became more important than the artist. Some singers, such as Madonna, Gloria Gaynor ("I Will Survive"), and Donna Summers ("Love to Love You Baby"), blossomed because of the exposure they received in the clubs, but many singers were merely vehicles for producers. In fact, many producers became artists.

A well-constructed remix will keep the dancers on the dance floor throughout an entire song. If the floor clears, the remix is a failure. The dancers listen to the music on superb sound systems, and the lighting is sometimes equivalent to that of theatrical productions. The audience is thrown into a surreal atmosphere that is controlled by the ability of the DJ to blend hours of recordings. In addition to merely mixing the records, the most skilled DJs add beats (with drum machines) and mix in loops and effects from other records.

Individual clubs became known for playing certain styles of dance music—garage, house, techno, and an array of subgenres. Since much of the music was not considered mainstream, only specialty retail stores sold dance music. Dance music has always been and still is an industry—a subgenre within the music industry. Many dance labels only record and distribute dance music. Most of the labels are not full-service independent dance labels but specialize in certain styles of dance music. Many of them are small, but over the years, mini-majors have developed from successful dance-oriented labels, notably Edel in Germany, and Tommy Boy and Strictly Rhythm in the United States. The success of dance labels has been cyclical. The genre has continued to be relatively healthy even with worldwide piracy problems.

Dance music is experiencing the same piracy and illegal-downloading problems that other forms of music are experiencing. The remixers are receiving one-fourth of a traditional fee, and sales are dramatically lower. Many of the dance labels are selling directly from Web sites and hoping to curb some of the peer-2-peer illegal file sharing by offering a price lower than traditional retail prices. The labels have no manufacturing cost on the Web and can, therefore, afford to offer a more attractive price to the consumer.

Disco had a distinctive sound. The most important difference between mixing a disco record and mixing music in almost any genre—with the exception of music for films—was that the music was primarily played on large sound systems. Consequently, the music had to be mixed so it sounded best on large audio systems. This principle still applies to today's dance music.

When mixing almost any other genre of music, the mix must sound best on an elemental sound system, since most listeners own basic systems. The mix must also sound balanced when heard on the radio. Most dance records sound best in clubs; consequently, separate radio mixes are produced. Dance labels usually record more than one style of remix. That helps the promotion team receive performances in clubs playing various styles of dance music; it also helps them get airplay on radio programs (Internet and Satellite radio) playing various styles of dance music.

> ♫ House music was the most popular style of disco music throughout the decade.

The following were typical elements of the disco sound of the 1970s:

- The average tempo was 120 beats per minute.
- Many tracks were orchestrated with strings and brass. Certain rhythm patterns, played by the strings and brass, became endemic to the disco sound.
- The bass drum (kick drum) played four quarter notes per bar. The bass drum was usually the loudest instrument in the mix.
- The bass parts were locked with the kick drum part to form a strong, pounding bottom end (low frequencies).
- Guitar parts comprised rhythmic single-line picking on muted strings and also playing rhythmic chord parts. All of the patterns were "catchy" rhythm patterns.
- Background singers were often featured performers. The background vocalists, singing in unison, often performed the lead vocal.
- Many of the lead vocalists were excellent singers and were prominently featured in the mix.
- The various instrumental parts were based on sequential patterns that gave the track a variety of hooks. For example, 2 hi-hat patterns were used on most disco records: (1) Four 16th notes per beat, or (2) an 8th note and two 16th notes per beat.

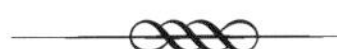

I produced many disco records during the heyday of the late 1970s. One such record is "Let's All Chant," by The Michael Zager Band, with worldwide sales reaching 5 million copies. From the standpoint of a music producer, it is important to try and retain both the publishing rights and the master sound recording rights of as many productions as possible. The publishing rights and the master sound recordings continually generate income derived from commercials, films, television, new recordings, digital sales, and compilation albums.

Pink Floyd

Pink Floyd formed in London in 1965. (The name was taken from the first names of 2 blues singers.) The original members were leader Syd Barrett (guitar and vocals), Roger Waters (bass and vocals), Nick Mason (drums and percussion), and Rick Wright (keyboards and vocals). In 1968, Syd was forced out of the band because of attitude problems. In 1968, Rick Gilmore (guitar and vocals) permanently replaced Syd.

♫ Pink Floyd's biggest U.S. hit was "Another Brick in the Wall" from the album *The Wall.* It reached the #1 position on the *Billboard* pop chart on December 8, 1979. It reached the #2 position in the UK on March 31, 1973. The album has sold more than 23 million copies.

Although this British progressive rock band started in the mid-1960s, the band's seminal album *Dark Side of the Moon* charted in 1973 and remained an unprecedented 27 years on the U.S. album charts—the longest tenure of any act since the charts were invented.

Dark Side of the Moon: *Production Elements*

The album was produced by Pink Floyd and engineered by Alan Parsons, one of the most respected engineers.

The album is overflowing with electronic effects and unusual sounds, creating a theatrical ambience. Spaceship effects and electronica were created with synthesizers and tape.

♫ Alan Parsons worked at Abbey Road Studios in London, where The Beatles recorded.

The musicianship is precise, and the arrangements are meticulous. This production can be compared to George Martin's productions of The Beatles. Each part fits and the recorded sound is impeccable.

- The album is somewhat unusual because of the number of instrumental sections included. Most are long introductions that have become mini-compositions, which eventually lead into a song.
- The lead vocals are frequently doubled.
- Most of the background vocals are ethereal and electronically processed. Four studio background singers enhance the band. An eclectic mixture of Rhythm & Blues, rock, and electronica is included throughout the album. A saxophone part is featured on 2 songs ("Money" and "Us and Them") and R&B vocals sprinkled throughout the album. "The Great Gig in the Sky" has a soaring R&B styled vocal, backed by a prominent organ part, which fades into a gospel-tinged piano before the song fades out. The album is truly a concept album and has a cohesive quality. The tracks were, obviously, designed to flow into one another.
- "Money" is a polyrhythmic song enhanced with sound effects and a hard-sounding R&B saxophone solo, which leads into a high-energy guitar solo. The song goes into a funky rhythm break that leads back into another high-energy guitar solo. The vocals reenter, and the song fades out with talking in the background of the track. The song achieved the #13 position on the *Billboard* pop chart on June 23, 1973.

- "Eclipse," the final song on the album, sums up its overall message: "Everything under the sun is in tune, but the sun is eclipsed by the moon."

A Brief History of Hip-Hop

The complex and inventive sounds and rhythms of contemporary R&B have made a major contribution to the newest form of African American music—hip-hop. Hip-hop began near the end of the 1970s. Hip-hop is, arguably, the most socially relevant music since the slaves sang spirituals. Some of the lyrics' messages, such as gansta rap, have a detrimental effect on society and the mores of young people. Other forms of rap send a positive message, such as the rhymes of Will Smith.

> ♫ The slogan "Rap the Vote" was used to help attract young voters for the 2004 presidential election. The recording credited with being the first rap hit was released in 1979 and called "Rapper's Delight," by The Sugar Hill Gang.

One form of hip-hop, called rap, is made up strictly of rappers who rap (talk in a rhythmic style) in rhymes; DMX is an example. Another form of rap includes singing and rapping, as done by Nelly and Jay-Z.

Rap rhythm songs have distinct rhythmic grooves and characteristic sounds. Many rap tracks have included old recordings and/or beats—these are the samples—as a basic element of the rhythm track. The signature sound of many recordings is a DJ scratching vinyl records on a turntable in time with the rhythmic groove. This creates inventive, percussive beats, which have become the defining element in many hip-hop tracks.

As with other popular music styles, there are subgenres, such as East Coast, West Cost, and Miami rap.

Author's Note: I worked with Grandmaster Flash, one of hip-hop's pioneer artists and producers. As is the case with many DJs who specialize in this genre, his uncanny ability to create inventive rhythms helped to define it.

In working with many other DJ musicians, I have seen that the DJ's ability to scratch has developed into an art form. Showcases are held to display individual scratching styles. DJ scratchers have distinct styles and individual traits similar to those of drummers. Scratching is the newest form of percussion.

1980s

Just as free-style FM radio made a major mark on the music industry in the 1970s, the introduction of MTV (Music Video Television) in 1981 made a similar, perhaps greater contribution to the music industry. (This subject was discussed in chapter 14.)

> ♫ A sequencer is a digital "tape" recorder (without the tape). After being programmed, the information is stored on a hard drive. (The editing capabilities are infinite because digital editing in nonlinear.) Another advantage is that, since it is digital technology, there is no quality loss, an issue that will be discussed later in the book.

> ♫ CDs eventually outsold vinyl and cassettes, becoming the most popular music format. Downloading is quickly making CDs obsolete. DVD audio and DualDisc have not attracted an audience. Will the consumer purchase new equipment? Will surround sound (used in movie theaters and also available for home use) take the place of stereo? As of the writing of this book, the answer is *no*.

For musicians, the technological advance of the 1980s that had the most prominent and permanent effect on the music industry was the advent of MIDI—an acronym for Musical Instrument Digital Interface. Sequencer programs, which are housed in either standalone units or as software sequencing programs, can trigger synthesizer sounds with perfect rhythmic and dynamic perfection. Today, a large majority of commercial recordings are either fully or partially programmed using a sequencer.

Digital sampling is equal in importance to MIDI. Programmers can digitally record anything and play it back by triggering the sample on a keyboard or another controller. Violins, drums, brass, woodwinds, pianos, percussion, and sound effects are just some of the sampled libraries available to music programmers. (Rap records are usually filled with sampled drum and percussion loops.) Like MIDI, this subject will be covered in more detail later in the book.

The introduction of the Sony Walkman (cassette and portable radio player), and later the Song Walkman CD player, afforded the listener a portable means of listening to music with audio quality equal to that heard on home systems. The Sony Walkman was partially responsible for the large increase in worldwide music sales throughout the 1980s.

Michael Jackson

Thriller, released in 1982 and produced by Quincy Jones, became the best-selling album in recorded music history. With *Thriller* selling more than 40 million copies, Michael Jackson became a megastar.

Not since The Beatles released the *Sgt. Pepper* album had there been a production achievement the magnitude of *Thriller*.

Quincy Jones had a well-established reputation as a jazz arranger and film composer. He brought his masterful skills to *Thriller*. It was the perfect partnership between a former child star (The Jackson 5) and an accomplished musician. The album spawned such hits as "Beat It," "Billie Jean," and "Thriller." The trend-setting videos from the album awakened MTV, which began playing R&B videos as well as rock videos. *Thriller* opened the door for black artists.

In 1987 *Thriller* was followed by another blockbuster album titled *Bad*. *Bad* generated seven hit singles and remained in the #1 chart position for 8 consecutive weeks.

Today, given the popularity of hip-hop and R&B, one could argue that MTV Neworks, owned by Viacom, is playing an excessive amount of black music and that the rock audience is not receiving enough attention. BET (Black Entertainment Television) is a major force in the promotion of black music in the United States. In reality, whatever generates an audience gets the airplay! The consumers of hip-hop and R&B are colorblind.

Thriller*: Production Elements*

Combining R&B with a jazz flavor provided *Thriller* with a unique sound. Outstanding arrangements, performed by the finest studio musicians, laid the groundwork for the exceptional talent of Michael Jackson. The superb engineering of multiple Grammy Award-winning Bruce Swedien made *Thriller* one of the best-sounding albums of all time. The hit songs, hit videos, production values, and engineering expertise made *Thriller* a benchmark.

Most producers working in this genre wanted to attain the same standards set by Quincy Jones. Quincy Jones is the quintessential musician and producer. The advantages of being a well-trained musician are exemplified in all of Quincy's productions.

The ability to specifically guide every element of a production and to shape it like a sculpture is the job of a producer.

"Thriller": Production Analysis

- The song "Thriller" is a combination of theatrics, R&B, and jazz. The voice of Vincent Price—the master of horror—adds an element of the bizarre.
- The song begins with ambient sounds of a creaking door, followed by footsteps and a howling animal.
- The rhythmic groove enters as more animals howl. A pulsating bass ostinato is the most prominent musical element.
- The track builds with the addition of a funky guitar riff and background vocal harmonies.

- The track builds with the addition of a synthesizer pad, horn accents, claps, and sound effects.
- The bridge provides a temporary respite from the groove. A synthesizer pad combined with horns creates a sonic smoothness.
- The original groove returns, propelled by the bass and guitar ostinatos. Sound effects are lightly sprinkled throughout the song.
- The chorus repeats and then leads into a C-section, with Vincent Price's menacing voice re-creating portions of what could be construed as a scene from a horror movie. The music track effectively enhances every word.
- The song ends with Price's famous "horror" laugh and a slamming door.

Listen to the placement of sounds throughout the track. The panning, effects processing, EQ, and level (volume) of each track enables the listener to clearly hear each musical component.

Madonna

In 1983 Madonna launched her first album, which landed in the top 10. Madonna's success in the dance market carried into the dance-pop market creating the first superstar from the disco era. Donna Summers was also able to cross markets, but her career dwindled, whereas Madonna has remained popular.

It is important to study Madonna's rise to fame because Madonna is a chameleon. The audience has remained curious about her persona. Her hair, clothes, and even her demeanor have continually changed. She is the ultimate marketer—marketing herself. Her intelligence and her marketing ability have served her well. (She also launched a successful record label called Maverick.)

An artist's image and image-building abilities are important factors in helping the sale of albums. Even though the record label, the artist's manager, and the booking agent assist in the process, an artist must ultimately create an identity for himself or herself. All concerned hope the image will be a natural outgrowth of the music. The group KISS is an extreme example of a calculated image. They have created a marketing empire based upon the band's image.

1990s

The most important technological achievement in the 1990s occurred in 1991, with the introduction of SoundScan, "an information system that tracks sales of music and music video products throughout the United States and Canada." When a consumer purchases an album in a retail store, an online store, or other sales outlets, the clerk scans the CD, or the online store automatically reports the sale. The information travels directly to SoundScan. Information is compiled from more than 14,000 sources, and the results are published weekly. *Billboard* uses the results to compile the charts.

Prior to SoundScan, it was rumored that there were ways to achieve chart positions that were not warranted. SoundScan changed that. Atypical albums began to achieve high pop-chart positions. The industry became healthier as a result of the information obtained from SoundScan. The reports help producers and industry people in general analyze the music market.

It is advisable for producers to be aware of trends. If a large segment of the record-buying public reacts to a certain sound, it can and often does influence a producer's approach to a recording project. (Smart producers use their awareness of trends merely as a guideline and not as a formula.)

The Music

The greatest effect that SoundScan has on the pop charts is the recognition of country music on a wider scale. Garth Brooks became one of the most successful record sellers, in any music genre, attaining sales of more than 65 million units. Country music radio stations now number more than 2,460, and the Country Music Association Awards television program is viewed on a worldwide basis.

Crossover country music has become increasingly popular. The music became more accessible to the pop music listener because of the rock elements mixed with traditional country music instrumentation and rhythms. The best example of a country-rock artist is Shania Twain. Her ex-husband, master producer Mutt Lange, achieved success as a rock, pop, and heavy metal producer. He produced megaselling albums for artists as diverse as Def Leppard, ACDC, Foreigner, and Bryan Adams. Shania's collaboration with Mutt brought glamour to country music and made Shania an international superstar, producing sales in the millions.

> ♫ Shania Twain is an example of an artist who not only has made extraordinary albums from a musical perspective, but also has developed a sexy and glamorous image both onstage and in videos. She is a marketer's dream. Taylor Swift now reigns as the Queen of the country crossover market.

From a production perspective, Shania's albums are some of the best produced in any musical genre. Lange's impeccable taste is showcased in all of her productions.

Alternative rock was the most significant musical development in the 1990s. Nirvana and Pearl Jam both sold more than 10 million albums.

Raves (drug-infested dance parties) took place in dance clubs, with Ecstasy being the drug of choice. The high-energy dance music (mainly techno) never achieved mainstream sales figures but retained a core audience. Raves with large numbers of people are called *massives.* At *massives* there are multiple rooms where different styles of dance music are played in each room. In addition to techno, some of the styles played are house, trance, drum and bass, ambient, and IDM.

Grunge, an amalgamation of many styles, found an audience.

From a sales perspective, Europe became the primary home of dance music. Although there has always been a dance-music culture in the United States, the European market allowed the music to become mainstream radio fare. Many dance tracks became pop hits, with sales figures to support the airplay. The Chemical Brothers, one of the most influential dance-oriented acts, combined traditional dance music with rock 'n' roll. Subgenres continued to develop.

Hip-hop continued to grow in popularity. Disruptive lyrics were heard in a subgenre of hip-hop called gangsta rap. A rivalry developed between West Coast and East Coast rappers, resulting in violent deaths.

> ♫ The fact that hip-hop continued to flourish is significant in the musical culture of the 1990s. It prognosticated the enormous popularity it would achieve after the millennium.

Conclusion

To date, the first decade of the 21st century has produced artists such as Lady Gaga, Katy Perry, Adele, and Rihanna. Pop/dance has had a recurrence. The industry has been turbulent because of the industry-changing technological alteration in the distribution of music (digital), the promotion of music (Internet and Satellite radio, cable, Facebook, YouTube, etc.), piracy issues (illegal peer-2-peer file sharing as well as physical piracy), and the experimentation with new music business paradigms, which continually evolve. There has been a resurgence of adult-oriented music, including artists such as Michael Bublé and Nora Jones. In 2004, according to Nielsen SoundScan, Usher's album, *Confessions,* sold nearly 8 million albums in the United States, making it the best-selling album of the year in the country; Norah Jones's second release sold 3.8 million copies, and Eminem sold 3.5 million units. Sales have continued to decrease throughout the years. Albums have become primarily a marketing device rather than a substantial income source for most artists. Successful recordings help artists get booked and sell merchandise.

As the baby boomers grow older, the music business is hoping that the rock 'n' roll generation continues to purchase recordings—in one format or another—and keep music and musicians alive and well.

♫ In 2010, album sales in the U.S. fell by 12.8%. Digital tracks increased by 1%.

Assignment

Choose a classic album and analyze some of the songs, using analyses of The Beatles' *Sgt. Pepper's Lonely Hearts Club Band* and *Pet Sounds* by The Beach Boys, described in this chapter, as models. Cite examples of recording techniques heard on your assignment album that are still used in contemporary recordings.

II

RECORDING TECHNOLOGY

16

The Studio

> The idea of separation (isolating instruments in the studio) is the total antithesis of rock and roll, which is a bunch of guys in a room making a sound and just capturing it.
>
> —Keith Richards (The Rolling Stones)

Music producers must have a thorough understanding of recording technology. *The creative use of technology* is essential to music production. Technology is nearly as important as the music in popular-music production. A musical ambience is created by the compositional style, the sound of the artist (a unique persona), and the application of audio technology. Producers communicate with engineers on an artistic level. Their conversations are based not on technology but on the application of technology used creatively.

The availability of digital technology at a reasonable cost has creatively transformed the music industry. Musicians can purchase professional-quality audio and sequencing programs at reasonable prices. Affordable technology has enabled musicians to change the sound of popular music. The sounds of MIDI instruments and sampled instruments have become commonplace. The audience does not expect or necessarily desire to hear all live instruments. Certain genres, such as techno, are based solely on electronic sounds, and primarily live musicians perform other genres, like classical and traditional jazz.

Composers, arrangers, and/or producers should consider the use of signal processing during the creative process. For example, if the producer wants a long reverb to trail the lead vocal, space must be left within the arrangement so that effect can be heard. If the arrangement is crowded, not only will the effect get lost, but the arrangement will also sound "muddy."

This book is not intended as a technical guide but rather an overview of the important areas of recording technology. The subjects that follow should each be studied in more detail.

The Studio

A producer ought to become familiar with the acoustical environment of various studios. The physical space (studio or venue) contributes to the final ambience of a recording. The natural reverberation in a studio telegraphs the size and acoustical treatment of the studio. A commonly used term, "live room," refers to the natural reverberation in a room. A recording sounds as if the session was recorded in a live venue and not in an acoustically treated studio. A "dead room" means that the room has been acoustically treated to absorb the natural reverberation, usually caused by hard, reflective surfaces.

> ♫ The section on studio design is included because most producers own project or home studios. Building a studio can be costly and requires expertise in the field of studio design. It is best to hire or consult a professional studio designer prior to building a studio.

Rock music and orchestral music are usually recorded in studios that contain high ceilings, isolation booths that separate drums, guitars, and so on, and natural reverberation. This helps capture a "live" sound. *Caution!* If the room is too "live," the sound will be muffled, and there will be little separation of individual parts.

For productions that are primarily synthesized, the acoustics of the studio room do not generally affect the final sound. Reverberation and additional effects are added during the mixing process; therefore, most producers prefer to work in a "dead" room.

Building a Studio

Because technology has made it possible to build a project studio at a reasonable cost, most preproduction is prepared in project studios. If a production is synthesizer-based music, a project studio might be sufficient. If a production involves live instrumentation, the acoustics of the room are critical, and a project studio might not be adequate.

When a professional studio is built, the acoustician and studio designers try to build a room devoid of outside noise. They accomplish that in several ways: *floating the room*, which is basically building an acoustically treated room-within-a-room, and by *tuning the room*, which is a scientific method of making the room sound "flat" (a realistic frequency response without acoustic coloration). Some studios might have an abundance of bass frequencies, contain too much midrange, or have any number of problems that will affect the final sound. Studio designers can eliminate most acoustical problems.

A professional studio (normally catering to outside clients) is much more costly to construct than a project studio, which generally caters to one artist, producer, and/or engineer. A professional studio can cost millions of dollars, whereas a project studio can be built for $10,000–$15,000 or less. Both budget and recording needs are determining factors when planning a studio, and what follow are items to consider when selecting a studio.

The Room Size

When recording a large orchestra, a room with high ceilings and natural reverberation will produce a more natural sound than a room with a low ceiling and no reverberation. Isolating instrumental sections is usually not a major consideration when recording an orchestra because the natural blend of the entire orchestra produces the most desirable result.

In other forms of live recording, isolation of the various instruments is necessary. *Leakage* occurs when unwanted sound is recorded on a microphone not intended to record that particular sound. For instance, if a distant-sounding saxophone is heard on a trumpet track, the track has leakage from a saxophone. Recorded on its own track, the sax should not also be heard on the trumpet track. There are several ways to avoid leakage:

- Some instruments or sections can be placed in isolation booths.
- Gobos (mobile sound panels) can separate instruments and sections, such as strings and brass. Gobos are essentially movable walls on wheels. They are constructed in different shapes and sizes.

Instrumental separation is preferred so that each track, containing only the desired audio information, can be equalized and electronically processed during the mixing session. For instance, the reverb and delay settings used for a snare drum will most likely not be the same ones used on the tom-toms. Panning tracks helps to create a stereo image. The panning positions are crucial for the overall musical clarity of a song/instrumental. With an abundance of *leakage*, panning tracks will create a muddled sound by masking

> ♫ *Print-through* (also called "bleeding") can occur when recording on multitrack analog tape. This means that information from an adjacent track can be heard in addition to the sound recorded on the adjacent track. For example, if track one is assigned to record an acoustic guitar and a distant-sounding acoustic bass can be heard on the same track, the bass would be bleeding onto track one. The engineer prefers to hear only the acoustic guitar.

other instruments. Panned tracks without leakage will create a "clean" stereo image.

Crosstalk

Crosstalk (digital distortion) can occur when a digital tape recorder is not aligned properly.

Acoustic Room Treatment

To record under optimum conditions, a studio should be acoustically treated and tuned. Highly paid acousticians design professional studios. They analyze the acoustics in the room and then design a sound treatment that helps eliminate any unwanted frequencies. Their goal is to design a room that is "flat" or has a flat response, which means that all frequencies are heard in a natural and balanced state.

Parallel walls produce the worst form of reflective sound. Sound bouncing from one wall to another creates an acoustical nightmare—chaos of reflective sound is not conducive to performing or to listening. The timbre of the reflected sound is altered by the characteristics of the surfaces it encounters.

To help solve acoustical studio problems, sound absorption and diffuser panels are attached to the walls in a scientifically designed manner. Sound panels come in various shapes and sizes and are made of a variety of materials. The following are some of the panels available:

- Convex diffuser panels
  Convex diffuser panels are designed to help solve problems caused by flutter (distortion of high frequencies), echo, hot spots (the amplitude of certain frequencies that are out of proportion to the rest of the sound), and dead spots (frequencies that are lost due to a phasing problem).
- Pyramid-shaped diffuser panels
  Pyramid-shaped diffuser panels diffuse sound into various angles of the room.
- Quadratic diffuser panels
  Quadratic diffuser panels are designed to diffuse sound equally throughout the room.
- Absorber diffuser panels
  Absorber diffuser panels absorb unwanted frequencies. The panels are unusually flat, made in various sizes and lengths, and are strategically placed throughout the studio.

Isolation Booth

Isolation booths are used to control leakage. Almost all studios, whether professional or project studios, have a vocal booth or a multipurpose isolation booth. The performer is placed in a glass-enclosed soundproofed booth, which is designed to block out undesired sounds. Quite often, a soloist records in the isolation booth while other musicians are recording simultaneously in the studio. If, for example, the background track becomes the final background track but the solo performance has to be rerecorded, there will be no leakage on the background track because the soloist was in the isolation booth; this permits the soloist to easily overdub a new part without hearing any leakage from the previous performance. It serves not only a creative purpose but a practical one as well. It is costly to keep musicians in the studio longer than necessary. The soloist can listen to the prerecorded music track and record numerous performances without incurring the unnecessary expenses of paying the musicians more money.

> ♫ Headphone leakage is common. If headphones are unusually loud, leakage will occur through an open microphone. Always solo a track to make certain leakage is kept to a minimum.

Drum Booth

Most professional studios have an isolation booth designed to record a full drum set. Drum booths are also used for multiple purposes, such as recording percussion, e.g., conga drums, or a tambourine.

The ceiling should be high enough to allow for the proper placement of microphones. Microphones must maintain enough distance from the source (e.g., snare drum) to avoid distortion. Many producers and engineers hang ambience microphones that pick up the entire drum set. Combined with the tracks that are closely miked, the ambience tracks help to create a "live" feeling.

Piano Booth

A piano booth is rare but exists in certain studios. Many engineers surround a piano with *gobos* (mobile sound proofing) and cover the piano with cloth blankets (used by movers to protect furniture). This helps to reduce and/or prevent leakage from other instruments.

Control Room

A control room is the "cockpit" of the recording studio. It is the center of the producer's- and engineer's recording universe. The acoustical treatment of a control room is of primary importance because the listening environment must be flat in order to judge the sound quality. The room should be acoustically tuned so that the recorded sound will remain constant when listening on speakers other than those in the studio.

Machine Room

Analog and digital tape recorders, computers, and other noisy machines are usually placed in a machine room, adjacent to the control room. This is done to isolate the noise created by machines. The noise interferes with critical listening that is essential during recording sessions. Not only is the sound distracting, but also the noise can mask frequencies, causing problems when mixing.

Some control rooms project too many low (bottom-end) frequencies or not enough low frequencies, such as bass or low kick drum; others have a lack of midrange or an excess of midrange frequencies (e.g., vocals, snare drum); some have a lack or excess of high-end frequencies, such as violins or bells. Choose a control room that has the most realistic response.

Listening to a familiar album in the control room enables producers and engineers to quickly become familiar with the "sound" of a room. It is best to choose an album that sounds good on multiple speaker systems. During the mixing process, producers should compare the sound quality of the familiar album with that of the new project; it is called A-B-ing. The album should be the benchmark against which to measure the sound of the new production.

Most producers and engineers frequent studios because they know the music will sound the same when played on multiple sound systems outside the studio. If the music does not sound accurate on three or four systems, the problem is either with the tuning of the control room or the speaker system, or creative problems with the mix.

Monitoring

Monitoring is the ability to listen back to a recording or to the music being recorded. There are many fine speaker manufacturers; therefore, purchasing speakers is a matter of artistic choice. Most professional studios offer at least two sets of monitors:

- *Near field monitors* are usually small in size and placed equidistant (left and right) in front of and relatively close to the engineer. They usually rest on a platform built above the meter bridge of the console.

- Large monitors, called *far field monitors*, are usually housed above the console and built into the wall (aka soffit mounted) behind the recording console. Far field monitors are also equidistant (left and right) from the engineer, who is seated facing the monitors.

The monitor placement, like the acoustic treatment of the control room, affects the ability to mix. If the control room and the monitor system do not have a flat frequency response, the mix will not sound the same outside the studio environment. Sound quality is a matter of personal choice; consequently, many engineers travel with personal near field monitors. That enables an engineer to compensate for discrepancies heard on far field monitors. For example, if the bass frequencies appear adequate in the studio but sound "bass heavy" outside of the studio, the engineer can make adjustments by equalizing the appropriate frequencies.

It is crucial that mixes sound good on the radio, which is why it is advisable to listen to mixes on several car-radio systems before giving final approval to the mixes. Most producers do special radio mixes in addition to an album mix. Certain frequencies may sound louder on the radio—than on an album on a home system—because radio station signals are compressed, which affects the sound. A radio mix is generally the format in which the listener first hears a new recording, and the producer must be aware of potential problems and compensate for the potential problems during the mixing process. Radio mixing is both a creative and business necessity. Producers and mixing engineers take pride in the sound of their mixes.

It is wise to monitor on inexpensive speakers. Certain frequencies will probably have to be re-equalized because the speakers are not capable of reproducing all of the frequencies on the original album mix. Special radio mixes are usually designed to appeal to a specific format. For instance, a mix geared to an R&B audience will generally have a prominent bass and kick drum in the original mix. A sub-bass and low kick drum might not be heard on the radio (or television), which means the low frequencies will have to be equalized. Some radio mixes have louder vocals than the album versions. Listen at a low level, making certain that the mix is as "hot" as possible in this format.

When remixing dance music for the radio, most producers make the mixes sound more pop than dance. For instance, there might be less of the kick drum, louder vocals, and new parts added that make the mix more appealing to top-40 radio listeners. Under certain circumstances, several radio mixes are designed, to appeal to a variety of radio formats.

When mixing, listen to the monitors at a low level. It is recommended that engineers listen at 85dB SPL. Listening at a loud level tires one's ears, which makes it is difficult to balance the mix. Radio mixes are usually compressed more than album mixes. Compression is an attenuation progress that allows the low dynamics (volume) and the high dynamics (volume) to meet in the middle of the mix, creating a generally more powerful sound. Since highs and lows are cut off at the radio station, the audience will have the experience of hearing frequencies that would be missing if compression were not used. Engineers who specialize in classical music use compression selectively because retaining the dynamics in that music is imperative.

> ♫ When a mix is completed, producers and engineers listen at several volume levels to see if the relative balances remain the same. They also listen on several speaker systems, both in the studio and away from the studio.

Recording Medium

A producer chooses the recording medium. The two main choices are surveyed here.

Magnetic Tape. For many years recording on magnetic tape was the standard for analog recording. It has been replaced by digital technology.

Analog tape recorders can record and play back multiple tracks. Twenty-four-track machines are the norm, but some engineers use eight-track and two-track machines. Two or more machines can be locked together to enable more tracks to play back in sync.

> ♫ Some producers and artists prefer the analog format because they consider the sound to be warmer than it is on digital recording; the lower frequencies are perceived as sounding deeper and rounder.

Magnetic tape breaks and is more difficult to edit than digital audio. Tape editing is performed with a razor blade; one miscalculated cut can ruin the tape. This form of editing is also more time consuming than digital editing and is destructive in nature. If the tape is not cut properly, it can be difficult to restore. Digital editing is flexible because it is nondestructive editing, meaning the original files can always be recalled as long as the "parent" (original) files have not been deleted.

> ♫ It is quite common to mix in a sequencing program and copy the digital mix onto analog 2-track tape before mixing.

Copying analog tape multiple times creates a generational loss in sound, resulting in a noticeable tape hiss; there is no generational loss when copying in the digital domain.

Digital Tape or Digital Hard Drive (Hard-Disk) Recording. Many producers and artists prefer the crystal-clear sound of digital audio and its easy editing capabilities. Others consider the sound harsh and, consequently, prefer analog recording.

Digital audio technology is offered in several recording formats. The most popular is recording on a computer using a music-sequencing audio and MIDI program, such as Pro Tools or Logic Pro. Editing is accomplished within the program. Nondestructive editing is one of the most attractive features of digital editing, since edits can be recaptured if the original files are not erased. Information is saved in several formats, but peripheral hard drives are the most popular—solid state external hard drives, optical drives, tape drive, DVDs, CDs, and cloud storage. Digital recording is also performed on dedicated hard-disk recorders, which are built into some synthesizer workstations, and also exist as stand-alone units.

Computer audio technology and hard-disk recording offer similar features, but computer-based audio recording is the most popular format. Since the advent of hard-disk recording, many producers do not use tape. With digital audio programs, the entire recording process can be recorded, edited, and mixed within the computer; there are also stand-alone hard-disk recorders. This process is referred to as *digital audio*. Converting an analog audio source into a digital waveform (ones and zeros) and having the ability to manipulate the sound and add effects such as reverberation and compression make this a versatile format. (Sound is first captured as an analog electrical signal and is then converted into a digital signal. This is referred to as analog to digital conversion. The signal is then converted back to an analog signal using a digital to analog converter. A digital signal cannot be heard.)

The ability to edit in a nonlinear format saves time. The engineer can locate any section of the production by clicking on a destination, rather than having to roll tape back and forth. Nondestructive editing enables producers to experiment without erasing original edits or takes.

Multitrack digital tape recorders were popular until computer-based programs developed and replaced the format. DAT (digital audiotape cassettes), DTRS, ADAT, and DASH recorders were primarily used for storage in professional audio environments. DAT never became popular with the general public. Making digital copies does not degrade the audio quality since there is no generational loss. (DVD, CD, hard drive, and cloud storage are the preferred methods of storing data. Always store on multiple devices. In a "flash" data may accidently be erased.)

Conclusion: Sound Media

As discussed, certain producers and artists feel that recording on magnetic tape produces a warmer sound than digital recording. Some producers like the sound of digital recording, which offers clarity. Most rock producers and artists prefer the sound of analog tape, whereas many R&B artists and producers prefer the sound of digital recording. The choice is a creative decision. (Unfortunately, unless tape is manufactured, multitrack analog recording will no longer be an option. Very few companies manufacture analog tape.)

The Recording Console

Recording consoles differ in sound and quality. Producers usually choose a console based on the overall sound they are trying to capture.

Numerous companies manufacture recording consoles. Consoles are analog, digital, or a hybrid of the two. With the advent of computer music programs, it is possible to complete a recording within a computer music program, never using a physical recording console, sometimes referred to as a *board*.

Sound is recorded from microphones, synthesizers, or other devices, which can be routed into the recording console or directly into the console with the use of a *direct injection* (D.I.) box. For example, an electric guitar can be recorded by either placing a microphone in front of an amplifier or by plugging the guitar into a D.I. box inserted into the input of the console. Some producers record a combination of signals and mix them together.

Consoles vary in size and optional expansion capabilities. Large, professional consoles are capable of recording numerous instruments/vocals simultaneously since they contain a sizable number of inputs. The recorded sounds can be processed through numerous outboard-processing devices, such as equalizers, compressors, reverbs, or delay units. Some consoles are equipped with effects, which are built into the console.

The console is the "command center" of the recording process. Recording consoles contain faders, equalizers, panning channel assignment switches, auxiliary sends and returns (including master sends and returns), trim knobs, master fader, group faders, solo buttons, and mute buttons. Some consoles contain limiters and compressors. What follows is a brief rundown of analog and digital consoles.

Analog Recording Console. *In analog consoles, the signal passes through physical components, which include capacitors, resistors, and wiring.* The sounds of consoles differ from manufacturer to manufacturer. Some engineer/producers think a Neve console sounds "warmer" than an SSL console, and so forth. Sound is a matter of preference.

Digital Recording Console. *In a fully digital console, the audio signal is converted into the digital domain. Ones and zeros represent the audio signal.* The sound quality depends on the quality of the analog-to-digital converters and the digital-to-analog converters; usually, expensive consoles have the best converters.

The digital process uses computer technology to route the audio signal. Most digital consoles have highly sophisticated switching devices that allow the user to scroll through various console pages where the engineer can adjust various parameters. Since a multitude of functions can be performed in a limited physical space, digital consoles have become much smaller than their analog counterparts with the same functionality.

A major advantage of digital consoles is that they provide *total recall. Total recall* means that all parameters that have been edited (especially during the mixing process) can be *saved* and *recalled* at any time—settings for reverberation, panning, equalization, signal processing. A multitude of mixes can be recorded and recalled without altering the original mix. For instance, the producer might move the panning position of the lead guitar from bar 32 to bar 33. The producer can move the position of the guitar from the one o'clock to the eleven o'clock position for that one bar only, and then automatically return to the original panning position, without affecting the remainder of the mix. (This is accomplished during the *automation* process; the console's *total recall* "remembers" the automated command.)

Digitally Controlled Analog Consoles. The signal path is processed in analog form, but the parameters of the console are controlled digitally. The consoles have total recall, which includes recalling levels, equalization, panning, and additional signal processing.

The choice of a console is a matter of personal preference. Some engineers prefer the convenience offered in a digital console; others feel that an analog console has a more appealing sound.

Console choice involves basically the same argument that goes on between those who like the sound of analog tape more than either digital tape or digital hard-disk recording. Some producers and engineers think that digital sounds harder and more piercing than analog recording; others prefer the sound of digital.

Computer Consoles. *Computer music-sequencing programs have virtual recording consoles built into the programs.* The majority of project studio recordings use this software console. They look and work almost exactly like their hardware counterparts. When project studio recordings are transferred to a system in a professional facility, the project will most likely be routed through a professional console such as an SSL.

Components of Recording Consoles

Recording-console types may vary, but some components are found in all recording consoles.

Faders (Input/Output Module). *Faders are used to control the input and output level of sound.* (The number of faders varies depending on the console.) The engineer records (input level) at the "hottest" (loudest) level, avoiding distortion (overloading). Adjusting the fader either raises or lowers the level. The fader is also used when *outputting* the recorded signal or live (microphone or line) signal.

When faders are used in an automation system (a system that saves adjustable console information and reproduces level and digital processing adjustments) the output levels can be adjusted throughout the mix, and the computer processes and memorizes the changes. All parameters can be continually updated.

Channel Input Knob. *The channel input knob is used to input the signal from either a microphone or another device.* The channel input knob is usually located above each input/output module (fader).

Trim. *The trim is designed to increase the signal level*; it is normally used after the gain from the fader has failed to meet the desired recording level.

Equalizer (EQ). *An equalizer offers the engineer the option of controlling the timbre of the input signal by boosting or cutting a specified frequency or general frequency range.*

Above each fader (on most consoles) is a set of equalization potentiometers (pots). The pots are marked with frequency information. There are 4 standard frequency allocations: low frequencies (between 20 and 200 Hertz, or Hz), low-middle frequencies (between 200 and 1,000 Hertz), high-middle frequencies (between 1,000 and 5,000 Hertz), and high frequencies (between 5,000 and 20,000 Hertz). (Hertz is a unit of measurement). Advanced consoles offer more varied and detailed adjustment possibilities, depending on the bandwidth. The two standard equalizers are graphic and parametric, designed to adjust the musical frequencies; the controls increase and/or decrease frequencies based on musical intervals. They are usually controlled by vertical slide controls that adjust the parameters in discrete steps.

- Parametric equalizers normally contain 3 or 4 frequency bands. The engineer is able to scroll through the frequency bands, rather than having to make adjustments in discrete steps.

- Third-party manufacturers sell outboard equalization devices. The output signal can be routed from the console to the input of a device, processed, and routed back into the fader's signal path.

Panning. Potentiometers (pan pots) are usually located directly above the fader. By turning a pan pot left, right, or anywhere in between, the sound will be placed within the stereo or surround sound sonic image. The placement of sounds is crucial to the final sound of a mix. Panning is part of the creative process.

To achieve a feeling of space, not only must the panning be varied from track to track, but the engineer and/or producer also has to find a sonic space for each instrument. If the panning is not thoughtfully planned, the individual nuances of each track will not be heard, and there might be masking of some sounds.

When recording contemporary popular music, the following are some suggestions:

- The kick drum and the bass are usually placed in the center of the mix.
- The snare drum is usually panned slightly off the center.
- The overhead cymbals and tom-toms usually have a stereo spread.
- Lead vocals are panned in the center, and the background vocals normally have a stereo spread.
- Do not pan stereo pianos hard left and right. It will sound unnatural. Arrive at the best panning position through experimentation.

Channel Assignment Buttons. Channel assignment buttons route the output signal of a fader to the input of a tape recorder or digital recording device.

Solo Button. *The solo button enables the engineer to solo a track(s);* this function is used only for monitoring. When working with multiple tracks, soloing is a convenient and easy method of either correcting errors or listening to sections of instruments without having to lower unwanted faders.

Cut or Mute Button. *The mute button mutes the signal on the selected fader(s).* This is a useful function when the intent is to instantly mute a track(s) and then reselect it. Some consoles have a master mute button, which enables multiple channels to be muted by using one switch.

Clipping. *Consoles are equipped with a small light, which indicates when a signal is clipping (distorting).* Overloading the input level usually causes clipping. Lowering the level of the input gain can prevent clipping.

Auxiliary Send (Aux Sends). *The* send *section of a console provides a break in the signal chain that enables the routing of various processors or functions* *through the selected send.* The number of sends varies between consoles. The sends have variable parameters and enable the engineer to increase or decrease the amount of signal routed through each send.

The line-level signal is sent to a processor and then returned back to the console by entering the signal path of a selected fader.

Some engineers like to route signal processors through the sends; they also use sends as a monitoring system. How sends are used is a matter of personal choice.

Master Send. The master send adjusts the overall level of the individual aux sends.

Return. The return returns the signals to the individual auxiliary sends.

Master Return. The master return adjusts the overall level of the returned signal.

Group Faders. *Individual faders can be bussed (sent) to group faders, to form submixes.* For example, the drum kit may be *grouped* to a stereo pair of faders. Adjusting the two faders retains the relative balance. (Listen to track 4 on the CD.)

Main Stereo Output. The master stereo output faders control the overall output level from the console.

Patch Bay. *A patch bay is used to route the various input and output devices used in a recording studio, without having to physically manipulate each wire from each device.* A patch bay is a routing system.

Most patch bays are custom designed to accommodate the needs of a particular studio. If, for example, an engineer wants the lead vocal track to be routed through a compressor: Patch a chord (using a small mini-patch chord) out from the vocal track (located on the patch bay) into the input of the compressor (also located on the patch bay), and from the output of the compressor back into the input of the vocal track, completing the signal path. This procedure is accomplished within the patch bay, rather than by physically taking quarter-inch cables, XLR cables, or digital cables out of each device and placing the cables into another device to create the same signal chain.

The patching system in a computer-based or digital console is contained in the software program. Working within this environment is easier, and usually less troublesome, than working with a hardwired, physical patch bay.

Signal Processing. *Signal processing includes the use of equalization (EQ), reverberation, delays, compressors, limiters, noise gates, and various hybrids.* Effects contribute to the overall sound of a music production and can be an intrinsic part of the arrangement. For instance, leaving room in the track to hear a delay on the lead vocal or adding various combinations of reverberation and echo affects the overall sound.

Signal processing was also discussed in Chapter 8. Reread Chapter 8 for additional information.

Reverberation and Echo. When sound is generated in a room, the sound that first reaches the listener is called the *direct sound*; following the *direct sound* are the *early reflections*. *Early reflections* reach the ear within 50 milliseconds, and they help forecast the size of the room. The longer it takes for the brain to perceive a sound, the larger the space. *Reverberation* occurs after the *early reflections*. The number of milliseconds it takes for reverberation to occur determines the size of the room. The sound that reaches a listener after approximately 50 milliseconds is called *echo*.

The sound bounces off of multiple surfaces and angles, and the size of the room determines the amount of *reverb*. The sound begins to decay. This is called *decay time*. The reduction in *decay time* is based on a 60 decibel (dB) level reduction. (A decibel is commonly used as a measurement in sound level, although that is not the technical definition of a decibel.)

Reverberation can be created in the digital mode. Digital effects are called *digital signal processors* or DSPs. Most studios, as well as computer and hardware-based sequencers, use DSPs for effects.

Compressor. *A compressor attenuates a predetermined threshold level.* This helps eliminate distortion. If a compressor is used on a mix, the bottom and top of the dynamic range are pushed to the center, creating a louder mix by eliminating factors that may cause distortion when the levels are too high. For pop recordings, a "hot" (loud) mix, when played at a low level, is extremely important for the product to be competitive in the marketplace. The sound quality contributes to the success of the recordings.

In addition to myriad other uses, compressors are frequently employed to raise and adjust the levels of bass drums, vocals, basses, and guitars, as well as to raise the level of a completed mix.

When dynamics are important, as they are in most orchestral music, engineers will most likely not use compression, or minimal compression, because it reduces the dynamic range.

Compressor Controls

- Threshold: The threshold setting signals the compressor to attenuate a signal that goes above the setting. The average range is between 0 dB and –40 dB.
- Ratio: The ratio is the setting that indicates how much to attenuate the signal when it passes the threshold setting. For example, if the ratio is set at 6:1, for every 6 dB above the threshold setting, the output signal will be raised by 1 dB.

- Attack: The attack time determines how quickly the compressor reacts to the signal when it exceeds the threshold setting. The attack setting is in milliseconds.
- Release: After the signal reacts to the attack time setting, the signal has a period of time to return to its previous gain setting. This is called the release setting; it is calculated in seconds and milliseconds.
- Coupling or Stereo Switch: The coupling or stereo switch couples both sides of a two-channel compressor so they react to the same settings.
- Hard knee/Soft knee: When the setting is in hard knee mode, the signal compresses at a rapid rate, causing quick gain reduction. This mode works with instruments, such as drums, where a quick compression sounds best. When in soft knee mode, the compression is slower and feels natural, as with vocals. (Not all compressors have this function.)
- Output Control: The output control setting adjusts the output level of the compressor.

Limiter. A limiter is a compressor that has a ratio over 10:1 and/or 12:1. The devices are usually called compressor/limiters. A preset level is set, and the compressor prohibits the incoming signal from exceeding that level. The input signal level does not affect the compression.

Expander. An expander increases a signal's dynamic range.

Digital Delay. *A digital delay processor records sampled audio into the RAM memory; the signal can be delayed in milliseconds, and when the signal is combined with the original signal, numerous effects can be created.* For instance, with a short delay time (15–35 milliseconds), a doubling effect occurs. This adds richness and fullness to a sound.

♫ Read chapter 8 for a discussion of noise gates, chorusing, flanging, microphone modeling, and auto-tune.

Microphones. Microphone placement and the choice of the proper microphones determine the quality of a sound. Microphones might be of the same type—dynamic, condenser, or ribbon—but each individual microphone, within each category, has unique sonic characteristics.

Since microphone selection is a creative choice, experimentation is necessary to find the precise microphones that are most appropriate for specific projects.

Engineers vary in the way they place microphones to record sound. With training and experience, they develop a style and a setup that achieves their sonic goals. Most engineers own a personal collection of microphones, which they rent to clients.

The following is a description of basic microphone placement:

- Ambient Microphone Position: Microphones are used to record the ambient sound of a room. For instance, to make an orchestra sound "live," most engineers place microphones in the room and mix in the ambient room sound with the sound of the microphones that are placed closer to the instruments. This helps to make the recording sound live. Without the room sound, the recording would sound drier—not as natural.

- Distant Microphone Position: Microphones should be placed far enough from the sound source to pick up the entire sound of the instrument, including some room ambience. For example, the sound of French horns expands into the room. The microphones have to be placed far enough from the bell of the horn so they capture the overall sound of the instrument. The direct sound of the instrument has to be prominent in the mix; if the microphones are placed too far from the source, the direct sound will not be prominent enough.
- Close-Up Microphone Position: Some instruments sound best when miked closely. For instance, an alto flute would not be heard if the microphone was too far from the sound source.

Microphone Configurations. The following is a description of basic microphone configurations:

- Condenser Microphone: Condenser microphones, also referred to as capacitor or electrostatic microphones, produce a clear and crisp sound. The condenser is powered either by a battery or (more often) by a 48 volt phantom power supply, which is housed in the recording console or a separate unit. Condenser microphones are the most popular microphones used for vocals, and they are excellent all-around microphones.
- Electret Microphones: Electret microphones, a form of condenser mike, are commonly used as lapel mikes. They are also used in computers and camcorders. Most of them do not require phantom power but may need a battery or possibly phantom power.
- Dynamic Microphone: Dynamic microphones are considered the sturdiest type of microphone. They are used to mike amplifiers and vocals, and can also be used to accomplish almost any result. They can take more abuse than other microphones, such as ribbon microphones, which can be fragile, although current ribbon mikes are sturdier than their predecessors.
- Ribbon Microphone: Ribbon microphones, a type of dynamic microphone, have a smooth sound. Singers and radio announcers often use them. Older ribbons are fragile and can easily break with misuse; the newer ribbons are sturdier. If a recording console contains a phantom power supply (a power source used to power condenser microphones), make certain the phantom power is turned off, or

it can destroy a ribbon microphone. They are bidirectional, which means they pick up the signal equally from both sides of the mike.

♫ Most engineers use the 3 microphone styles for a variety of purposes. Engineering is an art form, and there are no rules.

Preamplifier. Microphones' output signals need to be amplified because they generally have low output signals. This is accomplished by using a preamp (preamplifier). It is crucial that a producer/engineer use high quality preamps. Poor quality will result by using inferior preamps.

Polar Patterns (Polar Response Curve). Some microphones are designed to pick up information transmitted only directly in front of them. That means a vocalist would have to stand in front of the microphone to attain the best frequency response and the best vocal quality. This is referred to as *on-axis frequency response. Off-axis frequency response* means that the sound information is not hitting the microphone *on-axis*, and that can cause filtering and other unpleasant responses. The pattern in which the microphone picks up an optimum frequency response is called a *polar pattern.*

All microphones either have one polar pattern or can be adjusted to select a polar pattern. The following are descriptions of the most used polar patterns:

- Cardioid Pattern: A *cardioid pattern* is shaped like a heart. The heart-shaped area receives the best frequency response. Most microphones have a cardioid polar pattern.
- Supercardioid Pattern: A supercardioid pattern is similar in shape to a cardioid pattern but has a thinner on-axis area. This pattern is used when the engineer wants to capture ambience sounds from the sides of the microphone.
- Hypercardioid Pattern: A hypercardioid pattern is shaped like a cardioid pattern but picks up less on the sides; therefore, a hypercardioid pattern also records information emanating from the back of the microphone pattern. This pattern is often used on movie sets to keep out the ambient noise.
- Bidirectional (Figure 8) Pattern: The bidirectional pattern picks up sound information from the front and rear of the microphone. It does not pick up sound from the sides. This pattern is often used to record group vocals; for example, 2 singers on one side of the microphone and 2 on the opposite side.
- Omnidirectional Pattern: An omnidirectional pattern means that the microphone picks up sound from all directions. This pattern might be used to record a large group of singers.

The following are some concerns that engineers have when recording vocals:

- **Sibilant Sound**. Sibilance sounds like a whistle. Some singers naturally have sibilance in their voice texture. Microphones, which have an unusually high-end clarity, emphasize this problem. There are two basic solutions. A *de-esser,* which is a signal processor, is designed to compress a narrow range of high frequencies. Most often sending the vocal through a de-esser will either eliminate the sibilance or greatly reduce its sound. Also, changing microphones will often either eliminate or reduce the sibilance.
- **Plosive Sound.** Plosive sounds are popping sounds caused by singing certain consonants, such as Ps, Ts, and Ks. There are several ways to eliminate the sound. A pop filter is placed in front of or around the microphone. Most pop filters are made of either nylon or foam. Or professional singers turn their heads to the side before singing a plosive consonant.
- **Proximity Effect.** When singers move too close to a microphone, the lower vocal frequencies become prominent. This is especially true when using a ribbon microphone, although it is a characteristic of all microphones and often determined by the polar pattern. It is sometimes considered a desirable effect. Radio announcers move close to a microphone in order to sound more resonant and deep. If too many low frequencies are prominent in a singing voice, the singer might stand back from the microphone and try to achieve an equal balance of frequencies.

Conclusion: Microphones

Many singers and instrumentalists own microphones. Multiple microphones of the same make and model will each have individual characteristics. The entire sound of a production can change with slight variations in microphone placement. The study and use of microphones is part of an engineer's tool chest, and thus part of the art form.

It is advisable to experiment with condenser, ribbon, and dynamic microphones, as well as with microphone placement in standard recording setups. There are no rules when selecting microphones. Engineers select microphones according to personal preferences.

Recreating a Live Performance in the Recording Studio

Many producers and artists try to re-create a live performance in the recording studio. Audience reaction provides the adrenaline, needed by most artists, to stimulate a dynamic live performance. The producer must find a way to create a live atmosphere in the studio. That is sometimes accomplished by inviting a small audience—although it could be distracting to the producer and engineer. If the session is conducted in a professional manner, the audience can become the catalyst that fuels a dynamic performance.

It is generally wise for an artist to perform new songs live prior to recording. It affords an artist the opportunity not only to rehearse and edit new material but also to monitor the audience's response. Artists might change a song's format or arrangement as a result of information gained through this process. If a song does not receive a positive reaction from the audience, it might be deleted from the album. The audience *is* a focus group and can provide invaluable information.

Artists often rerecord songs years after the original recording was made. Performing live generally transforms songs into something not captured on the initial recording. That is the primary motive for issuing albums recorded in front of an audience. *Some songs (instrumentals) are like fine wine—they get better with age.*

Listen to Ike and Tina Turner's recording of "Proud Mary," and then view a video of them performing the song in front of an audience. The tempo is generally much faster than the one on the audio recording. Performing live brings an entirely different feeling to the song.

Some bands, such as Nine Inch Nails, are production-oriented artists, and the studio recordings must be re-created when they perform in concert. Technology has now made that possible. Most artists have massive technical requirements and travel with specialists called "techs" (technicians who maintain the electronic equipment). The gap between the sound of a studio recording and that of a live performance has narrowed. The sophistication of recording technology is truly staggering, and the creative results are governed only by an artist's imagination.

Audiences expect to "hear the album(s)" in a concert setting. The producer and artist, when preparing the sound concept of a recording, must address this. It is wise to keep the instrumentation as self-contained as possible. If the act is a band and additional musicians are used to enhance the recording, the band will not sound the same when playing live. This has to be of concern when the arrangements are conceived.

There are several ways to solve this problem when performing live:

- *Re-create parts on stage by using synthesizers, or record parts, and dump them into a sampler or a computer-sequencing program and trigger the parts to blend in with a live performance.* For instance, if the recording has a live string section, the parts could be played using string samples, or the live strings from the recording could be sampled and triggered in the appropriate places. (Music-industry writers and fans sometimes frown on the practice, although it is commonplace.)

- *Adapt the studio arrangements for live performance, which can be accomplished by a skilled arranger.* For instance, if a guitar player plays a solo on the album as well as an additional harmony part during the live performance, a keyboard player could play the harmony part using a guitar sample.
- *Hire additional musicians and singers to perform the extra parts—a common strategy of successful artists.* For instance, during concerts, The Rolling Stones usually perform with a horn section and additional background singers.

A competent *front-of-house engineer* (live-sound reinforcement) and high-quality musicianship help recapture the excitement and ambience that is heard on a recording, during a live performance. Engineers that adjust the earphone levels ("ears") of the performers are called *monitor engineers.*

♫ The study of sound reinforcement refers to the study of live-sound engineering. Understanding the sound in various venues should be of interest to a music producer because most producers will eventually produce live recordings. Various acoustical environments can be complicated, and a producer must consider potential problems prior to selecting an engineer.

Recording Live Performances

Bands and singer-songwriters often have different recording goals. Bands want to capture a live performance on a studio recording, à la The Rolling Stones. Beginning with *Sgt. Pepper,* The Beatles became a studio band and were more interested in the recording process than capturing a live performance.

Once a band has established a fan base, the label usually issues compact discs recorded during live concerts. The audience's interaction creates excitement, which translates into energetic performances. The A&R executives and the artist are usually responsible for choosing the songs and performances to be included on the album.

Recording live can be costly. Large trucks are designed to accommodate recording-studio control rooms. The equipment is expensive, and the rental is costly.

In a live venue, the recording engineer must contend with numerous problems that are not present in an acoustically treated recording studio. Sound reverberates between parallel surfaces such as walls. If there are no diffusers to help dissipate it or sound-absorption panels to soak it up, the sound can become muddled. The result is a lack of sonic definition, and the audience experiences an undesirable "Wall of Sound" instead of a clear definition of sound.

That can be distressing for the producer and the recording engineer. To help alleviate some of the problems, the engineer places microphones in front of instruments, amplifiers, and/or instrumental sections such as brass or strings and separates their effects by recording them on individual tracks. That gives the engineer control over each instrument or section when mixing. Ambient microphones are placed throughout a venue to capture the room sound, including the reaction of the audience. The ambience tracks are mixed with the individual tracks. The overall sound greatly enhances the listener's perception of a live concert and telegraphs the size of the venue.

To combat some of the acoustical problems found in a concert hall, engineers hang heavy draperies and give the venue extra acoustical treatment that helps absorb unwanted sound and diffuse the sound more evenly. Acoustically treated gobos surrounding the drums, percussion, or other selected instruments, also help isolate the sound.

Conclusion

A producer must become familiar with all aspects of the recording studio. Choosing a studio, a recording console, an engineer, signal processors, a monitoring system, studio musicians, background singers, songs, and arrangers, is the full or partial responsibility of a music producer.

Once a producer has decided on a *production concept* and a *sonic image*, all potential concerns dealing with the studio and the engineering must be addressed. Choice of studios and engineers will affect the overall production. Producers must be detail oriented, *dotting the* Is *and crossing the* Ts!

> ♫ When recording engineers record live performances, they sometimes share the "snake" (a connection that simplifies connecting microphones, amplifiers, and other equipment to the sound console) with the live-sound reinforcement engineer. That helps eliminate unnecessary wires; both engineers must be willing to compromise on the placement of the microphones.

Interview with Trevor Fletcher

Trevor Fletcher is the vice president and general manager of The Hit Factory Criteria Studios in Miami, Florida (more than 300 gold and platinum albums have been recorded in these studios).

MZ: How has the studio business changed in the past several years?

TF: It used to be that when you made a record, it involved . . . $400,000-plus consoles, expensive tape machines, and so forth . . . then the industry began to change a lot as digital technology became more prevalent. Pro Tools, Logic, Cakewalk, Abelton Live . . . all of these innovations drastically changed the concept of how to make a record. It essentially democratized the recording process. As a result, people were able to record, with reasonable quality, in environments different than the traditional recording environment . . . The technological advancement and the cost [of equipment] enabled them to do that . . . Now anyone can spend a couple of thousand dollars and make a record at home. There is no guarantee that it is going to sound good, or no guarantee that it is going to be made well, or that anyone knows what they are doing, but the technology now enables the layman to dabble in the recording process . . . Almost anyone can go home and make music. It is a matter of perceived value. If I'm going to go to studio ABC and record on a large console with engineers, assistants, producers, arrangers etc and the ability exists now where I can do it at my house for $5, where is the incentive for them to spend money in a recording studio?

MZ: Have professional recording studios lost clients because labels have lowered their recording budgets?

TF: . . . file sharing has had a tremendously significant [effect] for the reduction in volume of monetized music sales. . . . [Many] young adults think music should be free. They have no qualms about stealing it, downloading it, sharing it with their friends, or anything along those lines. [The compression used in MP3 technology has caused a lack of sonic quality,] "If you have nothing to compare it against . . . Then you are in a situation where that becomes the norm. So there is an entire generation of consumers that believe that A, music should be free and B, music is supposed to sound like crap . . . they [the consumer] don't even know it sounds bad. They [the consumer] have essentially traded fidelity for mobility.

MZ: What percentage of your business is mixing as compared to recording?

TF: A large percentage [mix only]. . . . A lot of people believe they can do their recordings at home and then they come to the studio and say, "Fix this . . . make this better . . . make it sound like band XYZ but band XYZ recorded in a multi-million dollar facility with highly trained professionals, acoustically correct rooms, the best equipment, the best technology, the best "ears" [producers and engineers] . . . but for the most part, it can't [sound as good]. [If an artist records a hit in a project studio, why should the record companies spend money for artists to go to a professional facility?] There are some boutique labels that go out of their way to keep the [recordings] in the digital domain at high sampling rates, bit depths—things along those lines . . . but it is not the rule but the exception.

MZ: What percentage of clients are recording on analog tape?

TF: 5 percent . . . the best of both worlds is to record the instruments that benefit from [the sound of analog] and then transfer it to the digital domain for digital editing while still retaining the sound of the analog signal path for those instruments that are most affected by it. Take into consideration that [very few companies manufacture analog tape.] . . . There are now plug-in companies that manufacture plug-ins to make the audio sound as though it has been recorded on analog tape.

MZ: What is the future of the professional recording studio?

TF: A large number of middle-tier studios have gone out of business . . . completely gone or perhaps to have become someone's project studio . . . The large studios that are able to cater to successful artists will continue to be a viable commodity. Target [your professional studio] to do things that can't be done in a small studio or project studio. Technology will continue to advance, the price point [of the equipment] will [also] drop . . . therefore, a studio must embrace that or your future will not be terribly bright.

MZ: Are most of your clients already established artists?

TF: Not necessarily. [We try to work [make affordable] with up and coming artists, producers, and engineers because one day some of them will be successful and be able to afford to work in a professional environment.] Some of our clients are not financially successful but value what we have to offer. [We are able to cater to anything our clients need, from technical assistance to dining and beyond.] When you come here, we have 5, 6, 7 studios of various sizes and varying acoustic spaces and they all sound fantastic . . . we have an [extensive] selection of microphones . . . our clients embrace that. If labels or production companies have ongoing relationships with the studios, they [labels or production companies] may ask for special financial considerations when recording a new artist. It is in everyone's best interest for the studio to attempt to work out a financially viable deal. One must recognize what the market will bear and work with the client. That is how relationships are built and maintained. It is a foolish venture [to build or purchase a studio] without knowing who is going to be using it and how they are going to pay for it . . . [In this industry environment, if a new state-of-the-art studio is built, someone involved should have a substantial revenue stream "to keep the doors open."] Most likely, successful producers and artists who write and produce [will attract clients.] With limited exceptions, the days when one producer will produce an entire album are over.

MZ: Are most successful producers recording tracks in their project studios and then mixing in your studio?

TF: It varies. The big difference, in my mind, of recording in a project studio or recording in a professional recording studio is primarily financial. It is my opinion, that if you are working at home, it is a lot easier to be distracted—and therefore less productive. Be it by your significant other, the dog, a movie, TV . . . there are always distractions if you are doing something outside of a professional environment. There are artists who have the financial resources to record at any recording studio, but choose not to. On the other hand, I have clients who already have their *own* studios but still choose to come here—because of the atmosphere, the level of service—whatever reason. My feeling has long been that the recording studio must be conducive to creativity . . . Clients don't have to worry about anything other than creating music . . . Our primary focus is to make people comfortable and elicit the best performances . . . the best music possible. *Recorded music is becoming a loss leader for touring.*

Assignment

Create a fictitious recording project (a complete album). Answer the following questions:

- Describe the attributes of an engineer who would be most appropriate for the project.
- Describe the studio of your choice. Why would you choose that particular studio? Your answer must include specifics about the control room and the studio room.
- Describe the signal processors you plan to use and how you plan to use them.
- Include any additional technical information you feel would enhance your production.

17

Audio Engineering

Most audio engineers specialize in a musical genre. They apprentice in recording studios, although many have studied audio engineering at universities or trade schools prior to apprenticeships. The training requires years of practical experience. Audio engineering is both a technical and artistic discipline. As previously stated, it is the *creative use of technology* that contributes to the success of a music engineer.

Some engineers work only *"in the box."* They record and mix in a computer audio program, such as Pro Tools or Logic Pro. Most professional engineers route the audio tracks from a computer program through an audio console. They use traditional outboard gear, such as hardware reverberation, compressors, and delay units, in addition to computer plug-ins, which are mostly software versions of the hardware counterparts for reverberation, compression, delays, and so forth.

If an engineer records on digital tape, the information is transferred to a digital audio program, such as Pro Tools, for editing and mixing.

> ♫ Several companies still manufacture audio tape.

Orchestral Engineering

- *Most engineers who specialize in orchestral recording try not to use excessive equalization (EQ).* Their goal is to make the orchestra sound natural. Most engineers own an array of microphones, and they have the ability to achieve a realistic sound through proper microphone placement and selecting the most appropriate microphones for each instrumental section.

- *The orchestra may contain prerecorded synthesizer parts, guitars, a rhythm section, or various other sounds that must blend with the orchestra, consisting of live musicians.* Engineers generally receive prerecorded tracks prior to the orchestra recording. During the recording process, the producer and the engineer must make certain that the orchestra blends with the prerecorded tracks. If necessary, the engineers can EQ the prerecorded material to blend with the orchestra. If the overdubs are recorded after the orchestral recording, it is easier to blend the sounds.

Orchestra Setup

Many albums are mixed in traditional stereo as well as in surround sound. Engineers develop individual microphone setups. There are traditional setups that work for recording orchestras. The following is one example:

- 4 microphones over the violin section. For a solo violin, place a solo microphone.
- 2 viola microphones
- 2 cello microphones
- A bass microphone for each double bass
- Stereo woodwind microphones and solo microphones for any solo instruments. Include an overhead stereo pair to record the ambience of the section.
- Record trumpets and trombones with a stereo pair. Use solo microphones if needed.
- Record French horns with a stereo pair placed far enough away from the bell to record the room ambience along with the direct sound.
- Tubas should have individual microphones. There is normally only 1 tuba.
- Use microphones to record the ambient sounds of the entire orchestra. Recording the ambient room sound of the orchestra makes the recording sound as if the listener was sitting in a concert hall.

Bob Fernandez Interview

Bob Fernandez has been a scoring mixer (a sound engineer for film music) for more than twenty-six years. He was the chief scoring mixer at Warner Bros. Studios (film) for approximately sixteen years, and he is currently an independent engineer.

♫ This interview was conducted on the Eastwood Scoring Stage at Warner Bros. film studios in Burbank, California.

MZ: What films have you have worked on?

BF: Most recently it would be *The Hulk, Fast & the Furious* and *Legally Blonde 2*. All in all there's probably a little over 300 films that I've done. And hundreds of television shows . . . probably a thousand.

MZ: How do the engineering techniques differ from recording records?

BF: The first thing is multichannel, dealing with more than two channels. People are talking up 5.1, but I've been mixing in surround sound for years.

MZ: Do you think surround sound mixing will extend to 6.1 or 7 [additional speakers]?

BF: It may. It's hard to say; I know there are a few films out in 6 and 7.1 format, but primarily it's still a 5.1 world.

MZ: Theaters would have to be reconfigured to accommodate a more complex system.

BF: The theaters would have to be set up for that. They would have to have the discrete surround sound channels. Discrete left, center, right, and front. Then you'd have to have discrete left side surround that discrete left rear, discrete rear center surround, and a discrete right rear, and a discrete right side surround. That becomes quite a big ticket for those guys to spend a lot of money like that. I can see them staying at 5.1 for a while now.

MZ: When you're mixing the music, are you using the entire surround sound system?

BF: Yes. I wouldn't consider mixing the film without the surround. Its just part of what we do. When you mike an orchestra you mike it so you have ambient surround microphones, which give you the fill in the back. And you can also create surrounds when you are mixing synthesizers. Basically all synthesizer samples are stereo, so you want to make them into 4.1. There are left-to-right fronts and the left-to-right surrounds.

MZ: How do you select the speakers for each instrumental section? Is your sonic picture from the audience's perspective while viewing a live concert?

BF: Yes. I mike it so the orchestra is in a traditionally classical setup. Violins on the left, violas center, woodwinds behind the celli, and basses on your right. And the brass on the right, French horns in the middle or on the left side, and percussion spread off in the back. That's pretty much how I do it. I've done several scores, where we split the strings. We have this sort of antiphonal effect, first violins on the left, second violins on the right.

MZ: Is that unusual?

BF: It is. A few composers that I work with like to do this. But you need to have a large string section to do that. I would say, twelve [violins per side] is the minimum size. That gives you twenty-four violins. We have had larger complements when we've had fourteen violas, ten or twelve celli, and eight basses. For violins to work that way [there should be] fewer divisions. It is better to lean heavily toward the unison side [especially if you have a small string section]; otherwise parts tend to stick out and make the sections sound smaller.

MZ: Have you ever changed the configuration of the studio because of the balance?

BF: No, because you plan everything with the composer. We talk about what we are going for. Are we going for a very open spacious sound, or a tight sound, or an intimate sound? The last thing you want to do is waste time when you are on the stage [soundstage], resetting everything. Once you step on the scoring stage—unlike a record session, where schedule is a little more lax, you have a little more time to do things—in a film environment if you go onto the stage at 10:00, you start at 10:00. You have as many as 100 people sitting out there, and that meter is running. It's very expensive. You have to be prepared when you come on the stage. How many synthesizer tracks are we bringing in? What format are they on, Pro Tools or Digital Performer? All of these things need to be addressed before you get to the stage.

MZ: What does a music editor do?

BF: The music editor starts on the project way before I do. He [she] comes on initially with the composer, and they work together. They'll meet with the director and watch the film for the first time. It's called a spotting session. They'll make notes of where they want the music to start and stop. Suggestions about "maybe we don't have music here, but how about we add music?" The music editor will make all those timing notes, write them all down, print them out, and give them to the composer. The composer now has an idea of where the director wants the music. The composer will go back to his home studio with a copy of the film, whether it is a digital video or a VHS copy. He'll sit there and have all the timing notes, and of course there is time code on the video, so he will know where each scene starts and stops. So the music editor provides him with all that information and keeps him abreast of all the changes. Then, on the scoring stage, we [music editor and scoring mixer] will notate everything that is going down. We both keep track of all the takes that we are doing on a specific cue and any pertinent notes that need to be addressed. We talked about adding some percussion stuff on this particular cue. So that's addressed, and all those notes are kept so we can systematically go through cue by cue and address any changes that have to be done to the cue. Then, when we get into the mixing process. I will mix off of whatever medium we record to. That could be a Pro Tools system, maybe analog tape or digital tape. We will mix back to a Pro Tools system. He will handle the Pro Tools while we are recording and mixing. He will keep track of all the takes and all the mixes. He will edit them together and take them off to the dubbing stage, where he lays them into the film with the rerecording engineers.

MZ: Do you hear the dialogue and/or the sound effects when you are mixing?

BF: We have a work track that we use. Unfortunately, it is only a mono work track, but yes, we play the dialogue track against the mixes we make to make sure we are not getting in the way of the dialogue. The effects in the work track, as well as the dialogue, are fairly crude, and they are not the finished effects [or dialogue]. The production dialogue, at times, could be replaced by ADR [Automated Dialogue Replacement] dialogue, but it gives us a good idea of where we are as far as anything getting into that range. If things are poking out or too loud, we can flatten them down a little bit, bring them down a level, give the music a better chance of getting through on the mix.

MZ: Do you find that more composers are taking home QuickTime [digital video] videos to work with?

BF: Yes. It's much easier and faster. It saves a lot of time on the stage [studio].

MZ: We're on the soundstage. You have a very high ceiling, which obviously gives you natural reverberation. Do you still use microphones to record the ambience in the room?

BF: Absolutely. For an orchestra we have three omni microphones around the podium over the conductor's head, then a couple of outrigger mikes left and right over the orchestra. For the surround I will have two mikes and set them back. We look at this from an audience perspective. For a room with restricted distance, add a delay to the mikes. I use a TC delay to do it either in feet, meters, or milliseconds. I want the mikes to be thirty feet behind the conductor. When you don't have space behind the conductor and are limited to twelve to fifteen feet, there isn't enough room to create a spacious feel.

MZ: Can you tell what the recorded ambience mixed with the music will sound like in a theater?

BF: Yes and no. What we try and do in an environment like this is to get as close to, or make the mix sound as well as it can possibly sound. You aren't going to be right on the mark because every theater is different. Obviously, there are times, because of sound effects and the new dialogue tracks, that they eat through the music a little differently than what we [originally] had.

MZ: Do the dubbing engineers have control over the gain on each output of the surround sound mix?

BF: Yes. We give the left and right surround. They have control of that. They can EQ it, raise the level, or lower the level.

MZ: Is it unusual for them to ask you to remix?

BF: It's rare but not unusual. Once in a while they'll say they are having trouble with one particular element [and ask us to] separate it. We will bring the mix up and put it on another set of tracks. It's just a matter of recalling the mix that has already been recorded in the computer. You bring it up, and make a new stem [grouping]. They have the mix as it originally was, plus that element they wanted separate. You need to give them some flexibility. Basically when you think of a 5.1 mix, the average person thinks a 5.1 mix is just 5.1. Well, it *is* in the sense that it is what you are monitoring. In a film, you are essentially monitoring up to twenty tracks, in a 5.1 configuration. You have an orchestra [LCR, LS-RS-LFE], then LCR choir [Left Center Right choir] with some surrounds. You may have some synthesizer [tracks] that could be a 4.1 [left front, right front, and your left surround, right surround, and LFE channel]—4.1 because most synthesizer samples, being stereo, do not have hard center channels . . . you have this phantom center [imagined center channel].

MZ: Are the synthesizers generally prerecorded before the orchestra is recorded?

BF: Yes. They are usually brought in already done, but they haven't been mixed. They are tracks that have been set up in a MIDI environment. For the most part, they haven't been balanced against the orchestra; they haven't been EQed. Some have been affected where the composer likes what he has, so let's not modify this; let it in against the orchestra.

MZ: Do you use the Pro Tools mixer or run the recorded material through the SSL console?

BF: There again, it depends where I'm working. I have mixed several films using the ProControl [Pro Tools mixing console], and from the SSL back into Pro Tools.

MZ: Are you using the console for balancing or effects as well?

BF: Sometimes effects. If I'm mixing through the Pro Tools console, I'm using the plug-ins there [virtual signal processing effects]. I may have the digital reverb connected to a 960 or TC6000. I may have that stuff connected to it. Mixing in a large studio, like Warner's, you are taking information from a Pro Tools system, bringing it in analog into the SSL, then analog out of the SSL through a high-end converter and back to Pro Tools.

MZ: Do you notice a big difference with plug-in effects compared to hardware effects?

BF: Yes. If you take some of their samples, plug-ins, like the Bomb Factory LA2A, and compare them, there is a bit of a difference.

MZ: Is one better than the other?

BF: I don't know if it's better. It's different. When I'm working in an all-digital domain, I don't mind using the plug-ins because I don't find them offensive. They are just a little different sounding than the actual hardware [but very good].

MZ: What plug-ins do you like?

BF: Filters, EQs, and compressors.

MZ: Have you compared the sound of Pro Tools HD system to what you are hearing directly through the console?

BF: Yes, and it sounds very good if I'm at 24-bit 96 k. I don't like working in lower bit rates and [lower] sampling rates. I have worked in 192 . . . great sounding.

MZ: How much memory do you need?

BF: You need an enormous amount of storage. With Pro Tools you can run out of DSP power pretty quick, especially with some of the newer reverb plug-ins.

MZ: Do you find in a major studio, like Warner Brothers, that you generally have enough of everything that you need? Do you have to call before the session?

BF: No, because I have a huge inventory of equipment myself. I have three monitor systems, sixty microphone preamps, one hundred and sixty microphones of my own, three processing racks of gear. I only worry about the console and the support team that is there. At a place like this, they have a great support team. You're never going to get stuck compared to smaller studios. You need a studio that caters to film.

MZ: What are your favorite microphones for recording strings?

BF: I use the original AKG C12. I'm a big tube mike fan. It's warmer...67s on violins and violas. On the condenser side, the Senheiser MK40. For woodwinds, Schoeps microphones, MK 40 for low woodwinds, bassoons, and clarinet. Percussion, I'll mix it up depending upon what it is. For big drums I use Omnis B&K4006 and MK40s cardioid microphones. The only adjustable patterns I would use: 414 BULS on vibes, K184, 84 on mallets. For brass I go from ribbons to condensers. Royers, AKG C12 VR on trumpets; Royer stereo; M50 on brass overall; Tuba 193, 414 and U87A. On low brass, M149—nice fat full sound.

MZ: You obviously have vast experience recording orchestras. Many young engineers only record into computer audio programs. Many of them do not know anything about miking a live orchestra.

BF: I would recommend that people like that go out and listen to as much live music as possible. Go to live concerts and hear what an orchestra really sounds like. Their only reference to orchestral music is samples, orchestra, string, brass, and woodwinds. You should hear what an orchestra sounds like. There are a lot of guys out there doing really great jobs, but for me, it doesn't sound like what an orchestra really sounds like. There is a huge amount of power when they are playing. Listen to as much orchestral music as you can. Submerse yourself. Listen to what's happening on the walls behind you. Listen to how the orchestra is filling up the room, the decays, and why an orchestra sounds a certain way.

MZ: How do you reproduce that sound?

BF: I spent years with orchestras setting up the console and doing assistance work. I was always exposed to music—live classical. It became a natural thing. The interesting part for me when I was assisting is that you could hear the difference between guys [who] really knew how an orchestra should sound [and those who did not]. There is a balance already [between] a good conductor and a good orchestra. It's not like a pop mix.

MZ: Can you explain the difference between a recording console designed for film recording and a console designed for normal music recording?

BF: First of all, this film panel [a section of the console] you wouldn't find in a record studio. This film panel allows us to monitor all the stems. If we are recording a mix that is twenty-four tracks wide, this will allow us to go through and listen to each stem individually. On a regular two-track stereo console, you wouldn't have that. You couldn't mix that way. What you'd have to do is mix using the tape buses and bring back your stems on some faders. This console is specifically designed to mix multiple stems as opposed to just mixing stereo. This allows us to mix in 5.1 surround sound. You wouldn't find that on a record console. You might find a subwoofer channel on all the subsonic stuff . . . 2.1 is what you would probably get.

MZ: What is a stem?

BF: A stem is a group of tracks mixed together, such as the Orchestra. That would be a 5.1 stem—LCR, LS, RS, LFE, The Choir, a five-channel stem—LCR, LS RS, the rhythm, percussion, synthesizers, etc. Each stem of the mix would come up in the monitor section. If I wanted to check the orchestra stem, I would check the LCR [left, center, right stem] or just the surround stem. The subwoofer [LFE] is a separate channel, percussion or choir. On a record console we don't have the ability to do that because you're not set up to mix twenty-four tracks wide [or in some cases even wider].

MZ: You don't separate the instrumental sections with gobos [portable soundproofing]?

BF: Sometimes. It all depends on the sound we are going for. If we have an instrument that is bleeding too much into the orchestra [we would use gobos]. For example: the celeste [might be] a little loud in the room. [If you put] gobos and a blanket around it, it will sound fine. Once in a while we do that, but for the most part we try not to. You want it to bleed, to sound live. That's the secret to a good orchestral recording, the bleed into all the microphones. This gives you the sound and space—your sound field. Your front-to-back, your left-to-right width, the sound traveling from one microphone to another.

MZ: Do you use outboard compressors or the compressors housed within the recording console?

BF: Both. I like compressors in both the Neve and SSL consoles. They are great. Basically, when I'm tracking, I'll use outboard compressors. I'll use things like LA2A or 1176. That's basically for rhythm tracking, percussion, and for orchestra. I'll use a rack of Summit DCL200 compressors, and Avalon EQ's. I run my film mix through them, sort of like mastering. My mix goes through that before it goes to the final Pro Tools mix rig.

MZ: Is there a special engineering term used for mastering a film score?

BF: Finalizing the mix. My mix goes through my compressors, and I set the ratio depending on what the mix is. A lot of the time I don't like the compression. I don't like that sound of things being squashed. I like that nice open sound. It all depends on what it is. For myself, I tend to put EQ after the compression so if there is any high stuff, I can put a little bit back in, brighten it up a little bit more. There is one thing you have keep in mind when you're mixing for film: The screen is a high-end filter. The screen is a big white perforated thing, and sound has to get through. Highs tend to roll off. We've measured that at Warner Bros. by putting microphones out in front of screen with the screen down and up. There is a marked difference in what the speaker produces without the screen. The speaker is just flat. You are listening to what comes out. It's basically what you're hearing in here. You're hearing the top end and things above 8K. Put the screen up, and that tends to roll off. So you need to add just a little more back in.

MZ: Is it similar to what happens when music is played on the radio? The top end is rolled off.

BF: Right, only this thing [screen] is a big white filter.

MZ: The majority of income from films is made through DVD sales. Do you have to remix the music for DVD, and are you concerned about the mix sounding good on small speakers, as you would be with a record production?

BF: No. I'm not. I've gone back in and remixed a series of films that were originally released in mono. I approached it as if I was mixing a film.

MZ: What do you normally put through the sub [low channel]?

BF: Specific instruments. If it's synthesizers I'll put some of the low hits, the impact, some of the real low-patch stuff. So you sort of feel the rumble in the room. You don't want to take the orchestra and drop it in there because of the subharmonic. It drops everything and gets very muddy. You have to be very selective. That's something I would say to guys just starting out: You've got to be selective as to what you put in there. Your mixes will come out much cleaner and brighter if you just put things in there selectively. Synth hits . . . the low stuff. You're not going to stick an oboe there. It's not going to sound right.

MZ: When mixing in surround sound, do you find it more difficult to get an accurate balance than if you're mixing in stereo?

BF: No. What I do like is to take some of the synthesizer parts and get the patch stuff moving around us. Add delays so it comes across you and goes into the surrounds. Again, that's another area where you need to be very selective. You can start to overload your surrounds with too much activity. For a film, it doesn't really work because what you're doing is drawing attention away from the screen. You don't want to do that. You want to have some ambience around you...maybe a little thing here and there in the left-right surrounds. Keep the activity down to a minimum because you're distracting the viewer from what's on the screen. You want [the audience] to be enveloped in the sound. You don't want to overload. You might want to shock them a little bit, keep the surrounds as an ambient track.

MZ: Do you use a lot of signal processing?

BF: Eqing, depending upon the environment—things that you want to take out. Every room has its own resonant frequency. Notes may tend to blossom a bit at that frequency. You want to be aware of that. Find out where that is, and notch it back a little bit. You want everything to sound like it's in the same environment. Oftentimes, if you want a different sound, it needs to be treated in a completely new way. On some scores, like *Fast and Furious*, we had a lot of electronics and a lot of delays.

MZ: What is the mixing process for film music? In records, sometimes you spend five days mixing one song.

BF: Well, in film we don't have the luxury of that time. Normally, I'll have to mix from 50 to 80 minutes of music for a score. When I'm asked how much time do I need, well, I say [it depends] on the complexity of the mix and how many synth tracks we have. That keeps getting bigger, and bigger, and bigger. Sometimes I'll have as many as eighty to a hundred synthesizer tracks in a mix.

MZ: How many faders do you use?

BF: Well, oftentimes we are using up the entire console; we use both sets of faders. [Sometimes] in order to assign everything out, we bring in a separate console. The complexity of the mix sort of dictates how much time I need. If it's a complex mix, then we're mixing twelve minutes a day. That's a lot of mixing in one day. The longest process has been two weeks. When you're mixing a song, you probably mix three or four different versions of one song; well, that's only one song. We have 40 to 50 cues; I'm [often] mixing three versions of that cue. We may start out with the cue as it was originally written, which may not go into the picture, and then there's the cue that was changed after the director heard it, and then there are alternates to that cue. In essence, you are mixing three, four, five versions of one cue that goes off to the dubbing stage, where they decide at that point which of those cues or mixes goes into the picture. So, again, not having the luxury of time that you have in the record industry, you have to really mix fast. So I'd say twelve minutes a day, based on a twelve-hour day. Depending on the budget, they don't give us the time to do what we need to do, so we are mixing around the clock. We are chasing the dub. If we start scoring on Monday, [on] Thursday you start mixing, and we have the music Saturday. That's when we are starting the dub [the final mix, including dialogue and effects]. That was the case with *The Hulk.* I worked on the second score with Danny Elfman. I was at Fox Studios, with Danny Elfman, recording the orchestra. Dennis Sands was here mixing the music. Every time we had something done we would send the hard drives over. Then Danny would show up here at night and go over the mixes with Dennis. The next morning Danny would be back there with me and we'd mix till seven or eight o'clock.

MZ: Is the film composer basically the music producer?

BF: Yes. He is dealing directly with you [the engineer] and the director. The director will talk directly to the composer. If it's something that pertains to changing the cue or adding something or rewriting, then obviously that doesn't pertain to me. That is Danny and the writing staff. That brings up a composer and having a crew that he works with, people that he surrounds himself with. A composer needs to establish a team of people around him that know their jobs and take away all the tasks and things that a composer doesn't need to worry about. Any composer I work with doesn't need to know what I'm doing here and how I set up there. We talk about the sound we're going for. It frees up the composer to do two things: write the score and deal with the director. He doesn't have to worry about what the rest of his team is doing. We are all professionals, and we all know what we have to do. We try to keep our questions to a minimum because we don't want to bother him while he is writing

MZ: Is the orchestrator usually at the session?

BF: Yes. Oftentimes the orchestrator may be the conductor. Some composers don't conduct, and they prefer to have the orchestrator right there.

MZ: How often do cues have to be rewritten?

BF: I've been on films where every cue is rewritten. I wouldn't say that it's a regular thing, but it does happen. I have not been on a film where every cue is thumbs-up approved. There are always one or two cues that could be lightened or darkened up.

MZ: Is that a matter of rewriting?

BF: It can oftentimes be fixed by orchestration, by changing something in the strings, or whatever. A lot of composers are really good at thinking on their feet, to change this and this, and then they rehearse it for their director, and the director will go, "That's exactly what I want." A lot of times it will be something a little more complex that calls for a rewrite, which is a little less uncommon.

MZ: How often do the directors refer to the temp tracks during a studio session?

> ♫ Temporary track is music written by other composers (or the film composer's music) to show the composer the style of music the director wants written.

BF: They do, and it's hell for the composer. One instance: working on a film—will remain nameless—where a composer had written this beautiful seven-minute cue, and he sat down. We played back the cue, and the director said, "That's not like my temp." The composer just looked at him and said, "If you really like that temp, then I suggest you hire the guy that wrote the temp, because this is what I wrote, and if you don't like it, then I'm out of here." Then the director did like it, but [the director said], "Can you do this and this?" I think the better approach of that whole situation would have been: "It's a great cue, but can you change this and this?"

MZ: When composing music for commercials, some creatives try to push the composer to plagiarize.

BF: That's an instance where they have been around their temp score so long that they can't wean themselves away from it. No matter how good the cue is, they are still falling back on the temp because they have lived with it for so long.

MZ: What makes a good score?

BF: A good score is one that brings you into the picture, doesn't distract you. It has a motion, movement, things that keep you glued to the picture. In the past, I've worked with people that overwrote for what was going on. A good composer will pick spots and write for what the scene needs.

MZ: Do you find that when you are mixing, you do have to mute some of the orchestration to make the cue work with the dialogue?

BF: That is something that used to happen in the past. The people I'm working with now are really good composers and orchestrators who are aware of that because they are listening to the dialogue too. They know to keep out of the way of the dialogue. You often have to throw away dialogue. If the audience hears it it's fine, but if the audience doesn't, that's also fine. We want the cue to enhance the scene, not detract from it.

MZ: How involved is the average director at the scoring session?

BF: Some directors are hands-on, and others will let the composer do what he [she] is doing. But they all have input, some more than others. Some will be a little too hands-on in guiding the composer. Other directors give input when they feel it is needed. If there is a scene that they feel strongly about, then they will have input. But again, they all have input; just the degree of input varies.

MZ: How much tension is the engineering staff under since budgets are so high? If you have a breakdown in the studio, it costs thousands of dollars.

BF: Yes, it does. The pressure is always there to make sure everything is working. The way I work: I will be here the day before setting everything up, will check everything out. If we start at ten, I will be here at eight. We will go through everything again. All the mikes are checked out, just to make sure. There is quite a bit of setup time and preparation. When ten comes, we start to roll. We start listening. With small-budget films you work a lot faster. With a big budget, you will take your time and go through each cue and get it right.

MZ: Do you normally listen back while watching the film?

BF: Absolutely. All the time. We never play back without it. We play back with film and dialogue. The way I run my sessions, I will play back the cue and listen to it with just the music. We are checking notes on our first playback. Then we play it back again with the dialogue to see where we sit. So we always have two playbacks.

MZ: Do you run a backup tape?

BF: Yes and no. Sometimes it's another hard-disk recorder.

MZ: Do you record using digital tape, analog tape, or direct-to-digital audio?

BF: Pro Tools HD. We record right into it.

MZ: Do you run a second Pro Tools backup?

BF: Yes. A second Pro Tools backup or a RADAR. It's a physical hard-disk recorder.

MZ: Do you still use tape?

BF: I do occasionally. I still love the sound of tape. When I'm not able to [work with high-resolution digital audio], I'll fall back to analog tape, two 24-track [recorders].

MZ: Do you think that 192 [high sampling rate] will become the standard?

BF: I hope so, unless they come out with something other than that. I would like to have 192 on all 48 tracks.

MZ: Have you compared 192 to 96 [sampling rate]?

BF: You will hear the difference. You will hear the difference between 96K compared to 48K and 44.1K. I was working on a classical record—classical guitarist with orchestra—and we had been recording for five days at 24-bit 96K. We were running 48K backup and had a DAT 16-bit 44.1. At the end of the session we hadn't heard the DAT yet, and we played back the DAT. How bad that sounds compared to 24-bit 96K. It was amazing, stereo mix in 24-bit 96K. The converters make a very big difference.

MZ: What sampling rate are you hearing in the theater?

BF: In some theaters you might be hearing 96K. In most theaters, I think you are hearing 44.1, but I'm not sure about that.

MZ: If you convert from 192 to a lesser resolution, does the lesser resolution sound enhanced since the original recording was recorded at a high sampling rate?

BF: Yes. In my opinion, it's always better to start in the highest resolution and then go down from there.

MZ: How much digital editing do you do?

BF: Each film is different. When you record a cue—say it's a three minute cue, and say there is a little clam [mistake] in there, trumpets or violins—you go back and make a pickup in that section. Some cues may have as many as three or four pickups, so you edit those pieces. You make one complete cue, but that doesn't happen on every cue. So you do have some digital editing. Sometimes the music editor and the composer get together and say this cue is a little long because the scene has been shortened. We will pick a section and [edit] that out, edit the cue, shorten it, or maybe add a few frames to the cue, just like a record. The Pro Tools operator, who is different than the music editor, will have all those cues in his rig, and he will take all those pickups and edit them all together, so when I start to mix them, I'm not mixing bits and pieces, I'm mixing the entire edited piece. It's done. By the time it comes up to me on the console, I'm mixing the cue, which has already been edited.

MZ: What percentage of cues are recorded using a click track [digital metronome]?

BF: Pretty much all of them. There are a few composers in town that don't use click tracks at all, or to a minimum. They work off streamers [markers put on the film]. They are the older composers. I don't know of any of the younger composers that work that way.

MZ: Do the conductors watch the picture on the big screen or on the monitor in front of them?

BF: Both. They have two monitors in front of them. One will be the picture, which is also up on the large screen. One monitor will give the bar counts [and sometimes the notation].

MZ: If I wanted to conduct while viewing Digital Performer, would I be able to view it?

BF: Absolutely. That would be generated from the music editor's rig or any other rig that was in here. Digital Performer will be coming off a hard drive. It has to be locked, and it has to start at a certain time-code point and end at a time-code point. Every cue is timed out for a specific scene. So it has to start at a certain point and end at a certain point.

MZ: Is it typical to work in digital?

BF: Yes, from the home studios into the bigger studios. The bigger studios now are actually supplying Pro Tools rigs. Warner, Paramount, and Fox all have Pro Tools HD rigs.

MZ: What kind of storage do they have?

BF: They are like 74-gig hard drives.

MZ: Are you working primarily on Macs?

BF: Yes.

MZ: Of course you don't eat up any power running on Pro Tools; they are all running on their individual computers. Is there any technology used more in film than in record production?

BF: Surround processing is really the only thing that comes to mind; you wouldn't find that, although record production is going that way now, SACD [Super Audio CD] and DVD Audio.

MZ: Titles mixed in surround sound [records] that sell five to seven thousand copies are considered hits.

BF: I have a home theater room that I rewired myself for 8.1. I did wire my audio room in anticipation of the SACD format and the DVD audio format. So I have a room that is wired for [surround]. It sounds great. The theater system—it's a great sound. I actually enjoy watching movies there more than in the theater. My sound is just as good or better than most of the theaters. My audio room is strictly audio.

MZ: Should a young engineer learn 5.1 or stereo mixing first?

BF: They should have a real understanding of stereo and how it works, how to separate things, and how to create that wide space. Learn that first, and then go to 5.1. 5.1 will be a little different in that you will have that hard center you didn't have before. Coming out in stereo you will have that phantom center. Then you have to decide, "What am I going to put in there?" The obvious things would be if you had vocals; vocals would be in the center. If you had an orchestra, if you miked it in a classical sense, that center mike would have to go. Solo instruments would go in the center.

MZ: When mixing a rhythm-section track, would you mix it like a record—the bass and the kick drum in the center and split the kit?

BF: Yes. That's how I normally do it. Bass and kick drum [center]. Oftentimes even the snare and hi-hat off to the right.

MZ: You have advised students to "listen" a lot?

BF: If you are a scoring mixer, the palette that you're dealing with is so varied. I've done scores where it's been rock. Example: [music] we mixed for *Queen of the Damned*—John Davis and Korn. That was really loud guitar with huge orchestra and smaller groups. Another example of orchestra with a small group is *The Hurricane,* a Denzel Washington film, where we had the B3 organ going on with a nice-size orchestra. So you need to be just aware of all the different styles. I will go out and buy research material—how [was that sound achieved]? That helps [because] you are not walking in cold.

MZ: If a popular band is recording music for a film, does the scoring mixer usually record the band?

BF: That is pretty much done by their own guys. We'll get the [finished tracks], and we add orchestra to it. Occasionally, we will do vocals and [other overdubs]. And that brings up another point. A lot of composers have friends or house engineers that work with them in their MIDI studios [who] haven't been exposed to a lot of live [recording]. They are good at mixing the MIDI tracks, so some composers [hire scoring engineers] who know how to mike orchestras, and to record [orchestras]. We will come in, and we'll do all the live orchestra [recording], mix that for them, and then take our mixes and balance it at their own home studio.

MZ: Would that become the final mix?

BF: Yes. A lot of the good composers have really nice studios at home, great places to work.

MZ: What is the difference between recording a score for a television show as compared to recording a film score?

BF: The big difference is that when you [record] a television score, you're on even more of a schedule than for film. Of course, you are probably working for one day. You come in, and you need to do the entire show in two sessions, which means you start at ten and break for lunch at one, come back at two, and you go till five. That's it.

MZ: How much music do you record in that time period?

BF: It depends on the show. An hour show will have forty minutes of music. [You record] as fast as you can go. When I first started out, I started off doing setup, working as an assistant on records. When I started mixing, I first mixed television. It taught me to be fast and accurate. There isn't any time to say, "I'm not ready for this."

MZ: Do you mix the music the same day?

BF: Sometimes you have to mix it live.

MZ: You have extensive knowledge of microphones. How does a young engineer get that kind of experience? Working in a MIDI studio is not going to do it.

BF: Again, you have to get yourself in an environment where you can do it. Even in a MIDI studio, they record things live occasionally. I would say try different microphones, microphone techniques. Read up on it—a lot of books on it. For me the best thing is to have hands-on, practical experience. If you can get yourself into a small recording studio or even as an assistant to somebody, you can pick up that knowledge. Mike placement is an art form.

MZ: Is it subjective what something should sound like?

BF: Again, that depends on the sound that you want. You listen to a French horn in a room; You don't put your ear next to the bell of the French horn. You listen to it in a room. That is the sound of the instrument.

MZ: Getting a smooth, angelic string sound is difficult in the recording studio.

BF: Two things come into play: How it is written and how it's miked. If you are too close, you are going to hear all [those unwanted sounds]. You need to get back and up a bit. You give the instrument a chance to breathe and a chance to develop a sound. There are times when you want that really close sound, when you [want] this sort of affected violin. But basically, for a very lush open-string sound, get back a bit. Let the strings develop a sound, because you don't want [to hear individual players]. You want to hear this big umbrella of sound going off.

MZ: Did you start as a musician as a kid?

BF: Yes.

MZ: How important is it for an engineer to understand music?

BF: I think it is rather important for them to understand music.

MZ: Do you generally get a copy of the score?

BF: Yes. I put it right up on the console. I make my notes on there for mixing; take numbers; how many takes; alternates; what we printed; what I have to mix, and what I have to raise or lower in the mix. I write that on the score and also write it in on the laptop.

MZ: What should be included in the training of scoring engineers?

BF: They should have a real understanding of what equalization is and how it works. Like anything else, it is a tool. The first mistake [made by young engineers] is that they want to add more EQ to [something]. That's not always the correct solution. Listen to what the problem is. You may find yourself saying, "You know what? I should be taking some EQ out here and there and open up the sound more." If it is not sounding right, adding more EQ is just going to make it sound worse. You want to figure out what the problem is. Oftentimes, I'll go through and listen to an instrument, and I'll sweep the EQ—turn the gain up and sweep the EQ—and find that bad spot, the thing that's real offensive. I'll play with the EQ, and set that, the width of that, and then—and then you have to be very selective that you don't notch too much out and affect the sound of it. Oftentimes, taking out is better than adding.

MZ: Do you EQ the microphones used to record the room ambience?

BF: Yes. If I'm in a room that has a real heavy resonant frequency, the basic frequency the room oscillates at—if that tends to be a problem, I'll find that, and I'll really turn the gain up on the EQ and sweep that frequency until I find it. Then I'll play with the EQ as to how much I want to take out. And then I will invert it. You would be surprised how all of a sudden it just cleans everything up because that unwanted frequency is not there any more. I will do that to each mike selected. I won't just say, "This EQ worked on the left overhead, so it will work on the center overhead." No, because where that microphone sits in relation to this other microphone, there is a difference in what the microphone is hearing. So you want to go through each one individually, find the offensive frequencies, and notch those out.

MZ: Do you go in and test the standing waves in a room, before recording?

BF: I don't have the time. I can hear it when the orchestra is playing. Certain notes will pop right out.

MZ: Do you use bass traps?

BF: Just open up those panels on the side, and you will have bass traps.

MZ: Is there anything else you would like to add?

BF: Again, having knowledge of EQs and compressors, that kind of thing. You have to be very selective in what you want. Do you want a solid-state or a tube compressor? What sound are you going for? That is always in the back of my mind.

MZ: Is there ever a time when there are instrumental sessions that you do not use EQ?

BF: Sometimes, I do not use EQ at all. Again, that goes back to selecting the right microphone. When you have the right microphone you don't have to use a lot of EQ. I'm not a big fan of EQ. I'll use it to brighten things up on the top end for my ambient mikes, so we are getting through the [movie] screen a bit. But as far as going in there and using EQ for the sake of EQing things, oftentimes, it works against you.

R&B, Hip-Hop, and Pop Music Engineering

Most R&B, hip-hop, and pop engineers have an extensive knowledge of MIDI, sampling, and *in-the-box* (computer) digital audio. They almost always work in an audio and sequencing program; Pro Tools has become the industry standard. There are instances where the artist or producer prefers to work in the analog domain. This becomes more costly, and most contemporary artists prefer not to incur the expense. Another reason for remaining in the digital environment is that most artists, engineers, and producers own project studios. Transferring MIDI and audio data from one computer and system to another is a relatively simple task; it is also cost-effective.

Engineers must be familiar with the market. The sound of mixes changes, and the sound of the individual instruments changes, as in the case of kick and snare drums. An engineer must achieve an overall ambience to a mix. Listeners become attracted to styles of mixes or trends in the sound of mixes—sub-basses, loud, dry vocals with slight delays, loud, deep kick drums, and the like. Engineers have to be on the cutting edge of the contemporary music scene. Their involvement in the music is essential to achieving success.

As mentioned, many engineers route audio tracks from the computer through a recording console. Some engineers travel with equipment they own, which includes signal processors, microphones, studio monitors, and additional gear. Working with personal equipment helps them achieve the highest technical recording quality, and the recording environment remains relatively stable from studio to studio.

Many young and successful engineers are not experienced in orchestral recording, since they have grown up in a MIDI and sampling environment. It is preferable to hire an experienced orchestral engineer to record orchestras and orchestral overdubs; the mixing engineer can then mix the completed tracks.

Some engineers mix and do not record. Mixing and recording are art forms, and just as physicians specialize, so do engineers.

Rock and Latin Music Engineering

Most engineers who specialize in rock and Latin music are a hybrid between engineers who specialize in live recording and those who work primarily with MIDI and samples.

Most traditional rock is recorded in a large studio, which provides a natural room ambience, especially for the drums. Rock bands, traditionally, like to capture the equivalent of a live performance in the recording studio. Rock engineers know how to mike drums, guitars, vocals, keyboards, and other traditional instruments used in popular forms of music. Some may also be seasoned orchestral engineers. Some engineers are mixing specialists, and others prefer to record and mix an entire project.

Latin music and rock engineers have similar backgrounds. Most Latin music is recorded with live instruments, and engineers who specialize in this style are generally well-seasoned professionals capable of recording all sections of the orchestra. They must be adept at capturing the sounds of a large variety of percussive instruments, as well as native instruments. Latin music comes from many countries, and the instruments and the music differ between countries. The engineer must be familiar with the general sound of mixes used in the various genres.

The sound of contemporary Latin pop and hip-hop is generally mixed with the same sonic ambience as American hip-hop and R&B. The engineers generally work in a digital audio program, such as Pro Tools, and the remainder of the engineering process is the same as the various processes previously discussed.

Conclusion

It is advisable for music engineers to study music as well as audio engineering. Attending live concerts is the best preparation for learning the natural sound of the instruments, and hearing the natural balance between them. Most often, an engineer's job is to replicate the sound of a live performance in a recording studio. If the engineer does not attend concerts and frequent clubs, it is difficult for them to reproduce the sound in the recording studio.

The term *creative use of technology* has been used throughout this book. The importance of using technology in a creative way cannot be emphasized often enough. *In commercial music, technology is a part of the music.* Arrangements are often designed with the inclusion of signal processing. A guitar can be assigned to use a particular *chorus* effect, or a trumpet might use a long *digital delay.* (The arranger will indicate the use of effects in the score.) If the effects were deleted from the arrangement, the arrangement would not sound the same. If a horn section was made up of a trumpet, a saxophone, and a trombone and the saxophone player did not play, the horn section would not sound the same. A signal processor must be considered an additional instrument.

Because of advancements in portable technology, many of the effects used in recordings can now be reproduced during a live performance. Signal processing has also expanded the creative palette of an arranger. The infinite number of sounds, which can be created on synthesizers and samplers, in addition to an infinite variety of effects, which can be created with signal processors, has offered contemporary musicians a new set of creative tools. Creative output is limited only by the author's imagination.

Michael Abbott Comments

Michael Abbott is the audio mixer for the television program The Talk, broadcasted daily on the CBS Television Network. He also works on the Country Music Awards and the Grammy Awards. (In his younger years, he was a violinist.)

I've been in the audio business since 1972. I started on the road doing live audio for rock 'n' roll acts such as Frank Zappa, MOR acts, Diana Ross. . . . I've had a lot experience over the years doing a variety of music. In the 80s, I started working in the TV Broadcast Audio business doing the 1984 Olympics in Los Angeles . . . sound reinforcement for the opening ceremonies . . . mixing in the booth for television shows, talk shows, music shows . . . the transitions of all those disciplines is very diverse. The time constraints to come up with a mix that's going be 3 minutes on a television show. . . . I've got about 15 to 20 minutes to dial up my mix depending upon the size of the act.

I'm honored to be the audio producer for the Country Music Awards, in Nashville, every year . . . working with country artists is really a phenomenal experience. . . . (Since the country artists are constantly performing on the road) they always come in prepared. The arrangements are going to be clean . . . we know that the mix that I feed to the network live is going to go through, what I call, "audio sodimization." . . . processing, compression, integration into commercials . . . then played into a server . . . a 5 second delay for obscenities . . . and knowing how the audio stream I publish is processed downstream from me I apply specific EQs. . . . I do a lot of low pass (filtering) on all the audio because of digital resolution. In the old days, you had roll-off naturally on the high end when you sent something live to the network . . . it was sent into a satellite) which de-emphasized the high frequency . . . otherwise you would have distortion from peak transients. Nowadays we have a digital datastream with very high resolution. (Referring to The Talk: We send the digital datastream) and the stream is ingested in the CBS Broadcast center in New York, it is integrated with the commercials and is then sent out (to the stations). There are latencies issues which occur with the many decoded and encoded paths and along with multiple data compression processes. . . . I try keep my audio levels the same as the commercials so that the listener does not have to adjust the volume on their television sets.)

For the Grammys, we have 2 music mixers, a production mixer, and a Audio Play Operator who sits behind the production mixer that does the nominee playons and playoffs. . . . (Although the Grammys are broadcast in 5.1-surround sound, we make certain that the television viewer that has only a stereo receiver, still receives a good sounding mix.) For 3 years in a row, the show has won an Emmy (Award) for sound.

(Referring to The Grammy Awards show) An audio coordinator interfaces with the network, all of the engineers on the show, the Artists, the Artist's engineers, the Producer (and so forth). I contact the artists who are going to be on the show (and get all pertinent audio information) . . . I am always looking at new equipment . . . we receive approximately 400 to 500 microphones that (manufacturers want us to use on the show).

[Mr. Abbott proceeded to say that the younger generation does not know what they are missing when it comes to high quality sound because they have grown up listening to MP3s.]

The following is an example of Michael Abbott's daily audio setup sheet for the CBS daily talk show *The Talk* (www.cbs.com/daytime/the_talk/). The show periodically has live music. This rubric shows the complexities of sound mixing on a daily television program. Since many composers are also engineers, they might mix television programs as well as compose and mix their music projects.

PGM	Audio Program Composite Mix.
TD	Technical Director, the operator of the Camera Switcher.

ESU	Equipment Set Up although now known as Everybody Shows Up, this is the period in the beginning of a shift when Cameras are turned on, Microphones are checked . . .
FAX	The origin of this is unknown. The actions are the checking of Technical Equipment for the use in the Production day.
Julie Main & B/U	This refers to the Host Mic, Julie wears (2) mics a "Main & a "B/U" B/U denotes a Back Up . . .
Hand #1, Hand #1 & Q&A	There are (3) Hand mics used by our Talent, (2) Hand Mics or handheld mics and a Q&A mic which typically denotes its use for Audience Question & Answer segments.
IFB	Refers to the function in the Talent Communication system where a Button on a Communications Panel has an IFB function. IFB is "Interrupt Feed Broadcast"; it is used by a Producer to speak to the Talent during the segment. To cue the Talent to go to a Comm'l Break or update with breaking news.
Warm Up	This a person who keeps the Audience motivated, he cues applause at the beginning and end of a segment.
FOH Mix	This is the Audio "Front of House" Mix position located on the stage; this operator provides a mix of all Production Elements for the audience in the studio.
Router	This is a device that can source various Video & Audio Feeds and assign to Destinations in the Video/Audio Signal Path. Typical routers configs can consist of 1100x1100 variables of sources to destination. With the variety of types of Audio & Video signal a Router acts a as a Hub for data, consider a bicycle wheel with the spokes running from the hub and the points on the rim serving as the destinations such as Video Tape Recorders, Video Monitors, Audio Console inputs . . .
Tone	Tone is an Audio Signal used to calibrate devices and confirm and identify Signal sent to different devices such as VTR's "Video Tape Recorders." Typically a 1Khz frequency is used for this set at an audio level of –0db VU or –20db dbu "Decibel Unit."
Aux	This is a utility feed sent for or to a device or location . . . it can be either a Video and/or Audio Feed.
SA	Stage Announce, this is a communication function, a button on the Communications panel, which is used by the Director to address the Audience via the Stage Sound System.
ATPB	Audio Tape Playback, any Audio Related signal that is played back for a music or VO Cue during a segment.
VTPB	Video Tape or Server Playback, any Tape or file played back during a segment.
OS	Off Stage.

DSL	Down Stage Left, from the perspective of standing onstage facing the Audience or Cameras.
DSR	Down Stage Right, from the perspective of standing onstage facing the Audience or Cameras.
DSC	Down Stage Center, from the perspective of standing onstage facing the Audience or Cameras: Camera Left, from the perspective of facing the stage from the Audience, and Camera Right, from the perspective of facing the stage from the Audience
VO	Voice Over is an announcer or talent-delivering dialog laid onto a VTPB or an ATPB.
Instant Replay	An audio device that records and plays back music or VO Cues
Fostex Dir & AD Hot Mics	This is a feed from the Communications system of the Director & Associate Director headset mics to allow their cues to be heard.
Rundown	This a quick view of the various segments to be produced for a Show.
Prompter	This is a device that has the dialog or bullet points of the script per a segment that the talent will read on camera.

6:45AM, ESU

- Ipod Music to PGM for TD to Check Dressing Room Feeds
- Bypass mics in Dugan for ESU
- Check Cedar Units are not Bypass. . . . We lose power over the weekend sometimes fax
- Check mics in the following order:
- Julie Main & B/U, Sara, Sharon, Holly, Leah, Hand #1, Hand #2, Q&A, Fishpole,

Warm Up

- Julie IFB via Julie Button
- Talent IFB via Talent Button (Sara, Holly)
- Warm up via Production PL button

FOH Mix FAX

- Set Router to Tone
- Select 3rd-layer inputs: Use RTR channel for FAX Feeds to FOH Mix
- Push Aux 1–4 Attention Button
- ATPB-Aux #1, VTPB-Aux #2, Remote-Aux #3, Dialog-Aux #4
- Push Aux 5–8 Attention Button
- On Air: Aux #5

- Check SA #1

NOTE: NEED TO BE IN BOOTH PRIOR TO 10:00 AM HAIR & MAKEUP CHECK TO PREVIEW FOR JULIE BTPBs

10AM Hair & Make Up Check

- Check OS Stage Mic prior to 10AM, Julie will be doing VOs from Stage
- Feed instant replay OS mic via Aux Stereo #8, make sure instant replay is not online, Post and VTR will also track, IR is backup to b/u. Select IR cues in the 900 cue numbers and label "VO [date], ex. VO 03311 . . .
- As talent comes out, open their respective mics to the Booth for Director to hear.

10:30AM VTPB QC

- Check all VTPB with Jill Tape AD on Tape Channel & Network for levels

10:30 AM 10:45 AM Pre Show

- Check the Talent IFB Julie: Talent for Sara & Holly
- Preset Cue #1 on Instant Replay
- Confirm Host mics go to PGM with a quick fade up online
- Preset Dugan with all Host mics online
- Turn on Fostex Dir & AD hot mic
- Set Dialog, A/R, At & VT "A" at Show Open Presets
- VTPB "E" is back up to all VT rolls
- Keep Audio Black 30 seconds out from start of broadcast
- Opening shot is camera #6, 2, 7, 5, 4, 2, 7, 6 & dissolve to 1; Camera 6 start fade Julie up & fade down VTPB . . . have a nice show!

Segment X-checks

- Check rundown for which hosts are in segment.
- Make sure previous mics are turned off.
- At programming music cue, double check AT DCA is down.
- Get dialog up before camera shot at top of segment.
- Watch prompter for the tease to open VTPB at end of segment.

III

THE MUSIC BUSINESS

18

A Combination of Art and Business

> Any great work of art . . . revives and readapts time and space, and the measure of its success is the extent to which it makes you an inhabitant of that world—the extent to which it invites you in and lets you breathe its strange, special air.
>
> —Leonard Bernstein

The marriage of art and business makes the music industry unique. The marketing and selling of artists and artistic endeavors is *not* selling widgets. Some music executives do not see the difference; therein lays a problem.

The most successful record executives are those who possess both a creative and business temperament. For instance, Clive Davis and Herb Alpert are two executives who know how to relate to artists.

Clive Davis began his career as a Harvard-educated lawyer who had an indefinable gift for picking hit artists and hit songs. Choosing hit songs (and instrumentals) is the foundation for a successful career in popular music. His admiration and respect for talent and his relationships with artists are legendary in the music industry. He is also one of the most respected record executives in the history of recorded music.

Herb Alpert, who became a success with The Tijuana Brass, cofounded A&M records in partnership with promotion executive Jerry Moss. Herb Alpert is an accomplished musician, producer, and executive, and he admires and respects talented artists. Talented people are attracted to executives they can relate to musically.

The history of the music industry has confirmed that artist-oriented executives are the backbone of the industry. Those who follow this example usually become the most accomplished and successful executives. John Hammond and Goddard Lieberson are examples.

John Hammond was one of the most accomplished A&R executives in the history of recorded music. He signed to recording contracts and discovered Bruce Springsteen, Bob Dylan, Billie Holiday, Benny Goodman, Count Basie, Robert Johnson, Bessie Smith, Aretha Franklin, and Pete Seeger. That is a remarkable achievement. After studying the violin and viola at Yale University, he dropped out to pursue a musical career. He had an eclectic background that provided him with the ability to understand what he was listening to, and he also had an innate ability to sign talent that appealed to the public. The gift of successful A&R executives parallels that of producers or recording engineers. They know what attributes make artists exceptional and also know how to nurture their talent.

> I have learned from experience that it is easier to make a businessman out of a musician than a musician out of a businessman.—Goddard Lieberson, former president of Columbia Records and a master record producer

Competent record executives not only listen to their labels' album releases but also attend concerts given by the artists; this conveys both moral and business support to artists. Since labels prioritize marketing and promotional expenditures, executive interest in artists is essential to their success. Executives should always attempt to make an artist feel supported and comfortable, since insecurity is common with artistic people. This creates an atmosphere for an artist to concentrate solely on the creative process.

Music Publishing

> ♫ It takes time and devotion to compose music and write lyrics for a Broadway show. Most shows take years of work until they are mounted, and then the chances of surviving the critics are slim at best. Creators who have had past success and are pursuing new projects rely on back royalties as a source of income. The income enables them to devote the time and energy it takes to create a new work. Copyright protection offers this opportunity.

Music publishing is the heart of the composer's and lyricist's business world. The following section, on music publishing, is intended to give a brief understanding of a very complex and interesting business. Before signing a publishing agreement, composers and lyricists are advised to seek counsel with an attorney who specializes in copyright law.

Copyright protection affords the authors of copyrightable works control over the works for a specified period of time. The works must be original enough to be copyrightable—sometimes a gray area. Copyright is accomplished when a work is in a tangible medium of expression. For instance, a song is automatically copyrighted if it is recorded or notated on music paper. This provides the creators with initial protection, but it is advisable to register copyrights with the U.S. Copyright Office or to register with the appropriate bureau in a territory outside the United States. If there is a claim of copyright infringement and the copyright is not registered, it is difficult to prove the date of creation, and it will be impossible to obtain damages and attorneys' fees from the infringer. (In the United States, the term of a copyright is life plus seventy years following the death of the last surviving author.)

Copyright protection gives the creators certain exclusive rights. These rights are described below in language from the U.S. Copyright Office. This protection affords the authors the opportunity to generate an income stream, which might enable them to pursue writing on a full-time basis, and also help them to achieve financial stability.

The following information is taken from the website of the U.S. Copyright Office:

> The Congress shall have Power . . . to promote the Progress of Science and useful Arts, by securing for limited Times to Authors and Inventors the exclusive Right to their respective Writings and Discoveries.—Article I, Section 8, U.S. Constitution

What Is Copyright?

Copyright is a form of protection provided by the laws of the United States (title 17, U.S. Code) to the authors of "original works of authorship," including literary, dramatic, musical, artistic, and certain other intellectual works. This protection is available to both published and unpublished works. Section 106 of the 1976 Copyright Act generally gives the owner of copyright the exclusive right to do and to authorize others to do the following:

- *To reproduce* the work in copies or phonorecords
- To prepare *derivative works* based on the "adaptation right"
- *To distribute copies or phonorecords* of the work to the public by sale or other transfer of ownership, or by rental, lease, or lending

The right to *Display the Work* publicly must be added to the above list. This can include sheet music or works of art.

> ♫ This means that the creators have the first right to choose who will record and perform a work and to use it on television programs or in motion pictures, and other media. *Phonorecords* refers to any form of audio reproduction. This is called the *First Sale Doctrine* (see section 109c of the Copyright Act). The term *first use* is also used, but this is not a legal term.

♫ This means that no one can use the author's work to create a new work without the permission of the original author. Examples: Broadway shows are sometimes adapted from films, books, dramatizations, or other such works from different media. A music arrangement of a work is considered a derivative work. Many rap songs use music tracks from existing compositions (sometimes samples from other recordings), and a rap (lyric) is written over the existing music. This combined work is copyrighted with a new title and is now considered a new work. The new title protects not only the new work but also the original authors, who have agreed to receive a percentage of the royalties generated by the new title.

♫ The creators must give permission to distribute the music and to have the work performed publicly. The owners of sound recordings must give the exclusive right to digitally transmit audio recordings of their works.

Transfer of Copyrights

Copyrights can be transferred, as in a sale, or bequeathed in a will. The length of the copyrights is based on the current copyright laws.

Compulsory Mechanical Licenses

Once a published song has been recorded (the authors have the right to choose the artist who records the work for the first time) and sold to the public, the publisher, with the consent of the copyright owner and the creators, is obligated to issue a compulsory mechanical license to U.S. record companies, and the license allows third parties to record "cover" versions of the song. Record labels must request a license. The record companies also have to agree to pay royalties based on the statutory licensing rate (or a negotiated rate), which as of January 1, 2004, is 8.5 cents per song, per disc manufactured and distributed. Beginning on January 1, 2006, the rate was increased to 9.1 cents or 1.75 cents per minute of playing time or fraction thereof, whichever is greater. (This occurs after the right of *First Sale* has taken effect. *The First Sale Doctrine* gives the creators the right to issue a license for the first recording.) Under negotiated compulsory mechanical licenses, the record companies are also obligated to account for, and pay royalties on, units sold by the licensees. The melody or fundamental character of compositions, or other works, cannot be altered without permission from the publishers and the creators.

Mechanical Licenses for Samples

Sampling is new usage of any prerecorded material. Without permission of the publisher and the record label, the user will be in violation of the laws governing mechanical licenses or other required licenses. If a party is not authorized to sample a work, he or she is infringing on the copyright.

Sampling became popular with the formation and popularity of rap/hip-hop music. Hip-hop producers and artists used portions of completed recordings to form the musical foundations of rhythm tracks. Generally, they looped (repeated) a four- or two-bar passage and proceeded to record a rap over the track. Aside from musical sounds, additional effects and sounds were also incorporated into the track. The practice was abused because they were using copyrighted material without paying the proper royalty fees or applying for a compulsory mechanical license (publishing license), performance license, or a license to use the sound recording owned by a record label or other owner. The practice changed when publishers and record companies began to police recordings by searching for unlicensed samples. Samples can include numerous identifiable sounds. Therefore, users should be aware that to use copyrighted works requires a license.

Sampling is a lucrative source of income for music publishers, record labels, and artists alike. Companies specialize in clearing and negotiating the use of samples.

♫ Various areas of compulsory licenses include forms of digital performances, including uses on the Internet, various cable television stations, public broadcasting, jukeboxes, and phonorecords (audio recordings) of nondramatic works. This does not include digital phonorecord deliveries to individuals. (See section 115a of the Copyright Act.)

Mechanical Licensing in Foreign Territories

Where mechanical licensing is concerned, most foreign countries (divided into territories) have copyright laws that are similar to the copyright laws of the United States; however, royalties are based on a percentage of the wholesale price of the recording rather than the retail price used by most U.S. labels. The number of songs on a CD does not affect the fee. In the United States, each song receives an individual royalty; foreign mechanicals are pro-rated based on the total number of compositions on the disc.

Music in Print

Most substantial music publishers have a print division that publishes sheet music. The royalties paid to the creators is based upon the standard retail price. The royalty rate is negotiated between the publisher and the creator(s) prior to release of the printed material; this also includes digital print rights.

Digital Performance Right in Sound Recordings Act of 1995 (DPRSA)

This act requires publishers and creators to issue mechanical licenses to companies wishing to digitally transmit and distribute musical downloads that are sold on the Internet. The DPRSA is important because it procured an exclusive right of public performance for digitally transmitted and distributed sound recordings, and also protected digitally transmitted and distributed musical works by adding to the compulsory mechanical license portion of the Copyright Act. Many Web sites sell music, represented on the Internet by online record stores, iTunes, Napster, artists' Web sites, and similar cyberspace digital distribution systems. Licenses are also required for digital subscription services. The fees are negotiable. As yet, there are no standard fees.

The Copyright Arbitration Royalty Panel (CARP) has established webcasting rates. Featured artists receive 45%, nonfeatured musicians receive 2.5%, nonfeatured vocalists receive 2.5%, and the record label receives 50%. Sound Exchange, an autonomous nonprofit performing-rights organization, collects the royalties for more than 300 record labels and other copyright holders of sound recordings. Sound Exchange receives a small collection fee for its services. The artists receive direct payments, which is significant because the record labels cannot deduct their payments from unrecouped advances.

> ♫ As the Internet grows, the laws and the business models will change. The information dealing with cyberspace continues to evolve at a rapid rate. All music-industry professionals and students should remain aware of the changing worldwide laws.

Digital Millennium Copyright Act

This is a complicated Act. The issues are complex and require constant study. Laws concerning the use of music on the Internet have not been standardized. The Act also addresses the illegal copying of albums and other copyright-protected software.

- Essentially, the Act punishes copyright piracy by making it illegal to use software to circumvent or defeat copyright-protected devices or any form of hardware that helps to "crack," or make operable, copyrighted software. For example, some CDs are encoded in various encryptions to prevent a consumer from copying a CD. DVDs have a coded encryption called *Content Scrambling System* technology. Programs—some developed by hackers—allow consumers to bypass or make unauthorized copies. Accessing television stations without paying a cable provider is illegal under the DMCA.
- Under special provisions, exemptions can be made for educational and several other related uses.

- Limitations exist for Internet service providers.
- Webcasting companies are required to pay licensing fees to record companies, which in turn must pay performers' royalties and publishing royalties.

The DMCA, although controversial because some feel it severely curtails Fair Use and public access to copyrighted works, is designed as a form of copyright protection. New laws will be established as business paradigms develop in various areas of Internet transmission and software protection.

Author's Opinion: The right to use copyrighted material in educational institutions and other carefully policed nonprofit uses should be more lenient, for example as regards libraries. This presents complex issues and requires continual study as the laws and industry practices change.

Synchronization Licenses

Synchronization licenses must be obtained when potential licensees want to synchronize (use music with a visual image) music with films, television programs, videos, commercials, video games, or other visual images. Sync licenses must be obtained on an individual basis; each usage requires a new license. The fees are negotiable. The process of obtaining a license is referred to as "clearing the rights." If the composer is contracted on a work-for-hire basis, a sync license is not needed because the original composer is not considered the author; the company issuing the work-for-hire agreement is the author and the owner of the work.

There are no standard fees, but industry practice enters into the negotiations. For example, a hit song used as a theme for a motion picture can generate fees between $250,000 and millions of dollars, depending on how important its use is to the director and producer. If the title or storyline of a film is based upon a song title, that song will generate a higher licensing fee than another song.

Sync licensing is complicated and should be negotiated by an attorney who specializes in this area. Opening and closing themes, source music, incidental music, broadcasting rights, and music used in trailers require individual licenses.

If the music is also going to be used on a CD, for downloading, video game, DVD, Internet site, or similar medium, a mechanical license must be obtained for each usage from the publisher. The fees are split between the publisher and the composer.

Music that requires a synchronization license can offer unknown composers an opportunity for exposure. Producers of low-budget, independent movies normally allocate a small percentage of the film's budget to music. Some composers license their music in return for retaining the publishing rights. If the film is broadcast on television (or cable) or plays in movie theaters (internationally), performance royalties are generated. (There are no performance royalties generated by performances in U.S. movie theaters.)

By retaining the publishing rights, the publisher(s) and creator(s) may generate additional income. If the independent film becomes a hit, the composer will most likely receive offers to score additional films. Composers have jump-started careers by scoring independent films, for either no fee or a meager fee. Many songs, new or old, have become highly successful because of exposure in a film.

> ♫ The manner in which performance royalties are divided and paid is complex and requires in-depth study. It is advisable for new publishers and writers to understand the various systems because there are instances where creators and publishers will not know if they are receiving an accurate accounting. For instance, television networks are expected to keep cue sheets (a log of music performances with timings) for each program. If a composer is supposed to receive payment for 24 minutes of music and the payment is for 16 minutes of music, it is relatively easy to track, assuming that the cue sheets are accurate.

Performance Rights Societies

Performance rights societies collect licensing fees generated by public performance income, such as in television and radio performances, live performances, motion picture performances in theaters (with the exception of the United States), nightclubs, and other streams of revenue directly related to the live performance or recorded public performance of music. BMI (Broadcast Music Incorporated) and ASCAP (American Society of Composers, Authors and Publishers) are nonprofit organizations; SESAC is for-profit. (BMI and ASCAP are much larger than SESAC.)

ASCAP and BMI issue blanket licenses. This enables the licensees to use the songs in their respective catalogues.

A composer can be represented by only one society. A publishing company usually has two companies with two different names: one company belongs to ASCAP, and the other belongs to BMI. (Some also belong to SESAC.)

Foreign Performance Royalties

Foreign territories have organizations (analogous to BMI, ASCAP, and SESAC) that collect performance royalties for writers and publishers. Writers' royalties are paid directly to BMI, ASCAP, or SESAC and distributed to the writer. The publisher's share is paid to the subpublisher; the subpublisher deducts a royalty percentage and pays the U.S. publisher.

The Harry Fox Agency

The Harry Fox Agency issues mechanical licenses for the majority of independent publishers in the United States. It collects and distributes royalties and conducts audits, when necessary. HFA receives roughly 4.5% of the collected royalties.

♫ The Harry Fox Agency is a wholly owned subsidiary of the National Music Publisher's Association (NMPA).

The National Music Publisher's Association (NMPA)

The National Music Publisher's Association (NMPA), a not-for-profit company, represents more than 900 publishers in the United States. The NMPA's goal is to protect publishers and authors from copyright infringement; when necessary, it initiates litigation. The National Music Publishers' Association's Internet Anti-Piracy Task Force is devoted to helping curb Internet piracy.

Income Distribution

When income is generated from a copyrighted song, most publishing agreements provide that 50%, referred to as the publisher's share, be distributed to the publishing company, and the remaining 50%, referred to as the writer's share, be split between the composer and lyricist. The composer/lyricist share can be divided in any manner agreed upon by the authors. More often than not, the composer and the lyricist split the writer's share 50/50. If the contributions by the authors are not equal, the authors must agree upon a royalty split. For example, if a composer and lyricist need help on the last verse of a song, they might call in a third party to complete the song. They may agree to a royalty split of 40% (composer), 40% (lyricist), and 20% (third-party contributor). Unequal splits are not unusual when there are multiple creators of one work. If a written agreement does not exist, the writer's share will be equally split between the authors.

Music Publishers' Services

Publishing companies in the United States perform the following services:

- *File musical copyrights with the U.S. Copyright Office, in Washington, D.C.* The forms are on the Internet, and the filing process is simple. As of this printing, individual copyrights cost $30.00. Multiple copyrights by the same writer or cowriters can be registered on one copyright form, but it is advisable to register individual copyrights because it affords the writers additional protection in case of any legal problems.
- *Collect and distribute musical copyright royalties, and issue royalty statements quarterly to the composers and lyricists.*
- *Register songs with the performance-rights organizations, BMI, ASCAP, and SESAC, in the United States, and with counterparts in countries throughout the world.*
- *Publish sheet music, and administer other forms of rights for various publications.* Sheet music can generate substantial income if a song is a hit or has wide commercial appeal, such as a simplified arrangement of a popular work that is performed in high schools. Most popular works are arranged and/or transcribed for various instrumental combinations. The arrangements vary in degrees of difficulty.
- *Negotiate synchronization and mechanical licenses.* Synchronization licenses and mechanical licenses must be issued before companies can use songs or instrumentals in film, television programs, commercials, or wherever the music will be synchronized with visual images. Synchronization licenses and mechanical licenses are not compulsory licenses. Each license must be negotiated separately. Once a musical composition has been recorded the publisher is obligated to issue a mandatory license after it has been recorded and released in a country for the first time. Copyright royalties must be paid.

> ♫ 50% is the publisher's share, and 50% is the author's share.

Synchronization licenses (the use of a recording) must also be obtained from any company interested in using a master recording in a film, on a television program, for a commercial, or for any other synchronized use.

> ♫ The authors have the right to choose the artist who will record and release the first recording of a composition. Most countries observe this rule. This is called *First Use*.

Mechanical publishing royalties are paid to composers and lyricists for the use of songs (instrumentals) on albums or single songs, which are distributed and have been sold and paid for. The following are the current rates paid in the United States:

- For digital downloads and physical product, such as CDs, the publisher statutory rate is 9.1 cents. If song is longer than 5 minutes, the rate is 1.75 cents per minute.
- These rates began on January 1, 2010 and are applicable through December 31, 2012.

Many labels negotiate to pay 75% of the minimum statutory rate. This is usually requested when dealing with compositions that are controlled by the artist ("controlled compositions"). This means that the artist has either authored the works or owns and controls the publishing of other songwriters. The compositions are referred to as *controlled compositions*. Labels usually cap the amount of publishing they are willing to pay on 1 album to 10 songs. For example, if an artist writes and records 10 songs and also records an additional 2 songs written by songwriters whose publishing is not controlled by the artist, the label will generally be obligated to pay the full statutory rate to the outside writers. The amount that is over and above the negotiated publishing agreement will be deducted from the artist's controlled compositions publishing royalties. For instance, if the label is willing to pay a total of only 85 cents per album to publishers and the total comes to $1.02, the extra 17 cents will be deducted from the artist's controlled compositions income.

- *Legally pursue musical copyright infringements.* Most major publishing companies pursue legal action against companies or individuals infringing on copyrights. The fees required to pursue legal action are generally deducted from the writers' royalties. For this reason, it is important that the company and writers have a strong case before incurring any legal expenses. The publisher has control over whether or not to pursue a lawsuit. Accurate accounting practices ensure composers and lyricists that royalties are collected and distributed pursuant to worldwide industry standards.

The following is a description of the revenue stream generated by music publishing companies:

Mechanical royalties. Mechanical royalties are royalties paid from the unit sales of records, tapes, CDs, and digital downloads. Mechanical royalties are a significant source of income for authors and publishers.

♫ The publisher retains 50% of the income and the authors split the other 50% of the income.

♫ The royalties are paid directly to composers and lyricists by the performance rights societies. The publishers also receive direct payments. The publishers and the songwriters split the royalty income equally.

Performance royalties. Performance royalties are the part of U.S. copyright law (as well as worldwide copyright laws in most countries) that requires users of copyrighted musical compositions to pay performance royalties. Performance royalties have to be paid when music is played on television and radio networks and individual stations, in concert venues, as background music, such as Muzak, "on hold" telephone messages, Websites, theme parks such as Disneyland, hotels, restaurants, and other venues that play music. Performance royalties are a significant source of income for both songwriters and music publishers.

Source Publishing Statements

Selection of trustworthy subpublishers is the best assurance of receiving accurate royalty payments. Publishers and authors should request *source statements* from subpublishers. A *source statement* means that the primary publisher's royalties are based on the gross income derived from the *source territory,* and not after the subpublisher in the local territory has taken commissions as well as the main subpublisher also taking commissions. Sometimes subpublishers collect in more than one territory, which means that if a contract does not read that the author and publisher are paid at the *source,* the subpublisher can deduct additional fees before paying the primary publisher. That is, the subpublisher and the subpublisher's subpublisher, in a local territory, both deduct commissions before paying the primary publisher. This cannot happen if the royalties are calculated at the *source.*

For example: XYZ Music Publishing, from the UK, agrees to collect European publishing royalties for the U.S. publisher CBA Music Publishing Company. XYZ (UK) is now the subpublisher for CBA Music Publishing (U.S.). XYZ (UK) has a subpublisher in France, who is paid a percentage of all royalties they collect as the subpublisher for XYZ in France. If CBA (U.S.) does not have a *source* collection deal with XYZ (UK), not only XYZ will deduct its normal collection percentage before paying CBA (U.S.), but the bottom-line payment by which CBA's French royalties will be paid will also include a deduction based on the percentage the French subpublisher charged against XYZ's overall subpublishing deal.

If the agreement says that CBA (U.S.) receives their royalties based on the gross royalties received at the *source* (which in this example is France), the U.S. company will not have to absorb the French company's commission. If $1.00 is collected in France and XYZ (UK) receives a 15% administrative fee, XYZ will base the royalty paid to CBA (U.S.) on 85 cents. If CBA (U.S.) is supposed to receive 80% of the gross royalties, CBA will receive 72.25 cents. If the French subpublisher deducts a 15% administrative commission before paying XYZ (U.S.), XYZ will receive 85 cents, deduct another 15% (XYZ's commission), which comes to 68 cents, and finally pay CBA (U.S.) 57.80 cents.

Copyright Administration

Some music publishing companies and authors operate publishing companies in the territories in which they reside. Outside of their territory, they make *subpublishing* or *administration deals* with publishing companies. The licensee is responsible for collecting the income from sources, which include mechanical royalties, performance royalties, synchronization licenses (income from films, commercials, etc.), print, and other income sources. They do not solicit business, which is the job of a publisher. To administer a catalogue, fees range from 10% to 25% of the gross receipts. The licensee provides the licensor with royalty statements twice a year. In the interim, the licensee might provide the licensor with prepayments.

> ♫ A prepayment is income derived from royalties already received by the subpublisher but is not yet due to be paid. This differs from an advance payment, which is recoupable.

Conclusion

The above information is a brief description of music publishing. All students interested in the music industry should become familiar with the continuously changing laws and industry standards that are developing, primarily because of the evolution of the Internet and its relationship to the music industry. Global boundaries are essentially nonexistent, and the music publishers must be as familiar with the international music publishing business as they are with practices in their home territories.

Assignment

Study the structure of a major publishing company. Design a business plan for a small publishing company. Consult a music business accountant for advice.

19

The Record Business

I wish there had been a music business 101 course I could have taken.

—Kurt Cobain

Google published *Google's Rules* to help their management executives become more efficient managers. These rules can apply to any business.

- **Be a good coach**
- **Empower your team and don't micromanage**
- **Express interest in team members' success and personal well-being**
- **Be productive and results oriented**
- **Be a good communicator and listen to your team**
- **Help your employees with career development**
- **Have a clear vision and strategy for the team**
- **Have key technical skills so you can help advise the team**

The following are "Pitfalls of Managers," according to Google

- **Have trouble making a transition to the team**
- **Lack a consistent approach to performance management and career development**
- **Spend too little time managing and communicating**

The following is a general description of how the record business operates. Most artists who sign agreements with record labels have several options.

Major Label Deal

Major labels—EMI Music, Sony BMG Music Entertainment, Universal Music Group, Warner Music Group and their imprints—sign artists who, in their opinion, have the potential of generating platinum and multiplatinum sales. It is costly to maintain a record company; therefore, they cannot afford to retain artists who spawn minimal sales. Popular forms of music, such as rock, hip-hop, country, and R&B, are the mainstays of the majors.

Generally, jazz and classical music do not generate sales on a par with popular artists. There are exceptions by artists such as Norah Jones and John Williams. By offering lower advances to artists and spending a minimum on promotions and marketing, the majors can make a profit or break even. For example, the renowned classical music division of Sony brings prestige to the overall label. Labels not only want to sell quantity, but they also enjoy associating with prestigious artists, not just the flavor-of-the-month variety. Some profits from multiplatinum-selling artists are allocated to artistic endeavors that will not necessarily be profitable. Fortunately, there are still areas in the recording industry where artistry is revered. Unfortunately, that is *not* the industry standard. The public dictates the market through buying habits. *The recording industry is a business first and an artistic venture second.*

> ♫ Movie soundtracks have been generating substantial sales due to the conscious effort by movie executives to hire popular recording artists to write for a particular film or license their recordings for use in the film and on the soundtrack album.

Author's Opinion: Throughout the history of the music industry, many artists have been artistically and commercially successful. In the contemporary music industry, country music and jazz music have consistently produced artists fitting the aforementioned description. The music is not dependent on recording technology, which enables producers to technically manipulate and improve artistically mediocre performances. Most country and jazz artists are signed to labels based upon the ability to perform, without relying on an excessive use of technology to help create performances. They are offered recording contracts based on their artistic ability.

Large Independent Labels

Large independent labels are usually financially stable and provide almost the same opportunities for artists that major labels offer. Many large independent labels do not distribute all genres of music; they generally focus on several styles. Some labels become as successful, and even rival, the major labels. For example, majors acquired both Zomba and A&M.

Small Independent Labels

Small independents usually specialize in one or two styles of music and operate with smaller staffs than large independents. They are distributed by independent distributors or through the distribution channels of the major labels. Their ability to promote music is limited by available funds, and they rarely specialize in music that requires substantial financing.

Dance music is an area of music that is dominated by independent labels. The independents promote the music primarily in the dance clubs by soliciting DJs to play their records. Since there are a limited number of radio stations playing dance music in the United States, one promotion person—and sometimes with the aid of independent dance radio promoters—can make a dance record a success.

In this particular example, one might ask, "Since dance music sales are minimal compared to high-profile major label artists like Britney Spears, why would a label specialize in dance music?" There are several answers: Small independents generally operate with two to ten employees, and their overhead is relatively low. With low overhead, moderate sales can generate substantial profits. The success of dance records internationally enables small labels to license hits to companies that release compilation albums. Dance hits are heard on numerous compilations; they are also licensed for use in commercials, motion pictures, television programs, and other outlets. Performance royalties, mechanical licensing royalties, and synchronization licensing fees, in addition to unit sales, can be lucrative.

> ♫ During the 1990s, major labels purchased small, boutique, independent labels for inflated prices. The practice did not generally prove profitable. Illegal downloading and pirating decreased the availability of cash, and the majors began downsizing.

Similar musical genres have mirrored the results dance music has generated. The various spin-off opportunities can make small label catalogues valuable. In the past, successful small independents have been sold to major labels for millions of dollars. Most small dance labels do not survive after being purchased by a major label. One reason is that the profitability is not enough to warrant the resources of a major label.

Evaluating a Label Offer

A logical question for an artist to ask is, "How do I decide on the proper label for me?" The question is complex and difficult to answer; there is more than one answer. Choosing a label is both a subjective and a business decision. The following are some of the pros and cons:

Major Label

Pros

Major labels have substantial financial resources, as well as the ability to promote and market artists. They can "break an act."

Cons

Artists may not receive the proper attention from the promotions and marketing staff. If an album begins to sell, the label takes notice; if it does not sell, the promotional dollars are usually redirected to albums that are selling. The label's commitment to an artist is paramount to the success of an artist's recording career.

Large Independent Labels

Pros

Large independent labels are usually well funded and generally only sign artists they are committed to breaking (achieving success). Each artist, normally, is considered to be an important signing. That is advantageous to the artist.

Cons

It can be difficult to receive proper royalty statements. If the artist is generating adequate sales, an accurate and prompt royalty payment is virtually assured. If the artist's music is not selling, the artist might receive late statements.

Independent distributors distribute some large independent labels. It is common for the distributors to experience collection problems from clients. This naturally filters down to the labels, resulting in late accountings and royalty payments to the artists.

Some independent labels are distributed through the distribution systems owned by major labels. In that case, independent labels can usually be assured of timely statements, which enable them to pay artists (and publishers) in a more timely fashion.

During contract negotiations, it is wise for an artist to request a *source statement* from the distributor. This means that the artist gets a copy of the same royalty statement received by the label. The artist does not usually have the right to audit the distributor. If a problem occurs, the artist must audit the label.

Small Independent Labels

Pros

Small independent labels cannot afford to sign an artist without promoting that artist. They generally have limited funds and therefore *must* try to produce a profit on their investment. They cannot afford to release three or four similar artists, see which one receives attention, and then put promotional efforts behind that one of the four. It is too costly for a small label.

Most small labels specialize in one or two genres of music; consequently, the label executives understand the music and know how to promote it. They are familiar with radio station formats and Internet and services that are genre specific. Established independents gain credibility in certain market areas, for example with new age, jazz, and dance music, which helps to attract future artists.

> ♫ Many small independents grow into large independents. Historically, successful small labels tend to grow too quickly, overextend financially, and eventually file for bankruptcy. Smart independent label executives tend to grow a business slowly, attempting to avoid the "Peter Principle," or rising to the level of being incompetent.

Cons

Limited finances are the leading liability of a small label. It is difficult for small labels to compete against larger labels, but since the operating costs are lower, they can generate a substantial profit with fewer sales. Small labels generally pay lesser advances to an artist and offer a lesser royalty rate than major labels.

Record Label Services

Record labels perform the following services:

- Sign artists and, sometimes, pay recording expenses
- Distribute CDs and music DVDs (cassettes are a rarity) by manufacturing hard copies, or enabling the music to be digitally downloaded from the Internet. (Although sales are not significant, vinyl has experienced a resurgence. It is purchased mainly by audiofiles.)
- Promote and market recorded music
- Pay artists' and producers' royalties
- Pay publishing royalties (mechanical royalties) on song copyrights on the recordings sold, and other revenue streams, such as ringtones and ringbacks used on mobile phones.
- License recordings that can be used on compilation albums, motion pictures, television programming, commercials, and additional outlets that require a license.

The following is a description of the revenue streams generated by record labels:

- CD sales of hard copies
- Downloading
- Mobile phone music licensing (recordings downloaded onto mobile phones)
- Internet sales (legally downloaded music)
- Synchronization licensing (films, television, and other special products)
- Mechanical and performance royalties, which include royalties generated from digital transmission (some labels own publishing companies)
- DVD/video sales
- Licenses by third parties; third parties license master recordings.

Internet

The business of music is as intricate as the music publishing business. Creative people, as well as music executives, must be familiar with all aspects of the business. Since the industry is rapidly evolving—primarily because of the digital revolution—business paradigms are continually changing. When formulating promotions and marketing plans, global considerations must be addressed. Regional and national releases are, to all intents and purposes, a business practice of the past. When an album is released, it becomes a global release, whether intended or not. Global communication is instantaneous. Legal and illegal Web sites enable consumers to instantly access most music (and films); Internet promotion has become as imperative as radio and television promotion.

Research has shown the most effective sales tool is releasing new music in the stores and on the Internet simultaneously. (Some music is tested on the Internet prior to releasing physical copies for sale.) Since the large record store chains have closed, and stores (e.g., Best Buy, Target, etc.) have record departments, unless an artist is successful or is signed to a company that had pledged considerable marketing and promotions for an artist, it is very difficult to release physical product because of limited shelf space.

In the past, foreign releases in most territories followed the release in the primary territory. Since legal downloading is becoming a worldwide paradigm, sales are lost if simultaneous releases are not scheduled. Internet stores contain territorial firewalls. For instance, a consumer in the UK cannot download a song that is offered on a French Web site and vice versa. Recording contracts are often territorial, and if the Internet businesses do not abide by each territorial agreement, the record industry could shrink to an almost monopolistic industry.

Author's Opinion: In the past, Internet computer codes were relatively easy to crack. Even with legal downloading, hackers will crack Web sites in foreign territories so they can purchase music that is licensed only to that particular territory. This violates territorial boundaries, which are included in most sound recording contracts. In the future there may be worldwide copyright laws, which would eliminate this problem.

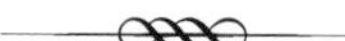

Complex issues in copyright laws and publishing statutory rates are endemic to particular territories. With the constant challenge battling illegal file sharing, it is to the industry's advantage to standardize as many industry issues as possible.

Author's Opinion: Publishing statutory rates and downloading prices will become relatively standard throughout Europe. Research has shown that ease of downloading and one-price structuring are the main ingredients for success on the Internet. In April of 2009, iTunes initiated three price tiers: 69 cents, 99 cents and $1.29. The most popular songs are sold at the highest price. As of the writing of this book, Amazon has more single MP3 downloads priced at 69 cents than iTunes.

Job Descriptions

The music industry is multifaceted. Managers, agents, accountants, and attorneys represent artists; record label personnel discover artists and promote, distribute, market, and publicize them; music publishers publish and promote compositions; stores—both brick and mortar—and Internet stores sell recordings; radio stations (terrestrial, cable, and HD radio) play recordings, and the Internet has created a digital world of music.

This chapter offers a brief description of some of the critical jobs in the music industry. Each job description is supported by entry level and mid level positions. Study the structure of record (production) companies. Basically, the only structural difference between a major label and a midsize independent label is the number of employees. One or two employees at a small or medium-size label might tackle the job of 10 employees at a larger label. All full-service record companies provide the same services.

♫ Major label distribution and independent distribution companies distribute small and midsize independent record labels. A sales executive from the label stays in daily contact with the distribution company. The executive keeps the distributor updated on the progression of airplay and the venues and cities in which the artists are performing. The distributor must keep the stores stocked with CDs, especially when an artist is performing in a specific geographical area. Consumers usually purchase albums immediately after attending a concert.

Artists' Representatives

Manager

A manager (personal manager or artist's manager) coordinates all facets of an artist's career. Strategic long-term planning should be a manager's primary goal. Managers who think only of short-term results are usually not successful. Record company contracts, publishing agreements, talent agency coordination, sponsorships, and public relations and marketing are all under one umbrella. Managers are, first and foremost, amateur psychologists. The ability to solve problems is vital to success. Managers and clients make strategic choices that can shape an artist's long-term career. They are compensated with an average commission of between 15% and 25% of the gross receipts, which include record royalties, publishing royalties, public performance income, merchandising, and additional sources of income. Managers' commissions are negotiable. They do not receive commissions on certain negotiated items, such as recording costs or tour support that is not recouped against artists' royalties.

Managerial decisions affect profit and loss. The business of music is complex, and, as in other businesses, there is a high degree of cross-pollination: Each business component links to something else. A manager not only coordinates all business and creative activities but also is often a referee. Numerous internal problems occur between band members, artists, record labels, concert promoters, and others who deal directly with artists. A manager has to assume the role of a CEO, overseeing and solving problems. Managers are not booking agents and do not solicit performances and other income-producing "gigs" for artists. In fact, if problems occur, a manager who acts as an unlicensed booking agent may be required to relinquish all commissions back to the artist.

Managers must make certain that artists' sound reinforcement equipment and lighting demands are adequate in each performance venue. There is usually a contractual addendum written into each agency agreement with a promoter that stipulates the terms and additional requests. Some managers refuse to allow artists to perform unless the promoter has met all contractual obligations.

The two most essential functions of a manager are to (1) secure record deals for clients, and (2) arrange for artists to be signed to contracts with talent agencies, which book artists for concerts, or other public appearances. Most successful managers have close personal relationships with talent agents and record label executives. This can be advantageous to clients, especially new artists.

When a manager or a management company represents successful artists, agencies and labels are anxious to be informed about the newest signings. *Success breeds more success!* It is not unusual for a manager to represent several artists on the same label.

The following are managerial responsibilities:

- *Managers work closely with agents to design tours for artists.* Tours equal sales. Strategic planning and guidance help provide maximum exposure for clients. Performing in inappropriate venues, and/or appearing with artists who have a different fan base can damage an artist's credibility with fans and harm their public image.
- *Regional radio exposure breeds performance opportunities.* Agents and managers seek out opportunities to promote sales of albums and merchandise and to generate live-performance income.
- *Public relations and advertising are crucial to building and maintaining an artist's career.* Print, television, radio interviews (terrestrial, Satellite, cable, and Internet), and Internet exposure are the most effective promotional tools. Awareness attracts ticket buyers. Managers oversee the process by working with radio and television promotion executives (either staff or independent promoters) to obtain airplay,

especially in a market where an artist will be touring. A manager informs the record label of an artist's performance schedule; this enables the label to prepare a marketing and public relations campaign prior to a performance.

- *It is essential for record stores to be stocked with an artist's catalogue prior to a performance.* The label's sales force is informed of artists' performance schedules. Live performances provide the sales force with a "story" to tell the retailers. Individual stores, sometimes called mom-and-pop stores, and chains usually stock an artist's catalogue prior to a performance in the market area. Audience members normally have a short attention span and want to purchase albums immediately following a live performance. If a store is out of stock, the customer will quite often not return to buy the album. Many fans purchase music online.
- *A manager works in conjunction with an artist's road manager (traveling manager).* While on tour, a road manager is responsible for managing the daily activities of an artist. Many managers select the *road manager*, who reports directly to the manager.

Some of a manager's jobs include the following:

- Arranging for transportation
- Arranging for sound checks before performances
- Collection of performance fees and merchandising income from products sold at performances
- Making certain a promoter is honoring the terms of the performance contract
- Storing equipment, when the artist is not on the road
- Setting up rehearsal schedules and coordinating the musicians' itineraries

♫ Some artists travel with a massive caravan of tractor-trailers, which contain a sound system, lighting, and scenery.

Managers pursue and negotiate publishing contracts. Many artists are songwriters. Representation by a publishing company is necessary in order to collect mechanical royalties, which are generated from record sales, performance royalties, which are generated by performances, and other income, including royalties and fees derived from music publishing, which are called synchronization fees. Since many neophyte artists need income, publishers are willing, under certain circumstances, to advance money that they will recoup against future royalty earnings. As artists develop and catalogues grow, mechanical royalties, synchronization fees, and performance income can generate millions of dollars. Publishers are sometimes willing to negotiate sizable advances in exchange for the rights to administer a catalogue.

Some managers participate in selecting producers for artists. Producers' royalties are often deducted from artists' "all-in" royalties (all royalties collected). Therefore, artists and managers must agree to the contractual terms negotiated by the producer. The producer has a contract with the record label, directly with the artist, or with both parties.

> ♫ Some labels pay royalties based upon 90% of the sales rather than on 100%. That is negotiable.

Managers—in conjunction with music-business attorneys—generally negotiate all contracts. This includes performance contracts, recording agreements, and merchandising contracts. Merchandising can produce a large revenue stream. Most ticket buyers spend as much money on purchasing memorabilia as they do for the price of a ticket.

Managers usually consult with artists' accountants. Music business accountants specialize in the intricacies of the music industry. It is advisable for music industry professionals to be represented by a specialist in all business dealings.

Management: Conclusion

Artist management is a risky job. If an artist's career is flourishing, the manager is hailed as a genius; if the artist is faltering, many artists claim that it is due to poor management. In reality, when an artist's album sales begin to decline and the ability to attract a concert audience diminishes, there are hosts of contributing factors. The problems include poor choice of songs, a fickle public, mediocre stage performances, substandard production values on albums and in live performances, internal business problems, and personal problems. Managers can attempt to guide artists, but artists do not always heed the manager's advice. *You can lead a horse to water, but you can't make him drink.* It is unusual for an artist to remain with one manager or agent throughout his or her career.

The popular-music business is cyclical and contemporary. Popular musical styles frequently change, as do subgenres, such as R&B (e.g., hip-hop), dance music (e.g., garage and house), and various pop styles.

Some artists are popular because of a sound (individuality) that the public has accepted, or because an artist has a unique musical personality: Louis Armstrong, Prince, and Barbra Streisand. Clones usually follow, but with minimal success. When the public becomes bored with an artist, the artist loses either some or all of his or her audience. Many artists retain a core following and are able to sustain themselves for many years, through public appearances. Doo-wop shows, oldies shows, and Motown revues are examples. In 2003, the Isley Brothers, one of the most successful of the old-school R&B acts, had a hit album, which was produced by contemporary R&B artist R. Kelly.

Unfavorable publicity can seriously harm an artist's career, as has been the case with Whitney Houston. She has experienced a decline in sales as a result of her continual lack of discretion.

Some managers offer services that are not traditionally performed by personal management. Record labels provide public relations and radio promotion. Some managers use personal contacts to help the labels. Any activity by a manager that is related to standard label services is usually coordinated with the label, prior to any involvement by the manager. Their efforts must be consolidated so the manager's and the label's efforts are not counterproductive.

It is imperative that a record producer develops rapport with an artist's manager. It is necessary not only for general business reasons, but also because, quite often, peripheral communications with an artist go through the management office. In case of a business dispute, the communication is with the manager, possibly the artist's attorney, and also the record label. The manager is generally the initial point of contact.

An accomplished manager can literally navigate an artist into a successful career; poor management decisions can do the opposite. Choosing a manager is a critical business decision, and requires due diligence on the part of the artist.

> ♫ Some managers represent producers. Often, a manager is necessary if a producer receives numerous production offers. It can be difficult for a producer to choose and negotiate new projects without interfering with the creative state of mind. A manager analyzes the offers and presents the opportunities, along with the manager's recommendations. Some managers guide both producers and artists; sometimes that synergy can develop into business and creative opportunities for both parties.

Talent Agent

Talent (booking) agents book artists for live performances, such as concert, club, and television appearances. Most large agencies will not represent an artist until he or she either signs a recording contract with a reputable label or becomes established. Some agents are willing to help unknown artists secure recording contracts.

Agents' relationships with consumers are crucial to the success of artists. Agencies send out press kits and CDs, which provide information

> ♫ Within the structure of a large agency, one agent is usually assigned to an artist. The individual agent signs an artist and is responsible for handling the artist's career. The agent's responsibilities are analogous to those of A&R representatives at labels. If the agent's client is not successful, the agent's job might be in jeopardy. Some agreements require an agent to produce a minimum revenue stream per year, or the artist is able to terminate the agreement.

about new artists, and update promoters and bookers on established artists. They also direct them to the artist's website, where the same information can be found. (The Internet has become the primary source of information.) Agents who represent popular artists command more attention than an agent handling nascent artists. New artists should vie to be handled by the most influential agent who is willing to sign them. One of the concerns, which must be addressed, is that an artist needs to receive ample attention from the agent and/or agency. Powerful agents are interested in developing new artists, but the primary obligation of an agent is to generate income from prosperous and signed clients. An agent's commissions are based on gross receipts from concerts and other revenue streams, such as television and film appearances. Successful managers usually have personal relationships with agencies and agents, and they encourage clients to sign with the most suitable agency.

In the United States, talent agents or agencies must be registered and licensed. Most agents charge a commission of 15% to 20% of the gross revenue, but commission rates are often negotiable. All national multistate agencies are signatories to the AFofM (American Federation of Musicians), AFTRA (American Federation of Television and Radio Artists), and additional applicable unions that affect clients. They must abide by union regulations, which include a minimum pay scale and proper working conditions.

Major labels and large independent labels work closely with agents. Advertising, marketing, and financial tour support provides that artist with exposure, which is meant to translate into sales. Support gives credibility to the artists and helps the agents "tell a story" to potential concert promoters and talent bookers. Concert promoters are entrepreneurs, and they rely on the labels to support their efforts to sell tickets. *Exposure sells albums,* which is the ultimate goal of record labels and artists. Financial tour support is usually considered a recoupable advance against an artist's royalties.

Tour support is sometimes financed by *corporate sponsorships* (e.g., Nike sneakers or Pepsi). In return for substantial exposure, a company will spend considerable sums to be associated with an artist, and artists generally agree to appear in commercials in return for tour sponsorship. Artists' representatives should give much thought before making a commitment to lending their name and likeness to a product. Representing an unsuitable product can permanently damage an artist's credibility with his or her fans.

Agents work with artists' managers to guide artists' careers. After an artist has been signed to a recording contract, it is essential that he or she eventually sign with a talent agency. Agents usually begin to build an artist's career by booking clubs and small concert venues. Eventually, the artist embarks on a concert tour, usually as an opening act.

Relationships between artists and managers are analogous to the relationships managers and artists develop with talent agents. If the agency or agent arranges for a productive tour that is organized and includes playing venues that are prestigious and attracts an audience that will be receptive to the artist, the agency is in good favor; if a tour is not organized properly, problems occur. As with management, it is unusual for an artist to remain with one agent or agency throughout his or her career.

> ♫ Booking a major tour normally requires some positive activity surrounding the client's album such as announcing a single has hit the charts, encouraging consistent airplay, positive reviews, and active public relations.

Some consumers prefer purchasing music online because it is more convenient than traveling to a retail outlet, and albums and singles cost less.

Online legal downloading and on-demand streaming keep increasing. Although the overall record industry is predicting a rapid growth spurt, the increase has not yet generated enough revenue to make up for the loss of physical sales. Labels can charge less in the digital domain because they do not have to absorb manufacturing costs and the return of physical CDs. The business model for the worldwide record industry has been in a state of flux because of illegal downloading and rampant physical piracy. Many of the large labels are now sharing in the revenue stream spawned by live appearances, merchandising, and music publishing, in an effort to protect the label's financial investment. Other platforms for hearing music are:

- *Pandora Radio,* which allows listeners to enter artists or song titles they enjoy and the service responds by suggesting music that is similar to the listener's request. The listeners can be linked to Web online stores to purchase the music.

- *Last Fm* is a "recommendation service . . . it helps you discover music based on the songs you play."
- *Numerous music apps for mobile devices.*

Most powerful music agents work for large talent agencies. The William Morris Agency, International Creative Management (ICM), and Creative Artists Agency (CAA) are three of the largest. One of the advantages of signing with a sizable agency is that it has divisions that specialize in all areas of the entertainment industry. They can help coordinate an artist's overall career. For example, some singers, such Jennifer Lopez, are also actors; therefore, she may have one agent representing her for films and another representing her recording career. The larger agencies generally want to control all aspects of an artist's career, although there are instances when several agencies perform different functions for one artist.

♫ Record labels that provide tour support for a headlining artist will generally not allow agents to choose an opening act. The label may insist that an artist signed to their label open the concert. The clout of the artist, plus the influence of the label, enters into the outcome. (Many promoters and labels allow local artists to perform a short set prior to the "opening act.")

Because large agencies represent established artists, they sometimes hold the power to force, or "suggest," to promoters that a "baby" or midline artist becomes the opening act on a specified concert, or concert tour. Opening a major artist's concert offers great exposure for a new artist. Many artists have jump-started careers after opening for a headliner.

Many powerful agents book developing artists as an opening act with a headliner. The agent tells the promoter that if he or she wants to book a certain headliner, then the agent's choice of an opening act is part of the entire package. Agencies are interested in promoting new and developing artists and are therefore willing to exert pressure when necessary.

Music-Business Attorney

In addition to performing legal work, music business attorneys are essentially business representatives. Powerful entertainment attorneys are predominantly dealmakers. Many of them have close relationships with record label executives and agents and are able to shop deals to labels and publishing companies, much in the manner as managers. Attorneys negotiate recording contracts, concert agreements, merchandising agreements, and music publishing agreements, in addition to myriad other contracts that require guidance and negotiation. Disputes are usually settled through arbitration or mediation. Court should be the last resort. It is not uncommon for attorneys to represent artists before a manager is involved. Attorneys frequently recommend managers to artists and vice versa.

The music industry is a worldwide industry with thousands of employees, but the powerful attorneys, managers, and agents belong to a rather small but elite club. They can present incredible opportunities to deserving artists, which can literally create recording stars. They are highly selective and put together the pieces of the entire organizational puzzle before the career-building machine goes into gear. There have been extremely successful record labels that have signed a majority of their artists because of business relationships with a select number of managers, agents, and attorneys. The label executives know when a promotional and marketing machine is in place.

The following is an example of how this machine operates: A manager finds an outstanding artist. The manager calls an attorney and asks him or her to negotiate a contract with record label Y. The manager knows that the attorney is friendly with the CEO of the record label. If the artist is as good as the hype, the deal will be consummated. The label then "suggests" that agent Z become the artist's agent. The agent knows the label has made a major commitment to the artist. The sum of all parts equals a whole—good business!

This sounds like a fairytale, but the information is accurate. The artist who is selective when choosing business representatives may be able to create a situation similar to the one just described. The choice of advisors can be crucial to an artist's overall career.

Attorneys are compensated in several ways: hourly fee, a retainer for a certain number of hours, or a percentage of profits from a deal the attorney negotiates on behalf of the client. Some litigators who try court cases in the entertainment industry are willing to work on a contingency basis, if they feel that there is a strong case. If they win, they are paid a percentage of the financial award; if they lose, they get nothing.

Many managers and/or agents have law degrees. Their legal background is often beneficial to the artists. As previously mentioned, music attorneys frequently act as business affairs representatives.

Artists and producers should feel comfortable with an attorney and respect not only their legal advice but also their overall guidance. Since many artists are not particularly interested in the business of music, the role of an attorney becomes even more significant. *Trust* is the paramount factor in the relationship.

Music Business Accountant

♫ Business affairs: Most major labels have business affairs departments, which are staffed by attorneys who negotiate deals and agreements—artists' contracts, publishing contracts, international licensing agreements, and the like. The results of their negotiations are forwarded to the legal department. Some labels combine both departments.

Music business accountants specialize in all financial matters an artist or producer might encounter. They understand the global record business, the live-performance business, as well as the global music publishing business. In addition to industry specific matters, they attend to traditional accounting duties that deal with taxes, accounts payable, and accounts receivable.

Their relationships with attorneys, managers, agents, and record executives can be advantageous to their clients. Many young artists do not know people in the industry and seek out business relationships in hopes of networking as a result of one important contact. Accountants quite often perform that function.

Accountants calculate royalties and income derived from the following:

- Master sound recordings
- Mechanical and performance royalties
- Merchandising royalties
- Artist's royalties
- Performance royalties

♫ Additional income is derived from the peripheral entertainment-oriented businesses.

Record company mergers, the Internet, and the ease of communication have made the 39 billion-dollar global music industry a relatively compact community. The major "players" know one another and relationships, as in any industry, perpetuate new relationships. In many ways, music business accountants perform the same peripheral functions that music business attorneys perform. They are *dealmakers!* Some are licensed financial advisors and help clients plan for a secure future. Since artists are notoriously inadequate financial planners, accountants and/or financial advisors perform a crucial role in protecting clients' financial futures.

Being an artist is a *business.* Many artists own record companies and publishing companies. Accurate records are necessary because of accountability not only to the government, but also to other artists and songwriters who are entitled to fees and royalty distributions from the record label or publishing company.

Artists and writers receive fees, advances, and royalty payments. The calculations can be complicated and must be handled by a qualified music business accountant.

Record Label Positions

A&R Executive

A&R (Artist and Repertoire) executives are responsible for signing artists to labels and guiding the artists' recording careers.

Skillful A&R executives work closely with artists to help guide them in making creative and, as everyone hopes, commercially successful recordings. As overseers, they are peripherally involved in the formation of marketing and advertising plans. Labels pay royalties or bonuses to A&R executives based on the performance of the artists. It behooves them to become involved in as many aspects of their artists' careers as time permits. A recording may be of the highest artistic quality, but without promotions and marketing its chances of achieving financial success are minimal.

In classical recordings, targeting a core audience is the main consideration. Marketing and promotional concepts are of primary interest when dealing with soundtracks for films such as *Star Wars* and *Titanic.* Catchy titles, such as *Bach's Greatest Hits,* can attract a consumer's attention. Unless the consumer is familiar with an artist or an orchestra, it is a difficult task to sell the artist's albums. Inventive selling techniques have proved to be successful. An average classical album that has been promoted sells between 5,000 and 12,500 units worldwide.

In all styles of music, albums must have an artistically cohesive quality. A set of random songs or instrumentals without a preconceived marketing image is usually a mistake. Record labels produce videos and design album covers that project an image. Most artists tour to promote newly released albums. The tours are often named with the titles of the albums. Labels, managers, agents, concert promoters, and public relations firms work as teams to help promote what they hope will become commercially successful albums. That is an expensive and time consuming undertaking, and the more harmony among the creative and business teams, the better chance the projects have of achieving success in the market.

Following are some of the responsibilities of A&R executives:

- *A&R executives usually help with the selection of producers.* They arrange meetings with various producers to determine if there is any

"chemistry" with the artist. It is unusual for an A&R executive to force an artist to work with a producer. The choice is usually a mutual decision.
- *It can sometimes be a mistake to place an artist with a producer simply because he or she is "hot" (has a current hit or hits) at the moment.* The producer might not necessarily be the best creative choice for working with a particular artist. Consider temperament, musical taste, and availability before committing to an artistic relationship.
- Artistic ventures inherently create a multitude of potential problems that would not necessarily occur in a purely business relationship. Artists "give birth" to their "creations" and do not necessarily value or want the opinion of others, even though a successful artistic relationship between an artist and a producer results in a better creative product. An outsider's view can bring new ideas and new perspectives to a project. It is the job of a perceptive A&R coordinator to mix and match until the most appropriate producers are found.
- *As mentioned several times, A&R executives are amateur psychologists.* Not only do they work with the artist, but they must also develop rapport with the artist's manager and agent.
- *Many decisions that could be beneficial to the label are not necessarily helpful to the artist.* For example, the label may suggest that the artist promote the album on a television program that has a large number of viewers, but the manager may feel that appearing on the program could hurt the artist's credibility with fans. Some labels are more interested in immediate success than long-term development. Unfortunately, artist development by labels has become almost extinct. The expense, coupled with the state of the music industry, has made the financial commitment almost impossible.

> ♫ Analyzing the weaknesses and strengths of new artists is the mark of a creative music producer.

Success is a team effort, and consequently, cooperation from the business team is essential.

Artist Relations Executives

Artist relations executives' duties include coordinating the label's activities with artists, managers, and booking agents. They address all aspects of an artist's development, including tour support, release schedules, public relations, promotions, marketing, and advertising.

At smaller labels, the A&R staff, or general management personnel, usually handle artist relations.

Promotion Executive

Promotion executives have one of the most grueling jobs at a record label—to get airplay. Airplay, especially on radio (terrestrial, Internet, cable, and HD) and music-television stations and websites, is the primary promotional tool for helping to create a hit record and developing artists' careers. The vice president of promotion oversees either a national staff or independent promoters who are hired to promote one or more albums or singles. Record promotion usually begins in a region and then spreads nationally. Superstars releasing a hot record might attract national airplay from the day of release. The more the "story" develops, the easier it is to spread a record. Success generates more success.

- *Terrestrial radio stations monitor stores to determine if the records on their playlists are selling.* Sales and advertising are important to radio program directors because they reflect the effects of airplay. If a record is not popular or is losing popularity, stations will usually drop the record from their playlist.
- *Internet, Satellite, and cable radio are all significant promotional devices.* Technology also affords consumers the ability to listen to music on Internet on-demand subscription services, or on a label's- or artist's Web site. Most oftern, the listener can instantly purchase the music from either the source or be linked to a retail outlet on the Web. The track is downloaded and logged; the pertinent information allows appropriate royalties to be paid to the artists, record labels, and publishers. The listener can listen to the selection either on a computer or on a digital player, such as Apple's iPod or on a mobile phone.
- *Videos are also an important promotional tool.* Performance ability and charisma are essential to an artist's success, since visuals help create an image. Lady Gaga is a formidable example of an innovative artist. She developed one of the most recognizable personas in the music industry. She is the 21st century version of Madonna. In addition to the basic artistic ingredients needed for commercial success, promotion becomes the significant factor. (YouTube is the primary outlet for music videos.)

****

Some of the most popular artists on YouTube were selected to be part of a 27 city tour organized by YouTube. It was called *The Digitour* and began in May, 2011.

♫ It is costly for new and midlevel artists to tour. Videos provide universal exposure without touring. Labels have tried to generate profits from music videos via DualDisc, the format that has music on one side of the disc and video on the other. The format failed with the public. They are now developing strategies to profit from videos on the Internet.

Marketing Executives

The job of a marketing executive has changed dramatically, mainly because of the increase in viral marketing. The next chapter, Marketing and Promotions, contains an in-depth discussion on this subject.

Advertising Executive

Strategically placed print, television, all forms of radio, and Internet advertising continue to be the traditional outlets for informing the public about the release of an album. An advertising executive(s) is responsible for the overall advertising strategy. The best

♫ *Promotion encompasses merchandising and public relations.* Promotion executives work closely with the label's marketing and public relations departments. The following are promotional tools:

Radio Promotion Radio is the most important marketing tool used to create sales. Radio stations are the equivalent of boutique stores that specialize in a product. Some boutiques sell designer clothes, others sell designer shoes, and some sell only men's clothes. Some radio stations play rock, others play R&B, while others play only the top 40. The list is extensive. Although there has been a decline in the listenership to terrestrial radio, in 2010 there has been resurgence in the popularity of terrestrial Top 40 radio. This is mainly due to the success of artists such as Katy Perry, Lady Gaga, Usher, Madonna, Rihanna, and other pop-dance artists.

With the advent of Internet and radio, the subgenres have become even more compartmentalized. Stations usually play one style of music. A listener can find almost any genre of music desired. The Internet is the most important technology since the invention of television. Internet and radio stations have become an important link in the promotional chain. Since downloading can be instantaneous, the listeners are able to purchase songs instantly without having to travel to a traditional brick-and-mortar store. The technology eliminates manufacturing costs and traditional distribution costs.

Producers, Songs, and Promotions Producers are concerned with the source and quality of artists' songs. Performers' primary assets are songs (instrumentals). Labels—both majors and independents—want artists to record songs/instrumentals that will be played on the radio. A&R executives are always scouting for artists who are songwriters. Artist/songwriters are essential to labels because the labels know they are a source of future material.

♫ To gain acceptance from radio, a recording must be competitive within the market. Radio airplay, Internet radio, Satellite radio, cable and terrestrial, and music videos are the primary sources of promotions. Hits lead to concert tours, and exposure leads to sales.

Some musical genres receive limited airplay on terrestrial radio stations. Internet and other radio outlets specializing in one style of music have opened up new opportunities in a way analogous to the channels on cable television, such as The History Channel, CNN, and the Food Network.

The question that must be addressed is this: If a station does not advertise, how does a consumer become aware of a particular radio station or new artists? Word of mouth, called social networking or viral marketing, has become the most affective tool used to inform potential consumers. Sirius XM is the giant in the U.S. They have bought print, direct mail, and television advertising, and have subsequently greatly increased their number of subscribers, although they are struggling financially as of the writing of this book.

An additional problem is that BMI, ASCAP, and SESAC, the performance-rights organizations in the United States that collect performance royalty income for writers and publishers, want the boutique Internet radio stations to pay blanket performance fees similar to performance fees paid by broadcast radio stations. The Internet stations claim they cannot afford the fees because their advertising revenue does not generate enough income. Many small Internet stations have ceased operating because they cannot afford the fees required by the rights organizations and the RIAA. There are many problems associated with not only writers' and publishers' royalties but also with royalties for performers. This topic is beyond the scope of this book.

Producers and Promotion The relationship that a producer develops with the label and the label's belief in the final product ultimately determines their commitment to an artist in terms of promotion.

advertisement has always been for the potential consumer to hear the music on the Internet, radio, television, or in a store, including the short snippets heard on legitimate Internet music stores, such as iTunes, which lets the consumer preview each selection. In recent years, advertisers have been showing television commercials in movie theaters. Some have packaged sample CDs along with a purchase at the food concession. Many retail chains run co-op print advertising, which is generally featured in newspapers on the weekends. They usually offer discounts for a limited time. In-store listening stations have proved to be a successful way of promoting CDs. It is a form of advertising. A fine line exists between advertising, promotions, and public relations.

Trade advertising is geared to attract executives from various areas of the music industry such as promoters, retailers, program directors at terrestrial, Internet and radio stations, video outlets, and other areas that have the potential of creating exposure for artists.

> ♫ Questions to ask when creating an advertising plan:
>
> - Where will the album be advertised? Is the advertising reaching the target audience?
> - Is co-op advertising being bought? The cost of the ad is pro-rated when an artist's album is included with other albums.
> - Is the media buy prudent? Buying airtime and print space is costly. Labels do not usually engage in these expenses unless an artist is generating sales. Advertising placement is crucial to effective advertising.

Public Relations Executives

Public relations is, essentially, a form of free advertising. PR representatives arrange for clients to gain exposure on television, radio, in print, on the Internet, and in other forums. The PR department assembles press kits, which consists of promotional and background material for writers or interviewers. A press kit, both physical and online (electronic press kit), consists of new and past reviews (magazines, television, radio, etc.) newspaper articles, radio and television interviews, and additional material that might be of interest. Electronic Press Kits (EPK) have become essential. If the promotion is for the release of a new album, the CD is included in the press kit. PR representatives assemble press parties, which are usually coordinated with a new release or a highly visible event, such as the beginning of a major tour. Most major labels assign a press representative to accompany artists on all important organized activities.

Public relations is a high-pressure job because it relies on PR agents' contacts. New and established artists need exposure. Controlling not only the amount of publicity but also the *appropriate* publicity is the publicist's job.

Most successful artists hire private public relations firms on a yearly basis or for a selected project. Many record companies have PR departments that are primarily responsible for promoting new releases. Since it is difficult to provide equal attention to each artist, the artist's personal agent usually assists the label.

Art Executives

Creating and/or supervising an album cover design is the primary job of an art and graphic-design executive. Portraying an artist's public persona is critical. Therefore, all artwork must be carefully crafted to graphically capture the album's theme or concept.

Art executives are also involved in the overall graphic branding of artists. A logo can be an effective tool; think about the Rolling Stones logo of

♫ To promote a new album, there must be a "handle"—something for the promotion, marketing, and advertising teams to "hold on to." When a new project is being designed, some of the key ingredients of concern to an artist, producer, and label are the album title, cover design, and the project's musical identity. Producers help formulate the overall ambience of a project. Many projects have musical themes, which helps the promotion department market an image. Questions to ask when preparing promotions and public relations plans:

- Which radio stations are being targeted?
- Are special radio promotions and giveaways being offered?
- Are Internet, satellite, cable, HD radio, and terrestrial radio stations all being targeted?
- Are newspapers (including college papers) being contacted to write stories about the artist? Are magazines that cover the artist's genre of music being targeted?
- Is the Internet being utilized for both promotions and sales?
- Is there a physical and electronic press kit?
- Has a one-page fact sheet been prepared?
- Are discount coupons being offered?
- Is there a sampler CD or a digital sampler?
- Are there any cross-promotions? (For example, buy 2 hamburgers and a soda and receive an artist's greatest hits album at a reduced rate.)

Mick Jagger's tongue and lips. Advertising and merchandising campaigns extensively use various forms of artwork and graphic design.

Some major labels employ staff artists, but independent artists do the majority of artistic work on a work-for-hire basis. Most photographers and videographers are also hired on that basis. Under work-for-hire agreements, labels retain ownership of the works.

Sales Executives

A sales director is in charge of the regional sales managers. Salespeople sell directly to large retail chains, rack jobbers, Internet companies, and other specialized sales outlets. When a new album is released or there is a special sales promotion, the label executives arrange for quantity discounts and special pricing structures. Wal-Mart, Best Buy, and Circuit City are the most important brick-and-mortar retail chains in the United States.

The United States is divided into sales regions, and the sales team works closely with the promotions department to maximize the impact of sales promotions. The sales director must make certain that, when an artist is touring, the stores in the vicinity of the concert sites are stocked with the artist's CD(s).

♫ Nielsen SoundScan, which tracks official sales in the U.S. and Canada, and Broadcast Data Systems, or BDS, which tracks airplay, serve as the guiding lights for sales personnel. Stores and labels rely on the information gathered from these services to determine the number of CDs that should be racked in the stores. The National Association of Recording Merchandisers (NARM) is a nonprofit organization that tracks sales figures, use of listening stations in record stores, Internet sales, and other related sales outlets.

Questions to ask when creating a sales plan:

- Have stores been approached to rack (sell) the CD? Stores have to be "sold," especially when an artist is new. There is very limited shelf space.
- Have special sales promotions been established with the retail chains? An example is offering a discounted price for a specific time period.
- Are listening stations being used so the consumer can hear portions of the CD? Listening stations are expensive to rent, but they are considered one of the most effective sales tools.
- Is in-store play being used to promote the CD? This is also one of the best sales tools. The CDs are usually displayed at the checkout counter.
- Is the CD exhibited on in-store wall displays, window displays, and end caps?
- Is the label advertising? The advertising must be strategically planned so that the target audience is reached.

Additional Information

- It is rare for a label to employ staff producers and engineers; most are hired on a freelance basis.
- Some labels own studios, but the majority of state-of-the art studio facilities are available for rent on a per-hour or daily rate.
- Some major labels own mastering labs.
- Video directors are hired on a work-for-hire basis.
- Music publishing is an exciting and creative career path. An understanding of domestic and international copyright laws, as well as the complex issues involving all aspects of music publishing, is the backbone of the music industry.
- Most labels own music publishing companies.

Conclusion

The occupations described in this chapter have numerous support positions. The music business is a complex, interesting, and exciting industry. It is advisable to choose a focused career path when first entering the industry because apprenticeships are rigorous and time consuming. It is also advisable to complete an undergraduate university education and, in some instances, an advanced degree, in addition to either an internship or industry experience. Most major universities offer courses of study that prepare students for industry-specific jobs. For example, Florida Atlantic University, The University of Miami, and New York University offer majors in music industry studies. Consult the Internet and university guidebooks to find similar academic programs.

♫ The studio business has become an increasingly difficult business primarily due to the availability of inexpensive, professional, or semi-professional home studio equipment. Most artists and producers have home (project) studios, which allows them more creative freedom. Renting studio space is costly and should be used, in most instances, to complete the work, not to create it.

For those interested in entering the creative aspects of the music business—producer, artist, arranger, or composer—it is wise to study music at the university level. Musical versatility can be an asset because of the volatile and varied nature of the business. For example, an arranger can arrange music for records, commercials, films, and television. Learning the various aspects of music production, which includes an understanding of audio engineering, prepares students to apply their skills in a variety of fields.

Often, creative people feel they can tackle any musical situation, which is highly unlikely. It is advisable to only accept jobs that showcase one's creative strength. *Second chances are rare!*

Assignment

Assume you are forming a small record label. To remain within the budget, you can hire only 5 employees. Outline all positions and describe the responsibilities of each position. The jobs should encompass all areas needed to run a small label.

20

Marketing and Promotions

> Without passion, you don't have energy; without energy, you have nothing. Nothing great in the world has been accomplished without passion.
>
> —Donald Trump

As noted by RIAA board member Tommy Silverman, "74% of all US-based albums sales came from CDs in 2010." Silverman noted even better statistics in certain genres. "84% Country . . . 85% Gospel and . . . 93% Latin album sales came from physical."

According to Nielsen SoundScan, 46% of U.S. sales in 2010 were digital downloads.

To develop comprehensive and, hopefully, successful marketing and promotions plans, artists and/or labels must have concise and targeted goals. The ultimate objective is to attract new fans, retain current fans, and interest them in purchasing music and merchandise and to attend concerts. The details of how to achieve these objectives will be discussed in this chapter.

The 4 P's of Marketing

- Product
  - This term originally referred to physical product. In the music industry, it also applies to digital product.
  - The name of an album, the artwork, the recording quality, etc. is all considered part of the "product."
- Price
  - iTunes is an example of a pricing strategy that changed. Originally, all individual songs were priced at 99 cents. After much

discussion with the record labels, they implemented a new pricing structure: $1.29 for very popular and mostly new recordings, some catalog songs that have remained popular sell for $.99, while older less desirable songs sell for $.69.
  - The price of albums varies.
- Place (distribution)
  - Today, distribution includes making product available to digital stores and mobile devices.
  - Physical distribution includes delivering to brick & mortar (retail) stores, warehousing, transporting the product, returns, etc.
  - Special Products: Albums that are either newly recorded or compiled from existing tracks and are specifically targeted for exclusive distribution, e.g., the album is only sold at Bed, Bath & Beyond.
- Promotion
  - Marketing the product to a targeted demographic
  - Public relations
  - Sales
  - Radio and television promotions
  - Web promotions
  - Inventive promotional strategies, some of which are described in this chapter.

> ♫ A "Greatest Hits" album could be considered a Special Product. Since the genre has decreased in sales, some labels now promote these albums as new product. For instance, the artist might be booked on television programs that attract the proper demographic such as the Late Night programs or the artist may record several new tracks for the album or include several remixes; a deluxe package might contain a music video and booklet. This marketing strategy has proved to increase sales. (Most record contracts limit the number of "Greatest Hits" albums that will be released within the term of a contract.)

Most marketing plans use these basic principles to develop marketing strategies.

The 4 P's rubric was assembled by E. Jerome McCarthy, which was taken from an article written by Neil H. Borden in 1964.

SWOT Analysis

Many businesses develop a SWOT Analysis, as an aid, prior to making business decisions concerning marketing, strategic planning, and other crucial aspects that must be considered when operating a business. SWOT is an acronym for:

- Strengths
- Weaknesses
- Opportunities
- Threats

A SWOT Analysis can be useful in marketing albums. The following is an example of some of the items that should be listed under each major category.

Strengths

- The executives are experienced in targeting the proper demographic
- An innovative marketing strategy
- Advantages over other companies marketing similar artists
- A substantial budget that will allow the company to conduct a thorough marketing campaign and sustain the campaign, if warranted
- Price the product to be competitive
- Quality (high quality reproduction and mastering)

Weaknesses

- May not have competitive distribution
- May be under-financed
- May not have experienced marketing managers in the record industry
- May not have the commitment and morale required by the top executives
- May not have the ability to distribute and market globally
- May not distribute physical copies

Opportunities

- Social networking (viral marketing), which is not necessarily costly.
- Unknown artists have many opportunities because they can be discovered through websites such as YouTube or Facebook. This was not possible prior to social networking, which was made available by innovative applications.
- Song videos can be produced at a relatively inexpensive production cost.
- Albums can be recorded in project studios, which present opportunities for many innovative artists that would, most likely, not be signed to major labels because they have a limited audience. (The equipment used in project studios is relatively inexpensive and produces high-quality results.)

- Artists can communicate directly with their fans and develop new fans by approaching them to help expand their audience.
- Synchronization opportunities

> ♫ In the 1960s and 1970s, Albert Humphrey, a management consultant, developed the SWOT Analysis Technique while working at the Stanford University Research Institute. He was in charge of a research team.

Threats

- Peer-2-Peer file sharing
- Physical piracy
- Limited radio play

Marketing Executives

Marketing executives, obviously, market recordings, hopefully in a creative manner. Marketing departments negotiate promotional deals with radio stations; they give away concert tickets and merchandise to listeners and expand the marketing as an artist generates income. They work closely with the promotion department. When a recording is receiving exposure, which includes airplay via terrestrial radio, the Internet, satellite radio, blogs, etc., or an artist is touring, the marketing department is responsible for supporting that exposure in various ways.

> ♫ Business models are changing at a rapid rate and it is difficult to predict how the current increase in Internet and mobile sales and decrease in traditional retail sales will affect overall sales. Some labels pay stores merely to have their product racked and prominently displayed. Most music pundits predict that brick-and-mortar stores will not be the primary source of purchasing music in the near future. To help combat the problem, many store chains and record labels have developed online stores.

In-Store Promotion Labels rent listening stations in retail stores so potential customers can hear portions of CDs; they also purchase space to hang promotional posters and to have their recordings played on in-store speaker systems. This is a costly marketing tool. End caps are located at the end of a rack so the CD is proximately displayed. Some CDs are prominently displayed where a customer pays for the product. This is called the Point-of-Purchase (POP) and can be costly. Artists sometimes perform in stores. This attracts new potential fans and the artists make themselves "available" to converse with their current fans. (As a result from the competition from the digital market, physical sales have decreased; therefore, most large stores devote less space for CDs.)

Tour Promotion and Tour Financial Support Concert appearances promote sales. To help support touring, record labels usually advance

♫ On average, record labels retain 20% to 30% of revenue generated by artists that sign "360" deals. Artists usually retain a minimum of 30% of the gross profits. Successful artists negotiate higher percentages.

♫ Swag (s.w.a.g.), an acronym for "stuff we all get," refers to merchandising such as t-shirts.

♫ When music videos first surfaced in the United States, some executives felt that depicting a song via visual images detracted from the listener's imagination. Apparently, they were mistaken. Almost all hit records are supported by videos.

money to worthy artists; the advances are recouped against record royalties. Tour support is 100% recoupable. (It is difficult for new artists to generate a profit while touring because there are numerous expenses.) Touring also helps to sell merchandise, such as t-shirts and hats. In general, revenue from merchandise produces the same revenue as ticket sales.

Music Video Promotion Music videos are an important marketing and promotional tool. (MTV popularized music videos, in the U.S., in 1981.) The production expenses are costly, which means the labels have to feel strongly about a song before committing financial support. Videos can cost anywhere from $5,000 to over $1 million. 50% of the cost of a video is generally recouped against artists' royalties and the remaining 50% is recouped from video sales. Artists with clout can sometimes negotiate more favorable terms.

Most consumers view the videos on artists' websites or sites such as YouTube.

University and College Promotion University and college promotion is a synthesis of sales, radio promotion, and merchandising. Most universities have radio and television stations; in addition, they present concerts by renowned artists. New recordings have "broken" (become hits) after receiving exposure on university radio and television stations. (Some labels hire college students, as interns, to promote their product on campus. Internships often lead to jobs upon graduation.)

Web Site Promotion Most artists (and producers) have Web sites. Web sites, or Internet sites (MySpace), are one of the most effective marketing tools. Some record labels' Web sites have direct links to the artists' personal Web sites. Create and register a domain name such as xyzband.com. The name should be simple and directly associated with the name of the artist.

An effective website begins with a thoughtfully designed homepage. The homepage is the most essential screen of a site because it establishes the image of the artist (producer). The site should be designed so that the artist's *brand* is identifiable. The site should be simple to navigate. Fans do not want to waste time attempting to find information that should be easily accessible. In addition to being graphically appealing, the menu should include links to the following content:

- New releases
- Bio
- Electronic Press Kit (EPK) (Include relevant press clippings.)
- Discography
- Tour schedule
- Newsletter
- Reviews
- Photos
- Sales Charts
- Chart Rankings (e.g., Billboard, iTunes, etc.)
- A request for the viewer's e-mail address
- A message board so that the fans can communicate with the artist or the producer
- MP3 samples of the latest CD and catalogue samples
- Purchase of albums (This is not always possible. If the album cannot be purchased on the Web site, links to other online stores, such as Amazon.com, should be included.)

It is essential to keep the Web site current and imperative that the questions on the message board be answered in a timely fashion. Gathering fan information is crucial to maintaining a solid fan base. Fans will attend more concerts and purchase additional CDs, downloads, and merchandise if they "connect" with an artist. Gather profiles of your fans, which should include information such as:

- What other artists do they follow?
- What blogs, e-zines, and traditional magazines do they read?
- Do they listen to a variety of music-based podcasts?
- Do they subscribe to social networks such as Apple's Ping, Facebook, and Twitter?
- Do they listen to terrestrial, Satellite, and Internet radio stations?
- Do they watch broadcast, cable, Direct TV, and Internet television programs?
- Do they communicate with others through music chat rooms?

♫ 70% of entertainment searches on Microsoft's Bing search engine, in the summer of 2010, were customers searching for song lyrics. This may become a lucrative source of songwriters' royalties.

The above information aids the marketing and promotions teams to target their audiences; therefore, it is cost effective.

Preparing a Marketing Plan The plan should include the following information in addition to traditional marketing plan information.

- In which bin will the CD be racked in a store (rock, pop, R&B, alternative, adult contemporary, etc.)?
- Describe the demographics and psychographics of the target audience. Provide a description of the music.
- How does the music differ from that of the competition?
- What is the artist's image? Does the artist have a musical identity?
- Is the image on the album cover being used as a general marketing logo? (E.g., Mick Jagger's tongue.)
- Visual branding is vastly significant because it helps to establish an artist's image.
- Does the artist publish a blog and/or podcast?
- Does the artist send an e-mail newsletter? (Newsletters should inform fans but in an entertaining manner. "Talk" to them as if one was conducting a private conversation.)
- Does the artist make music videos and post them on YouTube and other similar sites? What promotional tools are going to be used?
- Is there a "one sheet" (a brief description of the artist and the marketing and promotional plan)? This is important to retailers. If they rack (provide shelf space) the CD, it takes up store space; retailers want to be reassured that the label is committed to promoting the CD.
- Is there a music video? Will it be for sale? (Traditionally, music videos do not sell well but are effective for marketing.)
- Where is the artist performing and what promotional strategies are planned to help promote album and merchandise sales at concert venues?
- Does the artist have mailing addresses and e-mail lists?
- If so, how can they be used to help sell albums and merchandise? Are there sales incentives such as download 1 song and get another track for free? (These should be implemented for a limited time period.)

Nontraditional Alternative Marketing

- Have nontraditional retail outlets been approached for distribution; for example, stores other than traditional brick-and-mortar record stores, such as health-foods stores?
- Is there a plan to use direct marketing? The customer is contacted directly and provided with an opportunity to order the CD or download.
- Is there a plan to use direct mail or flyers? Most performing artists acquire a mailing list containing both e-mail and home addresses of their fans. They send out weekly reminders of upcoming concerts, as well as additional general information.

- Does the artist have a Web site? Most artists' Web sites present an opportunity for the customer to purchase albums (including merchandise), as well as providing them with a newsletter, which contains the artist's concert schedule and other news. Some link the customer to a traditional Web music store such as Amazon.com or iTunes.com. Allow the customer to print out a coupon that provides a discount on certain items. (In today's music industry, Web sites may be considered traditional marketing.)
- Link your Web site to a store(s), such as iTunes, so that fans can download or purchase physical copies of the artist's music. Some artists prefer to allow the consumer to download and/or purchase physical copies directly from their Web site.
- Is a one-page flier or brochure available? Most fliers and simple brochures provide fans with an opportunity to purchase artists' albums and other merchandise in addition to a listing of their concert schedule. An order form is usually included and it is either stamped or has a return envelope with the postage prepaid.

♫ iTunes Ping, which launched on September 1, 2010, is iTune's social network and is similar to Facebook and Twitter. The purpose of Ping is to allow iTunes customers to keep current with artists and share information. It is simple to use because while on iTunes there is a direct link to Ping. It can also be accessed on iPhones and iPod Touches.

- Is the album being licensed to record clubs? Record clubs sell albums at a discount but the volume of sales can more than compensate for the reduced royalty rate.
- Does the artist sell his or her CD(s) at live performances? This strategy can be lucrative, since the fans are most interested in purchasing an artist's music after attending a concert. The artist purchases the CDs at the wholesale price; however, labels limit the number of CDs an artist may purchase at that price.
- Have television programs, advertising agencies, and film companies been contacted to license songs from the album? Licensing music from an album can be a superb marketing tool as well as a lucrative revenue source.

♫ Study marketing techniques used in other industries and use them if they are applicable to marketing music.

Summary of Marketing and Promotions

Social networking, referred to as viral marketing, has become the predominant promotional tool used to sell music. It allows fans to communicate with each other as well as with their favorite artists. This tactic has always been used to market: *Word of Mouth.* It is important to target the proper demographic. For example, Katy Perry has a core demographic that most likely attracts teens through consumers in the their mid-20s. The Internet provides important information about consumers, which helps content providers target their audience. It also provides artists with global distribution. Marketing and promotions plans must include a budget.

- Determine when the CD and/or digitized recordings are scheduled for release and determine the territories. For instance, the digital distribution company IODA, previously mentioned, allows their customers to choose the territories they wish their product to be available. Planning ahead is necessary.
- Coordinate live performances with the release of an album. For instance, touring, television appearances and interviews, which may include podcasts, blogs, Ezine articles (online magazines), magazine articles, and additional forms of exposure.
- Target the proper demographic. The more pointed the marketing and promotion, the greater chance of reaching a core audience.
- Viral marketing is significant because fans want to become "friends" with the performers they admire. They do not want to be "preached to." For example, if a tweet, which is a short message (a part of the social networking service Twitter), is used to promote an artist, the tweet should only contain essential information about the artist such as, "The artist is performing this weekend from 9PM-10PM at the XYZ Club." (Twitter had 175 million viewers in 2010.)

♫ Some artists promote their new albums on Twitter rather than through traditional channels, which might involve managers and press representatives. This is yet another example of the influence and future of social networking.

Since consumers have complained that albums contain only 1 or 2 "good" songs, they have transformed the music industry, for the most part, back to the 1950s and early 1960s business model of selling singles; if the singles are hits, produce an album. This paradigm allows consumers to "cherry pick." (The ability to purchase only the songs they want to own.) The problem, from a record company's perspective, is that it does not warrant the cost of recording an album if the consumer does not have to purchase the album to get the song or songs they wish to own. As previously mentioned, consumers pay more for current hits and less for older recordings. Many artists offer a free download in order to entice consumers to purchase their album.

As a result of fewer sales and less profit, numerous artists view their recordings as marketing tools that help attract an audience to their live performances.

> ♫ "Facebook issued a warning to independent developers . . . in response to reports that some applications on the site were sharing identifying information about users." (Doug Cross CNN [October 2010])

- Music Web site design is one of the most essential tools used by artists that keep fans informed. It is essential that viewers have the ability to easily navigate the site and quickly access the desired information. The site must be frequently updated; the content should include:
  - Music
  - News
  - Videos
  - Photos
  - Music
  - Concert Dates
  - Updated Bio
  - Reviews
  - Chat Room (enables fans to communicate with each other and the artist)
  - Street Teams (fans who help promote the artists), log-in (provides e-mail addresses)
  - Available ringtones and ringbacks
  - Links to MySpace, Facebook, YouTube and Twitter, merchandise, videos, as well as links to additional essential Web sites. (Facebook had 500 million users in 2010.) Hire a web designer who will not only visually reveal your vision but will also help register a proper domain name and Internet address. List your site on the following search engines: Google, Yahoo, Bing, and About.com. There are also many additional search engines that are theme related.
- The objective is to appeal to fans so they will support the artist's career. Make them feel as though they have become a member of the artist's "family." Sometimes, artists offer backstage passes to fans that have helped sustain their fan-base and helped to increase their fan-base. The more interaction an artist has with his or her fans, the longer he or she will retain their support staff. Artists can no longer depend on labels and agents to guide and develop their careers. Managers have taken on a much more significant role than in the past partially because many new and established artists do not sign with labels; therefore, the manager becomes their "guiding light." Although the following statement might be construed as an insult, *artists are brands*. They must have the ability to survive in a competitive environment. This requires an unequivocal commitment to their careers, which is guided by a skilled support team consisting of a manager, road manager, agent, attorney, accountant,

public relations firm or individual, and others. Artists must project a very clear image so that the public associates their music with their personas. The record industry is a business, and their careers must be conducted as such.

When attempting to obtain public relations for an artist, the story or press release—a short synopsis containing pertinent information about the artist—should be targeted to the proper sources. (The story should be concise and the content clearly stated.) For instance:

- Do not send a story about a pop act to a new age magazine.
- The information should contain content that will appeal to the artist's audience. The headline should reveal only pertinent information about the content of the story. For example: XYZ TOURS EUROPE!
- Try to send information that is unique. Do not bombard the media with irrelevant stories.
- Send the story to multiple sources such as entertainment television programs, music blogs, music podcasts, etc. but be selective.
- Do not abuse relationships with media contacts. Use your acquaintances judiciously.
- Sometimes, it might be wise to give an "exclusive" interview, for instance, to one source but be prepared for the possible consequences. Other sources might get irritated and refuse to support the artist when the artist needs a favor.
- It is essential to build an e-mail list of fans. Develop a substantial list and use it to inform fans about all essential activities such as performances, merchandise, recordings, news, etc. Personalize each e-mail, e.g. Dear Bob, and create a message that is simple and short. (Personalized e-mails can be time consuming and therefore impractical.) E-mails should always provide a link to the artist's Web site.
- Approach retail stores, referred to as brick & mortar stores, only after a recording has created a "buzz." For instance, a buzz can be local or regional radio play that has resulted in confirmed online sales. Limited shelf space has made it difficult to place physical product in retail stores without some indication that the album will sell. Many stores will only accept CDs on consignment. Consignment means that the label only gets paid when the album sells. The store does not purchase the product.
- Streaming services: For example Rhapsody—the most popular on-demand streaming service in the U.S.—allows their subscribers to listen to unlimited music for a fee of $10.00 a month. The customers can also download as many songs as they wish but the songs cannot be burned to a CD or DVD. The content can be played on, for example, an iPod.

The iPod must be connected to the Internet at least once a month to verify that the customer has paid for their subscription. This is referred to as a non-tethered stream. If a customer stops her subscription, the songs no longer remain on the computer or other devices. A tethered stream means that the customer must be connected to the Internet to hear the stream. Rhapsody can also be downloaded to mobile phones. Napster (the legal version) is also a streaming service. Although record labels favor the streaming of music, as of the writing of this book, the paradigm has not proved to be financially viable.

- Some digital distributors, such as Bandcamp, allow the content provider to determine the sales price for a single or album and also retain all ownership rights. The content provider may set a minimum price and fans might choose to pay more than the minimum. (Most digital stores determine online prices.) The compensation for online distribution varies. (Bandcamp also allows artists to sell their merchandise.)
- "Sell Physical and Digital, Side-by-Side. You can sell both your physical merchandise and your digital music from Bandcamp, and better yet, you can sell them together." (Bandcamp website)
- IODA (Independent Online Distribution Alliance) is an example of a large online distributor of music and videos. They also offer a marketing service for additional compensation.
- ReverbNation permits artists, producers, and musicians to communicate and share their work with each other. They can market and promote music without a large investment. Topspin provides the same opportunities as many other Internet Web sites.

♫ Music publishers collect and distribute the royalties generated by all digital tracks; this includes streaming and downloading.

♫ Grooveshark is a free, ad based, music search engine that allows consumers to select songs and/or artists and stream their music. Downloading is not permitted. This is an unusual example of a music service because subscription services, such as Rhapsody, charge consumers to choose a specific song and stream it.

For a fee of $3.00 USD a month (for the first year), Grooveshark offers a VIP service, which removes banner ads, adds mobile applications, allows users to keep their playlists on their computer desktops, and additional features. Users can also upload content, which may increase the risk of copyright infringement. The content provider is personally liable for uploading illegal content. Major record labels have filed lawsuits against the company.

- Inserting an advertisement on a web page is called a banner ad. This can sometimes be very effective if placed in a location that attracts the proper demographic.
- Mobile marketing via ringtones and ringbacks generates substantial publishing and licensing income. Most mobile devices enable the user to create a ringtone library. Certain applications allow the user to illegally upload ringtones and ringbacks to mobile devices. This, obviously, is copyright infringement. Some mobile phones include generic ringtones and ringbacks and a free music library. The mobile market will continue to be an essential part of the evolving music industry. (In addition, there are many music "apps" available for mobile devices. This has become a lucrative business.)
- Synchronization licensing (licensing music for films, commercials, Internet use, etc.) and transcription licensing (e.g., radio commercials) are substantial sources of income.
- Game licensing can be a considerable source of income but mainly for established artists.
- Sell sheet music. Substantial revenue can be generated without much development cost. Most sheet music can be downloaded, which eliminates manufacturing costs. Larger works must be produced in a physical format.

> ♫ ReverbNation allows users to put music on other websites by using free music player *widgets*. (A music *widget* allows users to post notes on social networking sites.) In addition, the user might provide information on new artists and promote other web sites and blogs. Limitless information can be posted.

> ♫ Some Web sites, such as YouTube and Hulu, present a commercial prior to showing selected videos. This ad-supported model helps monetize the website.

Hulu shows television programs, films, and music videos in the U.S. only. Fox, ABC, NBC, as well as other networks and studios own it. They are able to provide content without infringing on copyright ownership.

Vevo is a successful Web site that shows music videos provided by the Sony Music Entertainment, EMI, and the Universal Music Group. Sony Music Entertainment, EMI, and Abu Dhabi Media own the site. (EMI is not an owner.) The site is monetized via advertising revenue. There is no illegal use of videos because the owners of the site, plus EMI, provide the content. The site also sells merchandise.

"Lift" is a new Vevo program that was designed to help develop emerging artists. They will select new artists and promote them on their website, Facebook, and Twitter in addition to providing additional social networking opportunities.

"Music Meter," launched by MTV, was designed to promote new artists. They rank the top 100 unknown artists. The chart is based upon interest from fans on social networks, the number of video streams, sales (physical and downloads), and radio play, including terrestrial, Internet, and Satellite radio. (Traditional charts are based upon sales and radio play.)

"Ultimate Chart," controlled by Big Champagne and "Social 50," owned by Billboard, base their rankings on artists that are popular on social-networking sites such as Facebook, Twitter, MySpace, and more. Most of these artists are well known and generally appear on traditional music charts. "Music Meter" and "Lift" provide music lovers with an opportunity to discover new music by unknown artists.

♫ As reported in the New York Times by Janna Wortham on September 6, 2010, "Viral videos tend to have a short lifespan online. The best ones might attract a few million views on YouTube and get a mention on a Late Night talk show before fading into oblivion." This statement might be accurate but what Ms. Wortham does not mention is that the exposure can lead to many opportunities.

- Instead of releasing an album, every several months release 1 single and promote it. Obviously, do not release all of the tracks. After a buzz has been created and there are respectable sales, compile the singles, add additional tracks, and release the album. This model allows the public to get to know the artist and to, hopefully, be en-

♫ One of the advantages of controlling content on the Internet is that artists are not necessarily willing to sign "360" deals (described earlier) with record labels. Artists and/or content owner/providers keep the majority of profits and have total control over their content, which includes merchandise. As this paradigm increases in popularity, the labels will, most likely, become weaker. When Web-based artists hit mainstream, global popularity, the music industry will have recovered from many years of reorganization. To date, this has not occurred. The major labels and mini-majors have the funds to market and promote artists into "superstardom." They can finance tour support, which is recouped against royalties. Will web-based artists without substantial funding be able to attain the same level of success? (Approximately 30% of sales are downloaded.)

As reported by Nielsen SoundScan (October 20, 2010), Lil Wayne's *I Am Not a Human Being* debuted on the Billboard 200 chart at number 2 based upon downloaded sales only. This is highly unusual as of the writing of this book. The release of the physical album increased the chart position to number 1 in its 3rd week on the chart. (Nielsen SoundScan tracks sales of music and videos in the U.S. and Canada. The information is used to determine the Billboard chart positions.)

couraged to purchase the entire album. Some albums have several album covers. For example, Lady Gaga's *Fame* album has several covers. The Deluxe Version, called *The Fame Monster* has 15 songs; the price is $14.99. The *Fame Monster* contains 9 songs plus a digital booklet; the cost is $7.99. The albums have separate covers. Labels must find new models that will increase monetization of their products. This is a creative example.

♫ According to Billboard, during the week of May 23, 2011, Amazon.com sold Lady Gaga's new album, *Born This Way*, for 99 cents for two days. The album sold approximately 1 million copies in its first week of release. Amazon's wholesale price is approximately $8.00. iTunes sold the album for $15.99.

The promotion was, most likely, sold for that price to promote Amazon's music service. Customers can store their music, for free, in Amazon's Cloud Drive Storaage.

- One of the advantages of digital distribution is that artists and labels can make their complete catalogues available without a substantial investment. Many formally established artists have had their careers revived because of the Internet, Satellite radio, ringtones and ringbacks, and the use of their music in commercials, films, and television. The same is true for new artists. Their songs are discovered online and licensed for various projects. This exposure can lead to multiple opportunities.

1. Performance on The Grammy Awards (After performing on the 2010 Grammy Awards, Pink's album *Funhouse* received the greatest increase in sales of any performer on the program.)
2. Synch Placement in a TV ad for Apple
3. Performance on *The Oprah Winfrey Show*
4. Song Featured as Free Single of The Week On iTunes
5. Album Displayed in Walmart Endcap
6. Song Performed on Fox's *Glee*
7. Album Featured As Amazon MP3 Daily Deal
8. Performance on *Saturday Night Live*
9. Single/Album Charting on iTunes
10. First Arena-Level Headlining Tour

♫ Billboard Magazine published a list of the 100 best ways to generate sales and a buzz (October 2, 2010). The following list is the top 10.

- Set goals. Set a time-line. For instance, by a specific date assemble an e-mail list that contains X number of addresses and also that a minimum of at least 150 fans attend each performance. These goals may be difficult to attain but it is the only means to build a loyal audience. Performances

♫ The Associated Press reported that in 2010 concert sales were poor due to elevated ticket prices. Concert promoters plan to lower ticket prices in 2011 and to promote the artists' merchandise in hopes of making up lost revenue. Pollstar Magazine reported that in the first half of 2010, concert attendance dropped 12% when compared to the same period in 2009. Live Nation Entertainment Inc. reported a drop of more than 12% in concert sales during the summer of 2010, even though they lowered ticket prices when sales were slow. Some productions are costly to produce: therefore, the promoters cannot afford to lower prices. In the future, some artists might not create massive, expensive productions. This will allow the promoters to lower prices.

and selling merchandise are the primary source of income for most performers unless they are superstars. Superstars can earn significant income from artist's, publishing, and performance royalties.

Conclusion

The producer and label know that a marketing and promotions campaign cannot be successful unless the songs and the production values appeal to the proper demographic. As previously mentioned, the songs are the foundation of any project. Producers and artists must spend considerable time and energy writing songs or selecting appropriate songs, "setting" the songs in the most suitable arrangement, and capturing the ambience of the music.

♫ The Top 10 Selling Albums in the U.S. for 2010 as reported in Billboard Magazine (Figures in millions) were:

1. Eminem, *Recovery* (3.42)
2. Lady Antebellum, *Need You Know* (3.09)
3. Taylor Swift, *Speak Now* (2.96)
4. Justin Bieber, *My World* (2.32)
5. Susan Boyle, *The Gift* (1.85)
6. Lady Gaga, *The Fame* (1.59)
7. Sade, *Soldier of Love* (1.30)
8. Drake, *Thank Me Later* (1.27)
9. Usher, *Raymond v. Raymond* (1.18)
10. Ke&ha, *Animal* (1.14)

As reported by SoundScan, total U.S. sales in 2010 dropped 9.5% when compared to sales in 2009. In 2010, total sales, which include CDs combined with downloads of complete albums, equaled 443.4 million units compared to 489.8 million units in 2009. The decline in sales is attributed to illegal downloading and diminishing shelf-space in retail stores.

The listener should be able to "hear" these elements in the final mix. The final "cherry on the cake" is mastering the project, which should capture the best possible sonic quality. Not all marketing and promotion plans are going to achieve complete or partial success. It is best to view your marketing strategy as a "living" plan, which means that the marketing managers must be prepared to make changes. Be flexible! It is the nature of any business venture.

Assignment

Create a fictitious artist. Construct a viral, Internet-based marketing and promotions campaign that is designed to support a new album. Include a budget but try to keep costs to a minimum.

21

Business Agreements and Creating a Business Plan

> Google, Apple and Amazon are all racing to provide cloud-based access to digital entertainment, including music, movies and books—Billboard Magazine (May 21, 2011)

The business of music is complex and should be studied as a separate subject. Numerous books are available. A student should become familiar with record company agreements and music publishing contracts, in addition to learning the general "deal points" associated with performance contracts, entertainment union contracts, merchandising contracts, managers' agreements, talent agency agreements, Internet agreements, mobile agreements, and additional music industry contracts.

Overview of a Production Agreement

In popular music genres, especially hip-hop and R&B, producers are often composers and arrangers. Frequently, producers scout for artists to record the producer's songs. The artist signs an agreement with the producer's production company and proceeds to record three or four songs. The producer then shops a deal (solicits labels for a recording contract). If the artist receives an offer to sign with a label, a representative of the production company—usually an attorney—conducts contract negotiations with the distributing label. Under this model, the production company collects all advances and royalties and distributes the allotted share to the artist after deducting the production company's share. Some artists receive royalties directly from the distributing label, although the production company usually signs the deal with the distributor. (These items are usually negotiable.) The distribution company normally asks an artist to sign an inducement

♫ The artist's deal is negotiated when he or she signs an agreement with a production company. The terms of the distribution contract are normally coterminous with the artist's deal with the production company.

letter, which states that the artist agrees to fulfill all obligations stated in the production company agreement.

In addition to signing with a production company, most record companies also require an artist to sign an additional contract directly with them. If business problems develop between the production company and the label, the label needs protection.

If a manager represents the artist, the manager—usually in conjunction with an attorney—negotiates an agreement with the production company. The negotiation involves royalty splits, publishing issues, and deal points relating to future recordings for a label and/or distribution company.

The deal points and signing of agreements should be concluded prior to any recording. This helps to avoid potential contractual problems. If an artist achieves success and is dissatisfied with his or her royalty rate and/or additional deal points, most labels and production companies will be willing to renegotiate certain terms. In fact, renegotiation is almost expected. If an artist does not uphold the terms of a contract, the courts will enforce the original agreement even if the agreement is not a fair contract, by industry standards.

As part of a renegotiation the label will generally ask for an extension of the terms of the current contract. Some managers will not negotiate a new contract until the current contract has almost expired; that helps to avoid potential conflicts with the label. From an artist's viewpoint, the more influential the artist, the better position the artist is in to renegotiate an agreement and receive more favorable terms than were provided in the original contract.

An artist who has achieved financial and artistic success will most likely be offered a substantial advance, an increase in the royalty rate, and other significant concessions. Bidding wars often occur after an artist's agreement has expired or the expiration of the agreement is imminent. Assuming everything is equal to competitive offers, if an artist has a fruitful relationship with a label or a production company, the artist will most likely sign a new agreement with that label or production company. Some artists have maintained multiyear label associations, as in the case of Barbra Streisand with Columbia and Paul Simon with Columbia and later Warner Bros. Simon's newest album, *So Beautiful Or So What* (April 12, 2011), is released by the Concord Music Group.

Producer's Agreements

Music business contracts are multifaceted, and a music business attorney should represent a producer. (Deals vary from country to country.) Producers sign production agreements with labels, artists, or production companies. Some producers own production companies and license their recordings worldwide. They retain ownership of the master sound recordings.

A number of artists own production companies and compensate independent producers directly. For example, if an artist receives an advance (against royalties) of $500,000, from the label, to produce one album, he or she may negotiate a deal with a producer to produce one song. The artist may negotiate a deal with a producer to produce the song for $25,000. The $25,000 is recouped against the producer's royalty rate, which is generally 3 or 4% of the retail price or the producer does not receive royalties until the record company has recouped the entire cost of the album through retail sales, which have been paid for. The $25,000 can be a creative fee, with the production company paying all recording expenses, such as studio time, musicians, engineers, and cover design, or the producer is responsible for paying all expenses out of the allotted budget. The producer's fee, or advance against royalties, is the currency remaining after expenses. (It is difficult to negotiate a fee for a producer. Most advances received by producers are recoupable against record sales.)

Most labels pay a producer and an artist separately. A record label may hire five producers to work on one album, and each deal is individually negotiated. Artists' deals and producers' royalty calculations may be intertwined, or they may be separate agreements; it usually depends on the track record of each entity and the contract negotiations.

The following general deal points are negotiable:

- The average producer receives a 3 or 4% royalty rate, which is calculated by using the U.S. suggested retail list price (SRLP) of units sold.
- Royalties in foreign territories are calculated in different ways, such as based on the wholesale price. The Published Price to Dealers (PPD) is usually double the retail rate. For instance, 10% of wholesale is the equivalent to 5% of retail.

Most producers do not receive royalties until all recording costs

♫ Standard deductions before calculating royalties are as follows:

- Free goods are used for promotion. Many contracts stipulate that no more than 3 "free goods" can be shipped with each 10 CDs. (Downloads are also used as "free goods.")
- Reserves—labels pay royalties only on sales and not on the number of units that have been shipped. The industry standard is for labels to accept returns of 100%. No reserves are applied to downloading.
- A packaging deduction of 25% is standard. There is no packaging deduction for music distributed online.

♫ Some producers' royalties are recouped at the combined artists' and producers' "all-in" royalty rate.

have been recouped. Some producers receive royalties from the first record sold, after recording costs have been recouped. Royalties are paid beginning from the first record sold. The deal depends on the clout of the producer.

Most producers usually receive an advance against royalties; the advance payment is deducted from the producer's royalties or against the producers' and artists' royalties combined. Highly successful producers may receive a fee (in place of an advance), which is non-recoupable. The amount of the advance depends upon how "hot" the producer is. A successful producer can receive substantial advances or fees. A novice producer may receive an advance of $1,000 per song whereas a successful producer might receive $100,000 per song or more.

Some labels buy completed master sound recordings (masters). If a producer owns master sound recordings, he or she usually licenses the masters for a specified period of time. Each territory (worldwide) negotiates a separate contract, which includes an overall royalty rate and payment schedule. The royalty rate is divided between the producer and the artist, in accordance with the terms of the production agreement.

If a producer or a production company owns a master sound recording of an artist and licenses it to a label (with options for the label to license or record future albums), most labels will not guarantee that the producer will continue to produce the artist, either on the current album (if tracks are added or replaced), or on future albums. To compensate a producer or a production company for their initial financial risk, the producer or production company usually receives an override royalty payment for a specified time. For example, the producer or production company may receive a 2% royalty override on the next two albums. The deals are not standard and require negotiation. The amount of the override—if applicable—depends upon the effectiveness of the producer or production company.

♫ The royalty override is calculated on the same basis as a producer's and artist's royalty. For instance, the record label must recoup all recording costs before the royalty override is paid.

Producers usually receive half of their royalty rate for the sale of videos. Video sales are meager compared to album sales, and this is usually a standard calculation.

A producer's royalty rate normally remains constant in calculations of additional income generated by the sale of the recordings. The royalties from Internet sales, master ringtone and ringback sales, and other nontraditional sales, might be calculated at a lower base rate than the traditional record royalty rate, but the royalty percentages remain the same. Individual projects may require specific alterations.

Most producers' contracts contain the following stipulations:

- Producers normally receive half of their fee, or advance (against royalties), prior to recording; the remainder is paid when the label has approved and accepted the completed master sound recordings.
- The length of the agreement and any options for future production services are stated. For instance, a producer might stipulate that if the album sells more than 250,000 units, the producer will have the option to produce either all or part of the next album. A label might also request this option. The agreement might not have any commitments past the current project. Most producers are hired on a nonexclusive basis.
- Producers must abide by the recording budget. In some contracts, the overage is deducted from either the producer's or the artist's advance. If a producer is likely to exceed the budget, the producer should get permission, in writing. This assures the producer that the overage will not be deducted from the fee or advance against royalties. A 10% "safety net" is built into most producers' agreements. The overage is usually not deducted from the producer's royalties but from the artists' royalties.
- The producer's royalty rate is stipulated. Some producers receive royalty escalations, also known as bumps, based on sales. For instance, for sales that range from 1 to 100,000 units, the producer receives a 3% royalty rate (based on the suggested retail list price referred to as SRLP) and, for units exceeding 100,000 units, the royalty will increase to 4%. That royalty might apply only to the units over and above the initial 100,000 units, or it may increase the royalty rate, retroactive to record one.
- The producer agrees to abide by the rules stipulated in all applicable union contracts, primarily the American Federation of Musicians (AFM). This includes timely union-scale payments, health and welfare contributions, reporting sessions prior to the session, confirming that all musicians are in good standing with the union, and that all performers all legally allowed to work in the United States.
- The record company must approve all aspects of the production, including the mix. Labels might request a remix and may reject a production. Contracts state that the productions must be "technically satisfactory," or "technically and commercially" satisfactory. "Commercially" means that the record

♫ When calculating album sales, 10 downloads of single songs is considered an album. The industry term is Track Equivalent Albums. Royalties are not paid on "free goods." These are recordings that are given for promotional purposes.

label can reject a master recording if it does not think that there is a market for the recording. It is better to avoid this clause in a producer's or artist's agreement.

- Prior to recording, the songs (instrumentals) must be approved by the label and/or the artist.
- Some producers submit the record packaging liner notes, but more often they submit information, and a professional writer writes the liner notes.
- The wording and placement of the producer's album credit are stated, as in "produced by" on the CD front and/or back cover and in all advertising.
- The producer must submit all credits for engineers, studio names, musicians, background singers, graphic artists, liner note writers, and label executives, as well as the timing for each song.
- The producer provides clearances for all samples used on the masters and other necessary clearances for items controlled by the producer.
- An influential producer might include a "guaranteed release" clause. This means that a producer's production must be released for sale to the public within a stated time period, and put on the shelf. This is a difficult clause to enforce. For instance, the label can release 200 copies and fulfill the agreement. The definition of the term *released* is stated in the producer's contract and must be clearly stated or it will be difficult to enforce a breach of contract if a problem occurs.
- Most agreements stipulate that the label has the right to replace a producer at the label's discretion; in such case, the producer still receives a producer's fee or an advance.
- All contracts give the producer and artist the right to audit the books and records of the production or the distribution company. It is costly to audit, and there is usually a significant reason(s) to do so. Reasons to audit might include considerable sales and suspicion of inaccurate accounting practices.
- The producer allows the label (production company) to use their name, bio, and likeness in all advertising and public relations concerning the project.
- The producer agrees not to produce or co-produce a song he or she produced on the album for a negotiated period of time. The average term is 3 to 5 years.
- The producer agrees to indemnify the company against any legal claims. The company has the right to withhold the producer's royalties if there is legal action, or potential legal action, taken against the company and/or the producer.

Additional Concerns

The following deal points should be taken into consideration when producers make deals with production companies.

- A producer might sign an agreement with a production company before the production company makes a label deal. This can present several problems such as the production company will receive the royalty payments (an "all-in" deal) from the record label, and pay the producer and the artist their royalties from that payment. If the production company files for bankruptcy, what are the consequences? It is wise for a producer be compensated directly from the record label, which is not always possible. At a minimum, the producer's attorney must address this scenario. Attorneys might request a Letter of Direction (LOD) to be signed by the producer (or artist) and the production company. The letter directs the distribution company to pay the producer (or artist) directly.
- The producer's agreement might stipulate that royalties on foreign sales, record clubs, and other sources of revenue—where it is standard to receive a reduction on the royalty base—are X percentage lower than the 3% to 4% royalty received on traditional retail sales. The production company might negotiate deals with the record label that are lower than the deduction it is asking the producer (and artist) to adhere to. For instance, the producer agrees to receive 50% of their base royalty for record club sales, but the production company is only charged a 25% reduction from the record label. The fairest way to solve this potential problem is to base the producer's royalty rate on the agreement the production company makes with the record label or the distribution company. If the terms with the label are more favorable than the economic terms in the producer's agreement with the production company, the producer shares in the more favorable terms, and vice versa. This is referred to as a flow-through or pass-through provision.
- A producer or production company may have to the right to assign the agreement to another entity as long as the producer or production company fulfills its obligations under the terms of the original agreement with the label and/or artist.
- If an independent producer funds an album, the producer may be obligated to have the album released within a certain time period or the artist's agreement is automatically terminated.
- If the artist breaches the producer's agreement with the artist prior to the producer obtaining a label deal or distribution deal, the producer

might be entitled to recoup all reasonable costs spent to develop the artist's career—including attorney's fees—from the artist.

- If a disagreement occurs between the producer and the artist, it is wise to consent to *binding arbitration*. It is generally too costly to initiate a trial. The agreement will stipulate in which state proceedings will occur. (Most cases are settled out of court.)

Producer's Production Agreement

Some successful producers sign agreements with major or large independent distribution companies. The average contract is 3 years with options, by the distributor, to extend the agreement. The option pickups, by both parties, are usually determined by the success of the relationship. *It is crucial that the producer/production company retains ownership of the master sound recordings.*

The following are general terms included in such agreements.

- If the distributor or label markets and promotes the albums, the producer receives a lesser royalty rate than if the distributor merely distributes the albums.
- The territory, e.g., the world or specific territories such as the U.S. and Canada only.
- The number of albums per year that will be distributed. This usually depends on the clout of the producer and, of course, negotiations. Each signed artist will be expected to deliver a certain number of albums as determined by the production agreement. The artist/producer is obligated to deliver the agreed upon number of albums even if the producer's agreement with the distributor expires prior to the artist and producer fulfilling their contractual obligation.
- Some producers are permitted to sign a certain number of artists without the consent of the distributor. It the producer wants to sign additional artists, he or she requires the distributor's permission.
- Some deals are based upon the label or distributor having "The Right of First Refusal." This means that if the label/distributor does not choose to distribute an album, the producer has the right to license it to another distributor.
- The amount of a recoupable advance, if any, is stated.
- The royalty rate—In most distribution-only deals, the distributor receives a 25% royalty and the producer (production company) receives 75% out of which they pay the artists' royalties, publishers, marketing costs, and so forth. If the distributor also markets and promotes the albums, the percentages are negotiable. The average split is 50/50.

- Do not agree to cross-collateraliztion. Each album should be handled as a separate project. This means that if one album is successful and others do not recoup the production and, possibly, marketing costs, the distributor may apply the profit from the hit album to recoup losses from the albums that are not profitable.
- Although an agreement expires, if the label/distributor has not recouped their investment, the agreement remains intact until the label/distributor has recouped its costs.
- In the current market, most distribution deals include both physical (CDs) and digital distribution (downloading). If the producer has a digital distributor and the album is selling, some labels will negotiate a deal to distribute the physical CDs.
- When an artist is signed to a producer's production company, all terms that might be included in a distribution agreement must be included in the agreement with the producer. If all terms are not included and the producer warrants that his or her company has the rights to distribute the artist's albums without any restrictions, there could be a potential lawsuit.
- Some successful producers receive "Record One Royalties." This means that they do not wait until production costs are recouped before receiving royalties. Many labels will not agree to include this clause in the agreement.

Composer/Producers' Agreements in Film and Television

Composers of film and video music often also produce the music. The following are some of the terms included in the contracts:

- The score must be written specifically for the film or video. The composer's music must be timed to the picture, as compared to using "library music" or "source music" (prerecorded music, such as records).
- The composer is required to write a minimum and a maximum number of minutes of original music. For instance, the composer is obligated to compose "a minimum of 30 minutes music and a maximum of 45 minutes of music." This provision is important for several reasons:
- If the film or video is a low-budget project, the composer/producer's fee will most likely be "all-in." "All-in" includes the cost of producing the music; the composer's/producer's fee is included in this budget. If, for instance, the maximum number of minutes is 45 minutes and the director requests an additional 10 minutes of music, the additional production cost could be substantial.

- If the composer/producer is hired to work for a certain time period—based on the length of time estimated to compose and record the score—and the composer/producer was contracted to begin a new project on the projected completion date of the current project, writing and orchestrating additional music can present a contractual problem. If there is a possibility that the director might need the composer/producer's services for a time period that exceeds the time period stated in the original contract, a provision to this effect should be included in the agreement, and an additional budget agreed upon.
- A composer of motion picture scores will frequently produce a soundtrack album, often coproducing with the music supervisor. A producer's royalty must be negotiated and included in the composer/producer's agreement.
- Composers of video and film music are usually hired on a work-for-hire basis. (The studio and/or production company becomes the "author" of the work.) This usually means that the original author(s) will not receive royalty income. For example, when composing music for national commercials, the advertising agency and/or the client becomes the "author" of the work; the composer receives a fee and waives all additional rights to the material. (Most composers receive performance royalties even though they are not legally considered the authors.)

♫ A composer's rights must be negotiated prior to signing a work-for-hire agreement. Some accomplished composers negotiate "back-end royalties," which include a participation in profits ("points"), mechanical royalties, music library royalties, and copyright ownership.

The composer's credit on screen, in advertising campaigns, and other media must be stated in the contract.

As a composer, some of a music producer/supervisor's responsibilities include supplying the cue sheets, hiring musicians, booking studios, hiring engineers and music copyists, paying union contracts, cartage and rental fees. The exact budget and expectations of the producer/supervisor is stated in the contract.

♫ Labels previously paid royalties based on 90% of the sales price rather than on 100%. This was due to breakage of records, which does not exist any more. Do not agree to being paid on anything less than 100% of a sales royalty base—that is, 100% of sales, minus returns.

Conclusion

Recording contracts include detailed terms that address many areas of the business of recording. The record labels and production companies can sometimes calculate royalties in very "creative" ways. A music-business accountant should closely review royalty statements. If economically justified, an audit may be necessary.

Music supervisors' agreements and producers' agreements are likewise complex and require the services of a specialized music-business attorney.

Music Publishing Agreements

Many recording artists and producers are also songwriters or instrumental composers. The compositions are called "controlled compositions" because they are "controlled" by the author. Publishing companies are generally interested in signing songwriters whose songs will be recorded and released. Therefore, recording artists and producers who are songwriters are generally offered contracts from large publishing companies. It is difficult for songwriters who are not artists to get signed to major publishers unless they have a track record. The exception is in Nashville, where songwriting flourishes. Many country artists do not write; they rely on outside songwriters to provide material.

> ♫ Read the section devoted to Music Publishing prior to reading the following section.

The territory stated in most music publishing deals is either worldwide or territorial. Deal points vary between countries. Some writers sign with one company for the United States and Canada, and with various foreign publishers for the remainder of the world.

> ♫ Some small labels, or production companies, will not sign a songwriter-artist without sharing in at least 50% of the publishing rights. This is called a co-publishing agreement.

Advances are given to established songwriters and composers who can guarantee recorded music releases. Unless a songwriter displays an unusual ability to write commercial songs, it is difficult to negotiate an advance against songwriter royalties.

Some large companies retain staff writers, who receive a weekly or monthly advance against royalties. Royalty statements are generally issued on a semiannual basis. The following general deal points are negotiable:

> ♫ Major film companies own the rights to all of the music specifically composed for the feature films and television programs they produce. (In rare instances, the composer might retain some of the publishing rights.)

- A writer assigns 50% of the copyrighted composition(s) to the publisher. Most publishers have the right to administer the compositions without permission from the writer, as long as the integrity of the copyright is protected. For instance, a publisher would not have the right to place a song in a pornographic movie without the writer's permission. In some contracts, the publisher needs permission from the writer(s) to place a song in a film or television program (synchronization license) or for uses other than standard recordings, which are governed by the law and require publishers to issue compulsory licenses.

Some publishing companies receive a fee for administering copyrights or a publishing catalogue. The fees range from 10% to 20%. The average rate is 15%.

♫ Administration includes collecting, paying writers, and issuing statements.

Publishers agree to pay royalties derived from the following sources.

♫ Publishing companies make administration deals with foreign sub-publishers to administer their catalogues in foreign territories.

- Mechanical rights, electronic transcription, reproducing rights, motion picture and television synchronization rights, performance rights (public performances), ringtones, ringbacks and other sources of publishing revenue.

Terms included in a Compulsory License Agreement

- Title of composition, also referred to as a musical work
- Name of author(s)
- Publisher(s)
- Date of Release
- Licensee Contact Information
- Licensee's Signature
- Fiscal Year of Licensee
- Date of Initial Distribution
- Label Name
- Catalog Number(s)
- Phonorecord Configuration, e.g., Digital Phonorecord Deliveries

If a client has a licensing agreement with the Harry Fox Agency, the licensing request will go direction to the HFA. The HFA will contact their client.

A client will receive a Notice of Intention to Obtain a Compulsory License. This license will include the manner in which the licensor will be compensated. If the master sound recording will also be used, the licensee will negotiate a separate agreement with the owner of the master sound recording as well as receiving a licensee from the proper performing rights society(s).

Synchronization License Agreement

The following are some of the terms included in synchronization (sync) licenses. Each of the following terms is explained in detail when the agreements are written.

- Composition—Name of composition
- Grant of Rights—Explains the content of the rights, e.g., non-exclusive, exclusive, any restrictions, etc.
- License Fee—States an agreed upon fee
- Out-of-Context Trailer Option—Agreement to use the agreed upon music in trailers. This paragraph states specifically how the music can be used. (Most often this refers to a song.)
- Performing Rights Requirements—PROs (BMI, ASCAP, and SESAC in the U.S.) must be paid when the content is performed on television, the Internet, cable, and additional content providers.
- Warranty—Licensor warrants that it owns the content.
- Indemnifications—Each party indemnifies the other party from any and all claims.
- The composition(s) cannot be altered without permission of the publishers and the authors.
- Screen Credit—The exact screen credit is stipulated such as "Name of Song," authors, publisher(s), and so forth.
- Options
- A music cue sheet must be presented to the Licensor within a stipulated time period, e.g., 60 days.
- If a party claims a breach of contract, the agreement stipulates in which state the disagreement will be adjudicated, e.g., California, New York, etc. The party claiming the breach must inform the opposite party and give them a short time period to settle the claim before the breach becomes an official breach.
- This paragraph states that the terms of the agreement are binding.
- Right to audit

Some very basic synchronization agreements are sometimes written, especially for television. These agreements are often referred to as Terms-of-Agreement. (These agreements are sometimes used to negotiate the seminal terms after which a more formal agreement is written.)

The agreement will typically state:

- The name of the program
- The episode number
- The name of the composition(s) being licensed and the publisher(s)
- The fee

- Term, e.g., 3 years
- A description of the scene in which the music will be used
- The timing, e.g., 1 minute
- Territory, e.g., the world
- Media, basic cable television, the Internet, DVDs, etc.
- Share, e.g., 25%
- Options

♫ BMI, ASCAP, and SESAC, the performance-rights societies in the U.S., collect performance income for artists and publishers.

- Sheet music sales
- "Fakebooks," folios, and similar publication sales
- Foreign rights (if included)
- Internet sales and general digitally transmitted sales, such as ringtones and ringbacks
- Additional publishing income derived from the songs or compositions

♫ When songwriters are hired to write a song for a film, they are usually paid a fee, in addition to receiving mechanical and performance royalties. A songwriter with clout might be able to retain ownership of a percentage of the publishing rights. The same is true of extremely successful film composers. In general, major film companies retain ownership of the publishing rights and always retain the administration rights. This enables them to conclude deals without having to consult with the authors.

Work-for-Hire

Songwriters and composers, such as film-music composers, are often hired as work-for-hire employees. The employer is considered the "author" and owns the work(s). Agreements to compose music for commercials, corporate videos, and other specific commissioned music, are usually written as a work-for-hire. The employers generally provide lump-sum, or flat-fee, compensation to the original authors if they do not participate in royalty income.

The U.S. Copyright Act describes work-for-hire as follows: "A work specially ordered or commissioned for use as a contribution to a collective work, as a part of a motion picture or other audiovisual work, as a translation, as a supplementary work, as a compilation, as an instructional text, as a text, as answer material for a test, or as an atlas, if the parties expressly agree in a written instrument signed by them that the work shall be considered a work made for hire."

Work-for-hire agreements call for the employer to become "the author." The original author has no future rights to the composition(s). When an author "assigns a copyright" to a third party, such as a publishing company or film company, the rights revert back to the original author after thirty-five years. This is called a "reversion right."

Conclusion

Most publishing deals that involve "controlled compositions" pay 75% of the minimum statutory rate; this is standard in the United States. It is advisable to consult a music-business attorney, specializing in music publishing, before signing a publishing agreement. The agreements are intricate and the author needs a competent negotiator.

Recording Artist Agreements

Recording artist agreements are lengthy and involved. Artists are advised to hire a music-business attorney to represent them.

With respect to recording agreements, the following general deal points are negotiable.

- Artists sign either a worldwide exclusive deal or territorial deals. Most major labels want to sign artists to an exclusive worldwide agreement. Territorial deals usually occur when a small or midsized label signs an artist and licenses the master recordings to various territories for limited negotiable time periods. Major labels might also license tracks for select territories.
- Artists usually sign 3 to 4 year recording contracts with an obligation to record 1 album per year. The label has the right to pick up successive 1 year options. After the initial contract period, if the option is not picked up, the artist is released from the agreement. The label only informs the artist if the contract agreement is being terminated. The label is not obligated to inform the artist that the agreement is still valid.
- Advances are given to deserving artists. Advances are not standard. They can range from $1,000 to over $1,000,000.
- An artist is generally expected to record a minimum of 50 minutes of music per album.
- Recording costs and recoupable advances are deducted from royalties. Labels generally pay the recording costs, unless it is a licensing deal, in which case there is normally no advance paid. If the album does not generate enough sales to recoup the label's investment, the artist is not obligated to return the advance. However, the advance is recoupable from later albums that make a profit.
- Net artists' royalties (after deductions of producers' royalties) vary between 8% and 12%, based on the suggested retail list price (SRLP) in the United States on records sold and not returned and are higher for established artists. Royalty rates increase as options are picked up or increases are based on sales.

If an artist signs with a production company and the company licenses the master recordings to a record label, the artist receives his or her royalties either directly from the distribution company or from the production company.

> ♫ Most foreign territories calculate royalties based on the wholesale price. With this formula, artists usually receive double the SRLP royalty rate.
>
> Classical music royalty rates are generally less than popular music rates. The average royalty is 7 ½% to 10%, and recording costs are not deducted from the royalties, but advances are recouped; royalties are calculated from the first record sold.

The record label or production company owns the rights to the master recordings.

Bands are usually signed collectively—as a group—and individually; each member is considered exclusive recording artists. If a group member wants to record a solo album, it must be distributed through the label. If the label is not interested, it will often grant permission for the artist to record for another label. Sometimes the parent label is willing to accept a royalty override.

> ♫ The artist's term of contract is usually coterminous with the terms of the distribution agreement.

> ♫ Sometimes, the rights to the master recordings revert back to the artist after a predetermined time period.

- In writing, a group member must notify the label if he or she plans to leave the group.
- The member cannot use the group name or a similar name.
- The member cannot advertise that he or she was a former member of the group until after 6 months following departure from the group.
- The label has the right to approve a new group member (for recording) but cannot unreasonably withhold approval. The new group member must sign the existing exclusive recording agreement.
- If the label does not approve a replacement member, the group has the right to terminate the agreement.
- Within a specified number of days, usually 90, following the departure of a group member, the label has the option to require the member to record for the label.
- If the group is financially unrecouped and the departing member remains on the label, a pro-rata share of the group's unrecouped position will be charged against the departing member's new royalties. For instance, if the group consists of three members, the new member will be charged one-third of the unrecouped deficit.

- If the group disbands, the label is required to pay royalties only for past albums and is under no other obligation to record new albums or to honor the terms of the recording agreement.
- The group must legally own the group name.

Most agreements contain a *controlled composition* clause. If the artist writes his or her songs or *controls* the compositions written by other writers, the record label usually pays 75% of the minimum statutory mechanical royalty rate. Artists with a substantial sales history might receive the full statutory mechanical royalty rate. On January 1, 2006, the statutory rate in the United States increased to 9.1 cents per song per disc (up to 5 minutes) for a 2 year period. This rate applies to records that are "made and distributed."

Artists cannot rerecord any composition recorded for the label for 5 years after the recording has been delivered to the label or three years after the contract has expired, whichever is later. This is called a "rerecording restriction." (This restriction is sometimes negotiable.)

Record labels pay royalties on the following:

- Units sold via normal distribution channels (not on free goods)
- Internet sales, video streaming, and additional digital sales, such as master ringtones and ringbacks (songs played on mobile telephones)
- Synchronization master sound recording use licenses (for film and television use and other audiovisual uses)
- Music video direct sales (no payments are received for music clips and other promotions uses)
- Foreign sales, including all third-party sales

Record labels do not pay royalties on "free goods," such as records or videos given to reviewers or DJs, or videos given for promotional purposes.

Record labels pay royalties on any additional income-producing agreements.

Royalty statements are issued on a semiannual basis.

Cross-collateralization, from album to album, is standard in most agreements. If an album has not recouped production costs, advances, or other costs, the expenses are cross-collateralized (recouped) against the next album(s) or a former album. Unfortunately, this can become a downhill spiral, and the artist might never receive royalties. (Artists should avoid having unrecouped record advances taken from publishing royalties.)

> ♫ Most artists' agreements deduct 50% of the cost of video production from their royalties, and also deduct 50% of the money spent on marketing and independent promotion.

Below is a possible model being considered by some record contracts:

- A 4 album deal.
- Advances will be paid throughout the length of the agreement. Currently, it is industry practice to pay advances upon the signing of a contract.
- Advances will not be recoupable.
- An equal split on nontraditional sales between the artist and the label.
- Monthly statements will be issued in place of biannual statements.
- A 15% royalty, which is high, will become standard. (Royalty rates currently average 12% in the United States, with increases based upon sales and the length of contract.)
- The standard 25% CD packaging deduction will be eliminated for all electronically distributed music, thereby increasing the base for determining artists' royalties.
- Reserves for returns will be eliminated for electronically distributed music.

Labels are realizing less income from recordings due to the problems previously stated. They are hoping to recoup their investments by creating new income-producing sources. New agreements are being structured as partnerships between labels and artists.

"360" recording contracts, previously discussed, have become the standard business model as of the writing of this book.

Overview of a Video Game Agreement

This overview is not intended to be a legal document. It merely states terms that are included in most agreements. All music producers/supervisors should be aware of the following:

A composer or music producer/supervisor working on a game, in any capacity, is required to sign a confidentiality (non-disclosure) agreement. A game developer will not disclose any information until this agreement is signed. The agreement remains in force even if the composer or supervisor rejects the projects or is not offered the project.

The agreement will state:

- The name of the game
- The characters
- The marketing, advertising, and promotions strategy
- Anything related to the graphics
- Technical information
- The game platform(s)

- The composer's fee
- The music budget, including the payment schedule
- The completion period
- A work-for-hire agreement (most game developers own the rights to the music)
- Ancillary rights
- Credits
- Litigation
- Expenses

Conclusion

The details of the agreement are beyond the scope of this book. Hire an entertainment attorney who has expertise in music for video games before signing a contract.

Personal Management Agreement

Music producers often have personal managers. Busy producers do not have the time to analyze prospective projects or to negotiate agreements. Managers and attorneys will, generally, get the best possible terms.

The following are the general terms included in most Personal Management Agreements:

- The length of the agreement, e.g., 3 years.
- The manager is exclusive. He/she may agree to only manage a producer's recording career. For example, if the producer is also a film composer, he or she might have a separate manager.
- The agreement will state the duties of the manager, e.g., analyzing projects, negotiating, compensation, and so forth.
- The manager's commission is usually off of the gross. This term may vary dependent upon the manager's performance. An average commission is 15% of the gross. (The gross must be defined.)
- The producer might agree that the manager has the right to handle all publicity and advertising, with the producer's written approval.
- The manager might receive all monies generated by the producer and distribute the income according to the terms of the agreement.
- Some managers make loans to their clients. For instance, a manager might finance demos for a new artist.
- The agreement will state that the manager is *not* a talent agent but represents the artist to the talent agent.
- Some managers are also business managers and invest a producer's money. (Some managers are often attorneys and/or CPAs.)
- If there are legal difficulties, most managers and producers agree to enter binding arbitration.

Conclusion

A Personal Management agreement contains many terms not mentioned above. Also, each category mentioned might have multiple sections, within the final agreement. An attorney should negotiate on behalf of the producer.

Business Plan

"360" recording agreements (explained in a previous chapter) have encouraged music business entrepreneurs to form, primarily, web-based record labels. Funding cash may be needed to cover recording, marketing and promotions, salaries, website development, and other related costs essential to operate a label. This requires a business plan. The following are items that must be addressed in the plan:

> ♫ Do not start a record label or music publishing company without experience in the industry(s) or hiring experienced executives.

- Mission Statement—What is the company trying to achieve? This statement should be brief and easy to comprehend. The writer must assume that numerous potential investors/lenders do not understand the music industry.
- Present an overall view of the music business.
- The Executive Summary provides information about the management team. This is the most essential section of the plan. If the executives do not have the proper experience and success, it will be problematic to attract investors/lenders. What percentage of stock do the owners control? This should be broken down into individual shares.
- Why should investors or lenders fund the label?
- Will they be equity partners or shareholders?
- Why and how will the label increase in value? State the strategic goals, and forecast revenues and expenses, which will most likely increase if the business grows.
- Does the company own both a label and a music publishing company? If so, explain the sources of revenue that can be obtained from publishing revenues such as synchronization and transcription licenses and mechanical royalties.
- Is the concept of the label unique?
- Identify the *Target Demographic*. For instance, the music will appeal to a young demographic between the ages of 14 and 21.
- State a *Projection of Profits* and *Possible Losses* over a determined time, e.g., 5 years. (Do not make the projections too aggressive.)

- How much capital are the principal executives personally investing in the company?
- List job descriptions, which should include the title, responsibilities, required education, and salary; include benefits and other pertinent information.
- What is the projected return for the investors and/or lenders and for how long will they receive a return on their investment? Not all investors receive a return in perpetuity.
- *Budget*—The budget includes such items as salaries, advertising, marketing and promotions, website development, maintenance, accounting fees, legal fees, rent/lease, phones, office supplies, and other essential items. Most projections cover a span of 5 years. It should also include a "cushion" for unexpected expenditures.
- *Break-Even Forecast*—Although it is a difficult task to project the future, potential investors/lenders want to study a forecast prior to reviewing a business plan. Be conservative!
- List the biographies of the artists signed to the label and the publishing company.
- List merchandising and touring opportunities.
- Use graphics, if necessary, e.g., pie and bar charts.
- Using bullet points and numbers makes it easier for a reader to navigate the document.

The plan should not be too verbose. Only include necessary information. Investors/lenders read many proposals and do not have time to read documents containing unnecessary material. State the facts as simply as possible. Use headings to aid the reader in finding seminal information.

As suggested by author Mike McKeever, a complete *Business Plan* should be organized in the following order. (An option is to write a condensed version and add information if requested.)

- Title Page
- Plan Summary
- Table of Contents
- Problem Statement
- Business Description
- Business Accomplishments
- Marketing Plan
- Sales Revenue Forecast
- Profit and Loss Forecast
- Capital Spending Plan
- Cash Flow Forecast
- Future Trends

- Risks Facing Your Business
- Personnel Plan
- Specific Business Goals
- Personal Financial Statement
- Personal Background
- Appendix

The potential of attracting funding is greater if the label has achieved some success prior to approaching potential investors or lenders. It may be advantageous to hire a professional business plan writer and consultant. For a small venture, it may be too costly; therefore, plan carefully and do not pursue any venture without thoroughly understanding the risks involved in starting and/or sustaining a business.

Conclusion

Due to the continuing evolution of the worldwide music industry, standard artists' contracts will continue to change. Illegal peer-2-peer file sharing, as well as physical pirating, has caused record labels to rethink the structure of artists' agreements. Some new agreements include labels sharing in publishing, merchandising, and live-performance income.

Music Video Agreements

The right to shoot music videos is included in all artists' contracts. When artists agree to sign a recording contract, they are simultaneously giving the label the rights to sell and distribute the artists' music videos. (The definition of the term "record" in a recording agreement includes the video rights.) Some contracts include separate provisions for music videos. The following are some of the deal points that are, or should be, included in record agreements.

- The label exclusively owns the rights to the videos and the artist cannot make music videos for other companies during the term of the recording agreement.
- Labels usually agree to finance one video per album. For superstars, labels commit to more than one video per album.
- Music publishers (and authors) must grant companies the rights (*mechanical licenses*) to use music in videos. *Mechanical licenses* are automatically granted for recordings but must be negotiated for use in videos. These rights allow the label to sell the videos.

- Recording agreements state that the video rights to compositions controlled by the artist, or controlled compositions, are automatically granted to the label without charge.
- Publishers issue *synchronization licenses*. Synchronization licenses allow labels to use the music with the videos. The license is automatically issued to the label (upon request) for any controlled compositions.
- On average, 50% of video production costs are recouped against artists' royalties. Most agreements state that if the costs are not recouped against the sale of the videos, the costs are then recouped against the artists' record royalties.
- Record labels absorb the remaining 50% of production costs. Recording contracts define the term *production costs*.
- Most artists' video royalties equal one-half of the label's net receipts. Music videos that are sold are normally licensed to third-party video distributors. If the label distributes the videos, artists' royalty agreements can become complicated, and some terms are negotiable. As in any contract, the terms of the agreement are dependent on the "power" of the artist.

Film composers often produce their scores. The music supervisor may co-produce. Film composers' agreements include the following terms:

- The score is defined as music that is used as background music, main and end title music, the orchestrations and arrangements, as well as additional required music.
- The composer is required to compose music that is in synchronization with the film.
- Composers, primarily working on independent film, may be required to also act as music supervisors. One of the responsibilities of a music supervisor is to select and license songs for the film.
- They may be required to attend the final dubbing session.
- The composer is required to write X number of minutes for an agreed upon fee. If extra music is needed, additional compensation is negotiated.
- The dates of the composer's services are stipulated.
- The studio usually owns the publishing rights. Composers of independent films might be able to retain the ownership of their music.
- The producer has the right to use the composer's name when publicizing the film.
- The wording of the screen credit is stipulated, such as full screen credit. Composers want their names included in all advertising and exploitation of the film.

- The composer agrees to allow the score to be used on a soundtrack album. Most composers receive performance royalties and producer's royalties from soundtrack albums.
- Studio films usually pay all expenses plus the composer's fee. Many independent filmmakers pay the composer one fee and the composer must deliver a complete score for that fee. This is referred to as a "buy-out."
- The composer must warrant that he or she has the right to enter into the agreement.
- If there is a breach or default of contract by the composer, the film company (producer) has the right to terminate the agreement. The same is true if the film company creates a breach or default of the agreement. Either party agrees to inform the other of a breach or default of contract and provides them with a time period to solve the problem.
- The film company is not obligated to use the music in the final film but must pay all fees and expenses.
- The state in which any legal matter will be handled is included in the agreement.
- The agreement is binding.
- Some composers receive "back-end" royalties. These consist of performance royalties (BMI, ASCAP, or SESAC) and mechanical royalties, from the sales of the music, which include album sales and music library sales and/or licenses.

Conclusion

Video agreements should be negotiated by an attorney. Video sales have proved to be disappointing, and music videos are generally considered to be a marketing tool. Artists receive exposure on television, in movie theaters, on the Internet, and in clubs. Radio play (terrestrial, Internet, cable, and Satellite), video play, and live performances are necessary to generate sales.

Record Distribution Agreements

Independent record labels are distributed either by the distribution arm of major labels or by independent record distributors. Distributors only "sell" the completed CDs to buyers; record labels are responsible for producing the recordings, advertising, marketing, promotions, public relations, tour support, video production, artwork, and so on.

Distributors sell to retail outlets, "one-stop" distributors that sell to small retail outlets, rack jobbers, or firms that lease floor space in stores, Internet companies that sell physical product, and additional outlets. Some labels manufacture the CDs and ship them to the distributor for distribution. This is done so that the label knows the number of CDs that have been manufactured and can therefore keep an accurate accounting of sales.

The following are some of the deal points included in distribution agreements.

- The label pays the distributor an average of 18% to 22% as a distribution fee and may pay as high as 25%, if the distributor also manufactures the CDs as part of a P&D (Pressing & Distribution) deal.
- The term of agreements is negotiable. If the deal is to exclusively distribute the label, the initial term might be for 2 or 3 years. If the product does not sell a minimum negotiated number of units per year, the distributor has the right to terminate the deal.
- Some distributors want to select only selected CDs for distribution. (The industry term is to "cherry-pick.") It may be wise to allow a distributor to distribute one CD and "test the waters." If the relationship is not successful, neither party is obligated to continue the relationship. If the product is successful, a long-term agreement might follow.
- Many distributors will not conclude a label agreement without investigating the finances of the distributed label. They want to be assured that the label has the financial resources to advertise, market, and promote the product.
- The territory might be North America (United States and Canada), selected territories, or for worldwide distribution. If the agreement states North America only, the label will most likely make either selected foreign deals or agree for one distributor to distribute in all territories outside of North America.

♫ Sony closed the company's largest CD manufacturing plant at the end of March, 2011. The closing is mostly due to the increase in digital downloading and a decrease in CD sales. Between 2008 and 2009, CD sales were down 18%. 300 employees were fired.

♫ Most distribution fees are calculated by using net sales as a base. The distributor is not paid on "free goods."

Conclusion

One of the dangers of manufacturing CDs is that the record companies may manufacture too many copies. Retailers are allowed to return 100% of unsold copies, and the record company must accept all returns. This can be costly. The agreement should state the number of CDs pressed. If radio stations in a region are playing a record, the video is getting substantial hits on YouTube, the market has been inundated with public relations and advertising, and the artist is touring, the risk of manufacturing too many copies lessens.

Distribution agreements should be negotiated by a music-business attorney.

Selling a Master Sound Recording

If a record label wants to purchase a master recording, the deal points can vary. The following are some of the possible scenarios.

- The production company may ask for a substantial advance, in addition to recouping the production costs. This means that if the artist has "made some noise" in the marketplace via radio, Internet, cable, television performances, regional sales, or performance income, several labels will most likely be vying to purchase, or license, the master sound recording. They will also want options to record additional albums. If the artist has an influential manager and/or agent, a major label might offer a large advance, although in the current market this is highly unlikely. The purchase price will be based on the industry standards at the time of the purchase. An agreement will include a price for the current album, plus an advance for additional albums.
- If an artist is new and has not been previously exposed to the public, a label might offer an advance equal to the cost of the production, or it may not offer an advance but offer a guarantee of promotion, marketing, advertising, and distribution; labels try to reduce financial risk.
- The label might not offer an advance but guarantee a release within a stipulated time period. Royalties will be paid beginning with the first royalty statement.
- Labels often lease a catalogue for a negotiated number of years after which the catalogue is returned to the owner. This could be viewed as "ownership" for a specified time period.

Conclusion

♫ This scenario is analogous to sub-publishing agreements, which involve licenses to sub-publishers for negotiated limited time periods.

Because of problems in the global music industry, labels are less likely to offer large advances for master recordings, unless there is a sensible reason to do so. For instance, if an album had sizable sales in a region, this indicates that it might attain significant sales nationally. Regional distribution acts as a test market. If a local band attracts a sold-out crowd each time the artist performs in a particular region, that indicates the artist has a loyal following, which can lead to sales. The artist might embark on a U.S. tour, opening for a headlining artist. Touring exposes artists to potential buyers.

Master licensing and purchasing agreements are complex and should be negotiated by a music business attorney.

Additional Agreements

In the United States, record labels and production companies have to adhere to certain union agreements, if they are signatories. It is advisable for producers to study the following agreements:

American Federation of Musicians (AFM)

The AFM protects the interests of musicians, music copyists, contractors, arrangers, orchestrators, and conductors. The union provides a list of scale payments for recording sessions, live performances, reuse payments for various forms of recordings, pension, health plans, and additional protections.

Screen Actors Guild (SAG)

SAG represents singers (as well as actors and other performers) when the singers' performances are used in film, television, commercials, industrials, corporate videos, and music videos. SAG negotiates and implements scale and reuse payments, pension and health plans, as well as additional protections for the membership.

American Federation of Television and Radio Artists (AFTRA)

AFTRA represents singers (as well as actors, broadcasters, and other performers) whose performances are used in live and taped television and radio programs, sound recordings, non-broadcast industrial programming, and new and emerging technologies, such as CD-ROMs. AFTRA negotiates and implements scale and reuse payments, pension and health plans, in addition to additional protections.

Concert Promotion Agreements

Concert promotion contracts are complex. Below is a list of some of the items included in most agreements:

- The financial terms—fees based on a percentage of gross receipts, a straight fee, and when the fees have to be paid.

- The name and address of the venue.
- The date(s) of the performance(s) and the length of the performance(s)
- If the promoter is paying for the transportation, the details must be incorporated in the agreement.
- The time of the sound and lighting check. The sound-reinforcement requirements (live sound) and lighting requirements are often addressed in a separate rider to the main agreement.
- Security arrangements for the venue and for the artists are also covered.
- Most popular artists arrive with truckloads of equipment. The promoter usually provides workers to load and unload the equipment. Enough time must be allocated to properly set up.
- In states adhering to union agreements, the promoter must agree to the terms of the agreements. (These are states with "no-right-to-work" under local law; those states do not require workers to be union members.)
- Space must be provided in the venue so that the artists' representatives can sell merchandise, such as programs, t-shirts, and hats. If the concert promoter shares in the merchandising profits, there is usually a separate agreement.
- Provide adequate parking attendants.
- Some agreements include a clause stating the number of advertisements the promoter is obligated to purchase and where the advertising will be placed.
- Some agreements state that the promoter will perform public relations services and launch special promotions designed to attract ticket buyers; this might include designing special posters and sending mailers and arranging for interviews at radio and television stations.
- Some large corporations, such as Pepsi, sponsor concert tours for popular artists. All details associated with a sponsorship are addressed in the agreement. The sponsors' names are included in all advertising and public relations surrounding the concert tours. The corporate names are also displayed in various locations within the concert venues.
- Popular performing artists always have riders, which include specific items that must be adhered to for the contract to be considered binding. Usually included are: food, dressing-room parameters, showers, and security guards. Almost anything can, and is, included in a rider.

Author's note: There is an artist who requires the toilet in the dressing room to be filled with rose petals!

Conclusion

In the United States, certain states do not require musicians or singers to join unions. However, if a production company is a signatory to union contracts, the singers and musicians are required to be union members or to receive the same scale payments as union members.

Calculating scale payments can be difficult. It is advisable to have people familiar with union agreements compute the payments and fill out and submit the contracts. Companies specialize in this process. Mistakes or late payments can result in large fines.

Assignment

Review publishing and artists' recording agreements, which can be found in numerous books and online. Construct a fair and realistic publishing contract and an exclusive artist's contract. Design the agreements for an artist-songwriter who is signing with a small independent label.

Assemble a budget to promote a band in a small theater.

♫ If possible, consult with a music-industry attorney. To learn contract negotiation, read numerous agreements and write your own agreements. Do not offer these agreements to artists without consulting with an attorney. Generally, your agreement will be used by an attorney as a model for a proper legal agreement.

♫ Request a copy of standard contracts issued by concert promoters. Call the unions (if applicable) and inquire about the cost of scale payments for workers in various jobs.

22

Album Production Budget

Budget items vary from project to project, but the basic line items rarely change. As a practical exercise, prepare two budgets: one based on paying union scale to musicians and singers and the other based on "standard" nonunion rates. ("Standard" nonunion rates vary from state to state in the U.S.)

Calculate the budget based upon a 12-song album recorded by a mixture of live musicians and synthesizer programmers. Submit a budget for each song and a total for the entire album. Not all tracks require the same line items or require the same number of hours to complete. Include applicable taxes, which differ in each state. The budget should be detailed. It must account for the following items, as well as any additional potential charges, that are specific to the project.

Studio Time

Divide the studio time into hourly charges.

- Recording time
- Mixing time

Albums might be recorded and mixed in numerous studios. Base your budget on an average studio's hourly rate or daily rate. Request rate cards from several studios. Most studios offer quantity discounts. It is cost effective to purchase studio time in blocks—usually 12-hour days.

Musicians

- Figure AFM (American Federation of Musicians) union-scale payments. The payments must include pension contribution, health and welfare contribution, Recording Trust Fund payments, and other applicable contributions. Request a copy of the AFM scale payment schedule. Study union payment procedures.
- Some musicians request double-scale union payments. (Calculating double-scale payments can be complicated. Study the union contract.) As part of the exercise, include several musicians at double scale. Contractors, leaders, and conductors always receive double scale, and contractors must be paid if a certain number of musicians are contracted. (Check union rules; not all additional contributions—health contributions are one example—are doubled as a result of a double-scale payment.)
- Overtime payments—Union scale provides for overtime payments; consult the union rules and scale payment schedule, and include several overtime payments.
- Cartage fee—Certain large instruments require the company to pay for instrument transportation (e.g., harp and double bass).

♫ Call the AFM and request a copy of the most current standard recording agreement. Request a schedule of payments.

Lead Singer Fee

Lead singers for sound recordings (albums or singles) are paid through the musicians' union (AFM). Royalty artists' fees differ from that of a singer who is a work-for-hire employee and receives no royalties. Overdubs warrant additional fees. (Singers are paid through SAG when recording music that will be used in films; they are paid through AFTRA when recording music that will be used on DVDs and radio projects, such as commercials.) Study union agreements for scale payment schedules.

Background Singers' Fees

Background singers for recordings used on records are paid through the AFM. There are additional fees for overdubbing. Consult the union agreement for proper rates. A contractor may be required, depending on the number of singers.

Tape Costs

If analog tape is used, which is highly unusual, substantial tape charges will be incurred. (Producers often record and edit in a digital program such as Pro Tools, and transfer the mixes to analog tape prior to mastering.)Estimate the number of tape reels needed for the album. If twelve songs are being recorded, at least twelve reels will most likely be used. Calculate the cost of making safety copies of tapes prior to shipping the original masters to various studios for overdubs or mixing in this scenario. Figure the cost of making a composite reel of the final takes before shipping; it might be possible to fit all of the takes (final recordings) onto two reels. (If you budget for digital tape, the calculations will be different.)

> ♫ It is cost-effective to create stereo mixes, or several stereo mixes, on the multitrack, before shipping a tape for overdubs. This leaves many open tracks for overdubbing. When the tape is returned, bounce the overdubs onto the master tape.

Copies

Include the cost of making digital or analog copies of the audio and the data. Estimate the cost of daily rough mixes, final mixes, and backup storage copies. The information, both audio and data, can be stored on DVDs, hard drives, and cloud storage. It is best to ALWAYS store data in multiple locations.

Mastering Costs

Include the cost of mastering and making copies in the budget. Call several mastering labs and request rate sheets. Mastering costs are usually based on an hourly studio rate, which includes the services of a mastering engineer. (For independent projects, some mastering engineers will negotiate an "all-in" deal and not charge an hourly rate.)

Music Copying

Music copyists' fees are paid based on the AFM union scale for copyists. The AFM agreement must be studied to determine the exact scale. The payment is based on the number of pages copied.

♫ Some copyists charge more than scale.

Producers' Creative Fees

Creative fees or advances against royalties vary, according to the demand for the producer and how in-demand he or she is at the time of the production. As part of this exercise, calculate an average fee (or advance against royalties) for a midline producer. Creative fees, or advances, are usually calculated on a per-song basis.

♫ Research producers' fees. Advances are recoupable against producers' royalties.

Orchestration, Arranging, and/or Programming Fees

It is possible that each of the above fees becomes a separate item within the budget. It depends on the requirements of the project. For instance, a Michael Bublé album might need the services of an orchestrator, an arranger, and a synthesizer programmer.

Engineering Fees

Most independent recording engineers charge an hourly fee. Engineers who are contracted to record and/or mix an entire album might offer a reduced rate. Negotiating an "all-in" rate (one fee) is rare because it is difficult to estimate the total number of engineering hours required. (It might be feasible if the engineer receives a royalty. The "fee" then becomes an advance against royalties.)

Instrument and Additional Rentals

Instrument-rental companies supply large and unusual instruments, additional microphones, and special signal processing gear for recording sessions. (High profile engineers usually own equipment and charge an additional rental fee.) Calculate the number of hours for which additional equipment will be needed. (The average union session runs 3 hours.) Musical-instrument rental companies are located in major markets; they also rent audio gear. (Search online for rate sheets.) Estimate additional gear rentals on a per-song basis.

Travel

Calculate all travel (airline tickets, auto rentals, car service, etc.), food, and hotel expenses. For this exercise, assume that a band has to travel to New York from the Midwest.

Miscellaneous Expenses

Figure at least 10% of the budget for unexpected additional expenses.

Video Production Costs

This is usually a separate budget.

Conclusion

All union contracts are intricate. It is wise to hire a professional who knows how to properly calculate the various union scale payments. If a contract is not filed on time or if there are mistakes, large fines might be levied against the production company.

All musicians and singers are required to be *in good standing* with the unions (e.g., dues are paid) prior to recording sessions. Companies are fined for hiring musicians or singers whose dues are delinquent, for not reporting a session prior to the session (informing the unions that a session is going to take place on a certain date and in a specific location), or additional reasons. The items included in this budget are standard. Add additional items, if necessary.

23

An Opinion

> The life of the arts, far from being an interruption, a distraction, in the life of a nation, is close to the center of a nation's purpose—and is a test of the quality of a nation's civilization.
>
> —John F. Kennedy

Global purchases of CD-Rs (recordable CDs) have far exceeded the purchase of prerecorded music albums. Like most music executives, I believe that this information confirms the seriousness of illegal copying of copyright-protected material.

It is ironic to think that an industry that has partially developed the technology to transform entertainment into a digital medium and made the technology available to the average consumer has also contributed to an economically disastrous and seemingly uncontrollable situation.

There are several reasons for the decline in global sales. The two most prominent are the free downloading of music (illegal peer-2-peer file sharing) from the Internet, and physical counterfeiting.

If illegal peer-2-peer Web sites are shut down, the doors will open on similar Web sites; many such services already exist. My view is that the problem will most likely not be tackled by combating technology with counter-technological solutions. Unfortunately, an answer to these problems has not been found.

> According to the RIAA (The Recording Industry Association of America) approximately 30 billion songs were illegally downloaded on file-sharing networks between 2004 and 2009.

The RIAA believes that three major factors have to be addressed if the recorded-music business is to begin to heal.

1. Educating the public. The public must be made aware that free downloading is illegal and tantamount to stealing.
2. More flexible music licensing. The public must be able to purchase music at a reasonable cost.
3. Tougher antipiracy enforcement.

Supreme Court Sides With Biz in Grokster Case

June 27, 2005, Susan Butler, New York

Grokster case in favor of the entertainment industry, reversing the Ninth Circuit Court of Appeals opinion.

The court held that developers of software violate federal copyright law when they provide computer users with the means to share unauthorized movie and music files from the Internet.

At issue in the case was whether Grokster and StreamCast, which operated—and continue to operate—the decentralized peer-2-peer file-sharing networks Grokster and Morpheus, respectively, should be secondarily liable for the copyright-infringing activities of their users who have shared millions of unauthorized music and movie files.

Counterfeiting CDs

Professional organized-crime rings manufacture counterfeit CDs in the millions of units per year. The majority of them are produced in Malaysia and Pakistan. Although governments throughout the world are trying to eradicate CD pirates, the amount of product that has made its way into virtually every country has contributed to a disastrous global downturn in legitimate sales.

In addition, the competition from other forms of electronic media, which includes video games, mobile phone ringtones and ringbacks, and DVD-videos, has contributed to the decline of revenue in the global music industry.

Ringtones and Ringbacks

It is believed that 85% of ringtones, used in mobile phones, are illegally downloaded. Ringtones and ringbacks is a lucrative business, and business models include downloading hit songs, along with music videos. This, once again, involves copyright infringement.

Transition

The music business has been going through a remarkable transition, which has affected the industry worldwide. The industry has been attempting to fight free downloading by offering legitimate, user-friendly legal downloading, containing a large repertoire of licensed tracks at a reasonable cost to the consumer. In my opinion, if a consumer can download music without paying, no matter how low the cost, the consumer will elect to illegally download the music. Children illegally download music and films for their parents who are often not Internet savvy. Parents are supposed to be role models, but unfortunately, many are not setting an example for their children.

Legitimate online music services, such as iTunes, offer licensed product for downloading. Companies such as Amazon.com are legitimate Web sites that allow consumers to purchase physical CDs and DVDs as well as download.

It is nearly impossible to stop hackers from breaking codes. Various companies are experimenting with new Internet business paradigms in hopes of finding solutions that will be acceptable to the consumer.

> **♫ Registering Logos and Other Protections**
>
> Register logos and company names. To protect a company name, the company logo, as well as any identifiable lettering associated with the company, contact the U.S. Patent and Trademark Office in Washington, D.C. for further information.
> Internet domain names can be registered with the Internet Network Information Center at www.internic.net and the Domain Registry at www.domainregistry.com.

Conclusion

Music piracy must be stopped. Only international cooperation can help facilitate a solution, and government intervention is helping to seize the fabrication of counterfeit music. At the risk of sounding naive, continuing to educate the public may be, at the least, a first step.

24

Epilogue

> Music gives a soul to the universe, wings to the mind, flight to the imagination, and life to everything.
>
> —Plato

Even with myriad problems facing the music industry, its future is encouraging and exciting. New business paradigms create new opportunities. Producers and artists have the ability to create and sell music without signing an agreement with a record label or production company. The Internet and the future of digital distribution present numerous opportunities. Ringtones, ringbacks, Satellite, Internet (which includes music streaming), cable, and HD radio and music for video games offer new opportunities to independent production companies, record labels, and other copyright owners and content providers.

> ♫ The free, ad-supported on-demand music streaming service *Spotify* has been highly successful in a number of European companies. In July 2011, Spotify launched its service in the United States. It is too early to tell if the company will achieve the same success in the U.S. it has elsewhere.

The fundamental difference between 2011 and the preceding eras can be reduced down to the phrase "control of your own destiny."—George Howard (former president of Rykodisc)

New business models offer outlets for music producers to sell music that is not considered to be in the mainstream. Music lovers seek out companies specializing in unusual and inventive music. Some musical styles may not be distributed through major outlets because the sales potential is limited. Small companies have low overheads and consequently can afford to sell fewer units than a major company, yet still derive a substantial profit. Digital downloading is less costly for the consumer since there is no manufacturing cost and companies can afford to sell the music for less than a traditional physical copy.

Learning record production helps a music producer produce all genres of music. Once the basic production concepts have been learned, adapting to the idiosyncrasies of producing music for films, corporate videos, game music, commercials, and additional musical genres is relatively simple.

A solid musical and technological background is not always necessary to a successful music producer, but a trained producer has more opportunities than someone with limited musical and technological skills. *Versatility can sometimes mean survival!*

Students who are willing to "woodshed" (a musician's expression that means a dedication to practice and study) develop the tools that will enable them to maintain a rewarding career in music.

Music production cannot be taught. It is based upon innate talent. What *can* be taught are the components of a well-crafted production. Executing this book's recommended assignments will help students develop their talent. The information and techniques discussed throughout this book, along with additional study, will become a part of a producer's creative psyche.

Current U.S. Music Industry Considerations

There are certain issues that music industry professionals should support since they affect the U.S. music business. As of the writing of this book, the following items are being discussed in the U.S. Congress:

- The Local Radio Freedom Act
  The United States is the only country in the developed world that does not permit performers and copyright owners of recordings (labels, etc.) from collecting royalties from terrestrial radio airplay. Because the U.S. does not pay this royalty, foreign territories withhold similar royalty payments to U.S. performers and copyright owners of sound recordings. Several hundred million dollars per year are being withheld.
- Creativity and Innovation Resolution
  This government mandate would force mobile device manufacturers and wireless carriers to include terrestrial broadcast radio tuners in new mobile devices. This should not be a law but a choice by the manufacturers.

- Combating Online Infringement and Counterfeits Acts (COICA)
  There are multiple websites that *sell* recordings without paying the proper royalties. Many of these websites are foreign and based out of the U.S. This infringement of trademark and digital piracy costs the U.S. an estimated one hundred billion dollars a year. Advocate that the U.S. government block these websites.
- The FAA Air Transportation Modernization and Safety Improvement Act
  When going through airport security, many musicians are prohibited from taking musical instruments on airplanes. It is possible that if their instruments are stored in the baggage area, the instruments could be damaged.
  A national policy, which would apply to all domestic carriers, would help musicians make a decision on how to transport their instruments.

Concern and involvement in current and future legislation that affects the music business is vital to the interests of all music industry professionals.

Bibliography

Adler, Samuel. *The Study of Orchestration*. 3rd ed. New York: W. W. Norton & Company, Inc., 2002.

Barkley, Elizabeth F. *Crossroads: Popular Music in America*. Upper Saddle River, N.J.: Prentice Hall, 2003.

Betts, Graham. *Complete UK Hit Singles 1952–2004*. London: Collins/HarperCollins, 2004.

Brabec, Jeffrey, and Todd Brabec. *Music, Money and Success: The Insider's Guide to Making Money in the Music Industry*. New York: Schirmer Trade Books, 2006.

Campbell, Michael, and James Brody. *Rock and Roll: An Introduction*. New York: Schirmer Books, 1999.

Cunningham, Mark. *Good Vibrations: A History of Record Production*. London: Sanctuary Publishing Limited, 1998.

Dahl, Bill. *Motown: The Golden Years*. Iola, Wis.: Krause, 2001.

Davis, Sheila. *Successful Lyric Writing*. Cincinnati, Ohio: Writer's Digest Books, 1988.

Editors of Rolling Stone. *Rolling Stone: The Decades of Rock & Roll*. San Francisco: Chronicle Books, 2001.

Field, Shelly. *Career Opportunities in the Music Industry*. 5th ed. New York, New York: Ferguson, 2004.

Garofalo, Reebee. *Rockin' Out: Popular Music in the U.S.A.* 3rd ed. Upper Saddle River, N.J.: Pearson/Prentice Hall, 2005.

Halloran, Mark. *The Musician's Business & Legal Guide*. Upper Saddle River, N.J.: Prentice Hall, 2008.

Huber, David Miles, and Robert E. Runstein. *Modern Recording Techniques*. 6th ed. Burlington, Mass.: Focal/Elsevier, 2005.

Hutchison, Tom. *Web Marketing for the Music Business*. Burlington, Mass.: Focal/Elsevier, 2008.

Joyner, David. *American Popular Music*. 2nd ed. New York: McGraw-Hill Higher Education, 2003.

Lewisohn, Mark. *The Complete Beatles Chronicle.* London: Hamlyn/Octopus Publishing Limited, 2003.

Malone, Bill C. *Country Music USA.* 2nd rev. ed. Austin: University of Texas Press, 2002.

Owsinski, Bobby. *Music 3.0.* Milwaukee, Wisc.: Hal Leonard Books, 2009.

Passman, Donald S. *All You Need to Know about the Music Business.* 5th ed. New York: Free Press, 2003.

Rapaport, Diane Sward. *A Music Business Primer.* Upper Saddle River, N.J.: Prentice Hall, 2003.

Rice, Tim, Jo Rice, and Mike Read. *The Guinness Book of British Hit Singles.* 2nd ed. Enfield, England: Guinness Superlatives Ltd., 1979.

Roberts, David, ed. *British Hit Singles and Albums.* 18th rev. ed. London: Butler and Tanner, 2003.

Schulenberg, Richard. *Legal Aspects of the Music Industry: An Insider's View of the Legal and Practical Aspects of the Music Business.* New York: Billboard Books, 1999.

Stuessy, Joe, and Scott Lipscomb. *Rock and Roll: Its History and Stylistic Development.* 5th ed. Upper Saddle River, N.J.: Prentice-Hall, 2003.

Wadhams, Wayne. *Inside the Hits.* Boston, Mass.: Berklee Press, 2001.

Whitburn, Joel. *The Billboard Book of Top 40 Hits.* 7th ed. New York: Billboard Books, 2000.

Zager, Michael. *Writing Music for Television and Radio Commercials: A Manual for Composers and Students.* Lanham, Md.: Scarecrow Press, 2003.

Index

About the Author

Michael Zager holds the positions of the Dorothy F. Schmidt Eminent Scholar in Performing Arts, Professor of Music and Director of the Commercial Music Program at Florida Atlantic University in Boca Raton, Florida. He previously taught at the Mannes College of Music, a division of New School University, in New York City. A graduate of the University of Miami and the Mannes College of Music, Zager has received 3 Fulbright Specialist Grants awarded by the U.S. Department of State Bureau of Educational and Cultural Affairs, 2 Visiting Professor Grants in Thailand, and served 3 terms as a member of the Board of Governors of the Florida Chapter of The Recording Academy (Grammy Awards). He is the author of 2 editions of *Writing Music for Television and Radio Commercials (and more): A Manual for Composers and Students* and the first edition of *Music Production: For Producers, Composers, Arrangers, and Students* (both published by Scarecrow Press).

He has produced, composed, and/or arranged original music in a wide range of musical idioms, including albums, commercials, and television, and source and theme music for major motion pictures.

Zager has produced Grammy Award–winning artists: Whitney Houston, Cissy Houston, Peabo Bryson, Luther Vandross, Denise Williams, Jennifer Holliday, Joe Williams, Arturo Sandoval, Herb Alpert, Olatunji, and The Spinners. Some of his original scores and original studio recordings of Whitney Houston, The Spinners, and The Michael Zager Band reside in the Rock and Roll Hall of Fame and Museum in Cleveland, Ohio.

His recording awards for producing, composing, and/or arranging include: 13 gold or platinum records, Golden Boot Award (France), Europe 1 Award (France), Olé Award (Spain), 2 BMI Citations of Achievement, given for most performed songs on radio in a given year, a Grammy Award nomination for "Cupid/I've Loved You for a Long Time," performed by The Spinners, and a nomination for producer of the year by the Golden Music Awards, in Nashville. Zager produced Daniel Ray Edwards, who was nominated for best new artist by the Golden Music Awards in Nashville, as well as "You Win Again," which was nominated for single of the year by the Golden Music Awards in Nashville. The Golden Music Award, in Nashville, also nominated his label for Best Independent Record Label of the Year.

His television awards include a Platinum Video Award for the ABC Television Network series *ABC FUNFIT* with Mary Lou Retton, and a Daytime Emmy Award for *ABC FUNFIT* with Mary Lou Retton. Jay-Z, Missy Elliott, 50 Cent, and many more artists have sampled his songs.

Zager has composed and/or arranged more than 400 commercials. His clients have included Dr Pepper, MCI, Masterlock, Cablevision, Buick, Acura, IBM, Schlitz Malt Liquor (sung by Kool & the Gang, The Spinners, .38 Special, and The Chi-Lites), Bounce (sung by Whitney Houston), Crystal Light (sung by Raquel Welch), Budweiser, Crest, Kodak, Ivory Shampoo, Maxwell House Coffee, Clearasil, Lancôme, Volvo, Burger King, Oscal (featuring Olympic Gold Medalist Peggy Fleming), and Burlington Coat Factory.

His advertising awards include a Clio Award, 3 International Film Festival awards, 3 Art Directors Club awards, and a Mobius Advertising award. For many years he produced the American Advertising Federation Hall of Achievement Awards in New York.

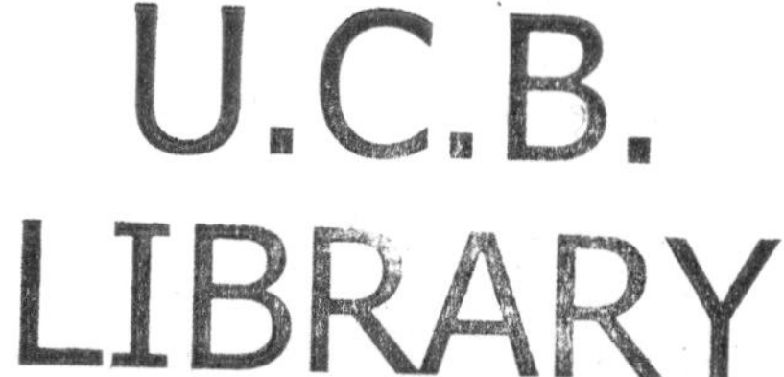